Poetry

An Introduction and Anthology

POETRY

An Introduction and Anthology

CHARLES S. FELVER

MARTIN K. NURMI

Charles E. Merrill Books, Inc.
Columbus, Ohio

Library of Congress Catalog Number: 67-15064

1 2 3 4 5 6 7 8 9 10 11 12 13—75 74 73 72 71 70 69 68 67

Printed in the United States of America

PREFACE

Most teachers of introductory courses in poetry, ourselves included, would probably prefer using a collection of poems instead of a textbook. Unfortunately, the usual academic term does not provide time enough for both the leisurely discussion of individual poems that is so profitable and pleasurable in studying poetry and the exposition of certain theoretical matters which must be understood before fruitful critical discussion can occur. The backgrounds of students also differ greatly, and those whose preparation is less than adequate should have something they can study at home. In the present book we have attempted to provide both a large collection of English and American poems ranging from Chaucer to the present day as well as an "Introduction" to the art of poetry.

The Introduction, which begins simply by reading a few poems without reference to any particular technical vocabulary, takes up in order: imagery, metaphor, diction, symbol, speaker and situation, tone, structure, metrics and sound, old poetry and new, judging poetry, and finally reading poetry aloud. This order of topics differs somewhat from that followed in many similar books, which often take up diction first. We have arranged our book in this way so as to minimize the impression, too often given to students in elementary school and high school, that poetry is a superior kind of rhetoric. Accordingly, the discussion of some matters, notably of metaphor, differs somewhat from those usually found in high school and college freshman rhetorics, because we wish to focus attention clearly on the *poetic* use of words and figures of speech. We make no claims to critical novelty, but are simply applying in a book for beginning students some of the ideas that are current in much excellent recent writing on poetics. Footnote references, more numerous than customary, indicate all the sources we could remember, and a Bibliography suggests works for further reading, many in paperback editions.

Although the order of chapters forms part of our strategy of exposition, we have tried to make the chapters more or less independent essays that can be read in almost any order the teacher prefers, and have given definitions of all important terms (printed in small capitals on their first appearance in the text) in the Glossary, together with cross-references to places in the text where they are most fully discussed. We have tried to avoid designing the teacher's course for him.

In the Introduction we have attempted to proceed as inductively and as concretely as possible, illustrating theory wherever we could through analysis of particular poems. We have tried to make the analyses of poems just full enough so a student could, while studying by himself, have illustrations of the matter under consideration but not so full as to discourage his own further study of the poem or to take away the freshness from later class discussion. The questions following poems bear on the topic under immediate consideration, but also bring up matters studied earlier.

At the end of each chapter are a number of poems for further study, some with questions and some without, as well as suggestions of other poems from the Anthology which seem to us interesting or useful to study in connection with a particular chapter.

In a section called "Three Poets at Work," following the Introduction, we have reprinted sections of three essays in which three poets discuss the process of writing poetry.

The Anthology includes over 200 poems in English, from all ages, with as many modern ones as we could manage. Most major poets are represented by several poems each, some with as many as a dozen or more. And, although inevitably most of the poems in a book such as this are shorter lyrics, there are some longer poems as well. The poems in the book are not all equally good, because they are intended for study and critical discussion. Indeed, some rather bad poems appear at various points in the book, as material on which the student can exercise his developing critical faculties — though we do not think that the end of the study of poetry should be making value judgments.

We have attempted to supply sound and accurate texts of all poems, modernizing spelling and, in a few cases, punctuation. We have not tampered with the punctuation of poets who are known to have used punctuation with care. A few poems are given in the old spelling, with slight modifications, to give the student some feeling of history.

What we have tried to provide in this book above all is simply a textbook that does not force a particular pedagogical or critical "approach" on a course and a teacher, but can be used in different ways, and one which does not, because of over-simplified or idiosyncratic definitions, shift most of the burden of basic explanation on the teacher after all.

In trying to make the book as useful as possible, we have sought advice and assistance from teachers of courses in poetry in a number of college and universities. We are especially indebted for help of various kinds to colleagues Glenn Burne, John White, Frederick Garber, and an anonymous reader (who are not, of course, responsible for the book's shortcomings), and to Marie Felver and Ruth Nurmi. We are also greatly indebted for help to Mr. Shigeru Taniguchi and Mrs. Betty Milburn.

C. S. F.

M. K. N.

CONTENTS

Introduction to Poetry

Poems and Readers

1

Lady Greensleeves

Alas my love, ye do me wrong,
To cast me off discourteously:
And I have loved you so long,
Delighting in your companie.
Greensleeves was all my joy,
Greensleeves was my delight:
Greensleeves was my heart of gold,
And who but Ladie Greensleeves.

Anonymous

The tune "Greensleeves" is so familiar that the music may come to mind as you read the poem. The association of words here with music is quite proper, because the poem was intended to be set to music. Soon after it was written by an anonymous poet sometime before 1580, it was printed on a large sheet of paper (a "broadside") with a suggested tune and peddled on street corners by singing ballad-mongers — the Elizabethan counterparts of our song-pluggers.

Most of the broadside ballads and songs of Elizabethan England have gone into the trashbaskets and fireplaces, just as most of our popular songs will disappear after their words and tunes have been stilled in the ears of the generations which listened to them. But somehow "Greensleeves" has continued to be popular. The speaker, or in this case the singer, whose words form the poem, complains of having been jilted, but he does so with grace, without self-pitying rancor. Instead of emphasizing how deeply hurt he was, he remembers how delightful it was to love Ladie Greensleeves and be beloved by her. Some of the delight is passed on to the reader.

It so happens that Ladie Greensleeves may not have been entirely respectable, but her social standing or morals do not affect the beauty of the song written for her. Indeed, though the tune of this song is primarily associated with the lady celebrated in the poem, it has also been traditionally associated with Christmas Eve, for the same tune has been used in a well known carol, "What Child Is This." The actual reputation of the lady in the original poem doesn't matter very much. What is important is the feeling expressed by the poet.

As a poem "Lady Greensleeves" is relatively simple. It is a song, indeed a popular song which has become something like a folk song. Because the texts of the songs are written in a way that allows them to be understood when sung—though a poetic song need not be set to music to be enjoyed—this poetic form is not usually very complex. Still, songs can deal with a variety of subjects, with humorous events, nonsense, matters of belief, love, and even death. The great songs say something about their subjects.

Let us consider another song, a dirge from Shakespeare's *The Tempest*, which, though it faces it squarely, manages to make death seem beautiful.

Full Fadom Five They Father Lies

Full fadom five they father lies,
Of his bones are coral made:
Those are pearls that were his eyes;
Nothing of him that doth fade
But doth suffer a sea-change
Into something rich and strange
Sea nymphs hourly ring his knell:
Burthen: Ding, Dong.
Hark, now I hear them—ding-dong bell.

William Shakespeare
From *The Tempest*

The song was originally written to be sung to musical accompaniment by Ariel, who in the play is consoling Ferdinand on the death of his father. But we do not really need to associate melody with this song, as we were inclined to do with "Lady Greensleeves," because the words are better able to stand by themselves. This song is better poetry than our first example.

But what makes it better poetry? The answer to this question is suggested in the rest of the present book. Poetry is an immensely rich and complex art, and we shall be taking up various aspects of it in the following chapters. For the present, however, let us simply look at this poem, and two others, to see what we can discover without reference to any special methods of analysis and without a technical vocabulary.

In an analysis of any piece of writing, one usually begins by finding out in general what the words say, so let us start with that here. A summary of the first poem might say something like this: It is wrong, lady, for you to be so rude to me since I have loved you so long and enjoyed myself so much with you. The sense of the poem is quite readily summarized, for the summary need be little more than a restatement of the first four lines. But notice what happens when the second poem is summarized: Your father is drowned in deep water, but his body is so changed by the effects of the sea that you would scarcely recognize it. The summary of this poem is less helpful in analyzing the meaning because the literal meaning does not really convey what the poem "says." Even adding to the summary some of the details that the poet gives us does not make it possible to get the full effect of the poem as a poem. The exact depth of the water (at least five fathoms) is not really very important in itself, for all one need know is that the water is deep. Nor can we take the other details literally at face value. Drowned persons' bones do not become coral or their eyes pearls. And their bodies do not become something "rich and strange," nor do sea nymphs ring their knell, hourly or otherwise.

And yet, as we read the poem, we almost believe that these things happen, because the poet has given us detailed and coherent sense impressions showing that they do happen. Furthermore, we rather want to believe this, because the changes described make death by drowning less unpleasant to contemplate. In Shakespeare's play, Ariel wants to diminish Ferdinand's grief by making the king's drowning seem a kind of marvelous transformation in which his body becomes a part of the life of the sea and thus in a sense continues to live. The poem does not come out and say this directly. We get this meaning from the IMAGERY, the imaginative sense impressions, in which the transformation of the king's body is described. (Actually, the king had not drowned, and Ariel knew it, but had to pretend that he had.)

The two poems considered thus far are songs, words intended for musical setting. In common usage words for songs are called lyrics, and the word lyric as applied to poetry originally did refer to poetry that was sung, or chanted, to musical accompaniment. Now, however, a LYRIC in poetry is any short poem in which there is one speaker and which is not primarily a poem that tells a story. A poem that tells a story is a narrative poem. Poems in which the effect depends a good deal on there being two speakers, whose discourse actually constitutes the poem, might be thought of as being dramatic. Poems in which a speaker's situation is of importance (as in W. B. Yeat's "Politics," to be discussed shortly) might be considered as a special kind of lyric that might be called dramatic lyrics. Distinctions such as these are hard to maintain rigorously (some narrative poems are in the form of dramatic colloquies, for instance), but they are worth keeping in mind because they sometimes suggest ways of looking at what is said in a poem. In a later chapter we shall have more to say about this matter.

Many of the great poems most of us are familiar with, at least by reputation (Homer's *Iliad* and *Odyssey*, Dante's *Divine Comedy*, Chaucer's *Canterbury Tales*), are narrative poems. And we all know ballads of various kinds ("Frankie and Johnny," "Sir Patrick Spens"), which tell stories, as do poems like Henry Wadsworth Longfellow's *Hiawatha*. Narrative poems, as this short list suggests, are of varying lengths and complexity and often involve much more than mere narration. Sometimes narrative poetry becomes lyric, as we become aware of the speaker's emotions. This happens in the ballad that follows, "The Falcon."

The Falcon

Lully, lulley! lully, lulley!
The faucon hath borne my make away!

He bare him up, he bare him down,
He bare him into an orchard brown.

In that orchard there was an halle,
That was hanged with purple and pall.

And in that hall there was a bed,
It was hanged with gold sa red.

And in that bed there lieth a knight,
His woundes bleeding day and night.

At that bed's foote there lieth a hound,
Licking the blood as it runs down.

By that bed-side kneeleth a may,
And she weepeth both night and day.

And at that bed's head standeth a stone.
Corpus Christi written thereon.

Lully, lulley! lully, lulley!
The faucon hath borne my make away.

ANONYMOUS

In reading this poem through, we may be puzzled at first by the two-line statement at the beginning and end, and by some of the strange words. But even without knowing fully what some of these old words mean, we can get the main sense of the story, which, unlike "Full Fadom Five," is told starkly, in grisly detail. Of course, if the poem is to be read for something more than a general impression—and one simply cannot read poetry for the "general idea"—we must find out what the puzzling words mean by consulting a dictionary, which will tell us that "make" means mate, that "pall" means a fine cloth, and that "may" means maiden. Even a reader without Latin should recognize that "*Corpus Christi*" means the body of Christ. With this information, we can read the poem again and see that it is a story of a knight who was mysteriously carried by a falcon into a richly decorated hall in a brown orchard, where he lies bleeding and dying, attended by a hound that licks the blood as it runs, and by a maiden who kneels weeping by his side. Thus far it is a simple but moving story of tragedy.

But it gives a disturbing feeling of being more than this, and we get a hint as to another possible level of meaning from the stone at the head of the knight's bed. The inscription on the stone, "*Corpus Christi*," the body of Christ, suggests that perhaps the story has a religious significance as well. Now this does not mean that the poem is, after all, an account of the death of Christ cleverly disguised as a story of a dying knight, and that our job as readers is to solve the puzzle and discover the "real" meaning of the poem. The poem has more than one level of meaning, and as we read it at the simpler level, we are aware of the other meanings. It *is* a story of a dying knight mourned by a dog and a maid, but it is also a representation of an image, in a sort of tableau, which calls to mind Christ's sacrifice and the grief of Mary. If we are aware of this broader meaning, it is as an overtone, or as background feeling to the scene sharply described in the poem. This additional meaning serves in a way to explain some of the mystery of the poem, but it also makes the mystery more significant by attaching the events in the poem to a broader human and religious context.

A poem can and usually does appeal to us on several levels of understanding and emotion at once. Unlike discursive prose which conveys information, such as is found in textbooks, poetry does not always state explicitly what a reader should get from it. It is often ambiguous, not because poets like to puzzle their readers, but because what poems communicate may not be explicitly stated. A poem does not state the meaning; it embodies it. In reading poetry, one must participate in the process of communication much more than in reading prose. A reader of poetry must half create the poem for himself from the hints that the poet has given, by responding intellectually and emotionally to story, picture, language, music, and so on. This requires attention and a good deal of effort sometimes, but the results are worth it.

There are still some aspects of the story of the dying knight that may be a little puzzling. What precisely is the relationship between the opening and closing COUPLETS and the story told between them? Knowing that the poem was intended to be sung, we can recognize "lully, lulley" as a REFRAIN, a portion of the song that is repeated, in this case after each two-line stanza, and does not advance the narrative. That is, the refrain does not tell us anything new. But it does build up the feeling that the poet wishes to embody in the poem, for it becomes a kind of incantation to which we progressively attach more meaning as we go through the narrative.

"Meaning" in poetry, of course, does not usually refer to the assertions made by the grammatical relationship between subject and predicate. To be sure, poetry is written in sentences, and the grammatical meaning is important. But a poem usually "says" more than its sentences do. And to hear and feel what it says, a reader must let the poem talk to him in its own way, through its IMAGES (the sights, sounds, smells it evokes), through METAPHOR (the associations in the poem), and so on, as well as through the words themselves. We shall be taking up these matters in some detail in later chapters.

We have read two songs and a ballad. Let us now consider a poem in which the speaker is directly involved in what is being talked about.

*Politics**

"IN OUR TIME THE DESTINY OF MAN PRESENTS ITS MEANING IN POLITICAL TERMS."—THOMAS MANN.

How can I, that girl standing there,
My attention fix
On Roman or on Russian
Or on Spanish politics?

---

*Reprinted with permission of The Macmillan Company from *Last Poems and Plays* by William Butler Yeats. Copyright 1940 Georgie Yeats. Also acknowledgments to Mr. M. B. Yeats, the Macmillan of Canada Ltd., and Macmillan & Co., Ltd.

Yet here's a travelled man that knows
What he talks about,
And there's a politician
That has read and thought,
And maybe what they say is true
Of war and war's alarms,
But O that I were young again
And held her in my arms!

William Butler Yeats

This poem was written by Yeats towards the end of his life, and more than the early poems it seems to show him reflecting to himself. He thinks of Thomas Mann's serious observation on twentieth century man and reminds himself that an old man should certainly be concerned with the state of the world in those troubled times. But a handsome young girl appears, and he is distracted from these pessimistic thoughts by someone more humanly and enduringly interesting. He knows that old men should concern themselves with the serious questions of the world, but nevertheless wishes he were young again and could hold the girl in his arms.

Poems can be mystifyingly complex, or they can sometimes be mystifyingly simple, like this one. On the surface it might appear that Yeats is celebrating youth, or making old age appear a little ridiculous. But in poetry the surface impression is often not the correct one, and in a poem which is IRONIC it can be utterly misleading. In reading this poem we might well recall that Yeats, in addition to being one of the greatest poets of our century, was also a playwright, a founder of the distinguished Abbey Theatre, an active force in the Irish movement for independence, an Irish senator, and a Nobel prize winner. The speaker in this poem, Yeats himself, is no ordinary old man longing for youth and girls. He is saying, in effect, that politics is of immense importance, and one ought to know more about it and be alarmed with the threat of World War II, but nevertheless phrases like "the destiny of man" do not adequately represent the real questions. Is not the blood and bone and root of man's destiny mixed up more with love than with politics? And is it not delightful that I, William Butler Yeats, the old poet and politician, can still be distracted from politics by a radiant girl and be sad only because I am no longer young enough to be her lover? The poem contrasts the abstract values of political thinkers and concrete human values, even though all we are given is a brief dramatic scene in which an old man sees a pretty girl.

Yeats can represent himself to us as an old man still very interested in pretty girls because he trusts us not to mistake his meaning. He trusts us to take the trouble to read his poem very carefully and sensitively and accepts us as equals, as it were, people to whom he is willing to talk very honestly about important things.

Reading poetry, therefore, like anything else worthwhile, takes a certain amount of effort and some knowledge of various aspects of the poet's art. But with a few tools to aid in reading poetry analytically, such as we propose to provide in the following chapters, the amount of effort should be decreased a little; or at least it can be more effectively directed.

Poems for Further Study:

To Robin Red-Breast

Laid out for dead, let thy last kindness be
With leaves and moss-work for to cover me:
And while the Wood-nymphs my cold corpse inter,
Sing thou my dirge, sweet-warbling chorister!
For epitaph in foliage, next write this,
Here, here the tomb of Robert Herrick is.

ROBERT HERRICK

Love's Best Sweet

He or she that hopes to gain
Loves best sweet without some pain,
Hopes in vain.

Cupid's livery no one wears
But must put on hopes and fears,
Smiles and tears.

And, like to April weather,
Rain and shine both together,
Both or neither.

ANONYMOUS

*The Heron**

The heron stands in water where the swamp
Has deepened to the blackness of a pool,
Or balances with one leg on a hump
Of marsh-grass heaped above a musk-rat hole.

He walks the shallow with an antic grace.
The great feet break the ridges of the sand,
The long eye notes the minnow's hiding place.
His beak is quicker than a human hand.

He jerks a frog across his bony lip,
Then points his heavy bill above the wood.
The wide wings flap but once to lift him up.
A single ripple starts from where he stood.

THEODORE ROETHKE

Remorse Is Memory Awake

Remorse is memory awake,
Her companies astir,—
A presence of departed acts
At window and at door.

It's past set down before the soul,
And lighted with a match,
Perusal to facilitate
Of its condensed despatch.

Remorse is cureless,—the disease
Not even God can heal;
For 'tis his institution,—
The complement of hell.

EMILY DICKINSON

Questions.

1. Compare and contrast the definition of remorse given in the poem with this conventional dictionary definition: the anguish, like gnawing pain, excited by a sense of guilt; compunction of conscience for a crime committed, or for the sins of one's past life; sympathetic sorrow, pity, compassion.
2. Which, among the dictionary definitions of remorse, does the poem seem to be discussing?

Images

2

Samuel Taylor Coleridge, in his account of how "Kubla Khan" was written, says that he fell asleep under the influence of an anodyne while reading in Purchas's *Pilgrimage* the words: "Here the Khan Kubla commanded a palace to be built, and a stately garden thereunto. And thus ten miles of fertile ground were inclosed with a wall."

> The Author continued for about three hours in a profound sleep at least of the external senses, during which he has the most vivid confidence, that he could not have composed less than from two to three hundred lines; if that indeed can be called composition in which all the images rose up before him as *things*, with a parallel production of the correspondent expressions, without any sensation or consciousness of effort.
>
> (PREFACE TO THE POEM)

Unfortunately, "a person on business from Porlock" came and detained the poet over an hour, with the result that only a fragment was written, the rest having been forgotten.

The separation of images and verbal expression into parallel things and words seemed so unusual to Coleridge that he reported the experience as a psychological novelty. It is even more unusual for a whole poem to come into the writer's mind that way. But in the initial stages of making a poem, it is not uncommon for poets to think in images. As C. Day Lewis remarks in "How a Poem is Made," the "seed or germ of a poem . . . may come in the form of a strong but vague feeling, a particular experience, or an idea: sometimes it first appears as an image: perhaps even—as a poetic phrase or a whole line of verse—already clothed in words."*

*The essay is reprinted on pp. 214-219.

Poetry is one of the most complex arts because it combines ideas, sound, rhythm, images, among other things. In it thought, perception, feeling, attitude work together in ways making it very difficult to isolate one element without distorting the role of that element in the poetic process. Even poetic imagery, which of all aspects of poetry seems the easiest to consider by itself because it is the easiest to examine apart from the actual language of the poem, cannot be thought of abstractly outside of the poem, especially as sense impressions: sights, sounds, smells, physical sensations. Poetic images are percepts, of course, but they are not merely that. Above all, they are not merely pictorial adornments of discursive sense. A poetic image is one of the forms in which a poet thinks, a perception in which feeling, attitude, thought come into a focus.

Thinking in images is by no means limited to poets, for we all do a good deal of thinking—or remembering—that way, giving form in images to important experiences. You can easily prove this for yourself. Clear your mind of verbal ideas and relax for just a moment. Then have someone give you a word as a stimulus referring to a common experience, such as "first day in school," "first love," "poverty," "death." Most people will see quite clearly in their minds eye a particular scene or visual image which they recall from their own direct experience: a cloakroom full of children, a girl riding a bicycle, patched clothing, the arrival of glum relatives. These images in which important memories are stored can be recalled with undiminished vividness over the years because they give form to experience.

This is not to suggest that everyone can be a poet if only he will dredge up the images of his experience—though most people who aspire to write poetry would be better off concentrating on these images than on regular meter and rhyme. Good poets are not only talented perceivers but have trained themselves to see things vividly and freshly. The point we wish to make is that anyone who has thought in images of his own—and most people have—can quite easily learn to read in such a way that he thinks, as he reads, in the images given in a poem. Unfortunately, many influences in elementary and high school discourage this kind of reading, and it may take a little conscious effort at first. But we have all had a great deal of experience with private imagery that will be of help.

To read James Schevill's "The Dancers with a Hop," for instance, we must respond to the extended images on which it is built. And the effectiveness of the poem depends entirely on the vividness with which the reader perceives its two contrasting scenes. It is hard not to see the scenes in this poem vividly.

*The Dancers with a Hop**

In that furious, final wake for Flannagan,
When they drained that booze and danced their babes,
They barreled with bulging rears; the Slang Angel
From the slum section danced with that old slick-hair,
Harry the Heel—together they performed the Hula
In honor of the Irish—the "Hula with a Hop,"
Harry explained as the Slang Angel leaped
High with flapping breasts and flopping hair . . .

While granite and grainfields away,
Flying to Arctic nesting grounds,
Soared to river-rest the sandhill cranes,
Male and female paired for life in luminous light,
Bowed to each other with brightest feathers,
Leaped in the air beating gravely their wings,
Circled again in the gracious, courtly dance and
Leaped! And the air glowed gala galore.

James Schevill

The poem is built around the contrasting images of the dancing humans—especially those of Slang Angel and Harry the Heel cutting a tastelessly grotesque caper in the "Hula with a Hop"—with the cranes dancing their much more graceful courting dance. Other contrasts add to these basic contrasting images. For one thing, there is a contrast in language. The humans "barreled with bulging rears," whereas the cranes very ceremoniously "bowed to each other with brightest feathers, / Leaped in the air beating gravely their wings." For another, the only pair of humans identified are the Slang Angel and Harry the Heel, who are certainly not "Paired for life in luminous light" as the cranes are.

By means of the contrast between the two sustained images of the dancing at Flannagan's wake and the courting dance of the cranes, the poem implies a criticism of crudeness among human beings. But the criticism is not given explicitly in words; the poet does not come out and preach. And though his attitude in the poem seems reasonably clear, the poem

---

*Reprinted from *Fifteen Modern and American Poets*, Holt, Rinehart & Winston, Inc., 1956.

should not be read as if it were a disguised attack on drunken wakes. What the poem says remains in the images. We may talk about the images, of course; in fact, doing so increases our appreciation of the poem because it helps us see them more clearly. But the meaning of the poem must be seen in a concrete picture of the grotesque humans as contrasted with the picture of the graceful cranes.

Although the images in "The Dancers with a Hop" emerge quite clearly, in other poems it may be more appropriate to the poet's intended effect to keep some of his images indistinct, suggestive. Consider the imagery of the following poem, especially in the last two stanzas.

*Green and Red and Darkness**

For twenty minutes between the end of storm
And the last of sunset, green became green and
All red roses stepped forward a little and burned.

Then from all over the world like an
Indeterminate number of dusk-robed figures
Evening walked to the center and made darkness.

And then it was my ancestors, for they said
'Now you have all the stars, surer than roses.'
'Damn you,' I said: 'damn you, you dead dead.'

WINFIELD TOWNLEY SCOTT

In the brief interval between the end of the storm and dusk everything becomes more vivid and clear. Then the dusk begins to close in. The poet here wants vivid imagery for the roses, which we shall discuss in a moment, but indistinct imagery for the dusk, identified with dead ancestors, "dusk-robed figures" who mysteriously "made darkness." Against this indistinct background of visual imagery comes a sharp cry for the life that was epitomized in the roses. The vague ancestors had said that stars are "surer than roses," but the speaker responds: " 'Damn you,' I said: 'damn you, you dead dead.' " The repetition of *d* sounds in *damn* and the word *said*, which rhymes with *dead*, when combined with the repetitions of the word *dead* both as an adjective and a noun, reinforce the feeling of the speaker.

---

*From *Collected Poems: 1937-1962*, by Winfield Townley Scott, (Macmillan Company, 1962).

In this passage, because the line is actually spoken by a character in the poem, the auditory effects are not only part of the sound patterns in the poem but also function as sound imagery. This speech is the only "heard" sound in the poem, and we should hear it.

In "The Dancers with a Hop," the images are evoked directly by descriptive names, by descriptions, and cumulatively by including every thing in two scenes. Poetic imagery can be related directly to the thing being talked about, as in this poem, or it can be obliquely related to it, as in metaphor or symbol (matters to be discussed shortly). Metaphor—connecting one thing with another unlike thing—often combines two or even more images at once, as in "Green and Red and Darkness," in which "All red roses stepped forward a little and burned." In saying that the roses stepped, the poet is attributing animate characteristics to the flowers, and in saying they burned he gives them yet another quality, thus making a new image which does not exist in nature but as an imaginative entity to be found only in the poem. In this image we do not see the roses very clearly as roses partly because the poet doesn't describe them very vividly as flowers (they are merely "red") and partly because the new synthetic image of roses that stepped forward and burned is more intense than the image of natural roses would be. The flowers are still roses, of course, in a particular setting, but because images other than the natural one of a flower have been associated with them, they are roses metamorphosed: the red roses at dusk after a storm are by the poet's metaphoric imagery made into something new. This new entity is used by the poet in the development of his theme. The animate burning roses come to represent the intense but transitory life that is in conflict with the cold permanence of stars.

Is the new image confused because three different images are combined? It is indistinct to the extent that the poet does not come right out and let us see roses walking in the manner of a bad comic cartoon. But that kind of distinctness would spoil the whole poem. The intensity of the image comes from the *combination* of new characteristics with the natural flower, from the synthesis of attributes. A red rose in the strange light of dusk after a storm does seem to step forward against its complementary color green, which, as the poem says, became very green indeed, and it does seem to burn. Thus the combination of imagery makes us see the roses at once more vividly as flowers and also gives to them characteristics that transform them into an imaginative entity. This newly-fashioned imaginative entity, with its special kind of artistic clarity, functions in a way that roses in nature cannot in the developemnt of the theme of the poem.

Poetic imagery is not ordinarily a mere adornment of discourse but one of the organic materials out of which poems are made. Often, as in the poems in this chapter, imagery is a more important material in the composition of a poem than verbal assertion, and sometimes the words do very little grammatically other than indicate relationships among the images. Of course the words are used musically and structurally, but so far as their predicative function is concerned, the poem verges on becoming wordless. For a poem is a construct, made of many things: verbal predications, rhythms, sounds, images, and so on. And it need not be regarded as a piece of discourse but as something else, which has only the superficial characteristics of a piece of discourse, and in which grammatical meaning is only one of several structural elements.

In the neoclassic period of English literature, poetry—at least certain kinds—was expected to have a solid discursive structure of argument. But it would be a mistake to view this poetry as being like prose, or, as used to be said in the nineteenth century in reacting against the age that had passed, that it *was* prose, devoid of imagination and imagery. If Samuel Johnson said that the things observed by the poet "must concur to store his mind with inexhaustible variety: for every idea is useful for the enforcement or decoration of moral or religious truth," he also said that it is through the poet's imagery, gained from great knowledge and wide experience, that the reader is furnished with "unexpected instruction."* Johnson had little patience with poetry that did not make fairly good logical sense, but this fact did not diminish the importance of imagery for him.

In stressing the importance of imagery in this chapter, we may have given the impression that without imagery there is no poem. Poems can be written without imagery and have been. In writing such a poem, a poet simply chooses not to avail himself of the resources of imagery and instead uses other resources. If he is a competent poet he does this and knows he is able to make the choice. (Unfortunately, a great deal of really bad poetry also tries to get along without imagery and relies on trite "noble sentiments.") Winfield Townley Scott consciously avoided images in the poem, "To L. B. S.," because in the situation being described images would be too painful.

*To L. B. S.***

Sometimes, tired, I imagine your death:
By childish illness, reasonless accident
Stopped still forever, gone: until I loathe
Fool dramatizations of the brain—I won't
Though I could, write them into pictures here.

**Rasselas*, Chapter X.

**From *Collected Poems: 1937-1962*, by Winfield Townley Scott, (Macmillan Company, 1962).

My child, outlive me! Stay beyond my times
Which—how I see now—could be worse than these,
As they are worse for many who had sons.
Death I can bear for myself once, not twice.
I am out of bed at midnight to beg this.

WINFIELD TOWNLEY SCOTT

Questions.

1. From your own experience describe a "Fool" dramatization "of the brain," line 4.
2. Describe as precisely as you can what is meant by "Death I can bear for myself once, not twice," in line 10.

We began this chapter by giving Coleridge's account of the composition of "Kubla Khan," and we conclude it by looking at the poem itself.

Kubla Khan: or, a Vision in a Dream

A Fragment

In Xanadu did Kubla Khan
A stately pleasure-dome decree:
Where Alph, the sacred river, ran
Through caverns measureless to man
  Down to a sunless sea.
So twice five miles of fertile ground
With walls and towers were girdled round:
And there were gardens bright with sinuous rills,
Where blossomed many an incense-bearing tree;
And here were forests ancient as the hills,
Enfolding sunny spots of greenery.

But oh! that deep romantic chasm which slanted
Down the green hill athwart a cedarn cover!
A savage place! as holy and enchanted
As e'er beneath a waning moon was haunted
By woman wailing for her demon-lover!
And from this chasm, with ceaseless turmoil seething,
As if this earth in fast thick pants were breathing,

A mighty fountain momently was forced:
Amid whose swift half-intermitted burst
Huge fragments vaulted like rebounding hail,
Or chaffy grain beneath the thresher's flail:
And 'mid these dancing rocks at once and ever
It flung up momently the sacred river.
Five miles meandering with a mazy motion
Through wood and dale the sacred river ran,
Then reached the caverns measureless to man,
And sank in tumult to a lifeless ocean:
And 'mid this tumult Kubla heard from far
Ancestral voices prophesying war!
  The shadow of the dome of pleasure
  Floated midway on the waves;
  Where was heard the mingled measure
  From the fountain and the caves.

It was a miracle of rare device,
A sunny pleasure-dome with caves of ice!
  A damsel with a dulcimer
  In a vision once I saw:
  It was an Abyssinian maid,
  And on her dulcimer she played,
  Singing of Mount Abora.
  Could I revive within me
  Her symphony and song,
  To such a deep delight 'twould win me,
That with music loud and long,
I would build that dome in air,
That sunny dome! those caves of ice!
And all who heard should see them there,
And all should cry, Beware! Beware!
His flashing eyes, his floating hair!
Weave a circle round him thrice,
And close your eyes with holy dread,
For he on honey-dew hath fed,
And drunk the milk of Paradise.

SAMUEL TAYLOR COLERIDGE

This is an enigmatic poem that puzzles even professional scholars, and it has been the subject of scores of critical studies, including one whole book. Though no critic has been able to interpret it in a way that will satisfy everybody, the poem continues to be read and continues to make a profound impact on its readers. But whatever the poem may "mean," its powerful effect is not produced either by its prose argument or by the mere vividness of its descriptions of scenery.

The prose argument is hardly more than a cryptic sketch of a story: Kubla Khan ordered a pleasure dome to be built in a garden, and both are described; then Kubla heard voices prophesying war. The poet recalls a vision of an Abyssinian maid playing a dulcimer and says that if he could revive the vision, he would be able to build the dome "in air," and everyone would think him bewitched. This summary does not really help very much.

Nor is the description in the poem, as description, really vivid enough to explain its strange power, for the objects described are interesting not so much for the accuracy with which they are described as for something else. We are affected in this poem by the same thing that affected Coleridge when he wrote it: the images *as* things, individually and in relation to each other. The images in the poem are not some kind of "audio-visual aid" to meaning; they are, or imply, the whole meaning. For the images communicate their meaning directly to our consciousness by what they are and how they function together.

Kubla's garden and pleasure dome are very peaceful and serene, with blossoming incense-bearing trees, ancient forests, sunny spots of greenery, and Alph, the sacred river, meandering five miles with a mazy motion. The spot is enclosed from the outside world by walls and towers. Still, whatever lies outside it is not entirely kept out, for in the garden is also a "deep romantic chasm," a frightening and savage place such as might be found in an old romance (this is what "romantic" means here), where the river enters the garden by boiling up in enormously powerful rhythmic surges from mysterious subterranean depths. There are also caverns "measureless to man," where the river plunges in tumult underground to a lifeless ocean. Amid this tumult Kubla hears ancestral voices prophesying war.

Except for the prophecy, all we are given in the first two-thirds of the poem is a description of what is enclosed in this unusual garden. The description is an interesting one, because the sights and sounds we are given are interesting in themselves. But it is interesting also because the images form themselves into a pattern. Whoever carried out Kubla's decree was able to enclose an area containing contrasts so strong as to be oppositions: The serene course of the river through the garden is in sharp contrast with its beginning and end, and the measureless caverns into which it plunges are contrasted with its meandering course, which is measurable (five miles), as is the garden itself (twice five miles). In the dome, oppositions seem to come together. The dome is at once sunny and icy, and its shadow floats on the waves of the river at precisely the point where is heard "the mingled measure" from the places where the meandering river turbulently erupts and tumultuously departs. Both sounds are heard; they are *mingled,* mixed but in a way that retains the identity of the sounds.

At this point the narrative account of things to be seen and heard in Kubla's garden breaks off, and the speaker shifts in the last third of the poem to another theme and another dome: a version of Kubla's that would be "made in air" by the speaker—were he able to revive vividly in his mind the imagery of an Abyssinian maid singing to the accompaniment of a dulcimer. An imagined scene shows what would happen if he were able to create the dome: people who heard him would be filled with awe and fear and would try to protect themselves from the unearthly power of the poet by magic. Oppositions brought into harmony also appeal in this section of the poem: those of male and female in the relationship of the poet to the maid and of the harmonious opposition in the music ("symphony" is used in its original sense and means a consonance of different sounds).

The shift from Kubla's dome to the poet's displays a contrast between the two domes that suddenly reveals the images of the first two-thirds of the poem in a different perspective. The imagery of what seemed at first merely a wonderfully exotic garden of an oriental potentate suddenly becomes charged with meaning when we learn that through an imaginative version of the garden the poet would be able to express a vision so powerful as to frighten ordinary people, though even they would recognize, without understanding how, that it was a vision gained by communication with a superior reality, indeed, with paradise.

The poet, however, is not able to "build that dome in air," and the poem is ostensibly about the poet's failure to do so. He cannot revive within him the imagery of the Abyssinian maid (who might be thought of here as a sort of muse), and he cannot therefore bring his soul to a condition in which his own music "loud and long" will create the poetical analogue of Kubla's dome. Yet, if the poet speaking the poem failed to create his transcendent dome, it cannot be said that *Coleridge* failed to give poetic form to the meaning he saw in the images of the garden. Coleridge's success is manifest in "Kubla Khan." Despite his offering the poem as a fragment and a psychological novelty, it seems complete, and it does build a dome in air. If generations of readers since 1797 (or 1799) have not been frightened by its meaning, they have nevertheless felt that a strange and powerful meaning is embodied, though ambiguously, in the images of Kubla's wonderful garden.

It is impossible to explain to everyone's satisfaction just what that meaning is.* And we shall not attempt to offer here an exhaustive or "correct" interpretation but merely some suggestions to give direction to your own reading of the poem. The river, with its mysteriously turbulent beginning and end and its peaceful course between, quite naturally suggests to many readers that it is rather like the life of man. We think it would be a mistake to say that the river Alph *is* the life of man, for to do that would tend to replace the river with an abstraction and begin a kind of interpretation in which the imagery of the poem becomes transmuted into a system of dry concepts. But the imagery may be left intact and still suggest certain things. We have already noted that the poem contains a number of opposites which are brought together without, however, being in conflict with each other, or at least not in a destructive conflict. The opposites, such as the sunniness of the dome and its caves of ice, are not synthesized, but retain their character while being reconciled. Indeed, the dome seems to be "a miracle of rare device" because, though sunny, it contains caves of ice. These oppositions create a tension that contributes to the marvelous quality of the garden as a whole and make it seem more perfect because in it conflict for the moment seems to have been suspended in harmony. The dome itself, a structure in which lateral thrusts are equally distributed so that the natural form supports the structure even when made of small blocks without a frame or external support, perfectly expresses a creative tension of opposition.

Still, the garden is not a secure place. Although inside it opposites are reconciled, there are other unreconciled opposites in the relation between the garden and the mystery lying outside, especially as suggested by the subterranean river, which, though it meanders peacefully within the garden, boils up turbulently and departs in tumult to a sunless sea. In the vision of the garden and the dome, the poet has a glimpse of a state of being which could be thought of as paradisiacal, Edenic (people would say that he had "drunk the milk of paradise"); but it is a paradise that is to be

---

*The range of critical opinion on this poem is very great. Critics are not agreed as to whether the poem is a whole or a fragment, whether the images are merely images or symbols, whether it was written under the influence of opium or not. One of the most sensible readings, and a trenchantly witty one, is that by Carol Woodring, "Coleridge and the Khan," *Essays in Criticism,* IX (1959), 361-368. See also Richard H. Fogle, "The Romantic Unity of 'Kubla Khan,'" *College English,* XIII (1951), 13-18; Elisabeth Schneider, *Coleridge, Opium, and Kubla Khan* (Chicago, 1953); Humphry House, *Coleridge* (London, 1953); Dorothy Mercer, "The Symbolism of 'Kubla Khan,'" *Journal of Aesthetics and Art Criticism,* XII (1953), 44-66; Marshall Suther, "On the Interpertation of 'Kubla Khan,'" *Bucknell Review,* VII (1957), 1-19; Alan C. Purves, "Formal Structure in 'Kubla Khan,'" *Studies in Romanticism,* I (1962), 187-191. This by no means exhausts the list of studies.

lost. For from the outside—i.e., in time—Kubla hears amid the roar of the departing river the ancestral voices prophesying war, a state in sharp conflict with the peacefulness of the garden and one which could very well bring about the destruction of the garden and dome. This pleasurable place seems as temporary as the span of the peaceful river is brief.

But the vision of the poet lasts long enough to afford him a glimpse of paradise. His own dome, made in the imagination, were he but able to make it, would not be subject to the ravages of war and death as Kubla's was but would embody more perfectly the full meaning of what he had only fleetingly seen in Kubla's. The ideal, temporarily embodied in an oriental garden either through the luck or skill of Kubla's landscape architect, would be eternally and fully realized in a transcendent work of the imagination. If Kubla's garden suggests a paradise to be lost—or one that has been lost—the poet's version of it will give an image of one that has, at least in imagination, been regained, or perhaps even one to be regained by mankind.

We have discussed the various features of Kubla's garden as images; to some critics—not all—these images are more than images: they are symbols—religious, cosmological, literary, even sexual. That is, the elements in the poem are said to "stand for" things other than what they are in themselves. The poem can be, and has been viewed either as a poem with unusually vivid images or as a poem in which the images, partly because of the poet's carefully systematic ordering of them, take on more meaning than images usually do. It would be an impertinence for us to try to settle the matter here, since many fine critics have written on both sides of the question. After you have read the chapter on symbolism (Chapter V), you might return to "Kubla Khan" to consider the poem from a symbolic point of view.

The distinction between images and symbols, as is suggested by the critical difficulties with this poem, is sometimes hard to draw. We have suggested that poetic images function as actually perceived—or imagined—sensory focal points for feelings, attitudes, ideas. Something of the same kind might be said of symbols.* In some cases, the difference between images and symbols may become a quantitative one—though literary study cannot quantify such differences numerically: when an image seems to take on so much meaning of a kind not relating directly to what the image is in itself that one is led to think more of these meanings than of the image, then perhaps the image could be said to function symbolically. At what point this happens it is hard to say: When is a man bald?

---

*George Whalley, in his superb *Poetic Process* (London, 1953), p. 166, says a symbol "is a focus of relationships."

Poems for Further Study:

Ode to Evening

If aught of oaten stop, or pastoral song,
May hope, O pensive Eve, to soothe thine ear,
Like thy own brawling springs,
Thy springs, and dying gales,
O nymph reserved, while now the bright-haired sun
Sits in yon western tent, whose cloudy skirts,
With brede ethereal wove,
O'erhang his wavy bed:
Now air is hushed, save where the weak-eyed bat,
With short shrill shriek, flits by on leathern wing,
Or where the beetle winds
His small but sullen horn,
As oft he rises 'midst the twilight path,
Against the pilgrim borne in heedless hum:
Now teach me, maid composed,
To breathe some softened strain,
Whose numbers stealing through thy darkning vale,
May not unseemly with its stillness suit,
As musing slow, I hail
Thy genial loved return!
For when thy folding star arising shows
His paly circlet at his warning lamp
The fragrant hours and elves
Who slept in buds the day,
And many a nymph who wreathes her brows with sedge,
And sheds the freshening dew, and lovelier still,
The pensive pleasures sweet
Prepare thy shadowy car.
Then let me rove some wild and heathy scene,
Or find some ruin 'midst its dreary dells,
Whose walls more awful nod
By thy religious gleams.
Or if chill blustring winds, or driving rain,
Prevent my willing feet, be mine the hut,
That from the mountain's side,
Views wilds, and swelling floods,
And hamlets brown, and dim-discovered spires,
And hears their simple bell, and marks o'er all
Thy dewy fingers draw
The gradual dusky veil.

While Spring shall pour his showers, as oft he wont,
And bathe thy breathing tresses, meekest Eve!
While Summer loves to sport,
Beneath thy lingering light:
While sallow Autumn fills thy lap with leaves,
Or Winter yelling through the troublous air,
Affrights thy shrinking train
And rends thy robes
So long regardful of thy quiet rule,
Shall fancy, friendship, science, smiling peace,
Thy gentlest influence own,
And love thy favorite name!

William Collins

Questions.

1. The descriptions of Spring, Summer, Autumn, and Winter, lines 41-48, involve PERSONIFICATIONS. How accurate are these as summaries of typical seasonal events?
2. Choose the most effective description in the poem, and justify your choice by its vividness, precision, and ability to suggest a mental picture.

The Night Piece, to Julia

Her eyes the glow-worm lend thee,
The shooting stars attend thee;
And the elves also,
Whose little eyes glow,
Like the sparks of fire, befriend thee.

No will-o'-the-wisp mislight thee;
Nor snake, or slow-worm bite thee:
But on, on thy way
Not making a stay,
Since ghost there's none to affright thee.

Let not the dark thee cumber;
What though the moon does slumber?
The stars of the night
Will lend thee their light,
Like tapers clear without number.

Then Julia let me woo thee,
Thus, thus to come unto me:
  And when I shall meet
  Thy silv'ry feet,
My soul I'll pour into thee.

ROBERT HERRICK

My Silks and Fine Array

My silks and fine array,
My smiles and languished air,
By love are driv'n away;
And mournful lean Despair
Brings me yew to deck my grave:
Such end true lovers have.

His face is fair as heav'n
When springing buds unfold;
O why to him was't giv'n
Whose heart is wintry cold?
His breast is love's all-worshiped tomb,
Where all love's pilgrims come.

Bring me an ax and spade,
Bring me a winding-sheet;
When I my grave have made
Let winds and tempests beat;
Then down I'll lie as cold as clay.
True love doth pass away!

WILLIAM BLAKE

From Sing-Song

The wind has such a rainy sound
  Moaning through the town,
The sea has such a windy sound—
  Will the ships go down?

The apples in the orchard
Tumble from their tree
Oh, will the ships go down, go down,
In the windy sea?

CHRISTINA ROSSETTI

Meeting at Night

I

The gray sea and the long black land;
And the yellow half-moon large and low;
And the startled little waves that leap
In fiery ringlets from their sleep,
As I gain the cove with pushing prow,
And quench its speed i' the slushy sand.

II

Then a mile of warm sea-scented beach;
Three fields to cross till a farm appears;
A tap at the pane, the quick sharp scratch
And blue spurt of a lighted match,
And a voice less loud, thro' its joys and fears,
Than the two hearts each to each!

ROBERT BROWNING

Parting at Morning

Round the cape of a sudden came the sea,
And the sun looked over the mountain's rim:
And straight was a path of gold for him,
And the need of a world of men for me.

ROBERT BROWNING

Sparkles from the Wheel

Where the city's ceaseless crowd moves on the livelong day,
Withdrawn I join a group of children watching, I pause aside with them.

By the curb toward the edge of the flagging,
A knife-grinder works at his wheel sharpening a great knife,
Bending over he carefully holds it to the stone, by foot and knee,

With measur'd tread he turns rapidly, as he presses with light but firm hand,
Forth issue then in copious golden jets,
Sparkles from the wheel.

The scene and all its belongings, how they seize and affect me,
The sad sharp-chinn'd old man with worn clothes and broad shoulder-band of leather,
Myself effusing and fluid, a phantom curiously floating, now here absorb'd and arrested,

effusing—pouring out

The group, (an unminded point set in a vast surrounding,)
The attentive, quiet children, the loud, proud, restive base of the streets,
The low hoarse purr of the whirling stone, the light-press'd blade,
Diffusing, dropping, sideways-darting, in tiny showers of gold,
Sparkles from the wheel.

WALT WHITMAN

Suggested Poems for Further Reading (ANTHOLOGY):

Andrew Marvell, "The Garden," p. 395
George Peele, "Gently Dip," p. 413

Metaphor

3

The Watch

Man is a Watch, wound up at first, but never
Wound up again: Once down, He's down for ever.
The Watch once down, all motions then do cease;
And Mans Pulse stopt, *All Passions sleep in Peace.*

ROBERT HERRICK

A careless paraphrase of this poem might say that man is like a watch, differing only in his inability to be rewound. But a citation only of the comparison and the very obvious difference between man and watch conveys more information about the ignorance of the paraphraser than about what is going on in the poem. Watches must be wound up, and one matter that an adequate paraphrase would have to explain is the implication about the kind of universe—its underlying outlook on life—that such a comparison involves. Also to be conveyed is the wry finality of the end of the second line, a finality which indicates a recognition of the inadequacy of the comparison. The third line seems to belabor the comparison by repeating the substance of the second line as it relates to watch rather than to man. But the fourth line leads us to the "discovery" of the poem, which is the distinction between man and watch, and this distinction is made in part by changing the verb from "down" to "stopt," a change which emphasizes the difference between a mechanical motion like ticking and the variant beat of the pulse and those "Passions" which affect its regularity. The poem asserts finally then that man is like a watch only in being "wound up," but his Master, having performed this action, allows him to run at his own pace and to establish his own rhythm in the running until, *requiescat in pacem,* he is overtaken by eternal sleep.

Even here, however, more is implied than may appear at first sight. For the poem clearly says that it is the passions that sleep in peace, and in the religious context implied by the metaphor of the Master who winds up the Watch Man, in the first place, we know that it is the restless motions brought on by the passions that sleep, along with the vessel of those passions, the body. The soul, which has nothing to do with watches, being individual and unmechanical, lives forever. This explication shows that when we try simply to translate metaphors from poems into prose statements we find ourselves in difficulty because the metaphors do much more than compare.

Yet, metaphor is usually defined as a comparison without the use of *like* or *as* ("My mind to me a kingdom is") and simile as a comparison in which *like* or *as* are used ("My luve is like a red red rose"). This definition may be adequate for most prose where metaphors and similes are used primarily to make logical meaning more vivid. To say that the Mississippi River is a great trough extending from northern Minnesota to the Gulf of Mexico helps to show the importance of the Mississippi in the topography of the United States. In this metaphor the reader's attention is fixed firmly on the river; the comparison of the river to a trough merely helps to show the functional importance of the river. In poetry metaphor also makes a comparison but it does more than that; it tends to fuse the elements used in the comparison. In Herrick's watch metaphor the elements are synthesized; the idea being illustrated cannot be thought of without the illustration. If this is a comparison, it has clearly got out of hand.

For the time being, let us concentrate primarily on metaphor (A is B, or some variation which presupposes such a relation: "Time, a maniac scattering dust") and take up simile (A is like or as B: "Life, like a dome of many-colored glass") later on (p. 38). Analogy, an extended comparison, is discussed briefly on p. 41. Much of what is said here about metaphor will be applicable to simile.

To define metaphor as a comparison is not incorrect; in poetry and imaginative prose, it is simply inadequate. For, as we have already seen, poetic metaphor can easily work in a way that makes its comparative function seem a little irrelevant. According to the *Oxford Universal Dictionary,* to compare is "to represent as similar; to liken . . . To mark the similarities and differences of; to bring together for the purpose of noting these." Implicit in these definitions is the idea of keeping the things being compared distinct and separate. In discursive prose, where the main concern is clear logical meaning, it is good to keep identities carefully separated. To be understood with perfect clarity, a writer must first make very explicit what he is talking about and then show how these things are related.

Metaphor and simile typically make the elements being combined in logical assertions as clear and as vivid as possible, and the reader does not lose sight of the fact that the writer is merely comparing—likening, showing similarities—when he says that one of the things being talked about *is* something different from what it ordinarily is. A writer of discursive prose does not usually want to do anything more than compare because the explicit statement does the work, and any figures of speech used must help it.

A metaphor can be used merely as a comparison, but as any student whose metaphors have been marked "inappropriate" can attest, it is a difficult figure to manage. Part of the reason for this is that metaphor has a tendency to call too much attention to itself, and when it does that it ceases to function properly as a logical comparison: It has diverted attention away from the thing it was supposed to be illustrating. It especially does this when it gets mixed with other metaphors.

In grammatical form a metaphor asserts an identity between two things of different kinds (the statement, Jane is a pretty girl, merely indicates membership in a class of similar beings and is not a metaphor). It asserts A is B, or makes some statement that presupposes this relation, such as,

> But at my back I always hear
> Time's winged chariot hurrying near,

in which Time is changed into a person with a chariot. In discursive prose, we are in a common-sense way concerned with identities and relationships outside the discourse, and when using a metaphor we merely pretend momentarily, for purposes of illustration, that two dissimilar and ordinarily unrelated things are the same. It is clearly a momentary pretense, for our main concern is that the identities and relationships outside the discourse be kept clear. The pretense is made only for the sake of an illustrative comparison, despite the grammatical form in which metaphor is expressed.

In a poem, conceived as a verbal structure, the relationships inside the poem are more important than the relationships of elements in the poem with things outside it. Of course, the poem as a whole has relevance to matters outside itself, and objects outside it are named and connected by statements contained in it. But a poem is an imaginative entity made out of words, images, metaphor, sound, more than it is a piece of discourse. In a poem we are interested more in what is happening inside than in what is being said about states of affairs outside. In poetry the pretense made in saying A is B, therefore, is not quite so much a mere pretense as it is in common-sense discursive prose. Rather, it is an imaginative identification that constitutes one of the elements of the poem. The identification is made within the poem only, to be sure. But within the poem a reader must suspend common-sense disbelief and accept metaphoric identifications with the same kind of belief that he used in accepting in a fairy tale a wolf's eating a grandmother without noticeable ill effects on the grandmother. If one submits himself to the world of imaginative relationships created by the poem, he must accept the way things are connected in that world while he is there. If, in the world of the poem, Time drives a chariot, the reader simply has to let him drive it. When we revert to common-sense and say, "What is meant here is that time seems *as if* it were driving a fast chariot," we step out of the poem. In a way, we are obliged to have a childlike faith in the possibility of strange relationships and transformations while reading the poem. If we cannot forget common sense and have this faith, the marvelous events going on in poetry will at most seem interesting, but untrue.

Whether a metaphor is a comparison or an identification, therefore, is partly a matter of perspective. From the point of view of common-sense, rooted as it is in ordinary relationships, a metaphor cannot be anything but a comparison. From the point of view of poetry, in which any kind of relationship is possible, things are what they are said to be.

Metaphor in poetry, instead of merely comparing, takes seriously the grammatical form in which metaphoric relations are expressed. Let us see what happens to metaphors of the brain, fabric, and yarn in a poem by Emily Dickinson. (In this poem a simile is used in the second line.)

*I Felt a Cleavage in my Mind**

I felt a cleavage in my mind
as if my brain had split;
I tried to match it, seam by seam,
But could not make it fit.
The thought behind I strove to join
Unto the thought before,
But sequence ravelled out of reach
Like balls upon the floor.

EMILY DICKINSON

What happens in this poem? The poem says that a cleavage occurred in the mind of the speaker, and she cannot mend it; when she tried to fit thoughts together, sequence ravelled out of reach like balls on the floor.

---

*From *Poems by Emily Dickinson*, Little, Brown & Co., 1937.

"Mind" and "sequence" are abstractions, but the poet makes them behave as if they were concrete. In one sense, of course, the poem describes the experience of a mental dissociation and does so by making implied comparisons between abstractions and concrete things. But the effect produced on a reader while he is reading the poem is not one of logical comparison. The abstractions do not merely seem *as if* they are concrete; in the poem, they *are* concrete. Logical analysis of the meaning of the poem reduces the strength of the identifications by translating them into comparisons. But analysis occurs outside the poem, after one has read and responded to it. Whatever the things in the poem, as long as they function within the poem, they do what they are said to do, and a reader is obliged to think of them that way. Not entirely perhaps: it is difficult to suspend one's notion of the world as it ordinarily is, and, of course, the poem does say something about human experience, describing very vividly a curious state of mind familiar to most people. But the poem tells us more about experience if we suspend analysis while reading and think as the poem asks us to instead of translating it at once into a form that makes logical sense. Through its metaphorical associations, the poem gives us a new and more vividly precise way of thinking about the experience described.

Metaphor in poetry is not then a kind of theoretical embellishment, but a primary mode of expression and even of thought. It would be misleading to say that metaphor is a language, for it is not separate from what is normally meant by language, but a special use of it, a special way of forming ideas in it. What it essentially does is to bring things together, whether it is considered as a mode of expression or of thought.

Thought for many means propositional statements and problem-solving. Unless an idea can be stated in propositional form it is not an idea. This is not the place to debate this issue, and it is mentioned here only to distinguish this kind of thought from metaphoric thought, which is associational and concrete instead of analytical and abstract. All of us use metaphor; we almost cannot help it, because people like to picture the things they think about if they possibly can. Furthermore, language is full of dead metaphors, to the extent that even in manipulating abstractions one is unable to avoid making statements like "A concept is *in* the mind." The metaphor of a spatial container for the idea is built into the words used. It is very difficult for most people really to think about verbal abstractions (the X's and Y's in mathematics may be another matter) purely as abstractions. Rare is the student, for instance, who can conceive the Platonic Idea of the familiar classroom chair as anything but another somehow vaguely superior chair, but an actual chair nevertheless. More than most of us are aware, our thinking about all kinds of ideas is governed by some concrete metaphorical image that we unknowingly keep referring to.

In sifting among abstractions for purposes of abstract thought and analysis of ideas, it is desirable to minimize the amount of metaphor involved, but a great deal would be lost, even from science and philosophy, if metaphoric thought were eliminated—were that, indeed, possible. For according to a distinguished logician, the late Morris Raphael Cohen, metaphors "are often the way in which creative minds perceive things." The rhetorical view of metaphor, according to Professor Cohen, "regards every metaphor as an analogy in which the words, *like*, or *as* etc., are omitted. This presupposes that the recognition of the literal truth precedes the metaphor, which is thus always a conscious transference of the properties of one thing to another. But history shows that metaphors are generally older than expressed analogies."*

Although Cohen's account of metaphor as a way of grasping new knowledge suggests that there is a good deal of truth to William Blake's aphorism, "what is now proved was once only imagin'd," metaphoric thought in poetry is valuable not because it may lead to useful discoveries in science. (It doesn't, except in psychology.) But it does help us to understand freshly and vividly, and with a kind of precision, matters of concern to human life that are represented in poetry. We don't usually get new information about them (poetry is not a reliable source of factual information); rather we gain new insights into human life which as often as not deepen its mystery because they enlarge our vision of it.

The suggestion that metaphor has clarity may be hard for the beginning student of poetry to grasp, because poetic metaphors have a good deal of ambiguity about them and are subject to various interpretations. Perhaps clarity is not the best word to use, since it suggests that metaphor has a clarity of reference to something outside of the poem, which it doesn't. Intensity is perhaps a better word, because what metaphor helps poetic language to do—metaphor and image and sound—is to gain a degree of concentration and intensity that metaphor rarely has in prose.*

The difference in the use of metaphor in poetry and prose may be seen in the attitudes toward mixed metaphors in each. In discursive prose a mixed metaphor is almost always a fault. Though a skillful prose writer may occasionally mix metaphors if they do not begin to attract too much attention, he will normally avoid doing so, because a mixed metaphor violates the kind of clarity needed by prose. But in poetry mixed metaphor is not a fault. Shakespeare, especially in his later plays, brings together

---

*Morris Raphael Cohen, *A Preface to Logic*. New York, 1944; 1956, p. 98. See also Jerome Bruner, *On Knowing*. New York, 1965, pp. 65-66.

*Many poets themselves say that one of the poet's purposes is to achieve a kind of clarity. See John Press, *The Chequer'd Shade: Reflections on Obscurity in Poetry*. London, 1958; and also George Whalley, *Poetic Process*. London, 1954.

metaphors from widely disparate sources and runs them together, sometimes two or more in a single line. Here is Cleopatra toward the end of the play, speaking of Antony:

His legs bestrid the ocean, his reared arm
Crested the world: his voice was propertied
As all the tuned spheres, and that to friends:
But when he meant to quail, and shade the orb,
He was as rattling thunder. For his bounty,
There was no winter in't: an autumn 'twas
That grew them more by reaping: his delights
were dolphin like, they showed his back above
The elements they lived in: in his livery
Walked crowns and crownets: realms and islands were
As plates dropped from his pocket.

Antony and Cleopatra
V. ii. 82-92

Shakespeare employs a half dozen different metaphors in this short passage. As John Press remarks concerning a similar passage, "We are expected to follow him unquestionably as he darts from one order of experience to another; to hold in our mind's eye a sequence of rapidly dissolving images; to retain in the memory the criss-cross of reverberating echoes."* For Shakespeare mixed metaphor is a device for increasing the intensity of a passage, and he uses it often. Percy Bysshe Shelley not only mixes metaphors but mixes different sensory impressions together (synaesthesia).

The sweetness seems to satiate the faint wind:
And in the soul a wild odor is felt,
Beyond the sense, like fiery dews that melt
Into the bosom of a frozen bud.—

From "Epipsychidion"

And William Blake metaphorically changes sound into sight in "London":

How the Chimney-sweeper's cry
Every blackening Church appalls;
And the hapless Soldier's sigh
Runs in blood down Palace walls.

Mixed metaphor in poetry grasps a multiplicity of relationships and packs them in as thickly as the structural limitations of language will allow, not

**The Chequer'd Shade*, p. 197.

to confuse but to concentrate the poem's meaning. "In prose," says J. Issacs, "all comparisons are simple and uncompounded. In poetry all metaphors are mixed metaphors."*

Sonnet 73

That time of year thou mayst in me behold
When yellow leaves, or none, or few, do hang
Upon those boughs which shake against the cold,
Bare ruined choirs where late the sweet birds sang:
In me thou see'st the twilight of such day
As after sunset fadeth in the west;
Which by and by black night doth take away,
Death's second self, that seals up all in rest:
In me thou see'st the glowing of such fire,
That on the ashes of his youth doth lie,
As the death-bed whereon it must expire,
Consumed with that which it was nourished by.
This thou perceiv'st, which makes thy love more strong,
To love that well which thou must leave ere long.

William Shakespeare

The poem suggests that the speaker is getting old and is not going to live forever, and that, therefore, the person who loves him will love him more. The poem implies this by developing the theme of aging in three basic metaphors: autumn, sleep, and a burned-out fire.

Thus far we have talked almost entirely about metaphor and have only touched on the other common figures. As was said at the beginning of this chapter, analogy does not in poetry belong with metaphor and simile. We shall discuss analogy in a moment. But metaphor and simile are close relatives, differing only in grammatical form and in the completeness of the metaphoric identifications.**

Metaphor says A *is* B, or otherwise substitutes A for B. Simile says A is like B. Students, who are asked to distinguish metaphor from simile on examinations, often attach an exaggerated significance to the difference as

---

**The Background of Modern Poetry*. London and New York, 1952; paperback, n. d., p. 16.

**This is not the view of all scholars, though it is a common one. For a discussion of the points of difference, see Christine Brooks-Rose, *A Grammar of Metaphor*, London, 1958, pp. 13-15, an extremely thorough and systematic study of the ways in which metaphors are formed.

defined above. A metaphor is usually more intense because it substitutes one term for another, but a simile can behave almost like a metaphor, when the terms of the comparison are overshadowed by the vividness of images used in it. In "I Felt a Cleavage in My Mind," as we saw, similes led to metaphor almost imperceptibly. Similes, on the other hand, may more easily function as mere comparisons than metaphors, because grammatically they assert a similarity rather than an identity and are more often used in discursive prose. Again, however, the extent of difference between simile and metaphor depends on the way simile is used, on whether a poet really wants a comparison in which identities are kept clear or wants to use the simile as a means of making a smooth transition from comparison to identification. Simply heaping up simile, as is done in the following poem, seems to produce a metaphoric effect. The reader is aware of the changes from simile to metaphor at the end.

Sic Vita

Like to the falling of a star;
Or as the flights of eagles are;
Or like the fresh Spring's gaudy hue;
Or silver drops of morning dew;
Or like a wind that chafes the flood;
Or bubbles which on water stood;
Even such is man, whose borrowed light
Is straight call'd in, and paid to night.

The wind blows out; the bubble dies;
The Spring entombed in Autumn lies;
The dew dries up; the star is shot;
The flight is past; and man forgot.

Henry King

Questions.

1. How many different similes are used?
2. Do they appear once or twice? If twice, how are they used the second time?

Another well-known device in figurative language is PERSONIFICATION, which is merely the name given to a very common kind of metaphor: those which identify inanimate objects and abstractions with people. Personifications are not different from metaphors; they are merely one species of metaphor. John Gay uses personifications in one of his songs.

Love in Her Eyes

Love in her eyes sits playing,
And sheds delicious death;
Love in her lips is straying,
And warbling in her breath.
Love on her breast sits panting,
And swells with soft desire,
No grace, no charm is wanting
To set her heart on fire.

JOHN GAY

Gay does not push the personification very hard, to make the metaphor too vivid, because a lightly suggestive quality is better to characterize the delicate beauty of the woman.

In some poetry, the poet does not worry about having his metaphor retain a TONE that is consistent with our normal attitudes toward the subject being talked about. In fact, he may stretch the metaphorical associations by making some surprising connections, or making them in a surprising way. Such far-fetched metaphors or similes, called CONCEITS, were especially popular in poetry of the earlier seventeenth century, but are also used in much modern poetry. In using a conceit the poet wants intensity, and he wants to delight us by his cleverness and WIT—a term which in discussions of poetry usually does not suggest humor but rather a complex association of disparate things.

There is a Garden in Her Face

There is a garden in her face
Where roses and white lilies grow;
A heavenly paradise is that place,
Wherein all pleasant fruits do flow;
There cherries grow which none may buy
Till "Cherry-ripe" themselves do cry.

Those cherries fairly do enclose
Of orient pearl a double row,
Which when her lovely laughter shows,
They look like rosebuds filled with snow;
Yet them nor peer nor prince can buy
Till "Cherry-ripe" themselves do cry.

Her eyes like angels watch them still;
Her brows like bended bows do stand,
Threatening with piercing frowns to kill
All that attempt, with eye or hand,
Those sacred cherries to come nigh
Till "Cherry-ripe" themselves do cry.

THOMAS CAMPION

Earlier in this chapter we removed analogy from consideration as an aspect of metaphor. To do so does not suggest that poems cannot use analogy, for many do. Here is one entirely based on an analogy:

That Women are but Men's Shadows

Follow a shadow, it still flies you;
Seem to fly it, it will pursue:
So court a mistress, she denies you;
Let her alone, she will court you.
Say, are not women truly, then,
Styled but the shadows of us men?

At morn, and even, shades are longest;
At noon they are or short, or none:
So men at weakest, they are strongest,
But grant us perfect, they're not known.
Say are not women truly, then,
Styled but the shadows of us men?

BEN JONSON

This is indeed a comparison, an extended one between shadows and women, which is logically developed throughout the poem.

There are virtually no limits to the range of metaphorical connections that are possible in poetry; anything is acceptable that will work. And it is impossible to say in advance of their appearance in a poem that some metaphors are good and others bad. Of course, our language is full of dead metaphors, associations that have become so conventional as not to summon anything but a vague cognitive response (the heart of the problem, off the top of one's head), and the discourse of most people is, alas, full of CLICHES, tired expressions, some of them metaphors breathing their last (fly in the ointment). Dead metaphors or cliches would not be used in poetry as a means of concentrating meaning, but they might be employed ironically, so even they cannot be ruled out.

The question to be asked in determining whether the metaphor in a poem is good or bad is simply the pragmatic one: Does it work, is it effective in that poem? Any answer is necessarily partly subjective, since in order for metaphor to be effective the reader must be able to respond to it. But the answer should also be objective enough so that the reasons why the metaphor does or does not work can be discussed with other readers on some common ground.

Poems for Further Study:

From *The Song of Solomon*

Behold, thou art fair, my love; behold thou art fair;
thou hast doves' eyes within thy locks: thy hair is as a
flock of goats, that appear from mount Gilead.
Thy teeth are like a flock of sheep that are even
shorn, which come up from the washing; whereof everyone
bear twins, and none is barren among them.
Thy lips are like a thread of scarlet, and thy
speech is comely; thy temples are like a piece of pomengranate
within thy locks.
Thy neck is like the tower of David builded for an
armory, whereon there hang a thousand bucklers, all shields
of mighty men.
Thy two breasts are like two young roses that are twins,
which feed among the lilies.
Until the day break, and the shadows flee away, I will
get me to the mountain of myrrh, and to the hill of frankincense.
Thou art all fair, my love there is no spot in thee.
Come with me from Lebanon, my spouse, with me from Lebanon:
look from the top of Amana, from the top of Shenir and Hermon,
from the lions' dens, from the mountains of leopards.

Thou hast ravished my heart, with one of thine eyes, with one chain of thy neck.
How fair is thy love, my sister, my spouse! how much better is thy love than wine! and the smell of thine ointments than all spices!
Thy lips, O my spouse, drop as the honeycomb: honey and milk are under thy tongue; and the smell of thy garments is like the smell of Lebanon.
A garden inclosed is my sister, my spouse; a spring shut up, a fountain sealed.
Thy plants are an orchard of pomengranates, with pleasant fruits; camphire, with spikenard,
Spikenard and saffron; calamus and cinnamon, with all trees of frankincense; myrrh and aloes, with the chief spices:
A fountain of gardens, a well of living waters, and streams from Lebanon.
Awake, O north wind; and come, thou south; blow upon my garden, that the spices thereof may flow out. Let my beloved come into his garden, and eat his pleasant fruits.

I Serve a Mistress

I serve a mistress whiter than the snow,
Straighter than the cedar, brighter than the glass,
Finer in trip and swifter than the roe,
More pleasant than the field of flowering grass;
More gladsome to my withering joys that fade,
Than winter's sun or summer's cooling shade.

Sweeter than swelling grape of ripest wine,
Softer than feathers of the fairest swan,
Smoother than jet, more stately than the pine,
Fresher than poplar, smaller than my span,
Clearer than beauty's fiery pointed beam
Or icy crust of crystal's frozen stream.

Yet is she curster than the bear by kind,
And harder-hearted than the aged oak,
More glib than oil, more fickle than the wind,
Stiffer than steel, no sooner bent but broke.
Lo! thus my service is a lasting sore;
Yet will I serve, although I die therefore.

Anthony Munday

Questions.

1. All the comparisons in the preceding poem are in the comparative degree (whiter, straighter, etc.). What would be the difference in the effect if they were made absolute ("I serve a mistress who's as white as snow")?
2. Are these comparisons similes?
3. Compare the description of the mistress in the first two stanzas with the description in the selection from The Song of Solomon, on p. 42.

On the Death of Mr. Robert Levett,

A Practiser in Physic

Condemned to hope's delusive mine,
As on we toil from day to day,
By sudden blasts, or slow decline,
Our social comforts drop away.

Well tried through many a varying year,
See Levett to the grave descend
Officious, innocent, sincere,
Of ev'ry friendless name the friend.

Yet still he fills affection's eye,
Obscurely wise and coarsely kind;
Nor lettered arrogance deny
Thy praise to merit unrefined.

When fainting nature called for aid,
And hov'ring death prepared the blow,
His vigorous remedy displayed
The power of art without the show.

In mis'ry's darkest cavern known,
His useful care was ever nigh,
Where hopeless anguish poured his groan,
And lonely want retired to die.

No summons mocked by chill delay,
No petty gain disdained by pride;
The modest wants of ev'ry day
The toil of ev'ry day supplied.

His virtues walked their narrow round,
Nor make a pause, nor left a void;
And sure the Eternal Master found
The single talent well employed.

The busy day—the peaceful night,
Unfelt, unclouded, glided by;
His frame was firm—his powers were bright,
Though now his eightieth year was nigh.

Then with no fiery throbbing pain,
No cold gradations of decay,
Death broke at once the vital chain,
And freed his soul the nearest way.

SAMUEL JOHNSON

Questions.

1. At first reading, this poem may not seem very metaphorical. Actually, it contains many personifications of abstractions, a kind of metaphor of which the eighteenth century was very fond. What effect do they produce?
2. Are the metaphors vivid? Are they meant to be?

*The Mind is an Enchanting Thing**

is an enchanted thing
like the glaze on a
katydid-wing
subdivided by sun
till the nettings are legion.
Like Gieseking playing Scarlatti;
like the apteryx-awl
as a beak, or the
kiwi's rain-shawl
of hair feathers, the mind
feeling its way as though blind,
walks along with its eyes on the ground,

*Reprinted with permission of Faber and Faber Ltd., London, and of The Macmillan Company from *Collected Poems* by Marianne Moore. Copyright Marianne Moore 1944.

It has memory's ear
that can hear without
having to hear.
Like the gyroscope's fall,
truly unequivocal
because trued by regnant certainty,
it is power of
strong enchantment. It
is like the dove-
neck animated by
sun; it is memory's eye;
it's conscientious inconsistency.
It tears off the veil; tears
the temptation, the
mist the heart wears,
from its eyes,—if the heart
has a face; it takes apart
dejection. It's fire in the dove-neck's
iridescence, in the
inconsistencies
of Scarlatti.
Unconfusion submits
its confusion to proof; it's
not a Herod's oath that cannot change

MARIANNE MOORE

*The Heavy Bear Who Goes With Me**

"the withness of the body"

The heavy bear who goes with me,
A manifold honey to smear his face,
Clumsy and lumbering here and there,
The central ton of every place,
The hungry beating brutish one
In love with candy, anger, and sleep,
Crazy factotum, dishevelling all,
Climbs the building, kicks the football,
Boxes his brother in the hate-ridden city.

Breathing at my side, that heavy animal,
That heavy bear who sleeps with me,
Howls in his sleep for a world of sugar,
Howls in his sleep because the tight-rope
A sweetness intimate as the water's clasp,
Trembles and shows the darkness beneath.
—The strutting show-off is terrified,
Dressed in his dress-suit, bulging his pants,
Trembles to think that his quivering meat
Must finally wince at nothing at all.

That inescapable animal walks with me,
Has followed me since the black womb held,
Moves where I move, distorting my gesture,
A caricature, a swollen shadow,
A stupid clown of the spirit's motive
Perplexes and affronts with his own darkness.
The secret life of belly and bone,
Opaque, too near, my private, yet unknown,
Stretches to embrace the very dear
With whom I would walk without him near,
Touches her grossly, although a word
Would bare my heart and make me clear,
Stumbles, flounders, and strives to be fed
Dragging me with him in his mouthing care,
Amid the hundred million of his kind,
The scrimmage of appetite everywhere.

DELMORE SCHWARTZ

*On Silence**

Silence is the pulling in of nets
on the sand. It is a tent
in a square. Silence is the covenant
of noise when the mind sleeps
in its neutral passion.

---

*©1960 by Ned O'Gorman. Reprinted from his volume *Adam Before His Mirror* by permission of Harcourt, Brace & World, Inc.

It is the bulb of a tulip
since silence looks in variety
And antecedes spring. Silence
rises to the high places
of the heart where meadows
flower and the dark passages
reach into light.
It is the power of a drum.
The interval of silence
is like a coiled rope.

In man an antiphon sleeps
facing the sun, bound foursquare
by a golden cord. Silence
is the desolation of the cord
and the waking of the antiphon.

NED O'GORMAN

Suggested Poems for Further Reading (ANTHOLOGY):

Margaret Cavendish, Duchess of Newcastle, "My Cabinets Are Oyster-Shells," p. 281.
John Fletcher, "Now the Lusty Spring," p. 337.
Emily Dickinson, "I Stepped from Plank to Plank," p. 316.

Words

4

*Pretty Words**

Poets make pets of pretty, docile words:
I love smooth words, like gold-enamelled fish
Which circle slowly with a silken swish,
And tender ones, like downy-feathered birds:
Words shy and dappled, deep-eyed deer in herds,
Come to my hand, and playful if I wish,
Or purring softly at a silver dish,
Blue Persian kittens, fed on cream and curds.

I love bright words, words up and singing early;
Words that are luminous in the dark, and sing;
Warm lazy words, white cattle under trees;
I love words opalescent, cool, and pearly,
Like midsummer moths, and honied words like bees
Gilded and sticky, with a little sting.

ELINOR WYLIE

One of the initial difficulties in learning to read poetry comes from the commonness of its medium, words. Words assault us every day from the various mass media in such profusion that to preserve sanity we close our ears to them. Words in practical use in daily life point away from themselves, as it were, to objects, events, courses of action, and are used as signs for things which are logically manipulated in sentences to say something

*Copyright 1932 by Alfred A. Knopf, Inc., and renewed 1960 by Edwina C. Rubenstein. Reprinted from *Collected Poems of Elinor Wylie* by permission of the publisher.

about relations among the things. Accordingly, in ordinary reading we try to get over the words as quickly as possible and concentrate on what they are saying.

This kind of reading simply does not work with poetry, which, as has been said, is not primarily discourse but a verbal structure—not something in which words point outside but something in which the various qualities possessed by words interact to produce a unified form. A poem is not, of course, completely an abstract self-contained form. Words in poetry refer to things—name, describe, indicate relationships—outside the poem, and some poems more than others make statements that can, as statements, be considered independently of the poem. But in reading the words and predications in a poem, one must see them in their proper context also as functional elements in a structure which, though it may contain statements, is in a very real sense independent of what is said in it.

One must, that is, become keenly aware of the way in which words work in poetry. Instead of simply trying to look quickly past the words to their referents, as in our routine reading, we must learn to see and hear words as perceptively as possible.

The words in a poem are referred to as its DICTION, and the words used by a poet are his diction. Since poems are made of words, all aspects of the art of poetry might properly be considered as aspects of diction. Words have meaning, evoke images, are combined in a special way to make metaphors, and are used to produce sound patterns. And though in this book some of these matters are considered in separate chapters, they are still related to diction. Thus far we have said very little about meaning, because we wished first to direct attention to some of the less well-understood characteristics of poetic language, especially image and metaphor, and to emphasize the importance of these characteristics in poetry. In this chapter we should like to concentrate primarily on meaning, but also make some incidental preliminary comments on sound, a matter which will be dealt with more fully in a later chapter.

Words are not inert counters with fixed limited meanings. Their meanings are not determined logically, but arise out of their histories: where they came from and how and where they have been used. And English is constantly changing, though of course it is not unique in this respect. As a result of its largely borrowed vocabulary, it has a great richness of verbal resources. Not only does English have a double and even triple vocabulary from which to select words for most situations, but many words can be used to convey a great range of meanings.

The meanings of words can be divided into two different kinds: DENOTATIVE and CONNOTATIVE. Denotative meaning is that given in the dictionary;

what the word designates or names, its most general meaning. Connotative meaning is what it suggests or implies. To take a simple example, the term *six-gun* denotatively means a large, single-action revolver, typically of .44 calibre, holding six cartridges. It connotes the Old West of movies and TV (for our generation), with dusty, sunbaked wooden towns, horses tied to a rail in front of the saloon, and slouchy men wearing big hats. There would be something wrong, or at least very strange, if a gangster of the 1920's referred to his pistol as a *six-gun,* even if it were the weapon of Wyatt Earp himself; more likely it would be a *gat* or a *rod,* terms appropriate to the 'twenties.

Connotations of words are commonly divided into three kinds: PEJORATIVE, NEUTRAL, and AMELIORATIVE, or bad, neutral, and good. The word *woman* would usually be neutral, *female* usually pejorative (except in very objective discussions), and *lady* ameliorative. The division of connotation into these broad categories is sometimes useful in studying poetry because pejoration and amelioration help to tell us about the tone of a passage, as they will in the discussion of a symbolic poem in the next chapter. But usually a reader must be concerned with subtler connotations than can be lumped together in these three categories.

Six-gun, gat, rod, are crude examples of connotation because the words are ephemeral, a kind of argot or specialized vocabulary used in special situations in which they have been memorable or frequently used.

Because words change in meaning, the meaning of borrowed words does not continue unaltered. The word *prevaricate* originally meant to walk crookedly, hence to deviate from the path of duty or obligation. By degrees it came to be associated with the way in which a person would deviate from duty or obligation, or to cover up such deviation: to speak deceitfully. In common usage now it is an elaborate way of saying *lie.* And yet in some words a good deal of the original meaning continues as connotation. The word *exalt,* for instance, originally meant to raise up physically. It is used in this sense in Isaiah XI.3 as translated in the King James Bible: "Every valley shall be exalted, and every mountain and hill shall be made low: and the crooked shall be made straight, and the rough places plain." The valleys will be raised as everything is being made smooth. This was an archaic usage even in 1611, when the King James Bible was published, for the word had come to denote, usually, an elevation in status, dignity, or power. It had become, as a matter of fact, a "dead metaphor" to express the idea of aggrandizement.

But, not entirely dead: John Milton, for one, retained something of its original Latin meaning of physical elevation when he described Satan on his throne:

High on a throne of royal state, which far
Outshone the wealth of Ormus and of Ind,
Or where the gorgeous East with richest hand
Showers on her kings barbaric pearl and gold,
Satan exalted sat, by merit raised
To that bad eminence: and from despair
Thus high uplifted beyond hope.

(*Paradise Lost*,
II. 1-7.)

Indeed, it is a little hard to tell whether Milton used the word primarily to mean elevate physically or in condition. Both meanings are present; denotation and connotation fuse.

To Milton, Oliver Cromwell's Latin secretary, Latin was very much a living language, and he consciously uses Latinate words in a way that conveys their original meaning. But with words like *exalt,* some of the meaning from Latin persists as a connotation for anyone, whether he knows Latin or not. In the most common use of *exalt* or *exaltation,* one still thinks of raising something up. Exaltation in its modern use often means a sense of intense well-being, not the kind felt after a good meal or a job well done, but another feeling which we can only describe by adjectives that recall the Latin meaning: a *heightened* sense of well-being, a state of being in *high* spirits.

Associations like this persist, perhaps not vividly enough to qualify as metaphor, but as connotations which are part of the total meaning of the word and which, if one is to use words with precision in writing or reading, cannot be ignored. Unfortunately, connotative components in the meaning of words are ignored even in educated usage—even black and white distinctions such as those between *infer* and *imply*—and few people seem to care about the difference between *uninterested* and *disinterested; aggravate* now seems to mean *annoy* or *irritate*. In such semantic blurring all sense of history and of precision is lost. The passage quoted from Milton above contained the word *gorgeous,* which meant magnificent, especially as concerns attire and appearance, and which now has been blurred simply to mean beautiful. We have no word for *gorgeous* and try to use *elegant,* which should mean tastefully refined rather than magnificent in dress.

Poets wage a war against the deterioration of the language occurring through loss of precision and richness. It is a great mistake to think of poetic diction as being merely suggestive—especially vaguely suggestive in a blurry way. Poetry demands enormous precision of language. In poetry the right word, with the right denotation and right connotation, must be found; synonyms just won't do. To an experienced and perceptive reader of poetry, the wrong word, denotatively or connotatively, sticks out like an out-of-tune instrument in a musical performance.

We belabor the point that denotation and connotation are both aspects of poetic diction because the distinction between the two kinds of meaning is apt to mislead students into thinking of denotation as belonging to prose and connotation as belonging to poetry, and sometimes even into thinking that some words are denotative and others connotative.

Occasionally poets love to heap up associations by playing on the connotative qualities of some words, as Keats does in this passage from "Ode to a Nightingale" (see pp. 376-377 for the complete poem):

> O, for a draught of vintage! that hath been
> Cooled a long age in the deep-delved earth,
> Tasting of Flora and the country green,
> Dance and Provencal song, and sunburnt mirth!
> O for a beaker full of the warm South,
> Full of the true, the blushful Hippocrene,
> With beaded bubbles winking at the brim,
> And purple stained mouth. . . .

This wine is called for on no ordinary occasion, and the wine that Keats describes with all the rich associations he brings to it is no ordinary wine. This passage forms part of a poem only, and in the rest of it both kinds of meanings are used.

But poetry can be written in which denotative meaning is more important than connotative, especially if sound is managed well. Songs, for instance, are often very explicit, with an exactness of denotation, which, combined with a smooth purity of sound, produces a beautifully modeled lyric. Great numbers of such lyrics were written in the Elizabethan period, when England had many composers writing for the singing voice. It has often been said that English is not a very singable language. To be sure, a great deal of English poetry has been written with a verbal music designed for speech that is not easy to sing. The beginning of one of Shakespeare's sonnets, as an example, would be almost impossible to set to

> When to the sessions of sweet silent thought
> I summon up remembrance of things past,

music, because the singing voice would be seriously hampered by prolonged *s* and *m* and *n* sounds. But sonnets are not intended for music. Shakespeare could and did write beautiful songs, as did any number of his contemporaries.

That poets were properly appreciative of a skilled singer-composer's ability to keep a just accent in the songs he set is indicated by the following tribute to Henry Lawes by Edmund Waller.

To Mr. Henry Lawes, who had then Newly Set a Song of Mine in the Year 1635

Verse makes heroic virtue live;
But you can life to verses give.
As, when in open air we blow,
The breath, though strained, sounds flat and low;
But if a trumpet take the blast,
It lifts it high, and makes it last:
So in your airs our numbers dressed,
Make a shrill sally from the breast
Of nymphs, who, singing what we penned,
Our passions to themselves commend;
While love, victorious with thy art,
Governs at once their voice and heart.
You, by help of tune and time,
Can make that song which was but rhyme.
Noy* pleading, no man doubts the cause;
Or questions verses set by Lawes.
As a church window, thick with paint,
Lets in a light but dim and faint,
So others, with divisions, *hide
The light of sense, the poet's pride;
But you alone may truly boast
That not a syllable is lost:
The writer's and the setter's skill
At once the ravished ear do fill.
Let those which only warble long,
And gargle in their throats a song,
Content themselves with *ut, re, mi:*
Let words, and sense, be set by thee.

*a famous lawyer

*Unskilled composers hide the sense of the poem with their setting

EDMUND WALLER

The following song, by an anonymous poet, has vowels ordered in a very easily singable sequence with consonants that can be easily articulated in a way that does not hamper the production of pure vowels. As a result it also has a liquid sound when read.

Love Not Me

Love not me for comely grace,
For my pleasing eye or face;
Nor for any outward part,
No, nor for my constant heart:
For those may fail or turn ill,
So thou and I shall sever.
Keep therefore a true woman's eye
And love me still, but know not why;
So hast thou the same reason still
To doat upon me ever.

ANONYMOUS

This lyric, written by an anonymous poet, was set to music by John Wilby and preserved in the musical setting. The words were selected, not for their suggestive quality in this context, but for their sound and clarity of denotation. These two qualities, together with the cleverly perceptive turn given the thought in the last four lines, which resolves the idea developed in the first six lines, work together to produce a delightfully graceful lyric. A song like this seems so simple and effortless that one might be tempted to undervalue the art that produced it. The words seem so clearly the right ones that the art in selecting them is concealed, but it is there.

Like the anonymous Elizabethan song-writer, the contemporary poet, Karl Shapiro, also relies a great deal on exact denotation to produce the effects in "Drug Store."

*Drug Store**

It baffles the foreigner like an idiom,
And he is right to adopt it as a form
Less serious than the living room or bar;
For it disestablishes the cafe,
Is a collective, and on basic country.

Not that it praises hygiene and corrupts
The ice'cream parlor and the tobacconist's
Is it a center; but that the attractive symbols
Watch over puberty and leer
Like rubber bottles waiting for sick-use.

Youth comes to jingle nickels and crack wise;
The baseball scores are his, the magazines
Devoted to lust, the jazz, the Coca-Cola
The lending-library of love's latest.
He is the customer; he is heroized.

And every nook and cranny of the flesh
Is spoken to by packages with wiles.
"Buy me, buy me," they whimper and cajole;
The hectic range of lipsticks pouts,
Revealing the wicked and the simple mouth.

With scarcely any evasion in their eye
They smoke, undress their girls, exact a stance;
But only for a moment, The clock goes round;
Crude fellowships are made and lost;
They slump in booths like rags, not even drunk.

KARL SHAPIRO

In talking about the exactness of Shapiro's diction in this poem it becomes necessary to use words like *suggest,* which implies that not only denotative but connotative meanings are at work. The line between denotation and connotation is a hard one to draw when words are actually in use. An exactness of denotation is not a bare precision but a rich one, in which not only the core meaning but the peripheral meaning of a word is satisfyingly right. Like the frictionless body of physics, the word which is merely used to denote and does not connote is to be found only in theory.

To pick but a few words, *disestablishes* does not mean to pull down in condition, but to take away from something its character of being firmly established, as for instance, the church is said to be an "established church" when it is connected with the state and "disestablished" when the state severs its connection. The drug store in the eyes of the foreigner, to whom the café is the social center, disestablishes the quasi-official position of the café. The word *hygiene* denotes exactly, but selectively, one of the characteristics that is associated with drugs, and its meaning is further sharpened and given force when it is put in conjunction with *corrupts,* a word which includes as an aspect of its meaning (again the history of the word is felt) the idea of infection. The word *hectic* is used with a great sense for its historical denotation when applied to lipstick, for it originally referred to a feverish condition and the redness of lips and cheeks that came with fever. And *wicked* in this context, used in contrast to *simple,* conveys more sharply but also more suggestively an impression of the kind of wickedness involved here as that which comes with experience. Again when the young boys are said to *exact* a stance, they take a position in the way that adolescent boys trying to impress girls do; they don't merely stand, they stand as if they insisted upon standing that way, as if they demanded the right to stand that way, assertively, aggressively.

Alexander Pope adds something else to sound and exact denotation in the following passage from "Rape of the Lock": a delightful IRONY in the tone. He gets this effect by a metaphoric treatment of Belinda's morning beauty preparations as a sacred ritual. Pope doesn't tell us directly that these are like a religious ceremony. The words he selects deftly suggest it.

From *The Rape of the Lock*

And now, unveiled, the toilet stands displayed,
Each silver vase in mystic order laid.
First, robed in white, the nymph intent adores,
With head uncovered, the cosmetic powers.
A heavenly image in the glass appears.
To that she bends, to that her eyes she rears;
The inferior priestess, at her altar's side,
Trembling begins the sacred rites of pride.
Unnumbered treasures ope at once, and here
The various offerings of the world appear;
From each she nicely culls with curious toil,
And decks the goddess with the glittering spoil.
This casket India's glowing gems unlocks,
And all Arabia breathes from yonder box.
The tortoise here and elephant unite,
Transformed to combs, the speckled and the white.
Here files of pins extend their shining rows,
Puffs, powders, patches, bibles, billets-doux.
Now awful beauty puts on all its arms;
The fair each moment rises in her charms,
Repairs her smiles, awakens every grace,
And calls forth all the wonders of her face;
Sees by degrees a purer blush arise,
And keener lightnings quicken in her eyes.
The busy sylphs surround their darling care,
These set the head, and those divide the hair,
Some fold the sleeve, whilst others plait the gown;
And Betty's praised for labors not her own.

The toilet or beauty cabinet, is "unveiled," and stands "displayed." Belinda "adores" the "cosmetic powers," and bends to her own image and "rears" her eyes to it, as she and her maid begin "the sacred rites of pride." This is superbly polished poetry, and every word is selected with care as to denotative and connotative meaning and sound. In the lines beginning "A heavenly image . . . ," we can see especially how individual words, as used in the lines, contribute to the effectiveness of the passage, for here the sound is, as Pope himself said it ought to be, "an echo to the sense." Pope's ear is so acute and his verse so carefully modulated that he can get results with very subtle rhythmical and semantic variations. The word *heavenly*, for instance, conveys Belinda's prideful response to herself in the mirror, and the rhythm of the word, which slightly alters the beat of the verse by introducing an elided extra syllable, imparts at just the right time a slight suggestion of awe. And when Belinda bends and rears her eyes, Pope gives the line a balanced cadence that suggests the movement in parallel phrases beginning with "to that," requiring the reader to pause in the middle and feel the balance. And when Betty, her maid, here "th' inferior priestess," "trembling begins the sacred rites of pride," the line trembles with an inverted accent pattern just at the point where Betty does. Sound, denotation, connotation, imagery, metaphor, all work together.

John Keats in "To Autumn" uses words suggestively to evoke the warmth of an autumn day. We can speak fairly confidently concerning his intentions here, because he talked about the poem to his friend John Hamilton Reynolds: "How beautiful the season is now—How fine the air. A temperate sharpness about it—I never liked stubble-fields so much as now—Aye better than the chilly green of the Spring. Somehow, a stubble field looks warm—in the same way that some pictures look warm. This struck me so much in my Sunday's walk that I composed upon it."*

To Autumn

Seasons of mists and mellow fruitfulness,
Close bosom-friend of the maturing sun;
Conspiring with him how to load and bless
With fruit the vines that round the thatch-eves run;
To bend with apples the mossed cottage-trees,
And fill all fruit with ripeness to the core;
To swell the gourd, and plump the hazel shells
With a sweet kernel; to set budding more,
And still more, later flowers for the bees,
Until they think warm days will never cease,
For Summer has o're-brimmed their clammy cells.

*September 22, 1819.

Who hath not seen thee oft amid thy store?
Sometimes whoever seeks abroad may find
Thee sitting careless on a granary floor,
Thy hair soft-lifted by the winnowing wind;
Or on a half-reaped furrow sound asleep,
Drowsed with the fume of poppies, while thy hook
Spares the next swath and all its twined flowers:
And sometimes like a gleaner thou dost keep
Steady thy laden head across a brook;
Or by a cider-press, with patient look,
Thou watchest the last oozings hours by hours.

Where are the songs of Spring? Ay, where are they?
Think not of them, thou hast thy music too,—
While barred clouds bloom the soft-dying day,
And touch the stubble-plains with rosy hue;
Then in a wailful choir the small gnats mourn
Among the river sallows, borne aloft
Or sinking as the light wind lives or dies;
And full-grown lambs loud bleat from hilly bourn;
Hedge-crickets sing; and now with treble soft
The red-breast whistles from a garden-croft;
And gathering swallows twitter in the skies.

John Keats

Of course, Keats does not merely rely on connotations to produce the precise kind of warmth that is communicated, but uses rich imagery, metaphor as well. But notice how many of the words suggest warmth even though they do not name it. Many of them suggest it simply because they identify qualities usually associated with warmth: fullness, sweetness, drowsiness.

We have looked at poems in which words were used primarily for denotation and sound; for denotation, sound and connotation; and for suggestive connotation. Let us now consider a passage which moves from denotation to connotation—remembering, of course, that these two kinds of meaning cannot always be found so sharply distinguished as they are here. Shakespeare, in a passage from *Measure for Measure,* modulates his meaning to reflect a dramatic progression in mood.

From *Measure for Measure, III.i.*

I, but to die, and go we know not where,
To lie in cold obstruction,* and to rot,
This sensible warm motion, to become
A kneaded clod; And the delighted spirit
To bath in fierie floods, or to recide
In thrilling Region of thicke-ribbed Ice
To be imprisoned in the viewlesse windes
And blowne with restless violence round about
The pendant world: or to be worse then worst
Of those that lawlesse and incertaine thought,
Imagine howling, 'tis too horrible.
The weariest, and most loathed wordly life
That Age, Ache, periury, and imprisonment
Can lay on nature, is a Paradise
To what we fear of death.

**obstruction*—stagnation

William Shakespeare

The first and last lines of the passage consist of a series of monosyllabic words whose meanings are primarily denotative, conveying a sense of the starkness of death in their shortness and their emphatic central meaning. But in the second, third, and fourth lines, words with richer associations begin to appear in contrast to words like *cold, lie, rot, and warm. Obstruction* suggests inertness in addition to stagnation, and this inertness is made even more horrible by its being extended into its final state of earth, whose only motion is the passive one of being kneaded like clay. This seems a terrible culmination to the *sensible warm motion* of life. *Sensible,* besides conveying human capacity for feeling, also suggests the inner purpose of man who consciously conducts his life from within, only to become a cold and motionless *clod,* kneaded perhaps not even by another human but by the slow movement of the crust of the *pendant world* about him.

As the body is reduced to clay in death, so the soul is disrobed of its conveyor, the body, whose senses once moved and lighted it as its substance made it visible. *Delighted* now, deprived not only of light (*de-lighted*) but of the joy in living, it is paradoxically imprisoned in invisibility in contrast to its former freedom in the body, and blown about without rest in contrast to its former restful delight in its outward habit, the body. Worse than these possibilities in death is the possibility of eternal torture in Hell. Even the weariest of lives is preferable to the fears in death, as the speaker considers it.

To a fleshly person like the speaker, Claudio, whose sentence of death has come about through incontinence, the absence of body or the death of body is the worst of fates. He cannot imagine any kind of consciousness as spirit being bearable without his sensible warm motion. He reveals himself in the passage as an unbeliever, or at the least a skeptic, about the comfortable nature of the after-life, and his religious beliefs are sharply modified by his fleshly desires.

In this passage, then, not only do we get a good deal of information about the speaker's psychological state of mind from his choice and use of words, but the diction also reflects, simultaneously, a psychological unity in the drama.

What characterizes the diction of poetry is not a special vocabulary that is somehow "poetic," but the precision and indeed efficiency with which words are used. Poetic language hits the mark more exactly than language as used ordinarily, and it does more. But it is not of a different kind. Some poets have used ARCHAISMS, old-fashioned locutions, especially the *thee* and *thou* forms of address together with the appropriate forms of verbs, as in "thou goest." And a few poets, notably Spenser, went much farther, using obsolete words such as *wight* for man and old grammatical forms such as *yclept* for called, so that one needs a glossary to read him. It is also true that poetry of the neoclassic period (1660 to roughly 1800) employed a diction that was, as Dr. Johnson described it, a "system of words at once refined from the grossness of domestic use, and free from the harshness of terms appropriated to different arts," and which also used a great deal of personification of abstractions, PERIPHRASIS (saying something in a rather roundabout way), adjectives ending in *y*, Latinisms, and archaisms. But these devices call attention to themselves mostly in the abuse through over-use.*

Reading poetry demands a keener word sense than is demanded by ordinary discourse, both for denotative and connotative meanings. And it requires as well an ear for the sound of words. These can be developed, partly with the help of a good dictionary, but mostly through much practice in close reading of poetry itself.

---

*For a discussion of this matter see Thomas Quayle, *Poetic Diction: A Study of Eighteenth Century Verse.* London, 1924; and James Sutherland, *An Introduction to Eighteenth Century Poetry.* London, 1948.

Poems for Further Study:

A Song for St. Cecilia's Day

(1687)

I

From harmony, from heav'nly harmony
This universal frame began:
When Nature underneath a heap
Of jarring atoms lay,
And could not heave her head,
The tuneful voice was heard from high:
"Arise, ye more than dead."
Then cold, and hot, and moist, and dry.
In order to their stations leap,
And Music's pow'r obey.
From harmony, from heav'nly harmony
This universal frame began;
From harmony to harmony
Through all the compass of the notes it ran,
The diapason closing full in Man.

II

What passion cannot Music raise and quell!
When Jubal struck the chorded shell,
His list'ning brethren stood around,
And, wond'ring, on their faces fell
To worship that celestial sound:
Less than a god they thought there could not dwell
Within the hollow of that shell,
That spoke so sweetly and so well.
What passion cannot Music raise and quell!

III

The Trumpet's loud clangor
Excites us to arms,
With shrill notes of anger,
And mortal alarms.
The double double double beat
Of the thund'ring Drum
Cries: "Hark! the foes come;
Charge, charge, 'tis too late to retreat."

IV

The soft complaining Flute
In dying notes discovers
The woes of hopeless lovers,
Whose dirge is whispered by the warbling Lute.

V

Sharp Violins proclaim
Their jealous pangs, and desperation,
Fury, frantic indignation,
Depth of pains, and height of passion,
For the fair, disdainful dame.

VI

But O! what art can teach,
What human voice can reach,
The sacred Organ's praise?
Notes inspiring holy love,
Notes that wing their heav'nly ways
To mend the choirs above.

VII

Orpheus could lead the savage race;
And trees unrooted left their place,
Sequacious of the lyre;
But right Cecilia raised the wonder high'r:
When to her Organ vocal breath was giv'n,
An angel heard, and straight appeared,
Mistaking earth for heaven.

GRAND CHORUS

As from the pow'r of sacred lays
The spheres began to move,
And sung the great Creator's praise
To all the blest above;
So, when the last and dreadful hour
This crumbling pageant shall devour,
The Trumpet shall be heard on high,
The dead shall live, the living die,
And Music shall untune the sky.

JOHN DRYDEN

From *The House of Life*

A sonnet is a moment's monument,—
Memorial from the Soul's eternity
To one dead deathless hour. Look that it be.
Whether for lustral rite or dire portent,
Of its own arduous fullness reverent:
Carve it in ivory or in ebony,
As Day or Night may rule; and let Time see
Its flowering crest impearled and orient.
A Sonnet is a coin: its face reveals
The soul,—its converse, to what Power 'tis due:—
Whether for tribute to the august appeals
Of Life, or dower in Love's high retinue,
It serve; or, 'mid the dark wharf's cavernous breath,
In Charon's palm it pay the toll to Death.

DANTE GABRIEL ROSSETTI

To Helen

Helen, thy beauty is to me
Like, those Nicean barks of yore
That gently, o'er a perfumed sea,
The weary way-worn wanderer bore
To his own native shore

On desperate seas long wont to roam,
Thy hyacinth hair, thy classic face,
Thy Naiad airs have brought me home
To the glory that was Greece,
And the grandeur that was Rome.

Lo, in yon brillant window-niche
How statue-like I see thee stand,
The agate lamp within thy hand,
Ah! Psyche, from the regions which
Are holy land!

EDGAR ALLAN POE

I Taste a Liquor

I taste a liquor never brewed,
From tankards scooped in pearl;
Not all the vats upon the Rhine
Yield such an alcohol!

Inebriate of air am I,
And debauchee of dew,
Reeling, through endless summer days,
From inns of molten blue.

When landlords turn the drunken bee
Out of the foxglove's door,
When butterflies renounce their drams,
I shall drink the more!

Till seraphs swing their snowy hats,
And saints to windows run,
To see the little tippler
Leaning against the sun!

EMILY DICKINSON

Questions.

1. Describe as specifically as you can the nature of the liquor being drunk in the poem.
2. For how long has this spree been going on and how much longer will it continue?

The Latest Decalogue

Thou shalt have one God only; who
Would be at the expense of two?
No graven images may be
Worshipped, except the currency:
Swear not at all; for, for thy curse
Thine enemy is none the worse:
At church on Sunday to attend
Will serve to keep the world thy friend:

Honor thy parents; that is, all
From whom advancement may befall;
Thou shalt not kill; but needst not strive
Officiously to keep alive:
Do not commit adultry;
Advantage rarely comes of it:
Thou shalt not steal; an empty feat,
When it's so lucrative to cheat:
Bear not false witness; let the lie
Have time in its own wings to fly:
Thou shalt not covet, but tradition
Approves all forms of competition.

ARTHUR HUGH CLOUGH

When Icicles Hang by the Wall

Winter

When Icicles hang by the wall,
And Dick the shepherd blows his nail,
And Tom bears logs into the hall,
And milk comes frozen home in pail,
When blood is nipped, and ways be foul,
Then nightly sings the staring owl,
Tu-whit, to-who,
A merry note,
While greasy Joan doth keel the pot.

When all aloud the wind doth blow,
And coughing drowns the parson's saw,
And birds sit brooding in the snow,
And Marian's nose looks red and raw,
When roasted crabs hiss in the bowl,
Then nightly sings the staring owl,
Tu-whit, to-who,
A merry note,
While greasy Joan doth keel the pot.

WILLIAM SHAKESPEARE

One Person

Sonnet VII

O love, how utterly am I bereaved
By time, who sucks the honey of our days,
Sets sickle to our Aprils, and betrays
To killing winter all the sun achieved!
Our parted spirits are perplexed and grieved
Severed by cold, and change that never stays;
And what the clock, and what the season says
Is rumor neither valued nor believed.
Thus absence chills us to apparent death
And withers up our virtue, but together
We grow beyond vagaries of the weather
And make a summer of our mingled breath
Wherein we flourish, and forget to know
We must lie murdered by predestined snow.

ELINOR WYLIE

Fritz and Eli as Death and Life

I

Old Fritz, who rolls his mower through
The emerald and endless lawns of my dreams
Is whiskered and sour-toothed, more peevish
By the moment, sick and surly enough
For all of us. His rigorous swathes are
Cursed for every inch, his head is perishable
As peaches, and his days are easily bruised.
Devious bicycles stir his surface to a froth,
Rocks burr his temper and his blades,
And children constrict his impressible bowels.
Where he cuts the grass must learn to grow again.
A boiling, knotting man, Fritz stops his blades
For nothing be it worm, beetle, sibling, dream, or egg.

Neighbor, do not love or picnic on the grass
Too long, for Fritz mows with enough resolve
And angry precision for all of us.

II

Eli enriches the soil with his fingertips.
Sweet shoots twine through his ribs,
And the air smells green about him.
Children grow in his presence. Weeds gag.
Eli sends worms excreting and swallowing
Through his garden. Roses rise in their dung.
Phlox are warmed and nourished by decay.
Eli is orderly as regiments, tender as nurseries.
He peers at shrubs and they burgeon
At his breath. Grass springs back where
He steps, rain collects and drops at his bidding,
And the tightened earth is unpeeled.

In my dreams Eli sews me in the ground,
He starts me from my husks and pushes me
Through earth until I burst from sod to the sun.

PAUL ZIMMER

Suggested Poems for Further Reading (ANTHOLOGY):

Thomas Lovell Beddoes, "We Do Lie Beneath the Grass," p. 253
William Blake, "The Little Black Boy," p. 258
Lewis Carroll, "Jabberwocky," p. 280
A. E. Housman, "Reveille," p. 364

Symbol

5

To a Locomotive in Winter

Thee for my recitative,
Thee in the driving storm even as now, the snow, the winterday declining.
Thee in the panoply, thy measured dual throbbing and thy beat convulsive,
Thy black cylindric body, golden brass and silvery steel,
Thy ponderous side-bars, parallel and connecting rods, gyrating, shuttling at thy sides,
Thy metrical, now swelling pant and roar, now tapering in the distance,
Thy great protruding head-light fixed in front,
Thy long, pale, floating vapor-pennants, tinged with delicate purple,
The dense and murky clouds out-belching from thy smoke-stack,
Thy knitted frame, thy springs and valves, the tremulous twinkle of thy wheels,
Thy train of cars behind, obedient, merrily following,
Through gale or calm, now swift, now slack, yet steadily careering;
Type of the modern—emblem of motion and power—pulse of the continent,
For once come serve the Muse and merge in verse, even as here I see thee,
With storm and buffeting gusts of wind and falling snow,
By day thy warning ringing bell to sound its notes,
By night thy silent signal lamps to swing.

Fierce-throated beauty!
Roll through my chant with all thy lawless music, thy swinging lamps at night,
Thy madly-whistled laughter, echoing, rumbling like an earthquake, rousing all,
Law of thyself complete, thine own track firmly holding,
(No sweetness debonair of tearful harp or glib piano thine,)
Thy trills of shrieks by rocks and hills returned,
Launched o'er the prairies wide, across the lakes,
To the free skies unpent and glad and strong.

WALT WHITMAN

Walt Whitman celebrates the steam locomotive, calling attention to the parts and movements that interest him. But the poem does not stop there. Though Whitman goes into great detail in describing the locomotive, he does not merely describe it as a historian of railroading would. For one thing, he personifies it, making it an animate being, by the words he uses in his description and by addressing it as the ostensible object to which he addresses his remarks. The poem is an APOSTROPHE to a locomotive in winter.

In thus writing a poem about the locomotive, Whitman is doing what virtually any poet does in a descriptive poem; he not only makes the object of his description vivid in one way or other as what it is, but also he sees a significance in it. But Whitman makes the significance more explicit than many others would have done. To him the locomotive is not merely an engine but stands for or represents certain aspects of modern life—modern in the latter half of the nineteenth century. He tells us exactly what it is to him, what he is doing:

> Type of the modern—emblem of motion and power—pulse of the continent
> For once come serve the Muse and merge in verse . . . .

He calls it a "type" and an "emblem," a visible sign of an idea. Had he used language a little more loosely, he might have called it a SYMBOL.

The word symbol comes from two Greek roots, *sym* (together) and *balein* (to throw), and etymologically, therefore, means to put together. Practically and very generally speaking, it means using one thing to represent another. In this very general sense, all kinds of things are symbols: flags, stop-and-go signs, wedding rings, the X's and Y's in algebra, numbers, even words themselves. We are familiar with certain symbolic objects and pictures of objects which stand for meanings that are very important to us—the dove, for instance, as a symbol of the Holy Spirit.

In one sense, of course, any picture of a dove (or a pigeon), whether in a dictionary or a stained glass window, "stands for" or represents the bird.

But the picture of a dove in the dictionary is intended to do nothing more than to depict the bird so that if we see a pigeon we will know what it is, whereas the picture of the dove in the stained glass window or in the religious painting represents not only the bird but something else, the Holy Spirit. It is impossible to represent something as mysterious as the Holy Spirit directly in an illustration because it is not something that can be apprehended by the senses. But people want to grasp as concretely as possible difficult ideas like that of the Holy Spirit, so they use images, which in themselves often have nothing directly to do with the ideas which they represent, to symbolize these ideas. They bring together, as it were, two different orders of experience in symbols: the world of the mind and the world of the senses.

In a preceding chapter, in our discussion of metaphor, we said that metaphors do something very like this. Symbols can, indeed, be thought of as being like metaphors with one of the terms missing. In a metaphor both terms, the thing being talked about and that with which it is being connected, are very clearly implied. In the sentence, "The crowds upon the pavement/ Were fields of harvest wheat," *crowds* and *wheat* are named. And in "Time watches from the shadow/ And coughs when you would kiss," a submerged metaphor, the living being with which Time is compared or connected is implied by the activities of watching and coughing. But a symbol usually stands alone. The meanings it represents, or embodies, are not usually specified, but are left for the reader to get for himself as he responds to the suggestions of the symbol.

The Silver Swan

The silver swan, who living had no note,
When death approached, unlocked her silent throat,
Leaning her breast against the reedy shore,
Thus sung her first and last, and sung no more:
Farewell all joys! O death, come close mine eyes;
More geese than swans now live, more fools than wise.

ANONYMOUS

In this poem, for example, we are not *told* what the swan represents, but we know that it embodies symbolic meaning because of its curious color—swans are usually white—and because of its gift of speech. The TONE of the words it speaks also contributes to its symbolic role. And if we know the swan-myth that swans are mute until their dying day when they sing, the swan becomes even richer as a poetic symbol. Indeed, we might say that the silver swan in a sense interprets herself as a symbol in her concluding song.

Whitman's locomotive, however, is not properly a symbol, at least not a literary symbol, but, as he himself says, an emblem. Because the term *symbol* is used in so many different ways in different contexts, any complete definition of even one kind of symbol, the literary symbol which is of interest in this book, would be impossible to make here. The most we can hope to do is to indicate in a very general way how a symbol is used in poetry. We might begin by making some distinctions that will illustrate what is meant by symbol.

Philosophers and semanticists usually distinguish between signs and symbols, of both of which there is a bewildering variety. Since we are interested only in the literary symbol, let us instead pick up the term used by Whitman and try to separate sign, emblem, and symbol (literary symbol) from one another.

A sign points to something definite, usually some one thing. There is a 1-to-1 relationship between a sign and what it represents. A class bell is a sign indicating that the class session is beginning or ending. A treble clef might be thought of as a sign which means that the note on the bottom line of the staff on which it appears is E. A check drawn on a bank where the writer of the check has an account (not overdrawn) is a sign that stands for or represents money to the amount specified on the check. Words, when they are used merely to point to an object or something definite, such as in the sentence, "The tree fell down," could be thought of as signs. A sign represents something other than itself, but it does so in a simple, limited relationship.

The relationship between an emblem and what it represents is somewhat complicated, but it is still essentially a limited one. Whitman's locomotive emblem represents modern life, stands for it, especially those aspects of modern life which the characteristics of the locomotive reflect: speed, power, etc. It *could* be called a *metonymic symbol*, after METONYMY, a special kind of metaphor in which one element or aspect of a thing is used to represent the whole. It represents a complex of characteristics, but one that is limited. The word *emblem* was originally applied to an object or a picture of an object expressing a moral fable, or, according to the *Oxford Universal Dictionary*, "representing symbolically an abstract quality, an action, a class of persons, etc." It was also used to mean a badge or other device signifying an officer. A device used to stand for a government, such as the hammer and sickle of the U.S.S.R., might be thought of as an emblem. An emblem is like a symbol, but a symbol that refers to something fairly definite, though possibly very complex. According to an eminent art historian (*emblem* is a word used in art history), an emblem "partakes of the nature of the symbol (only it is particular rather than universal."* An emblem may "contain" a great deal of meaning, but its meaning is limited, exhaustible.#

Unfortunately, many students interpret literary symbols as if they were emblems or even signs, and practice an almost algebraic substitution in which the symbol is completely replaced by what they think is its referent. In order to talk about literary symbols, we have to use verbal shorthand to identify in a general way what we are talking about. But if we limit their meaning by making exact and circumscribed equivalences, the symbol ceases to function as a symbol for us. Whereas a sign can be said to have a 1-to-1 relationship with what it represents and the emblem a one-to-many relationship, the symbol has almost a one-to-infinity relationship with its meaning. There are virtually no limits to its meaning—virtually because the qualities in the symbol itself lead the mind in contemplation of the symbol's meaning, but if it is a good symbol one feels that its meaning is inexhaustible.

The Sick Rose

O Rose thou art sick.
The invisible worm,
That flies in the night
In the howling storm:

Has found out thy bed
Of crimson joy:
And his dark secret love
Does thy life destroy.

WILLIAM BLAKE

*See Erwin Panofsky, *Meaning in the Visual Arts* (Garden City, N.Y., 1955), p. 148.

#The term *public symbol* is sometimes used to mean what we here describe emblem to mean, with *private symbol* being used to refer to literary symbol. This does not seem to us a good pair of terms, because *private symbol* connotes—and indeed is used to *denote*—a symbol that means a great deal to one person but not to others. If a poet uses something of significance to himself as a symbol in a poem but makes the symbol accessible to others, especially in a poem that is intended for the public, the symbol could hardly be said to remain private. In using *emblem* to make the distinction we are making, we do have the precedent of D. H. Lawrence. See his *Selected Literary Criticism*, ed. Anthony Beal (London, 1956. p. 158). See also George Whalley, p. 171.

The subject of this poem, the object being talked about, is a rose, just as the subject of Whitman's poem was a locomotive. But Blake's rose is much less a rose than Whitman's locomotive was a locomotive. Whitman's description is recognizably accurate and satisfying as a characterization of the object being described. Blake, on the other hand, describes the flower in a way which does not make too much sense on the literal level. Roses are subject to diseases, but any attempt to account for the invisible worm flying in the night as some kind of rose blight simply will not work. There are too many strange associations with the words of the poem.

Having read the poem and pondered it a bit, many readers will feel quite uneasy. "Here is a poem written in what appears to be plain English," they may think, "and yet I'm not quite sure what it says." At this point some people will insist on trying to make some kind of sense out of it at any cost. They recognize that the poem is probably talking about something other than roses, for it teases the mind into areas of speculation that have little to do with flowers as such. But perhaps because we have been so thoroughly trained in the so-called "problem-solving" kind of thinking, most people will begin to try to solve the poem as if it were a puzzle. They will at once start to guess and try to substitute various meanings that come to mind from outside the poem for the elements in the poem. The rose is a woman, one will say, and the worm is a destructive disease like cancer. Or another, sticking to the possibility that the rose is after all a rose, will say that the worm is the frost, and so on.

The poem is a troubling one, but treating it as a riddle, using the method of Little Jack Horner, will not bring relief. It is troubling because it is supposed to be, because the reader must become involved with it. The poet has given us the symbolic rose; the reader must see its meaning. That meaning is not a limited one, which can be guessed at once or supplied by a chance substitution for the objects in the poem by the first notion that pops into one's head. The poem will take on its proper meaning only if we respond to the associations which the poet has given to the symbol, and to do this we must read with a keen sense of connotation, letting the words do their work in context.

The words in this poem are ordinary ones, but in the context of the poem they are strange. Worms are not invisible, nor do they ordinarily fly at night in storms or at other times, and we don't usually think of worms as having dark secret loves which destroy roses, nor do roses live in beds of crimson joy. The poet combines these things in his poem in a way that makes the very strangeness evoke in the reader a powerful expansive response. Worms in poetry, especially since the poetry of the seventeenth century and Shakespeare, are traditionally associated with death and the consumption of corpses. Sometimes they are dragons. The worm in this poem, however, is a special one which flies dragon-like through stormy nights. Night, again, has traditional associations with death, ignorance, and so on; and storms, especially howling ones, suggest some kind of chaos. One more characteristic of Blake's worm is that he is invisible, a quality that makes him even more mysterious and ominous in connection with his other characteristics. He is more than a worm in the ordinary sense of the word and may be some kind of principle of corruption associated with ignorance and chaos.

Now let us consider the rose. Again, we do not ordinarily consider roses as being "sick" when they are diseased, and the rose's sickness here, therefore, connotes something human. Furthermore, this rose lives in a bed of crimson joy and is destroyed by the special kind of love that the worm feels, a "dark secret love." More than most flowers, the rose is associated with love, especially red roses. In the phrase, "bed / Of crimson joy," Blake combines the natural impression given by a bed of red roses with the connotation of crimson, bed, and joy in connection with love.

There are, therefore, two kinds of love in the poem: the worm's, dark and secret; and the rose's, associated with bright joy. Evidently there is a conflict between these kinds of love, since the worm's love destroys the rose. Blake does not explicitly say so, but in context it would appear from the contrast between these two kinds of love that the rose's love is not dark and secret, but bright and forthright. The words *crimson joy* and *bed* suggest that it is joyful nuptial love, passionately innocent and pure, as was the love of Adam and Eve before the Fall. Blake could have used other words to denote redness, *scarlet,* for instance; but scarlet would have connoted a debased or wicked sensuality. *Crimson* does not, for we associate this hue of red with the freshness of the new day or the beauty of sunset or with the color of natural cheeks. So we are safe in assuming that Blake approves of crimson joy—and of the bed in this connection. These words have AMELIORATIVE or good connotations, whereas scarlet would have had PEJORATIVE or bad connotations.

The poem appears, then, to be about two kinds of love, and about a conflict between the two in which the dark, secret and—by implication—shameful kind destroys the warm, forthright kind. But it does not stop there either. If we contemplate the poem a little after having closely examined the associations which we bring to it, we are led to further ideas, concerning, for instance, the kind of attitudes toward life that are implied by the two kinds of love: one rigid, repressive, dark, and the other free, joyful, bright. And if we pursue our contemplations a little farther still, we can think of all kinds of instances in which life is characterized by the conflict between forces that resemble in a general way one or the other of these two attitudes towards life.

By now, if not before, some readers are asking "Did the poet really mean to put all that stuff into this poem?" The answer in this case is yes. Further reading of Blake would reveal that even in a lyric as short as this he wants to give an insight into two radically different ways of looking at life. But the answer is yes for another reason. Or, rather, the question may be answered by saying that the poet wrote a symbolic poem, because he had too much to communicate to talk about his meaning directly. He is thinking in symbols, and he wants us to think in symbols with him. He invites us not to limit our thought to the restrictions of rational discourse, but to let it expand.

And symbols tend to be expansive. "In the Symbol proper," writes Thomas Carlyle, "what we can call a Symbol, there is, more or less distinctly and directly, some embodiment and revelation of the Infinite; the Infinite is made to blend itself with the Finite, to stand visible, and as it were, attainable there."* We can say with some confidence that Blake's intention was to be very expansive, for he often said so.

Of course, there are dangers here: discovering symbols where there are none, or exaggerating the importance of some symbols at the expense of others or of other elements in the work under consideration. We wish it were possible to lay down clear ground rules for the interpretation of poetry to guard against interpretations which lose contact with the work being interpreted, but all we can do is to urge the use of common sense, and to remind the student that any interpretation must be firmly supportable from the text of the poem itself. It often happens that students who discover the heady pleasures of free-wheeling interpretation of symbols begin to see symbols everywhere, and very little else.

Symbolism is sometimes confused with ALLEGORY, and it is worth keeping the two distinct. They are distinct, but it is hard to contrast them without going the long way around and first distinguishing allegory from myth, which might be thought of as a narrative made up of symbols. On the simplest level at least, allegory is a narrative whose elements have fairly definite and usually moral meanings outside of the story. These elements interact in the story in such a way that their parallel or allegorical meanings communicate some sort of argument. Myth is also narrative, and the elements composing it also have other than literal meanings, for they are symbols. But whereas the meanings attached to the elements of the narrative in an allegory are fairly definite and, therefore, in a sense limited, the meanings to be seen in the elements of a myth are not thus limited. An allegory invites interpretation that is a kind of translation of the story into a discursive

---

**Sartor Resartus*, Bk. III, ch. iii. See also Samuel Taylor Coleridge, *The Statesman's Manual* (London, 1816), p. 37.

argument—and the maker of an allegory hints at the kind of a translation this should be by giving his characters suggestive names. But a myth resists such an interpretation because its elements, being symbols, cannot be readily pinned down. D. H. Lawrence uses the god with two faces, Janus, to point up the difference: "An allegorical image has *meaning*. Mr. Facing-both-ways has a meaning. But I defy you to lay a finger on the full meaning of Janus, who is a symbol."*

The writer of an allegory wants obliqueness to enrich his meaning, but he also wants his meaning to be clearly understood. The maker of a myth—or a writer who adapts an existing myth for his purposes—also has a meaning in mind, but it is a meaning that cannot be easily separated from the mythical and symbolic form in which he perceives it. Sometimes he cannot be quite sure just what the meaning is but knows only that it is there, expressed in the myth or symbol. This is not to suggest that poets when in doubt resort to symbol and myth and that clear-headed poets write allegory when they want to talk obliquely, but that allegory and myth express different kinds of meanings and express them in different ways.

Definitions and distinctions such as these are hard to maintain rigorously when applied to actual works. Spenser's *Fairie Queen*, though an allegory, also has some of the characteristics of a mythical and symbolic poem.#

In reading symbolic poetry we must be especially receptive to suggestion given by relationship and verbal connotation, meeting the poet more than halfway. Learning to do this responsibly takes disciplined practice in seeing how poets manipulate relationships, and it takes a keen word sense—which, once developed, will also be useful in other reading and in writing. Before leaving this topic, let us see how another poet, very different from Blake, manipulates relationships in a poem about a tree at a window of a bedroom.

The Oft-Repeated Dream
From *The Hill Wife*

She had no saying dark enough
For the dark pine that kept
Forever trying the window-latch
Of the room where they slept.

**Selected Literary Criticism*, ed. Anthony Beal (New York, 1956), p. 157.

#For excellent studies of this matter, see Edwin Honig, *Dark Conceit: The Making of Allegory* (London and New York, 1960) and Angus Fletcher, *Allegory: The Theory of a Symbolic Mode* (Ithaca, N.Y., 1964). Northrop Frye, from another point of view and in another context, minimizes the distinction between allegory and other kinds of structures of ideas. See *Anatomy of Criticism* (Princeton, 1957), pp. 89-91 especially.

The tireless but ineffectual hands
That with every futile pass
Made the great tree seem as a little bird
Before the mystery of glass!

It never had been inside the room
And only one of the two
Was afraid in an oft-repeated dream
Of what the tree might do.

ROBERT FROST*

Questions.

1. What devices does Frost use to give the pine tree human attributes?
2. What quality about the tree frightens the woman despite its ineffectual hands and futile passes?

The woman experiences a fear and hatred for the pine while lying in bed, where most of us are as imaginative as we ever get to be. In that state of consciousness just before a person drops off to sleep, one is perfectly capable of transforming pine trees rubbing at the window into fumbling creatures trying to get in, and of focusing attitudes and states of mind into images of objects. Giving imaginative form to fears, apprehensions, worries, joys is a way of representing them to oneself. Robert Frost gives us an insight into ourselves in the woman's imaginative reaction to the tree. She has fears and projects them symbolically into the tree. The qualities of the tree itself characterize her fears as being of some kind of blindly purposeless force, for the tree can only fumble. And the glass that keeps the tree from entering suggests something of her defense against the threat. As glass is transparent, so is she able to know the threat; and as glass is fragile, so does she know that at best her safety depends on keeping intact the barrier between herself and whatever threatens her. She hates the tree ("She had no saying dark enough") because it has come to represent the threat. Exactly what the threat was, we are not told, nor does the woman herself know, having in her dream an unformulated fear "Of what the tree might do."

Frost has given a perfectly naturalistic explanation of the woman's fear by setting the poem as something occurring in bed, but that fact does not diminish the impact of the symbolic tree on her or the reader. It merely makes it easier for us to accept the symbol from her point of view, which is the point of view we must adopt in this poem.

This poem illustrates another aspect of symbolism that we might notice before leaving this topic: the gradual emergence of symbol from metaphor. Except for the initial suggestion in the first two lines of the poem that the woman hated the tree, we are not aware that the tree is going to be anything more than a metaphor, a personification, until we are almost through the poem and both the personification and the woman's feelings are developed to a point where the tree becomes something more than a personified tree. It is hard to say just where this change occurs; that would depend on the reader. But it does occur. Earlier we suggested that formally a symbol might be thought of as being like a metaphor with one term missing. It is not merely that. But occasionally a metaphor is used in such a way that one of the terms of the metaphor produces an intensely vivid imaginative response in the reader and seems to take on a life of its own, as the personification of the tree does in this poem, with the result that metaphor assumes the character of symbol.

We have attempted, in this chapter, to distinguish symbol from sign and emblem and have suggested that sign and emblem are limited ways of representing meaning, while symbol is an expansive one. Sometimes, indeed, even the creator of a symbol is not fully aware of all it can suggest to a perceptive reader. We add the qualification in the previous statement to remind the student once more that literary symbol is not a Rohrschach ink blot, whose interpretation is entirely up to the interpreter. Symbols function within a work, and any sound interpretation of a symbol must be consistent with the poem as a whole.

Poems for Further Study:

The Tyger

Tyger Tyger, burning bright,
In the forests of the night;
What immortal hand or eye,
Could frame thy fearful symmetry?

In what distant deeps or skies
Burnt the fire of thine eyes!
On what wings dare he aspire?
What the hand, dare seize the fire?

And what shoulder, & what art,
Could twist the sinews of thy heart?
And when thy heart began to beat,
What dread hand? & what dread feet?

What the hammer? what the chain,
In what furnace was thy brain?
What the anvil? what dread grasp
Dare its deadly terrors clasp?

When the stars threw down their spears
And watered heaven with their tears:
Did he smile his work to see?
Did he who made the Lamb make thee?

Tyger, Tyger burning bright,
In the forests of the night;
What immortal hand or eye,
Dare frame thy fearful symmetry?

WILLIAM BLAKE

Questions.

1. Which qualities of the tiger are selected for the description? What other qualities might have been used? Are the qualities that were used ameliorative or pejorative?
2. Who is the *he* in line 7? What is his chief characteristic?
3. In the fifth stanza, the symbolism of stars and spears is baffling to readers unfamiliar with the rest of Blake's work, in which stars are almost always symbols of repression and heaven is not the conventional reward after death but a symbol of repressively self-righteous morality and even oppressive political power. In the light of this meaning, what is the connection between the tiger and stars and spears?
4. To what extent is the creature of this poem *felis tigris,* the real tiger, and to what extent symbol?
5. The whole poem is composed of questions. Are we supposed to answer each question? What do the questions contribute to the poem? Would the poem have been more or less effective if Blake had used assertions instead?

6. The tiger is said to have "fearful symmetry," and he is portrayed mostly as being fearful. What is the other side of the symmetry? (See question 1.)
7. Is the last stanza identical with the first?

Awake, Awake!

Awake, awake! thou heavy sprite
   That sleep'st the deadly sleep of sin!
Rise now and walk the ways of light,
   'Tis not too late yet to begin.
Seek heaven early, seek it late;
True Faith finds still an open gate.

Get up, get up, thou leaden man!
   Thy track, to endless joy or pain,
Yields but the model of a span:
   Yet burns out thy life's lamp in vain!
One minute bounds thy bane or bliss;
Then watch and labour while time is.

THOMAS CAMPION

Silent is the House

Silent is the House—all are laid asleep;
One, alone, looks out o'er the snow-wreaths deep;
Watching every cloud, dreading every breeze
That whirls the 'wildering drifts and bends the groaning trees.

Cheerful is the hearth, soft the matted floor;
Not one shivering gust creeps through pane or door;
The little lamp burns straight, its rays shoot strong and far:
I trim it well to be the Wanderer's guiding-star.

Frown my haughty sire; chide my angry dame,
Set your slaves to spy, threaten me with shame:
But neither sire nor dame, nor prying serf shall know
What angel nightly tracks that waste of winter snow.

What I love shall come like visitant of air,
Safe in secret power from lurking human snare;
Who loves me, no word of mine shall e'er betray,
Though for faith unstained my life must forfeit pay.

Burn, then, little lamp; glimmer straight and clear—
Hush! a rustling wing stirs, methinks, the air:
He for whom I wait, thus ever comes to me;
Strange Power! I trust thy might; trust thou my constancy.

EMILY BRONTE

Terminus

It is time to be old,
To take in sail:—
The god of bounds,
Who sets to seas a shore,
Came to me in his fatal rounds,
And said: 'No more!
No farther shoot
Thy broad ambitious branches, and thy root.
Fancy departs: no more invent;
Contract thy firmament
To compass of a tent.
There's not enough for this and that,
Make thy option which of two;
Economize the failing river,
Not the less revere the Giver,
Leave the many and hold the few.
Timely wise accept the terms,
Soften the fall with wary foot;
A little while
Still plan and smile,
And,—fault of novel germs,—
Mature the unfallen fruit.
Curse, if thou wilt, thy sires,
Bad husbands of their fires,
Who, when they gave thee breath,
Failed to bequeath
The needful sinew stark as once,
The Baresark marrow to thy bones,

But left a legacy of ebbing veins,
Inconstant heat and nerveless reins,—
Amid the Muses, left thee deaf and dumb,
Amid the gladiators, halt and numb.'

As the bird trims her to the gale,
I trim myself to the storm of time,
I man the rudder, reef the sail,
Obey the voice at eve obeyed at prime:
'Lowly faithful, banish fear,
Right onward drive unharmed;
The port, well worth the cruise, is near,
And every wave is charmed.'

RALPH WALDO EMERSON

Poems for Further Study (ANTHOLOGY):

Ben Jonson, "Slow, Slow, Fresh Fount," p. 366
Herman Melville, "Father Mapple's Hymn," p. 397

Speaker and Situation

6

On First Looking into Chapman's Homer

Much have I travell'd in the realms of gold,
  And many goodly states and kingdoms seen;
  Round many western islands have I been
Which bards in fealty to Apollo hold.
Oft of one wide expanse had I been told
  That deep-brow'd Homer ruled as his demesne;
  Yet did I never breathe its pure serene
Till I heard Chapman speak out loud and bold:
Then felt I like some watcher of the skies
  When a new planet swims into his ken;
Or like stout Cortez when with eagle eyes
  He star'd at the Pacific—and all his men
Look'd at each other with a wild surmise —
  Silent, upon a peak in Darien.

JOHN KEATS

This poem was written by John Keats, but Keats is not the speaker. The speaker is a man who has travelled a good deal and seems to have lived sometime in the Renaissance, since he uses feudal terms ("fealty," "demesne") but also knows about Cortez (though he should have said it was Balboa who discovered the Pacific). The old traveller is, of course, a metaphor-persona who represents Keats, and the travels are Keats's reading. We are aware of this to the extent that the anachronism of Homer's ruling a medieval "demesne" doesn't bother us. Still, it will not do to strip the poem of its metaphor by saying that the speaker really is Keats, masquerading as the traveller, even though we know from Keats's biography that Homer and the Greeks in general made a powerful impression on him and, since he did not read Greek, he relied on translation, finding Homer admirably presented in George Chapman's translation. Keats wants to communicate his sense of discovery in reading Homer, but he does not do it directly, immediately. He does so by making a poem which is spoken by someone else who gives a metaphoric and, in a way, dramatic projection of Keats's attitudes.

Poems have the form of speech and, typographically, of writing, but of the two speech is most important. Many of them, indeed, seem like little dramas or self-contained scenes of dramas.* The sense of hearing speech is strongest in poems in which a speaker addresses one or more other auditors who are silent, a kind of poem called the DRAMATIC MONOLOGUE. The reader overhears the talk. In poems like this the speaker's situation is important, because it governs what he says, and we should try to hear what he says in the setting in which he speaks.

Soliloquy of the Spanish Cloister

G-r-r—there go, my heart's abhorrence!
Water your damned flower-pots, do!
If hate killed men, Brother Lawrence,
God's blood, would not mine kill you!
What? your myrtle-bush wants trimming?
Oh, that rose has prior claims—
Needs its leaden vase filled brimming?
Hell dry you up with its flames!

At the meal we sit together:
Salve tibi! I must hear
Wise talk of the kind of weather,
Sort of season, time of year:
Not a plenteous cork-crop: scarcely
Dare we hope oak-galls, I doubt:
What's the Latin name for "parsley"?
What's the Greek name for Swine's Snout?

oak-galls—used to make ink

Whew! We'll have our platter burnished,
Laid with care on our own shelf!

*See Reuben Arthur Brower, *Fields of Light* (New York, 1951); paperback, 1962, a study that applies this approach to a number of poems.

With a fire-new spoon we're furnished,
  And a goblet for ourself,
Rinsed like something sacrificial
  Ere 'tis fit to touch our chaps—
Marked with L for our initial!
  (He-he! There his lily snaps!)

Saint, forsooth! While brown Dolores
  Squats outside the Covent bank
With Sanchicha, telling stories,
  Steeping tresses in the tank,
Blue-black, lustrous, thick like horsehairs,
  —Can't I see his dead eye glow,
Bright as 'twere a Barbary corsair's?
  (That is, if he'd let it show!)

When he finishes refection,
  Knife and fork he never lays
Cross-wise, to my recollection,
  As do I, in Jesu's praise.
I the Trinity illustrate,
  Drinking watered orange-pulp—
In three sips the Arian frustrate;
  While he drains his at one gulp.

Oh, those melons! If he's able
  We're to have a feast! so nice!
One goes to the Abbot's table,
  All of us get each a slice.
How go on your flowers? None double?
  Not one fruit-sort can you spy?
Strange!—And I, too, at such trouble
  Keep them close-nipped on the sly!

There's a great text in Galatians,
  Once you trip on it, entails
Twenty-nine distinct damnations,
  One sure, if another fails:
If I trip him just a-dying,
  Sure of heaven as sure can be,
Spin him round and send him flying
  Off to hell, a Manichee?

Or, my scrofulous French novel
  On gray paper with blunt type!
Simply glance at it, you grovel
  Hand and foot in Belial's gripe:
If I double down its pages
  At the woeful sixteenth print,
When he gathers his greengages,
  Ope a sieve and slip it in't?

Or, there's Satan!—one might venture
  Pledge one's soul to him, yet leave
Such a flaw in the indenture
  As he'd miss till, past retrieve,
Blasted lay that rose-acacia
  We're so proud of! *Hy, Zy, Hine* . . .
'St, there's Vespers! *Plena gratiâ,*
  Ave, Virgo! Gr-r-r—You Swine!

Hy, Zy, Hine—perhaps an imitation of the bell

ROBERT BROWNING

The physical setting of the poem can be readily inferred to be the cloister garden, where the speaker watches Brother Lawrence care for his garden just before vespers. The sight of Brother Lawrence triggers the outburst that forms the poem. As in many dramatic monologues, the speaker gives a characterization of another person that reveals more about his own character than the one being talked about, and the dramatic tension in the poem grows out of the relationship between the speaker and the other person. At no point in this poem are we told directly what relations between the two monks are like, for we hear only one side of the story, privately spoken by the angry monk who hates Brother Lawrence. But most of us have had enough experience with enviously hateful people to evaluate the monk's characterization of Brother Lawrence as being distorted by his envy and thus can guess that Brother Lawrence is not such a bad sort. From the speaker's observations we learn that Brother Lawrence raises flowers, is a pleasant if somewhat conventional conversationalist, is a fastidious man who burnishes his platter, and a pious one (who does not read French novels). It is doubtful that his eye glows when he sees "brown Dolores" rinsing her black hair in the tank, but the speaker's description of her certainly suggests that his own does, kindled by his scrofulous novels.

In this poem the speaker and the situation in which he speaks are of almost equal importance, for the particular words are spoken in a particular physical and human setting. Indeed, the poem might be made into a little sound film without any changes—though a pictorial and dramatic realization might diminish its impact because it would leave less for our imaginations to do.

In the following poem the speakers actually participate in a little drama, because we have two characters talking to each other.

As You Came from the Holy Land

As you came from the holy land
  of Walsinghame
Mett you not with my true love
  By the way as you came?

How shall I know your true love
  That have mett many one
As I went to the holy lande
  That have come, that have gone?

She is neyther whyte nor browne
  Butt as the heavens fayre
There is none hath a forme so divine
  In the earth or the ayre.

Such a one did I meet, good Sir,
  Suche an Angelyke face,
Who lyke a queene, lyke a nymphe, did appere
  By her gate, by her grace.

She hath left me here all alone,
  All alone as unknowne,
Who somtymes did me lead with her selfe,
  And me lovde as her owne.

Whats the cause that she leaves you alone
  And a new way doth take;
Who loved you once as her owne
  And her ioye did you make?

I have lovde her all my youth,
  Butt now ould, as you see,
Love lykes not the fallyng frute
  From the wythered tree.

Know that love is a careless chylld
  And forgets promyse paste,
He is blynd, he is deaff when he lyste
  And in faythe never faste.

His desyre is a dureless contente
  And a trustlesse joye
He is wonn with a world of despayre
  And is lost with a toye.

dureless—brief

Of women kynde such indeed is the love
  Or the word Love abused
Under which many chyldysh desyres
  And conceytes are excusde.

Butt true love is a durable fyre
  In the mynde ever burninge;
Never syckes, never ould, never dead,
  From its selfe never turnynge.

SIR WALTER RALEIGH

Questions.

1. The shrine of Our Lady of Walsingham was a famous place of pilgrimage in Roman Catholic England. Is the poem interested in religion in the conventional sense?
2. What attitude does the poem convey toward women?
3. State as specifically as you can the two kinds of love discussed in the poem.

The reader here becomes, in a sense, another detached observer, like the passerby stopped by the question of the aging man, but when passerby and reader hear the history of his false love they become involved.

A part of this involvement comes about through the appeal of the lady's beauty to the pilgrim who has met her on the way back; when she is described to him "as the heavens fayre," who "Hath a form so divine / in the earth or ayre," the detached observer continues the rapturous description: "Suche an Angelyke face, / Who lyke a queene, like a nymphe, did appere / By her gate, by her grace." The three comparisons, angel, nymph, and queen are not ordinarily encountered in one lady. *Nymph* especially conveys overtones of fickleness and wantonness that contrast sharply with the lady's angelic face. Herein, of course, lies the paradox, a paradox which is made sharper by the lady's venturing on a pilgrimage and abandoning her lover along the way. In this poem the setting is not sharply realistic as it was in Browning's poem, and quite possibly it partakes of the metaphoric character of the setting of "On First Looking into Chapman's Homer." For one does not ordinarily associate ladies on pilgrimages with lovers, and the question arises as to the nature of the pilgrimage itself. Somehow or other it does not turn out to be a very religious kind of pilgrimage, or at any rate religious in the customary sense of the word. Perhaps the shrine is that of love, and the lover who ages becomes unfit for the journey and must drop out along the way. Another assertion is made about the lady, at least in her angelic and nymph-like aspects. The poem suggests that unlike her lover she is ageless (like angels and nymphs), and that her beauty is eternal. She seems almost to become a Venus with all the fickleness and sensuality of that pagan embodiment of physical love.

The aging man's love, then, presents a sharp contrast to that of the lady. His is bound up by mortality and needs to grow into a different state of existence as he matures and becomes old, but her love exists only on the youthful plane of sensuality; and when the physical factors on which it is based are waning or absent, her love wanes and disappears. The temporary nature of her love is conveyed by the aging lover's words in lines 29 through 36, which are an accurate description of Venus's child Cupid, conventionally represented as a blind boy shooting his darts of love wherever he will, careless of the consequences. The poem concludes on a note of hope rather than one of despair in its assertion of the existence of a higher kind of love which can be attained by maturing and can be retained in the mind as a fire of the spirit even as the fire of the body wanes. But the note of hope also conveys a renunciation of this love, for the speaker recognizes that he must suffer his love alone because the lady is incapable of enjoying it on this less physical plane with him.

In a poem like the preceding one, the poet is not talking in his own voice, but has created characters who speak the poem. The same is true in a poem which is spoken in the first person by someone who could not possibly be the poet, as in " 'I heard a fly buzz when I died.' "

'I Heard a Fly Buzz When I Died'

I heard a fly buzz when I died;
The stillness round my form
Was like the stillness in the air
Between the heaves of storm.

The eyes beside had wrung them dry,
And breaths were gathering sure
For that last onset, when the king
Be witnessed in his power.

I willed my keepsakes, signed away
What portion of me I
Could make assignable,—and then
There interposed a fly,

With blue, uncertain, stumbling buzz,
Between the light and me;
And then the windows failed, and then
I could not see to see.

EMILY DICKINSON

However, in a very real sense, any poem is spoken by someone other than the poet, even when the speaker is ostensibly the poet and talks in the first person. A poet may *write* a letter but he *makes* a poem, even if the poem is included in a letter. And in the process of making a poem there is enough objectification of the speaker so that even if the speaker actually is a direct representation of the poet, the poet to some degree stops talking in his own identity and becomes objectified as "the speaker." He becomes, as it were, a dramatization of himself.

The term often given the speaker, the character whom the poet creates to represent himself in the poem, is PERSONA. The persona is not only the agent who expresses the words in the poem; he is almost like a character in a miniature drama. According to George T. Wright, "The poet not only contrives a speaker for his poems; he also contrives a personality that the reader can abstract from the poem."*

*George T. Wright, *The Poet in the Poem* (Berkeley, Cal., 1960). The word *persona* is Ezra Pound's. See also Brower, *Fields of Light*, cited earlier, p. 85.

It should not be too surprising that a poet doesn't portray himself completely in his own person. In fact, it would be surprising if he did, or were able to do so. For one thing, a poem is public. For another it is a work of art, an emotion given a form it did not have when originally experienced, and hence in a way is artificial. A poem does not ordinarily spring into the poet's mind fully formed but often takes time to develop—and most of the time a good deal of work too—to take on the form which it finally has.

That a poet speaking in his own person as "I" is to some degree a dramatic projection need not eliminate him completely in a consideration of his work. It is sometimes an interesting experience to read poems as if they were anonymous (as I. A. Richards has students do), but most of us want to know who wrote a particularly good poem and probably want to know something more about him. With poets like William Blake and W. B. Yeats, and indeed with any poet whom we are going to read seriously, we gain a great deal by reading his other works and bringing to any one poem perspectives gained from others.

In reading poems known to be autobiographical, there is certainly no harm in remembering that the experience being described was intimately connected with the life of the poet. Milton's sonnet "On His Blindness" becomes more poignant when we learn that Milton was blind, and Coleridge's "Dejection: An Ode" takes on some additional significance when we learn that it embodies a complex spiritual crisis for Coleridge himself. A poet's life and his work can illuminate each other, if we keep clearly in mind the nature of the relationship. The relationship is a very complicated one, because what we are given in the work is not private confession but public art. To identify flatly the speaker even in an autobiographical poem with the poet denies him his art because doing so puts the poem in a perspective never intended by the poet, changing it from a work of art into a fragment of autobiography. Though in the serious study of the work of a poet we will want to know as much about him as we can, any given poem must be allowed a kind of autonomy. This means that we must be able to submit ourselves to the poem as the poet gave it to us, and be able, however much we may know about the poet's life, to see the speaker not literally as the poet but as the person who speaks the poem.

The following poem written by poet-teacher Theodore Roethke is an ELEGY for a student killed in a riding accident. The speaker represents Mr. Roethke in the sense that the experience and emotion were Roethke's and he gave them form in the words of the poem. But in the poem the speaker becomes almost independent of the poet. And the speaker's response to the situation as it emerges in the poem is more important to the reader than the actual experience of the poet. For the experience is given autonomous poetic objectification in the words of the speaker, so that even Jane's last name becomes a matter of no concern to us.

*Elegy for Jane**

(My student thrown by a horse)

I remember the neckcurls, limp and damp as tendrils;
And her quick look, a sidelong pickerel smile;
And how, once startled into talk, the light syllables leaped for her,
And she balanced in the delight of her thought,
A wren, happy, tail into the wind,
Her song trembling the twigs and small branches.
The shade sang with her;
The leaves, their whispers turned to kissing;
And the mold sang in the bleached valleys under the rose.

Oh, when she was sad, she cast herself down into such a pure depth,
Even a father could not find her:
Scraping her cheek against straw;
Stirring the clearest water.

My sparrow, you are not here,
Waiting like a fern, making a spiney shadow.
The sides of wet stones cannot console me,
Nor the moss, wound with the last light.

If only I could nudge you from this sleep,
My maimed darling, my skittery pigeon.
Over this damp grave I speak the words of my love:
I, with no rights in this matter,
Neither father nor lover.

THEODORE ROETHKE

Questions.

1. From what point of view has the poet "no rights in these matters"?
2. Describe as precisely as you can the events recorded in the last three lines of the first stanza.
3. What information does the kind of imagery used by the poet convey about the kind of girl Jane was?

We do not feel equally strongly in all poems that someone is actually talking. Sometimes, as in the following sonnet by Wordsworth, the words seem to be the thoughts of the poet. Even here, however, the situation is important, for the thoughts are those produced by looking at London from Westminster Bridge.

Composed Upon Westminster Bridge, Sept. 3, 1802

Earth has not anything to show more fair:
Dull would he be of soul who could pass by
A sight so touching in its majesty:
This City now doth, like a garment, wear
The beauty of the morning; silent, bare,
Ships, towers, domes, theatres, and temples lie
Open unto the fields, and to the sky;
All bright and glittering in the smokeless air.
Never did sun more beautifully steep
In his first splendour, valley, rock, or hill;
Ne'er saw I, never felt, a calm so deep!
The river glideth at his own sweet will:
Dear God! the very houses seem asleep;
And all that mighty heart is lying still!

William Wordsworth

The words here do not seem to be spoken to anyone at all, not even to the reader, but constitute a kind of soliloquy which has an external form in the poem—somewhat as soliloquies in motion-picture versions of Shakespeare's plays are heard as the projected thoughts of characters who either are not seen directly or do not move their lips.

The situation and character of the speaker in poems often determine how we should take what is being said. In other words, they affect the poem's tone, a matter which is intimately involved with speaker and situation but which we shall have to take up in a separate chapter.

Poems for Further Study:

My Last Duchess

Ferrara

That's my last Duchess painted on the wall,
Looking as if she were alive. I call
That piece a wonder, now: Frà Pandolf's hands
Worked busily a day, and there she stands.
Will't please you sit and look at her? I said
"Frà Pandolf" by design, for never read
Strangers like you that pictured countenance,
The depth and passion of its earnest glance,
But to myself they turned (since none puts by
The curtain I have drawn for you, but I)
And seemed as they would ask me, if they durst,
How such a glance came there; so, not the first
Are you to turn and ask thus. Sir 'twas not
Her husband's presence only, called that spot
Of joy into the Duchess' cheek: perhaps
Frà Pandolf chanced to say "Her mantle laps
Over my lady's wrist too much," or "Paint
Must never hope to reproduce the faint
Half-flush that dies along her throat:" such stuff
Was courtesy, she thought, and cause enough
For calling up that spot of joy. She had
A heart—how shall I say?—too soon made glad,
Too easily impressed: she liked whate'er
She looked on, and her looks went everywhere.
Sir, 'twas all one! My favor at her breast,
The dropping of the daylight in the West,
The bough of cherries some officious fool
Broke in the orchard for her, the white mule
She rode with round the terrace—all and each
Would draw from her alike the approving speech,
Or blush, at least. She thanked men—good! but thanked
Somehow—I know not how—as if she ranked
My gift of a nine-hundred-years-old name
With anybody's gift. Who'd stoop to blame
This sort of trifling? Even had you skill
In speech—(which I have not)—to make your will
Quite clear to such an one, and say, "Just this
Or that in you disgusts me; here you miss,
Or there exceed the mark"—and if she let
Herself be lessoned so, nor plainly set

Her wits to yours, forsooth, and made excuse,
—E'en then would be some stooping; and I choose
Never to stoop. Oh sir, she smiled, no doubt,
Whene'er I passed her; but who passed without
Much the same smile? This grew; I gave commands;
Then all smiles stopped together. There she stands
As if alive. Will't please you rise? We'll meet
The company below, then. I repeat,
The Count your master's known munificence
Is ample warrant that no just pretence
Of mine for dowry will be disallowed;
Though his fair daughter's self, as I avowed
At starting, is my object. Nay, we'll go
Together down, sir. Notice Neptune, though,
Taming a sea-horse, thought a rarity,
Which Claus of Innsbruck cast in bronze for me!

ROBERT BROWNING

Discipline

Throw away thy rod;
Throw away thy wrath:
O my God,
Take the gentle path.

For my heart's desire
Unto thine is bent:
I aspire
To a full consent.

Not a word or look
I affect to own,
But by book
And thy book alone.

Though I fail, I weep:
Though I halt in pace,
Yet I creep
To the throne of grace.

Then let wrath remove;
Love will do the deed:
  For with love
Stony hearts will bleed.

Love is swift of foot;
Love's a man of war,
  And can shoot,
And can hit from far.

Who can scape his bow?
That, which wrought on thee,
  Brought thee low,
Needs must work on me.

Throw away thy rod;
Though man frailties hath,
  Thou art God:
Throw away thy wrath.

George Herbert

Go, Lovely Rose!

Go lovely rose,
Tell her that wastes her time and me,
That now she knows,
When I resemble her to thee,
How sweet and fair she seems to be.

Tell her that's young,
And shuns to have her graces spied,
That hadst thou sprung
In deserts where no men abide,
Thou must have uncommended died.

Small is the worth
Of beauty from the light retired:
Bid her come forth,
Suffer herself to be desired,
And not blush so to be admired.

Then die, that she
The common face of all things rare
May read in thee;
How small a part of time they share,
That are so wondrous sweet and fair.

EDMUND WALLER

It is a Beauteous Evening, Calm and Free

It is a beauteous evening, calm and free.
The holy time is quiet as a Nun
Breathless with adoration: the broad sun
Is sinking down in its tranquillity;
The gentlessness of heaven broods o'er the sea:
Listen! the mighty Being is awake,
And doth with his eternal motion make
A sound like thunder—everlastingly.
Dear Child! dear Girl! that walkest with me here,
If thou appear untouched by solemn thought,
Thy nature is not therefore less divine:
Thou liest in Abraham's bosom all the year;
And worship'st at the Temple's inner shrine,
God being with thee when we know it not.

WILLIAM WORDSWORTH

Dirge from Cymbeline

To fair Fidele's grassy tomb
  Soft maids and village hinds shall bring
Each opening sweet of earliest bloom,
  And rifle all the breathing spring.

No wailing ghost shall dare appear
  To vex with shrieks this quiet grove:
But shepherd lads assemble here,
  And melting virgins own their love.

No wither'd witch shall here be seen:
  No goblins lead their nightly crew:
The female fays shall haunt the green,
  And dress thy grave with pearly dew!

The redbreast oft, at evening hours,
Shall kindly lend his little aid,
With hoary moss, and gather'd flowers,
To deck the ground where thou art laid.

When howling winds and beating rain,
In tempests shake the sylvan cell;
Or 'midst the chase, on every plain,
The tender thought on thee shall dwell;

Each lonely scene shall thee restore;
For thee the tear be duly shed;
Beloved till life can charm no more,
And mourn'd till Pity's self be dead.

William Collins

From *Vision and Prayer*, Part II*

I turn the corner of prayer and burn
In a blessing of the sudden
Sun. In the name of the damned
I would turn back and run
To the hidden land
But the loud sun
Christens down
The sky.
I
Am found.
O let him
Scald me and drown
Me in his world's wound.
His lightning answers my
Cry. My voice burns in his hand.
Now I am lost in the blinding
One. The sun roars at the prayer's end.

Dylan Thomas

Suggested Poems for Further Reading (ANTHOLOGY):

William Blake, "To the Evening Star," p. 259
Robert Burns, "Willie Brewed a Peck O'Maut," p. 277
Samuel Taylor Coleridge, "The Rime of the Ancient Mariner." p. 287
Thomas Dekker, "Haymakers, Rakers," p. 315
Robert Graves, "A Love Story," p. 343
Ben Jonson, "To the Memory of My Beloved Master William Shakespeare," p. 369

Tone

7

On the Late Massacre in Piedmont

Avenge, O Lord, thy slaughtered saints, whose bones
Lie scattered on the Alpine mountains cold,
Even them who kept thy truth so pure of old
When all our fathers worshiped stocks and stones,
Forget not: in thy book record their groans
Who were thy sheep and in their ancient fold
Slain by the bloody *Piemontese* that rolled
Mother with infant down the rocks. Their moans
The vales redoubled to the hills, and they
To heaven. Their martyred blood and ashes sow
O'er all the *Italian* fields where still doth sway
The triple Tyrant: that from these may grow
A hundred fold, who having learnt thy way
Early may fly the *Babylonian* woe.

JOHN MILTON

In 1655 the Waldenses, a protestant sect living in the mountains of Piedmont in northern Italy, were persecuted by the Duke of Savoy, and some of them were killed. Milton, an English protestant, wrote this sonnet in anger. It is a sectarian poem and an occasional one, written in response to a particular event, now almost forgotten; but we continue to read it because it is a good poem and an eloquent utterance of an angry man.

The attitude expressed in a poem is called TONE.* Tone in poetry may be thought of in general as being like the tone of voice in conversation. A

**Tone* was first used in this sense by I. A. Richards, and has been adopted in modern criticism.

person may say the word *great* in a half dozen different ways and communicate something different each time, by varying the pitch and emphasis with which he speaks. A poet, however, has only the printed word and not the speaking voice to modulate. His tone, therefore, must be communicated by connotation, sound, rhythm, but especially by the context in which the words appear.

Just as the tone of voice in which we say something in conversation is governed by where we are, what we are talking about, and to whom we are talking, so the tone of a poem depends on the speaker, the situation, the subject, and the auditor (or audience). In conversation, of course, the person talking is the one whose attitude is conveyed by the tone in which the discourse is delivered. In poetry the situation is more complicated, because the poet may not be talking directly as the speaker; the speaker may, as we saw in the previous chapter, be a character in a dramatic monologue or another speaker different from the poet, even if he is identified as "I." Often the tone of what the speaker says is different from the tone of the poem as a whole.

In the following poem, "Holy Willie's Prayer," for instance, the speaker is not even a projection of the poet but a character identified in the title as Holy Willie. The tone of his discourse is earnest, smugly and self-righteously pious, vindictive. This is not the tone of the poem, which is humorously, but devastatingly, ironic and satiric.

Holy Willie's Prayer

"And send the godly in a pet to pray."—Pope

O Thou, that in the heavens does dwell,
Wha, as it pleases best Thysel',
Sends ane to heaven an' ten to hell,
   A' for thy glory,
And no for onie guid or ill
   They've done afore Thee!

I bless and praise Thy matchless might,
When thousands Thou hast left in night,
That I am here afore Thy sight,
   For gifts an' grace
A burning and a shining light
   To a' this place.

What was I, or my generation,
That I should get sic exaltation.
I wha deserv'd most just damnation
For broken laws,
Sax thousand years ere my creation,
Thro' Adam's cause.

sic—such

When from my mither's womb I fell,
Thou might hae plung'd me deep in hell,
To gnash my gooms, and weep and wail,
In burnin lakes,
Where damned devils roar and yell,
Chain'd to their stakes.

Yet I am here a chosen sample,
To show thy grace is great and ample:
I'm here a pillar o' Thy temple,
Strong as a rock,
A guide, a buckler, and example,
To a' Thy flock.

O Lord, Thou kens what zeal I bear,
When drinkers drink, an' swearers swear,
An' singing here, an' dancin' there,
Wi' great and sma';
For I am keepit by Thy fear
Free frae them a'.

But yet, O Lord! confess I must,
At times I'm fash'd wi' fleshly lust:
An' sometimes, too, in wardly trust,
Vile self gets in;
But Thou remembers we are dust,
Defil'd wi' sin.

fash'd—troubled

O Lord! yestreen, Thou kens, wi' Meg—
Thy pardon I sincerely beg;
O! may't ne'er be a livin plague
To my dishonour,
An' I'll ne'er lift a lawless leg
Again upon her.

Besides, I farther maun allow,
Wi' Leezie's lass, three times I trow—
But Lord, that Friday I was fou, *fou*—drunk
   When I cam near her;
Or else, Thou kens, Thy servant true
   Wad never steer her. *steer*—touch

Maybe Thou lets this fleshly thorn
Buffet Thy servant e'en and morn,
Lest he owre proud and high shou'd turn, *owre*—over
   That he's sae gifted:
If sae, Thy han' maun e'en be borne,
   Until Thou lift it.

Lord, bless Thy chosen in this place,
For her Thou has a chasen race:
But God confound their stubborn face,
   An' blast their name,
Wha bring Thy elders to disgrace
   An' public shame.

Lord, mind Gaw'n Hamilton's deserts;
He drinks, an' swears, an' plays at cartes,
Yet has sae mony takin arts,
   Wi great and sma',
Frae God's ain priest the people's hearts
   He steals awa.

An' when we chasten'd him therefor,
Thou kens how he bred sic a splore, *splore*—uproar
An' set the warld in a roar
   O' laughing at us;—
Curse Thou his basket and his store,
   Kail an' potatoes. *Kail*—colwort, cabbage

Lord, hear my earnest cry and pray'r,
Against that Presbyt'ry o' Ayr;
Thy strong right hand, Lord make it bare
   Up' their heads;
Lord, visit them, an' dinna spare,
   For their misdeeds.

O Lord, my God! that glib-tongu'd Aiken,
My vera heart and flesh are quakin,
To think how we stood sweatin, shakin,
  An piss'd wi' dread,
While he wi' hingin lip an' snakin,
  Held up his head.

Lord, in Thy day o' vengeance try him,
Lord, visit them wha did employ him,
And pass not in Thy mercy by them,
  Nor hear their pray'r.
But for thy people's sake destroy them,
  An' dinna spare.

But, Lord, remember me an' mine
Wi' mercies temporal and divine,
That I for grace an' gear may shine,
  Excelled by nane.
And a' the glory shall be thine,

Amen, Amen!

ROBERT BURNS

Questions.

1. Does Willie think he has been elected for salvation? If so, on what basis? Does he say?
2. He confesses a few sins. How serious are they? Does he mention mitigating circumstances?
3. How do his sins compare with those of Gaw'n Hamilton, and how would he mete out punishments?

We said the tone of the poem as a whole is ironic, by which is meant that the tone as perceived by the reader is the reverse of the tone of the discourse. Willie is in dead earnest, talking to God in prayer, but what he says shows him to be such a hypocrite (as judged by us according to commonly received standards of fair play, Christian virtue, and simple consistency) that he can be blind to his own sins. Despite the Calvinist doctrine that one does not know whom God will "elect" for salvation, Willie is so smugly certain that he is among the elect—because of his exemplary virtue—that he is able to regard his sins, which are worse than the drinking, swearing, singing, and dancing that he condemns others for, as fleshly thorns to keep him from becoming too proud. And, certain that he has God on his side regardless of what he does, he asks God to punish Gaw'n Hamilton and Aiken by withering their crops and refusing to hear their prayers for laughing at and frightening the Auld Licht (the strict branch of the Scottish Kirk) "Presbyt'ry o' Ayr."

The poem has a tone of satiric irony (not sarcasm, which is a kind of irony intended to hurt someone's feelings, usually in person). And the laughter exposing Willie to ridicule arises from the same source as the *satire:* from the disproportion between what Willie represents himself as being and what he actually is. Satire shows someone or something as deviating in a ridiculous way from a norm or standard that the writer assumes will be known and accepted by his reader, usually one of commonsense rationality of some kind. Humor of the kind seen here derives from a disproportion between what seems and is, or a reversal of intention in someone we don't approve of.

The poem is ironic both because of the satiric disproportion and because of the reversal of intention. These two aspects of the poem display two different meanings of the word irony. Irony is very hard to define in a way that would clarify how the word is used in any particular situation. It has been most satisfactorily defined in connection with drama, where it originated; it is derived from a character in Greek drama, especially comedy, who was known as the *eiron:* a naive person whose discourse, in the situation of the play, had more significance than he knew, and who unwittingly brought about the comic effect. Often the audience at a play is unaware of the significance of a character's remarks when he himself is not, and this is called, rather loosely, dramatic irony. When someone who is far from naive or ignorant assumes the mask of ignorance, the pose is called Socratic irony, after Socrates, who practiced it to draw his interlocutors into logical traps. The term is harder to pin down as it is used in discussing lyric poetry, where it can mean reversal or simply an important complexity of meaning, especially one arising from a disproportion between what is said and what is meant.*

In poems in which the speaker talks to someone else, and is overheard by the reader, the character of the speaker has a greater effect in governing the tone of the poem than it does in a poem in which the speaker addresses the reader, whether the speaker is the person of the poet or a character

---

*For discussions of irony, mostly in drama but also generally, see G. C. Sedgewick, *Of Irony, Especially in Drama.* University of Toronto Studies, Philology and Literature, Series No. 10. Toronto, 1935; and Alan Reynolds Thompson, *The Dry Mock: A Study of Irony in Drama.* Berkeley and Los Angeles, 1948. For satire, see David Worcester, *The Art of Satire.* New York, 1940.

completely separated from the poem. When the speaker addresses the reader directly, there is a closer relation between the speaker and the tone, as there is a closer relation between the reader and the speaker. The speaker's situation is still important—when the situation is identified—but perhaps more important is the mood of the speaker, and the relation between what is said and the mood in which it is said.

Mood is not the same as tone, but is one element in the poem that affects the tone. In the following poem the tone derives from the interplay between the mood of the speaker and the subject.

On the Life of Man

What is our life? a play of passion,
Our mirth the musicke of division,
Our mothers wombes the tyring houses be,
Where we are drest for this short Comedy,
Heaven the Iudicious sharpe spectator is,
That sits and markes still who doth act amisse,
The graves that hide us from the searching Sun,
Are like drawne curtaynes when the play is done,
Thus march we playing to our latest rest,
Onely we dye in earnest, that's no Jest.

Sir Walter Raleigh

Questions.

1. What is the underlying attitude toward life conveyed by this analogy? Define it as carefully as you can.
2. Does the fact that the play is a comedy affect this attitude?
3. What is the effect of the modifier "searching" on the word "Sun"?

The poet, who here talks as from a position of remove as he considers human life, sustains a mood of amused detachment. The play of life is a comedy, and Heaven is represented as a "Judicious sharp spectator," as a sort of ideal discriminating audience, who judges life as if it were a comedy. And although the play ends with death—"and that's no jest"—it remains a comedy, at least up to the end. But what is said about life? That it is a comedy, a tragedy, or merely absurd? Actually none of these. *What* the poet says in the analogy he develops is less important than his attitude, as it can be inferred from the combination of serious and amusing elements in the poem. What the poem really says, in other words, is not directly stated at all but lies in the tone, which is a complex one.

There are as many different tones in poetry as there are poems, for each poem has its own, produced by the interaction of all its elements. Our own age seems to prefer poems with a complex tone to poems that are sentimental and one-dimensional in tone. We are speaking now of sophisticated readers, of course; sentimental poetry is the poetry that is popularly read and is often read aloud to musical accompaniment. What do we mean by "sentimental"? Not emotion, certainly, but an attitude toward emotion: one that relishes emotion for its own sake, especially emotion which through conventional tenderness and nostalgia can moisten the eye of someone who likes to weep.

What seems sentimental depends a good deal on the response of the reader. To some people the following poem will seem to express an attitude, have a tone, of strongly felt piety; to others it will seem to have a tone in which piety largely serves to indulge emotion.

From *Divina Commedia*

Oft have I seen at some cathedral door
A laborer, pausing in the dust and heat,
Lay down his burden, and with reverent feet
Enter, and cross himself, and on the floor
Kneel to repeat his paternoster o'er;
Far off the noises of the world retreat;
The loud vociferations of the street
Become an undistinguishable roar.
So, as I enter here from day to day,
And leave my burden at this minster gate,
Kneeling in prayer, and not ashamed to pray,
The tumult of the time disconsolate
To inarticulate murmurs dies away,
While the eternal ages watch and wait.

HENRY WADSWORTH LONGFELLOW

Questions.

1. Is there any reason why the man selected for the first five lines be a laborer?
2. The poem contains little metaphor. What is the effect of this?

Both mood and tone of the previous poem are relatively simple. In the next poem both are complex.

Bathsabe's Song

Hot sunne, coole fire, tempered with sweete air,
Black shade, fair nurse, shadow my white haire — *white haire*—fair hair
Shine sun, burne fire, breath aire, and ease mee,
Black shade, fair nurse, shroud me and please me
Shadow (my sweet nurse) keep me from burning
Make not my glad cause, cause of mourning.
Let not my beauties fire,
Enflame unstaied desire, — *unstaied*—uncontrolled
Nor pierce any bright eye,
That wandreth lightly.

George Peele

Questions.

1. Explain the appropriateness of the personification of shade as a fair nurse.
2. In how many senses is shadow to keep Bathsheba from burning?
3. Define "coole fire" in line one.

Bathsheba, as her song reveals, is quite aware of the danger of her own beauty—its ability to get her into trouble— and she is also a woman whose passionate nature half frightens her and yet pleases her. Although she hopes that her beauty will not "pierce any bright eye,/ That wandreth lightly," she is aware that it has the power to do just that, and the mood of the poem is that of breathless hot suspense to be followed by torrential passion. The poem makes use of paradox to achieve its effect with a very few words. Observe how the progression of "coole fire" of the first line becomes "burne fire" in the third line, and then a request to shadow "to keep me from burning" in the fifth line. But this beauty of Bathsheba's, variously called in the poem "cool fire," "glad cause," and "beauties fire," is igniting itself, as the poem makes clear, even as it ignites a fire in the mind of David through his eye that "wandreth lightly."

Some of the complexity of mood and tone in "Bathsabe's Song" comes from a complexity of imagery. The imagery of Longfellow's poem, which has a simpler tone, does nothing to distract from the clear representation of the experience of standing before a cathedral in Italy and going in to pray, and the poem contains only one metaphor, a rather indistinct, conventional one. Complexity of tone is often produced by a complexity of metaphor and imagery.

Indeed, tone is produced by the interaction of all elements in the poem. In the following poem, for instance, a sort of blues rhythm, which helps to characterize the shoe salesman, who is in fact "humming the blues," contributes to the tone of the poem as a whole, because it helps to communicate the way the speaker sees the salesman.

*Sale**

Went into a shoestore to buy a pair of shoes,
There was a shoe salesman humming the blues
Under his breath; over his breath
Floated a peppermint lifesaver, a little wreath.

I said please, I need a triple-A,
And without stopping humming or swallowing his lifesaver away
He gave one glance from toe to toe
And plucked from the mezzanine the very shoe.

Skill of the blessed, that at their command
Blue and breathless comes to hand
To send, from whatever preoccupation, feet
Implacably shod into the perfect street.

JOSEPHINE MILES

Questions.

1. Explain the appropriateness or inappropriateness of the jazzy rhythm of this poem.
2. How are the words "implacably" and "perfect" of the final line related, and what do they contribute to the tone of the poem?

The relation between tone and symbol is harder to talk about because in a symbolic poem the real "subject" is not the visible symbol itself but everything it suggests, and in order to grasp the meaning of the symbol we need to have some notion of the tone of the poem. It would seem as if

---

this were a circular process. Actually it is not. As we saw in the analysis of Blake's "The Sick Rose," a symbolic poem will not in any satisfactory way yield its meaning until a reader has begun to look at it as what it is, a poem in which the things that are directly represented are not what it is about. But the poem makes this felt very quickly, and in making it felt already communicates something of its tone. Other elements in the poem—the speaker, situation, imagery, metaphor, connotation, rhythm, sound—naturally also contribute to the tone and indicate the direction in which the reader should allow the symbolism to lead him; hence, these elements affect what he is going to see in the poem as a whole.

What he finally sees depends on the effectiveness with which the parts of the poem interact, the richness of the symbol, and his own perceptiveness. But when a symbolic poem suggests so much that the reader is allowed to see in it something of human life in a strangely comprehensive and revealing way, it might be said to have almost a prophetic tone. Now when the word *prophecy* is used in this connection, it doesn't mean prediction. Even in Biblical prophecy, prediction is a superficial and incidental aspect of something else: the communication, usually through symbolic vision, of a perspective gained from a superior kind of knowledge. In saying that a symbol can become in a way prophetic, we are not suggesting that the poet is divinely inspired, but that in his symbol he brings to bear on life a superior kind—or degree—of imaginative perception. To put it quantitatively, so much imagination is involved in the symbol that it takes on something of the character of a vision—*not* a hallucination, which is involuntary and mistakes what is seen in the mind for external reality. That is, the symbol is something seen with tremendous intensity and clarity, and becomes enormously significant in a way which, according to W. H. Auden and many others, may not be fully understood even by the poet.*

Let us examine a symbolic poem to notice as well as we can in a brief analysis what its tone is like. Because we cannot consider the poem in context with the rest of Yeats's work our analysis must necessarily be partial.

The Black Tower

Say that the men of the old black tower,
Though they but feed as the goatherd feeds,
Their money spent, their wine gone sour,
Lack nothing that a soldier needs,
That all are oath-bound men:
Those banners come not in.

**The Enchafed Flood.* New York, 1950, p. 65.

There in the tomb stand the dead upright,
But winds come up from the shore:
They shake when the winds roar,
Old bones upon the mountain shake.

Those banners come to bribe or threaten
Or whisper that a man's a fool
Who, when his own right king's forgotten
Cares what king sets up his rule.
If he died long ago
Why do you dread us so?

There in the tomb drops the faint moonlight,
But wind comes up from the shore:
They shake when the winds roar,
Old bones upon the mountain shake.

The tower's old cook that must climb and clamber
Catching small birds in the dew of the morn
When we hale men lie stretched in slumber
Swears that he hears the king's great horn.
But he's a lying hound:
Stand we on guard oath-bound!

There in the tomb the dark grows blacker,
But wind comes up from the shore;
They shake when the winds roar,
Old bones upon the mountains shake.

WILLIAM BUTLER YEATS*

Questions.

1. What effect is achieved in the refrain by changing the words of the first line?
2. What is the relationship between the refrain and the events in the rest of the poem?
3. Who and where is the speaker whose words form the poem? Does his situation and, therefore, perspective change at any points in the poem?
4. What do "those banners" of lines 5 and 11 refer to?

Obviously the events described in the poem are set in a bygone age, and the black tower is a relic from some dim past, unrecorded in history. The rough men and their cook, with whom the poet's imagination has peopled the tower, are in a bad way, "Their money spent, their wine gone sour," and relying for food on the small birds that the cook still manages to catch at the top of the tower. The soldiers, however, are committed to their charge to keep the invaders out and feel that they "Lack nothing that a soldier needs," since they are able to maintain the tower against the enemy. The men seem to know that their lord the king is not coming, though the cook swears he hears the king's horn.

They are committed to a lost cause. And the refrain seems to give portents of an end to it all; for the black tower progressively becomes blacker as even the "faint moonlight" dies away, the dead stand up in their tombs, and the wind roaring up the mountainside from the shore shakes their old bones.

On one level it might be said that the poem is about lost causes, but this does not adequately account for the disturbing feeling the poem gives as one reads it over and over, nor does it explain even the things described—the dead standing in their tombs, for instance. Images such as these invite us to make associations, and one of the associations we would most likely make with the bodies standing is that with the Judgment. But there is nothing in the poem other than this image to suggest the Last Judgment of the Christian tradition, so perhaps we are not justified in pursuing this association any further than to say that some kind of judgment, or some new period of history, is about to begin in which the outworn cause defended by the men in the tower will disappear completely. Or possibly the dead stand upright in their tombs, like ghostly sentries shivering, but steadfast, in some vague expectancy. The blackness of the tombs and the blackness which increasingly envelops the tower, as well as the fact that both the tower and the bones of the dead are old, may link the conditions of the dead and the living and suggest some kind of change to come which could affect them both. Certainly the men in the garrison cannot long endure with such wretched provisions, and the growing darkness seems to be a final one.

But what, precisely, is the nature of this change? The poet does not say—here. We can get a great deal out of the poem without knowing what Yeats may have thought of the matter, for the symbolic tower stimulates our imaginations in a way that lets us see all kinds of meanings in it, and the tone of the whole poem becomes in a strange way prophetic. It so happens that Yeats can give us help in reading this poem and others of his, if we will go farther in his work and read more. With many poets we can better catch their tone in any given poem by knowing their other work. This is especially true of Yeats, who regarded all his work (even his letters, which he revised after they were published!) as constituting a whole, and much of whose work fits into an elaborate symbolical system. Read in context with this system, which views history as being a cyclic process, "The Black Tower" does indeed represent a turning point in history, and the king's horn heard by the cook may well be the trumpet heralding the new era which the others will hear after the old one has disappeared in the complete darkness.*

The prophetic tone is strong enough in the poem itself, however, so that the reader almost cannot help seeing the dark tower and its abandoned men in growing darkness as but one image of a vastly more comprehensive vision.

Tone in poetry is hard to talk about explicitly because, as was said, the tone of a poem arises from the interaction of all its elements and cannot be attached to any one element. Furthermore, the tone a reader feels the first time he reads a poem modulates everything in the poem on a second reading, with the result that the tone he gets the second time through may be different from the first time. One's perception of tone, especially in a difficult poem, may be gradually cumulative, even cyclical. Fortunately, tone is harder to describe and account for than it is to feel, if a reader commits himself to the poem and lets it speak. A receptive reader will usually know quite early in his experience with a poem how, in general at least, the poet feels about his subject.

Poems for Further Study:

Sonnet to Mrs. Unwin

Mary! I want a lyre with other strings;
Such aid from Heaven as some have feigned they drew!
An eloquence scarce given to mortals, new,
And undebased by praise of meaner things!
That, ere through age or woe I shed my wings,
I may record thy worth, with honor due,

In verse as musical as thou art true—
Verse, that immortalizes whom it sings!
But thou hast little need: there is a book,
By seraphs writ with beams of heavenly light,
On which the eyes of God not rarely look;
A chronicle of actions just and bright!
There all thy deeds, my faithful Mary, shine,
And since thou own'st that praise, I spare thee mine.

William Cowper

---

*The interested student should see *The Collected Poems of W. B. Yeats*, New York, Macmillan, 1956, and John Unterecker, *A Reader's Guide to William Butler Yeats*. New York, 1959, a useful paper-back guide.

To—

Music, when soft voices die,
Vibrates in the memory—
Odors, when sweet violets sicken,
Live within the sense they quicken.
Rose leaves, when the rose is dead,
Are heaped for the beloved's bed;
And so thy thoughts, when thou art gone,
Love itself shall slumber on.

Percy Bysshe Shelley

Dover Beach

The sea is calm tonight,
The tide is full, the moon lies fair
Upon the straits;—on the French coast the light
Gleams and is gone; the cliffs of England stand,
Glimmering and vast, out in the tranquil bay.
Come to the window, sweet is the night-air!

Only, from the long line of spray
Where the sea meets the moon-blanched land,
Listen! you hear the grating roar
Of pebbles which the waves draw back, and fling,
At their return, up the high strand,
Begin, and cease, and then again begin,
With tremulous cadence slow, and bring
The eternal note of sadness in.

Sophocles long ago
Heard it on the Aegean, and it brought
Into his mind the turbid ebb and flow
Of human misery; we
Find also in the sound a thought,
Hearing it by this distant northern sea.

The Sea of Faith
Was once, too, at the full, and round earth's shore
Lay like the folds of a bright girdle furled.
But now I only hear
Its melancholy, long, withdrawing roar,
Retreating, to the breath
Of the night-wind, down the vast edges drear
And naked shingles of the world.

Ah, love, let us be true
To one another! for the world, which seems
To lie before us like a land of dreams,
So various, so beautiful, so new,
Hath really neither joy, nor love, nor light,
Nor certitude, nor peace, nor help for pain;
And we are here as on a darkling plain
Swept with confused alarms of struggle and flight,
Where ignorant armies clash by night.

MATTHEW ARNOLD

The Old Man's Comforts and How he Gained Them

"You are old, Father William," the young man cried,
"The few locks which are left you are gray;
You are hale, Father William, a hearty old man,
Now tell me the reason, I pray."

"In the days of my youth," Father William replied,
"I remembered that youth would fly fast,
And abused not my health, and my vigor at first,
That I never might need them at last."

"You are old, Father William," the young man cried,
"And pleasures with youth pass away;
And yet you lament not the days that are gone,
Now tell me the reason, I pray."

"In the days of my youth," Father William replied,
"I remembered that youth could not last;
I thought of the future, whatever I did,
That I never might grieve for the past."

"You are old, Father William," the young man cried,
"And life must be hastening away;
You are cheerful, and love to converse upon death,
Now tell me the reason, I pray."

"I am cheerful, young man," Father William replied,
"Let the cause thy attention engage;
In the days of my youth I remembered my God!
And He hath not forgotten my age."

ROBERT SOUTHEY

Father William

"You are old, Father William," the young man said,
"And your hair has become very white,
And yet you incessantly stand on your head—
Do you think, at your age, it is right?"

"In my youth," Father William replied to his son,
"I feared it might injure the brain;
But now that I'm perfectly sure I have none,
Why, I do it again and again."

"You are old," said the youth, "as I mentioned before,
And have grown uncommonly fat;
Yet you turned a back-somersault in at the door—
Pray, what is the reason of that?"

"In my youth," said the sage, as he shook his gray locks,
"I kept all my limbs very supple
By the use of this ointment—one shilling the box—
Allow me to sell you a couple."

"You are old," said the youth, "and your jaws are too weak
For anything tougher than suet;
Yet you finished the goose, with the bones and the beak;
Pray, how did you manage to do it?"

"In my youth," said his father, "I took to the law,
And argued each case with my wife;
And the muscular strength which it gave to my jaw
Has lasted the rest of my life."

"You are old," said the youth, "one would hardly suppose
That your eye was as steady as ever;
Yet you balanced an eel on the end of your nose—
What made you so awfully clever?"

"I have answered three questions, and that is enough,"
Said his father; "don't give yourself airs!
Do you think I can listen all day to such stuff?
Be off, or I'll kick you downstairs!"

LEWIS CARROLL

Suggested Poems for Further Reading (ANTHOLOGY):

William Blake, "Holy Thursday, I and II," p. 255
Robert Browning, "Confessions," p. 263
Robert Burns, "To a Louse," p. 273
Emily Dickinson, "Sweet is the Swamp with its Secrets," p. 318

Structure

8

People are very quick to perceive patterns. The following group of numbers, for instance, becomes almost instantly organized into a pattern.

1 2 1 2 3 4 3 4 5 6 5 6 7 7

Two consecutive numbers are each repeated once, then the next two, for three pairs of numbers, and the number following is repeated to end the sequence. If this pattern were given with letters instead of numbers, many students would quickly recognize it as that of the rhyme scheme of the SHAKESPEAREAN SONNET:

ABAB CDCD EFEF GG

It has three quatrains (groups of four lines) and a couplet (two lines that rhyme).

This is not the only pattern found in this kind of sonnet. The lines themselves have a basic stress pattern of an unaccented syllable followed by an accented one, which is repeated five times to form lines with five IAMBIC FEET, or IAMBIC PENTAMETER. Thus the sonnet is organized into units by its basic beat, by the length of the lines, by stanzas (quatrains) marked by rhymes, and finally closes when the end of the pattern is signalled by a concluding couplet.

The sonnet is called a poetic FORM, an abstract form, as can be seen by our being able to consider it completely as an abstract pattern of stresses, number of feet, rhyme. The minute one starts using terms like *form, structure,* and so on, as we shall have to do in this chapter, there is a danger of creating the wrong kinds of pictures in the reader's mind. A form should in this case not be thought of as something that contains, a mold into which the sonnet is poured. It can be thought of this way, but preferably not until there is something "in" the form. It would be better to consider the abstract sonnet form as a sort of paradigm or pattern that the poet follows: quatrain, quatrain, quatrain, couplet.

A sonnet, abstractly conceived as a pattern, could be composed using names from a telephone directory. Indeed, even one of the less elaborate computers could be instructed to put together a sonnet with the right stress patterns and rhymes. Such sonnets would accurately follow the sonnet form, but probably would not have a very good organic form. Earlier in this book we have used the word *structure* to refer to overall poetic form, a word which suggests that a poem is something that is built. *Organic form* is a term referring to the individual form—as opposed to the abstract form, or general form—of a poem; and it stresses, in the biological analogy implied in the word, that the form of an individual poem is not rigidly mechanical but something seen in the way that the parts and elements of a poem interact, how the poem works. *Structure* is a term used primarily when the poem is looked at from the outside, as it were, when we note the way the parts fit together.

Both terms are useful, and both refer to a fact about poetry: as the parts and elements of a poem are unique, so the relationships among these parts and elements are unique; and the relationships in a good poem give it an organization and a shape in which everything seems to be in a uniquely satisfying order. This is true even when the poem follows a general pattern such as that of the sonnet. The abstract form of the sonnet is the genus, but each good sonnet is in effect a new species having its own order. "Form," says the American artist Ben Shahn, "is the very shape of content."* Or we might say for poetry that the structure of a poem is the order of what occurs in it.

Poetry, like music, is a temporal art; a poem, like a piece of music, must be apprehended sequentially in time. Perhaps a few comparisons between structural process in music and in poetry might be helpful. Music, as everyone who has listened to it at all perceptively knows, relies very heavily for its structure on the device of repetition and variations. Many popular songs consist of a tune sung twice with different words, then a chorus (a segment with a different tune), and then a return to the first tune, which gives a form of A A B A. Repetition and variation can be seen even in the way in which musical motifs (small segments of musical ideas) combine to make up a tune. Here is a portion of the theme of the first movement of Mozart's Symphony in G Minor (catalogued by Koechel as No. 40 of his works). Notice the pattern of two eighth-notes followed by a quarter note three

*Ben Shahn, *The Shape of Content*, (New York, 1960), p. 62.

times, then tied quarter-notes, then a repetition, but with a change in the notes, of the rhythmic pattern of eighths and a quarter:

Repetition and variation in music is not usually a structure (except possibly in the theme-and-variations form), but a way of proceeding, a process by means of which a structure is developed. In a piece of music a theme—a subject, a musical idea—is announced near the beginning and then is developed through the composition by changing it in various ways but not so drasticallly as to make the theme unrecognizable. What emerges is a musical structure in which the parts are related by being developments of a common idea, but are different because they alter the theme. Similarity or relationship and difference are both necessary for a structure, because a structure implies a unity, and unity implies a relationship among different kinds of parts. If there were no similarity among the parts, we would have a collection of disparate elements; and if there were no differences among the parts, we would have mere repetition.*

Poetic structure could also be viewed as resulting in part from repetition and variation. Repetition is most obvious in the metrical beat, in stanza patterns, in recurring rhyme patterns in abstract forms such as the sonnet. And there is variation in the changes from the prevailing metrical patterns, in the changes of rhyme words (a repeated rhyme word is dull unless used for special effects with other variations), and in the progression within the abstract forms like the sonnet. A poet uses variations, especially metrical variations, to work against the basic beat to create a tension that leads the movement of the poem onward, playing tricks with rhythms somewhat as the jazz musician does in an improvisation. And there is often a satisfying surprise in the cleverness with which a poet will manage to vary his rhyme words. An extreme example is Lord Byron, who sometimes commits himself to an outlandish rhyme word of five syllables and then delights the reader by managing to rhyme it, as in the following passage from *Don Juan:*

---

*An extremely interesting book that deals, among other things, with musical structure, and to which we are indebted, is Leonard B. Meyer, *Emotion and Meaning in Music* (Chicago, 1956) available in paperback as a "Phoenix Book."

'Tis pity learned virgins ever wed
  With persons of no sort of education,
Or gentlemen, who, though well born and bred,
  Grow tired of scientific conversation;
I don't choose to say much upon this head,
  I'm a plain man, and in a single station,
But—Oh! ye lords of ladies intellectual,
Inform us truly, have they not hen-peck'd you all?

The reader wants to continue to the next stanza of OTTAVA RIMA (an eight-line stanza of five-foot lines rhyming A B A B A B C C) to see what will happen.

Repetition and variation in meter and rhyme are purely formal. A kind of repetition and variation that contributes more to the overall structure of a poem is that in which the treatment of the theme is varied in units of progression having a discernible relationship with each other. One kind of poetic development of a theme by variation that is fairly easy to recognize is that of changing the imagery of metaphor by means of which the thematic idea is expressed. This is what Shakespeare used in his 73rd sonnet (see p. 38). Usually something else is also involved in changing imagery; as the image is changed, another aspect of the subject or theme is taken up. Allen Tate's "Mr. Pope" is composed structurally of four main images.

*Mr. Pope**

When Alexander Pope strolled in the city
Strict was the glint of pearl and gold sedans.
Ladies leaned out, more out of fear than pity;
For Pope's tight back was rather a goat's than man's.

One often thinks the urn should have more bones
Than skeletons provide for speedy dust;
The urn gets hollow, cobwebs brittle as stones
Weave to the funeral shell a frivolous rust.

And he who dribbled couplets like the snake
Coiled to a lithe precision in the sun,
Is missing. The jar is empty; you may break
It only to find that Mr. Pope is gone.

---

*Reprinted from *Poems 1920-1945* by Allen Tate, Eyre & Spottiswoode Ltd., London. In addition, "Mr. Pope" is reprinted with the permission of Charles Scribner's Sons from *Poems* by Allen Tate, (1960).

What requisitions of a verity
Prompted the wit and rage between his teeth
One cannot say: around a crooked tree
A mortal climbs whose name should be a wreath.

ALLEN TATE

The poem develops through four main images: Pope taking a walk in orderly eighteenth century London and being feared for his tongue more than pitied for his deformed back by the ladies in sedan chairs; the image of the funeral urn, not full enough of mortal remains, indeed becoming hollow and covered with cobwebs; then the image of Pope as a lithe snake rather than a twisted little man, who cannot be found in the empty urn; and finally the image of a crooked tree around which "a mortal climbs whose name should be a wreath." The poem is an encomium to Pope, but the theme developed by the images is that of the contrast between Pope's mind and body: his actual body; the disproportion between what is found in urns and what should be found there; the lithe and supple form of the essential Pope; the empty urn; and along with these a new image that brings together both aspects of Pope, his physical grotesqueness and his imaginative subtlety. Some of these images may seem like rather strange ones for a poetical tribute, for those in the first part of the poem show Pope in an unfavorable light. The reason for this is that the poem presents Pope from two contrasting points of view: a generally unsympathetic one and a sympathetic one, based on transformations of the unfavorable images into favorable ones. From a reductively unsympathetic point of view, Pope could be represented by images like that of a man with goat's back (he was deformed physically), a dusty funeral urn (in a sense he has been entombed by the dust of history), and as dribbling couplets like a snake (his verse was so polished that it might seem to come with ease, and his satire was deadly). Images such as these are not wholly unrelated to Pope, but they reflect attitudes in which the essential Pope is missed. Tate uses these images, or aspects of them, as a basis for the contrasting view of Pope shown in the last third of the poem. First he develops the emptiness of the urn:

...The jar is empty; you may break
It only to find that Mr. Pope is gone.

Then, in the first two lines of the last stanza, we get a hint of a passion in Pope that has been lost sight of ("rage between his teeth") and of a vitality that is in sharp contrast to brittle cobwebs and frivolous rust and empty urns. This vitality is given beautiful form in the concluding image, which also contains a motif from the snake image used earlier, for now a vine climbs around a crooked tree. But this is no ordinary vine, for it is associated in the clause, "whose name should be a wreath," with the wreaths used to crown heroes and true poets.

Although the poem presents two contrasting views, its image structure is progressive: the London scene, the urn, the snake, and finally the crooked tree and vine. At first reading, the images may seem unrelated to each other and a little hard to apply to Alexander Pope, but once we reach the fine climax, the earlier images come into perspective. This poem, like many poems of the seventeenth century and our own day, is characterized by its wit—a term which in poetry means bringing together disparate things. The images seem disparate at first, but come together once we see the poem's progressive structure.

Although most good poems do not follow abstract forms and employ more than one structural principle, there are certain very general overall patterns that may be commonly noticed in poetic structures. We are a little reluctant to bring this matter up for fear that it may be misunderstood, for we do not wish to suggest that poetic structure may be mechanically schematized. Still it is useful to have some categories in mind when studying something as complex as poetic structure in order to develop one's perceptions. As rough instrumental categories, we might use the following general forms:

(1) A progression, or development proceeding by the variation of some element, such as imagery. The sections are usually parallel, but varied, and lead to a climax.

(2) A balanced or two-fold form based on a contrast: then and now; there and here; A-B. In music such a form is called "binary."

(3) A three-fold form in which there is a development of one theme, a change to another, and a return to the first. Again in music a form like this is called "ternary," and is schematically represented A-B-A.

(4) Logical form, in which the structure of the poem follows the structure of argument, often a syllogism (a major premiss, minor premiss, conclusion). Such a form obviously has no musical analogue.

These four forms or patterns of development are fairly common in poetry, but they by no means exhaust the possibilities. Psychological structure, for instance, is governed by associations which the speaker makes, and this kind of structure will not necessarily fall into any of these patterns. And some poems will be built up from a combination of our four patterns in a way that defies schematization.

Let us now consider some poems whose overall structure generally does fall into one of these categories.

The first kind of structural development we mentioned, a progressive rise to a climax or goal, can proceed either continuously or in units of stanzas. Building up the effects in units of stanzas or other formal divisions is the more common method. This is the method used by Shakespeare in Sonnet 55, "Not Marble, Nor the Gilded Monuments."

Sonnet 55

Not marble, nor the gilded monuments
Of princes, shall outlive this powerful rhyme,
But you shall shine more bright in these contents
Than unswept stone, besmeared with sluttish time.
When wasteful war shall statues overturn,
And broils root out the work of masonry,
Nor Mars his sword nor war's quick fire shall burn
The living record of your memory.
'Gainst death and all-oblivious enmity
Shall you pace forth, your praise shall still find room
Even in the eyes of all posterity
That wear this world out to the ending doom.
So, till the judgment that yourself arise,
You live in this, and dwell in lovers' eyes.

William Shakespeare

The sonnet begins with the image of marble and gilded monuments, which are made dusty and smeared. In the second quatrain, the stones are overturned and burned by war; in the third, they are forgotten completely in death and oblivion, and the poem shifts more attention directly on the rhymes memorializing the person to whom the poem is directed, but carries the theme of temporal oblivion to its logical end in the "ending doom" of the world. The couplet brings the poem to a conclusion by taking the positive aspect of the "ending doom," the Resurrection, saying that until that event the person addressed will live in the poem and "dwell in lovers' eyes."

A tight, brief form like the sonnet lends itself either to development by units (in the Shakespearean sonnet by quatrains and closing couplet) or to continuous development, in which the internal divisions of the poem are not so pronounced. Milton's sonnet "On His Deceased Wife" is an example of a climactic development that gives the effect of being continuous.

On His Deceased Wife

Methought I saw my late espoused Saint
Brought to me like Alcestis from the grave,
Whom Jove's great Son to her glad Husband gave,
Rescued from death by force though pale and faint.
Mine as whom washt from spot of child-bed taint,
Purification in the old Law did save,
And such, as yet once more I trust to have
Full sight of her in Heaven without restraint,
Came vested all in white, pure as her mind:
Her face was vailed, yet to my fancied sight,
Love, sweetness, goodness, in her person shined,
So clear, as in no face with more delight.
But O as to embrace me she declined
I waked, she fled, and day brought back my night.

JOHN MILTON

Milton's sonnet is an Italian one, composed of two main parts, an octave (eight lines) and a sestet (six lines), rhyming *abba abba cdcdcd.* Typically, the Italian sonnet states and develops one aspect of the theme in the two quatrains making up the octave and then in the sestet takes up another aspect of it, or perhaps applies what has been said in the octave. Milton's first quatrain is a complete sentence, stating the situation and giving a classical allusion. The second quatrain takes up the idea that Milton's wife died in childbirth and uses an allusion to the religious ceremony of ritually purifying women after childbirth ("churching") to introduce the theme of her purity. Then in the sestet he gives a vivid and concrete picture of his wife, white, veiled, shining; and the poem comes to a climax in the last two lines, when the poet attempts to embrace her, but wakes to be returned to grief.

In reading this poem, one does not get the impression that Milton is following an established form but rather that he is using the form to express what he wishes. We are most aware of the form in the first quatrain, where grammatical sense coincides exactly with a formal division. The second sentence of the poem, which runs for seven lines, carries the sense over from the second quatrain to the sestet in a progressive intensification of the emotion, but even so, Milton uses the form, because in the ninth line, at the beginning of the sestet, his vision of his wife actually appears. Milton gets something of the cadential effect of the Shakespearean sonnet's closing couplet when he puts the climactic action in the closing two lines. He intensifies the closing of the poem by using a PARADOX, "and day brought back my night," ending it dramatically and poetically.

Milton's sonnet, which is built on a single incident, develops that incident up to a climax when the speaker awoke and "day brought back my night." The story is over, though, of course, we are aware that the speaker's grief is not over for him. The progressive structure of some poems, on the other hand, seems to lead not so much to a conclusion of what has been represented but to the beginning of a different kind of experience. Formally, of course, such poems come to an end, often with a change to a different image, but in the change our thoughts are led to a different perspective. Shakespeare's sonnet, which moves from monuments, to the effects on monuments of war, and finally to the doom of the world, does something like this. The pattern of development is one of a kind of progressive revelation.* The typical progressive pattern is one not too much unlike the pattern used most often in paragraphs, that of development by accretion or addition. In "The Sick Rose," for instance, the poem starts out saying, "O Rose, thou art sick!" The rest of the poem shows what the sickness is. There is a real kind of revelation that occurs in this poem too, of course, but that occurs in the poem as a whole, not as a result of the structure of thought, which develops the theme of the rose's sickness by giving the history of the sickness.

Whe can see progressive revelation at work in a sonnet by Keats.

When I Have Fears

When I have fears that I may cease to be
   Before my pen has gleaned my teeming brain,
Before high-piled books, in charactery,
   Hold like rich garners the full-ripened grain;
When I behold, upon the night's starred face,
   Huge cloudy symbols of a high romance,
And think that I may never live to trace
   Their shadows, with the magic hand of chance;
And when I feel, fair creature of an hour,
   That I shall never look upon thee more,
Never have relish in the faery power
   Of unreflecting love;—then on the shore
Of the wide world I stand alone, and think
Till love and fame to nothingness do sink.

John Keats

*This phrase was used by Earl Wasserman, who shows a pattern of progressive revelation in a fine study of Shelley's "Adonais," *ELH* [English Literary History], (1948). We are also indebted to Frederick Garber for illuminating suggestions.

The imagery of the first quatrain (this is a Shakespearean sonnet, the first that Keats wrote) is of harvest, that of the second moves to the sky, that of the third to love and time. In the couplet, finally, the image shifts to "the shore / Of the wide world," and we are brought by the speaker's thought to apprehend a state of mind in which the images previously represented are transcended. The poem was built to produce this effect, not only in its imagery, which becomes progressively less connected with the world of space and time, but also by grammatical structure, for the poem consists grammatically of a series of introductory adverbial clauses leading to the main clause in the couplet (when A, when B, when C, then X). The structure of Allen Tate's "Mr. Pope" gives a somewhat similar progressive effect through the change of image that occurs at the end. After the images of death in the empty funeral urns, the closing image brings us back to think of life. But this new image of the mortal climbing around the crooked tree "whose name should be a wreath" gives us a strikingly new glimpse of Pope that is radically different from the one we got at the beginning of the poem, where the physical Pope, with his tight, twisted back, was shown concretely being looked at by ladies in sedan chairs in an eighteenth-century London street. The new image, transforming some of the elements of the earlier one, shows us the essential Pope and makes a comment on mortality.

Any good poem moves toward some point of conclusion, which may come about through realization of what is implicit in the theme or, as we have just seen, through a progress to a changed perspective in which things look strangely different. This movement toward a conclusion is easiest to see in poems whose structure is progressive. But there is a kind of progression also in poems that are built on the principle of contrast—poems which have a balanced structure: then and now, there and here, and so on. This kind of structure is readily discernible in Edgar Allan Poe's "Romance."

Romance

Romance, who loves to nod and sing
With drowsy head and folded wing,
Among the green leaves as they shake
Far down within some shadowy lake,
To me a painted paroquet
Hath been—a most familiar bird—
Taught me my alphabet to say
To lisp my very earliest word,
While in the wild wood I did lie,
A child—with a most knowing eye.

Of late, eternal Condor years
So shake the very Heaven on high
With tumult as they thunder by,
I have no time for idle cares
Through gazing on the unquiet sky.
And when an hour with calmer wings
Its down upon my spirit flings—
That little time with lyre and rhyme
To while away—forbidden things!
My heart would feel to be a crime
Unless it trembled with the strings.

EDGAR ALLAN POE

Contrasting structure here is very clear, for the poem is divided into two almost equal sections, the first developing the attitudes of youth and the second those of maturity, mostly through contrasting bird imagery. The progression is simply from the past to the present.

A poem which develops the same general theme and also by contrast, but one in which more of the contrast is implied, is Edwin Muir's "The Gate."

*The Gate**

We sat, two children, warm against the wall
Outside the towering stronghold of our fathers
That frowned its stern security down upon us.
We could not enter there. That fortress life,
Our safe protection, was too gross and strong
For our unpracticed palates. Yet our guardians
Cherished our innocence with gentle hands,
(They, who had long since lost their innocence,)
And in grave play put on a childish mask
Over their tell-tale faces, as in shame
For the fine food that plumped their lusty bodies
And made them strange as gods, We sat that day
With that great parapet behind us, safe
As every day, yet outcast, safe and outcast
As castaways thrown upon an empty shore.
Before us lay our well-worn scene, a hillock
So small and smooth and green, it seemed intended

For us alone and childhood, a still pond
That opened upon no sight a quiet eye,
A little stream that tinkled down the slope.
But suddenly all seemed old
And dull and shrunken, shut within itself
In a sullen dream. We were outside, alone.
And then behind us the huge gate swung open.

EDWIN MUIR

The basic structural contrast in the poem is between the way things look to the children in the first twenty lines of the poem and the way they look in the last four lines. The two children sit outside the fortress which protected them, "safe yet outcast," envying the adults inside and looking at the small green hillock, the still pond, and the tinkling stream. They are not allowed inside because the fortress is "too gross and strong" for their "unpracticed palates." Then suddenly comes the experience of seeing their "well-worn scene" outside turn old, dull, shrunken, shut up within itself, when the gate opens to allow them to go in. In the first part of the poem, the children, who look at things in innocence, do not understand that the adult world within the fortress *has* to be inside a fortress because adult life, like the scene outside after the change, is "shut up within itself." They do not understand that the fortress is stern and severe because adult life requires these qualities. But after line 20, when everything suddenly changes and shrinks for them and the gate opens, they will understand.

The structural contrast reinforces the symbolic contrast of inside and outside. In this poem Muir reverses the usual relationship of the inside as expressing the warm sheltered world of innocence and the outside as expressing the "world." In their earlier years children venture *outside* of the home, of which they think themselves the center. Later on, as they become more aware of being excluded from various aspects of the adult world, they tend to feel that they are on the outside looking in, denied admission to a mysterious but fascinating life within. As a simple example, they are denied admission to certain movies and excluded from adult discussions. Muir's use of inside and outside here, therefore, rather then dealing with early childhood, expresses more accurately the desires of later childhood and early youth to be admitted to the mysterious world of adulthood and also expresses something of the confining and dangerous character of that world.

The typical ternary form in music is the rondo (or rondeau), in which the sections of the composition are arranged as A-B-A. In poetry there is also a RONDEAU, an intricate French verse form consisting of ten or thirteen lines, two rhymes, and with the first line used twice. Leigh Hunt's familiar "Rondeau" is not a strict rondeau, but it illustrates ternary form, since the opening words make the closing line.

Rondeau

Jenny kissed me when we met,
  Jumping from the chair she sat in;
Time, you thief, who love to get
  Sweets into your list, put that in:
Say I'm weary, say I'm sad,
  Say that health and wealth have missed me,
Say I'm growing old, but add,
  Jenny kissed me.

LEIGH HUNT

Here the ternary form is an abstract one. As the ternary type of structure is used in poems not following a prescribed pattern, it derives more functionally from the situation. It may consist of a situation, a flash-back, a return to the situation. Sometimes the opening and closing of the poem forms a frame for the middle part, which is often the main part of the poem, as it is in "The Rime of the Ancient Mariner" and in Keat's "La Belle Dame Sans Merci." Keat's poem opens with a speaker addressing the knight:

O what can ail thee, knight-at-arms,
  Alone and palely loitering?
The sedge has withered from the lake,
  And no birds sing.

He inquires further what happened. The knight then tells his tale of love and enthrallment by the beautiful lady, and ends by using a slight variation of the words with which the poem began:

And that is why I sojourn here,
  Alone and palely loitering,
Though the sedge is withered from the lake,
  And no birds sing.

Thus the attention is returned to the present and the poem comes to a close. (The complete poem may be found in the Anthology.)

In "Ode to a Nightingale" Keats uses a ternary type of structure more functionally—or rather the character of the experience emerges naturally in a ternary type of structure. For the significance of the situation in the poem as a whole arises out of the tension between the speaker's situation or state of mind in the opening and closing sections and that in the middle section.

Ode to a Nightingale

1

My heart aches, and a drowsy numbness pains
My sense, as though of hemlock I had drunk,
Or emptied some dull opiate to the drains
One minute past, and Lethe-wards had sunk:
'Tis not through envy of thy happy lot,
But being too happy in thine happiness,—
That thou, light-winged Dryad of the trees,
In some melodious plot
Of beechen green, and shadows numberless,
Singest of summer in full-throated ease.

2

O, for a draught of vintage! that had been
Cool'd a long age in the deep-delved earth,
Tasting of Flora and the country green,
Dance, and Provençal song, and sunburnt mirth!
O for a beaker full of the warm South,
Full of the true, the blushful Hippocrene,
With beaded bubbles winking at the brim,
And purple stained mouth;
That I might drink, and leave the world unseen,
And with thee fade away into the forest dim:

3

Fade far away, dissolve, and quite forget
What thou among the leaves hast never known,
The weariness, the fever, and the fret
Here, where men sit and hear each other groan;

Where palsy shakes a few, sad, last gray hairs,
  Where youth grows pale, and spectre-thin, and dies;
    Where but to think is to be full of sorrow
      And leaden-eyed despairs,
  Where Beauty cannot keep her lustrous eyes,
    Or new Love pine at them beyond to-morrow.

4

Away! away! for I will fly to thee,
  Not charioted by Bacchus and his pards,
But on the viewless wings of Poesy,
  Though the dull brain perplexes and retards:
Already with thee! tender is the night,
  And haply the Queen-Moon is on her throne,
    Cluster'd around by all her starry Fays;
      But here there is no light,
  Save what from heaven is with the breezes blown
    Through verdurous glooms and winding mossy ways.

5

I cannot see what flowers are at my feet,
  Nor what soft incense hangs upon the boughs,
But, in embalmed darkness, guess each sweet
  Wherewith the seasonable month endows
The grass, the thicket, and the fruit-tree wild;
  White hawthorn, and the pastoral eglantine;
    Fast fading violets cover'd up in leaves;
      And mid-May's eldest child,
  The coming musk-rose, full of dewy wine,
    The murmurous haunt of flies on summer eves.

6

Darkling I listen; and, for many a time
  I have been half in love with easeful Death,
Call'd him soft names in many a mused rhyme,
  To take into the air my quiet breath;
Now more than ever seems it rich to die,
  To cease upon the midnight with no pain,
    While thou art pouring forth thy soul abroad
      In such an ecstasy!
  Still wouldst thou sing, and I have ears in vain—
    To thy high requiem become a sod.

7

Thou wast not born for death, immortal Bird!
No hungry generations tread thee down;
The voice I hear this passing night was heard
In ancient days by emperor and clown:
Perhaps the self-same song that found a path
Through the sad heart of Ruth, when, sick for home,
She stood in tears amid the alien corn;
The same that oft-times hath
Charm'd magic casements, opening on the foam
Of perilous seas, in faery lands forlorn.

8

Forlorn! the very word is like a bell
To toll me back from thee to my sole self!
Adieu! the fancy cannot cheat so well
As she is fam'd to do, deceiving elf.
Adieu! adieu! thy plaintive anthem fades
Past the near meadows, over the still stream,
Up the hill-side; and now 'tis buried deep
In the next valley-glades:
Was it a vision, or a waking dream?
Fled is that music:—Do I wake or sleep?

JOHN KEATS

The opening and closing stanzas show the speaker bound to reality (though with a difference in the two), and the middle section of the poem shows him trying to identify himself with the immortal bird, which he succeeds in doing, but only for a moment.

Actually, the middle section of the poem (stanzas 2 through 8) is progressive, moving by means of association. In stanza 2 the speaker longs for the wine of Provençal so that he might "leave the world unseen" and fade with the bird "into the forest dim." The word "fade" suggests in stanza 3 what it is that the speaker would fade from: the mortal world of weariness, fever, fret, aging, and sorrow. In stanza 4 the speaker develops the theme of moving *away* (the word immediately following "fade" at the end of stanza 2); he has no need of wine, for he is brought to an imaginative union with the bird on "the viewless wings of Poesy." In this state of mind—and in the darkness—he is led to see the flowers by their fragrances. In stanza 6 he thinks how rich it would be to die and thus pass permanently out of his mortal state, but he is brought up short with the thought that if he were dead he would "have ears in vain." Here the tension between the speaker's longing for the immortal beauty of the nightingale and his own mortality suddenly increases. For death, the only means whereby he could escape mortality, is not an escape *to* the immortality symbolized by the bird. Indeed, the only way he can gain even this glimpse of immortality is through his mortal perceptions. In stanza 7 he goes on to develop the bird's immortality, and by implication, to contrast his own mortality with it. He lets his fancy carry him associatively from ancient Rome, to the biblical story of Ruth, to thoughts of romance. A phrase that occurs to him in connection with romance brings up another word, "forlorn," which returns him to the reality from which he started. He bids the bird adieu and wonders ambiguously after the experience, "Do I wake or sleep?"

We have looked at progressive climactic structure, contrasting structure (which might be called binary structure) and ternary structure. These, as was remarked earlier, are types of structure which can be seen quite often in poetry, but they are not abstract forms or patterns which a poet will follow. A poet does not say to himself, "I think I shall cast my poem into a ternary type of structure," as he might say, "I think I shall write a sonnet," or "This poem looks as if it will become a sonnet." When, in this chapter, we pick out these typical structures, we do it not to suggest that all poems fall into these categories, but to furnish the student with a preliminary general notion of what to look for in investigating poetic structure. The poems selected for this chapter fit the various categories reasonably well in overall pattern, grossly considered. Perhaps these categories could be used to classify quite a few poems by structural pattern. But this is not what we intend here. The study of poetry is defeated by classification, a process which necessarily disregards what is unique about a thing and concentrates only on the features relevant to the class. Structurally, individual poems may generally be ternary or whatever, but what is important about the poem's structure is what happens in the poem: what is structurally unique about this poem. The categories we have sketched here should be used only to help direct attention to what is going on in the individual poem.

The structural types described here will not always be found in as pure a form as they are in the poems used to illustrate them, and even in these poems the categories are not entirely pure. More than one kind of structure can operate at a time. Stanzas in a generally progressive poem may be built on contrast, or may even be ternary. There often is progression within sections of a generally ternary structure, as there is in "Ode to a Nightingale"; the variations are almost limitless. We cannot stress this point enough. These categories are a crutch to be kicked away as soon as possible.

With this much warning, we can turn to consider one other popular type of structure, that based on discursive logic. Since poetry is made of words and sentences, the forms of logical discourse can be used to unify the parts of a poem. Andrew Marvell's "To His Coy Mistress" shows this kind of overall structure very clearly, because its three sections are really a kind of syllogism, a very strict one:

Major premiss: "Had we but world enough, and time,
This coyness, lady, were no crime. . . ."

Minor premiss: "But at my back I always hear
Time's winged chariot hurrying near. . . ."

Conclusion: "Now therefore, while the youthful hue
Sits on thy skin like morning dew
. . . .
Now let us sport us while we may. . . ."

To His Coy Mistress

Had we but world enough, and time,
This coyness, Lady, were no crime.
We would sit down, and think which way
To walk, and pass our long love's day.
Thou by the Indian Ganges' side
Shouldst rubies find: I by the tide
Of Humber would complain. I would
Love you ten years before the Flood:
And you should, if you please, refuse
Till the Conversion of the Jews.
My vegetable love should grow
Vaster than empires, and more slow.
An hundred years should go to praise
Thine eyes, and on thy forehead gaze.
Two hundred to adore each breast:
But thirty thousand to the rest.
An age at least to every part,
And the last age should show your heart.
For Lady you deserve this state;
Nor would I love at lower rate.
 But at my back I always hear
Time's winged chariot hurrying near:

And yonder all before us lie
Deserts of vast eternity.
Thy beauty shall no more be found,
Nor, in thy marble vault, shall sound
My echoing song: then worms shall try
That long preserved virginity:
And your quaint honor turn to dust;
And into ashes all my lust.
The grave's a fine and private place,
But none I think do there embrace.
  Now therefore, while the youthful hue
Sits on thy skin like morning dew,
And while thy willing soul transpires
At every pore with instant fires,
Now let us sport us while we may;
And now, like amourous birds of prey,
Rather at once our time devour,
Than languish in his slow-chapped power.
Let us roll all our strength and all
Our sweetness up into one ball:
And tear our pleasures with rough strife,
Thorough the iron gates of life.
Thus though we cannot make our sun
Stand still, yet we will make him run.

ANDREW MARVELL

The *overall* structure is a syllogism. But that is not all there is to the poem. The syllogism is concerned with sex, but this is not the main theme of the poem. A more important theme is time, which is developed in the imagery within the three sections formed by the logical overall structure. Indeed, to talk about the structure of the poem in any useful way, we must see what the imagery does: how it carries on its own kind of discourse from section to section in a sort of counterpoint between logic and image.

Poetic structure works to give the poem unity by bringing all the elements of the poem together into a coherent whole. Why is this important? Why not have poems that delight by variety and not bother about trying to make them wholes? There is no denying that variety is pleasant, and we want it in certain art forms such as adventure stories and musical reviews. And, in fact, a number of very fine poems cannot be said to be unified works of art for the simple reason that they are incomplete, fragments—or at least they have the form of fragments if they are not fragments in fact. "Kubla Khan" is an example. But if people like variety and enjoy poems that are and give the effect of being fragments, they also find unity satisfying in art and elsewhere. The word *unity* itself seems to have strong ameliorative connotations, whatever it is applied to. A poem or story that is structurally unified is a better poem, other things being equal, than one that is not.

One of the reasons for this is that a unified structure helps a poem to take on that kind of autonomy and completeness which makes it a work of art, a self-contained entity that can be contemplated in itself. Or, to use the comparison that has been employed, off and on, to characterize structural unity in poetry since Aristotle, a really unified poem becomes like a living organism, with all parts in vital interaction.* A poem which is thus vital and whole is not only more satisfying, but also seems to lend itself to that kind of steady and prolonged contemplation we want to give to serious works of art.

Structural unity is important for another reason. It gives a maximum of order to experience and hence to those ideas that cannot be adequately formulated apart from some kind of experience. It does not give order, of course, to *our own* experience and ideas, but to those expressed by the poet, which are given form in the poem and thus are made capable of being grasped. Even if the experiences are those of another, we are nevertheless enlightened by being able to perceive them represented in a coherent form, because poetry deals with matters that have more than private interest to the poet—death, love, man's relation to God, the order of creation, politics, nature, and so on—and because, in being able to grasp a difficult and subtle matter clearly formulated, we gain new ways of thinking. This is not to suggest that a reader will be able to apply practically a characterization of love from a poem by John Donne the next time he falls in love, but that in having seen love as formulated in the poem his understanding of love will have been enriched.

Perhaps the most remarkable thing about unified poetic structure is that it *can* order experience and give it a form in which it can be understood. The act of grasping experience thus ordered is itself an experience quite different from those we usually have. As the saying goes, experience is the best teacher, but we profit from it most if its teaching is formulated somehow. What we learn from ordinary experience is fairly easy to put into a form that makes it possible to reflect on it. But there are some experiences, often those affecting us most deeply, like grief, that seem to defy clear thought. Experiences such as these are assimilated without being really understood. There is a kind of form to them, to be sure, but more often than not it is a form that makes them assimilable, a rise and fall of emotion that diminishes as we learn to live with it. Once it has been assimilated, we can recollect it "in tranquility," to use Wordsworth's phrase, but most of

*See *The Poetics,* xxiii.1.

us find it hard to give our recollections a form clear enough to confer understanding of what the experience meant. This poetry does, not usually by imitating the natural form of grief, or whatever other emotions are dealt with, but by giving grief an imaginative context in a structure (as in Roethke's "Elegy," p. 93) where it can be contemplated almost objectively. Few of us could give form to grief as Emily Dickinson has done in "After Great Pain," and we learn something from seeing grief represented with imaginative coherency in the poem.

After Great Pain

After great pain a formal feeling comes—
The nerves sit ceremonious like tombs;
The stiff Heart questions—was it He that bore?
And yesterday—or centuries before?

The feet mechanical
Go round a wooden way
Of ground or air or Ought, regardless grown,
A quartz contentment like a stone.

This is the hour of lead
Remembered if outlived,
As freezing persons recollect the snow—
First chill, then stupor, then the letting go.

EMILY DICKINSON

Poems for Further Study:

*God's Grandeur**

The world is charged with the grandeur of God.
  It will flame out, like shining from shook foil;
  It gathers to a greatness, like the ooze of oil
Crushed. Why do men then now not reck his rod?
Generations have trod, have trod, have trod;

And all is seared with trade; bleared, smeared with toil;
And wears man's smudge and shares man's smell: the soil
Is bare now, nor can foot feel, being shod.

And for all this, nature is never spent;
There lives the dearest freshness deep down things;
And though the last lights off the black West went
Oh, morning, at the brown brink eastward, springs—
Because the Holy Ghost over the bent
World broods with warm breast and with ah! bright wings.

GERARD MANLEY HOPKINS

Questions.

1. In which of the traditional forms is this poem written?
2. Does it depart from this form in any way?
3. What means does the poet employ to knit the poem into a tight fabric?
4. Is the imagery appropriate to the theme of the poem, and does it progress in any way?

To Daffodils

Fair Daffodils, we weep to see
You haste away so soon:
As yet the early-rising sun
Has not attained his noon.
Stay, stay,
Until the hasting day
Has run
But to the even-song;
And, having prayed together, we
Will go with you along.

We have short time to stay, as you,
We have as short a spring;
As quick a growth to meet decay,
As you, or anything,
We die,
As your hours do, and dry
Away
Like to the summer's rain;
Or as the pearls of morning's dew
Ne'er to be found again.

ROBERT HERRICK

Ode
Intimations of Immortality from Recollections of Early Childhood

The Child is Father of the Man;
And I could wish my days to be
Bound each to each by natural piety.

I

There was a time when meadow, grove, and stream,
The earth, and every common sight,
To me did seem
Apparelled in celestial light,
The glory and the freshness of a dream.
It is not now as it hath been of yore;—
Turn wheresoe'er I may,
By night or day,
The things which I have seen I now can see no more.

II

The Rainbow comes and goes,
And lovely is the Rose.
The Moon doth with delight
Look round her when the heavens are bare.
Waters on a starry night
Are beautiful and fair;
The sunshine is a glorious birth;
But yet I know, where'er I go,
That there hath past away a glory from the earth.

III

Now, while the birds thus sing a joyous song,
And while the young lambs bound
As to the tabor's sound,
To me alone there came a thought of grief:
A timely utterance gave that thought relief,
And I again am strong:
The cataracts blow their trumpets from the steep;
No more shall grief of mine the season wrong;
I hear the Echoes through the mountains throng,
The Winds come to me from the fields of sleep,
And all the earth is gay;
Land and sea

Give themselves up to jollity,
And with the heart of May
Doth every Beast keep holiday;—
Thou Child of Joy,
Shout round me, let me hear thy shouts, thou
happy Shepherd-boy!

IV

Ye blessed Creatures, I have heard the call
Ye to each other make; I see
The heavens laugh with you in your jubilee;
My heart is at your festival,
My head hath its coronal,
The fulness of your bliss, I feel—I feel it all.
Oh evil day! if I were sullen
While Earth herself is adorning,
This sweet May-morning
And the Children are culling
On every side,
In a thousand valleys far and wide,
Fresh flowers; while the sun shines warm,
And the Babe leaps up on his Mother's arm:—
I hear, I hear, with joy I hear!
—But there's a Tree, of many, one,
A single Field which I have looked upon,
Both of them speak of something that is gone:
The Pansy at my feet
Doth the same tale repeat:
Whither is fled the visionary gleam?
Where is it now, the glory and the dream?

V

Our birth is but a sleep and a forgetting:
The Soul that rises with us, our life's Star,
Hath had elsewhere its setting,
And cometh from afar:
Not in entire forgetfulness,
And not in utter nakedness,
But trailing clouds of glory do we come
From God, who is our home:
Heaven lies about us in our infancy!
Shades of the prison-house begin to close
Upon the growing Boy

But He beholds the light, and whence it flows,
He sees it in his joy;
The Youth, who daily farther from the east
Must travel, still is Nature's Priest,
And by the vision splendid
Is on his way attended;
At length the Man perceives it die away,
And fade into the light of common day.

VI

Earth fills her lap with pleasures of her own;
Yearnings she hath in her own natural kind,
And, even with something of a Mother's mind,
And no unworthy aim,
The homely Nurse doth all she can
To make her Foster-child, her Inmate Man,
Forget the glories he hath known,
And that imperial palace whence he came.

VII

Behold the Child among his new-born blisses,
A six years' Darling of a pigmy size!
See, where 'mid work of his own hand he lies,
Fretted by sallies of his mother's kisses,
With light upon him from his father's eyes!
See, at his feet, some little plan or chart,
Some fragment from his dream of human life,
Shaped by himself with newly-learned art;
A wedding or a festival,
A mourning or a funeral;
And this hath now his heart,
And unto this he frames his song:
Then will he fit his tongue
To dialogues of business, love, or strife:
But it will not be long
Ere this be thrown aside,
And with new joy and pride
The little Actor cons another part;
Filling from time to time his "humorous stage"
With all the Persons, down to palsied Age,
That Life brings with her in her equipage;
As if his whole vocation
Were endless imitation.

VIII

Thou, whose exterior semblance doth belie Thy
  Soul's immensity;
Thou best Philosopher, who yet dost keep
Thy heritage, thou Eye among the blind,
That, deaf and silent, read'st the eternal deep,
Haunted for ever by the eternal mind,—
  Mighty Prophet! Seer blest!
  On whom these truths do rest,
Which we are toiling all our lives to find,
In darkness lost, the darkness of the grave;
Thou, over whom thy Immortality
Broods like the Day, a Master o'er a Slave,
A presence which is not to be put by;
Thou little Child, yet glorious in the might
Of heaven-born freedom on thy being's height,
Why with such earnest pains dost thou provoke
The years to bring the inevitable yoke,
Thus blindly with thy blessedness at strife?
Full soon thy Soul shall have her earthly freight,
And custom lie upon thee with a weight,
Heavy as frost, and deep almost as life!

IX

    O joy! that in our embers
    Is something that doth live,
    That nature yet remembers
    What was so fugitive!
The thought of our past years in me doth breed
Perpetual benediction: not indeed
For that which is most worthy to be blest;
Delight and liberty, the simple creed
Of Childhood, whether busy or at rest,
With new-fledged hope still fluttering in his breast:—
    Not for these I raise
    The song of thanks and praise;
  But for those obstinate questionings
  Of sense and outward things,
  Fallings from us, vanishings;
  Blank misgivings of a Creature
Moving about in worlds not realised,
High instincts before which our mortal Nature

Did tremble like a guilty Thing surprised:
But for those first affections,
Those shadowy recollections,
Which, be they what they may,
Are yet the fountain-light of all our day,
Are yet a master-light of all our seeing;
Uphold us, cherish, and have power to make
Our noisy years seem moments in the being
Of the eternal Silence: truths that wake,
To perish never:
Which neither listlessness, nor mad endeavor,
Nor Man nor Boy,
Nor all that is at enmity with joy,
Can utterly abolish or destroy!
Hence in a season of calm weather
Though inland far we be,
Our Souls have sight of that immortal sea
Which brought us hither,
Can in a moment travel thither,
And see the Children sport upon the shore,
And hear the mighty waters rolling evermore.

X

Then sing, ye Birds, sing, sing a joyous song!
And let the young Lambs bound
As to the tabor's sound!
We in thought will join your throng;
Ye that pipe and ye that play,
Ye that through your hearts today
Feel the gladness of the May!
What though the radiance which was once so bright
Be now for ever taken from my sight,
Though nothing can bring back the hour
Of splendour in the grass, of glory in the flower;
We will grieve not, rather find
Strength in what remains behind;
In the primal sympathy
Which having been must ever be;
In the soothing thoughts that spring
Out of human suffering;
In the faith that looks through death,
In years that bring the philosophic mind.

XI

And O, ye Fountains, Meadows, Hills and Groves,
Forbode not any serving of our loves!
Yet in my heart of hearts I feel your might;
I only have relinquished one delight
To live beneath your more habitual sway.
I love the Brooks which down their channels fret,
Even more than when I tripped lightly as they;
The innocent brightness of a new-born Day
        Is lovely yet;
The Clouds that gather round the setting sun
Do take a sober colouring from an eye
That hath kept watch o'er man's mortality;
Another race hath been, and other palms are won.
Thanks to the human heart by which we live.
Thanks to its tenderness, its joys, and fears,
To me the meanest flower that blows can give
Thoughts that do often lie too deep for tears.

William Wordsworth

Questions.

1. Account for the shifts in tone and mood in the poem. Do these shifts divide the poem into parts?
2. Does the verse in stanzas 3-4 sound forced?
4. How does the return at the end to the opening images show the structural progression of the poem?
4. Images of light and of sound recur in this poem. Does the imagery serve a structural purpose?

Poems for Further Study (ANTHOLOGY):

Michael Drayton, "Agincourt," p. 324
George Herbert, "Easter Wings," p. 356
Christopher Smart, "From Jubilate Agno," p. 439

Sound and Rhythm

9

Break, break, break
On thy cold gray stones, O Sea!
And I would that my tongue could utter
The Thoughts that arise to me.

The opening stanza of this poem by Alfred, Lord Tennyson has an insistent sound quality which has made it familiar to several generations of readers. In discussing these lines we are inevitably led to talk about hearing rather than reading them. Poetry is written for the ear as well as for the mind and imagination, and if one doesn't get in the habit of reading poetry aloud, or hearing it mentally, he will not only miss a great deal of its pleasure but also miss what is going on.

In reading the first line of Tennyson's poem aloud, one may notice the strength with which the word *break* asserts itself. Although in ordinary speech, speakers deliberately vary somewhat the stress given to different words or parts of words, as meaning or emphasis requires, some words actually require a particular stress on certain syllables for meaning, and words in certain places in sentences demand more stress than others. A poet consciously uses the stresses of speech and controls them to give his poetry a more highly organized rhythmical pattern than is found in ordinary speech. The phrase, "buying some apples," for example, seems to ask us to stress *buy* more heavily than *-ing; some* requires a light stress, while *apples* requires a heavier stress, followed by another light stress. The conventional notations of ˘ for a light stress and a / for a heavy stress, would show the light and heavy stresses in the phrase *buying some apples* as follows: /˘˘/˘. Our speech pattern in Tennyson's opening line would be notated as three strong stresses: ///. The poet, in other words, through his arrangement of speech patterns in the poetic line, forces us to speak them his way, whereas the prose writer ordinarily allows us greater freedom. Of course, it is true that the prose writer influences our speech patterns to a certain extent by the length of his sentences and the choice and placement of his words, but the poet is much more conscious than the prose writer of speech patterns, and he expects us to speak his words in a way that follows fairly closely the particular pattern he has chosen for them.

To continue our analysis of the sound patterns of this stanza of "Break, break, break," we observe that the stresses seem to fall into a speech pattern somewhat as follows:

> B´reak, b´reak, b´reak,
> Ŏn thy̆ ćold ǵray śtones, Ŏ Śea!
> Ănd Ĭ ẃould thăt my̆ t́ongue cŏuld ut́tĕr
> Thĕ T́houghts thăt ărise ĭn mé.

The punctuation is actually a part of the rhythmical pattern, because it affects the length of the pause. Sometimes it affects the tonal quality as well, for instance, when question marks and exclamation points cause the reader to modulate the tone of his voice. The end of each poetic line, even if unpunctuated in the usual sense, needs a brief pause to mark the underlying patterned length of the line. We can say, then, that most of the time Tennyson's stanza calls for three strong stresses in each line, with a possible exception in the second line, which some readers might read differently.

To determine the underlying pattern of the poem, however, one must look at the whole poem, for poems are not merely aggregates of individual lines and stanzas, but organic wholes with carefully integrated parts.

Break, Break, Break

Break, break, break,	/,/,/,
On thy cold gray stones, O Sea!	˘˘///,˘/!
And I would that my tongue could utter	˘˘/˘˘/˘/˘
The Thoughts that arise in me.	˘/˘˘/˘/.
O, well for the fisherman's boy,	˘,/˘˘/˘˘/,
That he shouts with his sister at play!	˘˘/˘˘/˘˘/!
O, well for the sailor lad,	˘,/˘˘/˘/,
That he sings in his boat on the bay!	˘˘/˘˘/˘˘/!

And the stately ships go on ˘˘/˘/˘/
To their haven under the hill; ˘˘/˘/˘˘/;
But O for the touch of a vanished hand, ˘/˘˘/˘˘/˘/,
And the sound of a voice that is still! ˘˘/˘˘/˘˘/!

Break break, break, /,/,/,
At the foot of thy crags, O Sea! ˘˘/˘˘/, ˘/!
But the tender grace of a day that is dead ˘˘/˘/˘˘/˘˘/
Will never come back to me. ˘/˘˘/˘/.

Alfred, Lord Tennyson

The general pattern of three strong stresses per line, with several exceptions, may be seen in operation throughout the poem. The lines also tend to begin with lighter stresses, although the opening lines of the first and last stanzas do not. Finally a pattern of light-and-heavy stress alternates with one of two-lights-and-a-heavy stress. These alternations are varied even more by the punctuation, which affects the lengths and the tonal qualities of pauses. The poem, we begin to observe, is a careful arrangement of various sound patterns. However, there are other sounds at work in the poem which must be taken into account. There is, for example, the repetition of the word *break* three times at the opening of the first and last stanzas. The repetition calls attention to the sound of the word, and the word itself, especially as repeated, may suggest both the insistent rhythmical surge and the cruelty of the sea in the *br* and *k* sounds. The three comma pauses also remind one of the sea's motion, forever mounting up as a wave, falling over with a crash, and withdrawing to the sound of pebbles and shells washing in its wake.

To the relentless surging which may be suggested by the first line, we must add the sensory effects of coldness and grayness of the second line. The repetition of the "o" sound, which occurs four times in the line, may serve to reinforce this feeling of coldness, since the sound was directly associated with *cold* earlier, so that we feel from the tone, as produced by sound effects in the first three lines, the thoughts of the poet, which remain unexpressed directly until the third stanza.

Of course, in order to read the poem properly, we must be conscious of the underlying pulsation of the stress pattern and give this pattern due weight in listening to our own reading. We must also pronounce the words fully, not slurring them as we sometimes do in ordinary speech. The recurrent consonants, or ALTERNATIVE sounds, and the open vowel repetitions, or ASSONANCE, must all be heard. Nor can we speak lamely and unemphatically at those points where exclamations call for emphasis, or hurriedly where commas require a pause between repetitions of the word "break." If a reader is to make the poem mean something to a person who has no copy before him and is not familiar with it, he must also speak the words with more variation of pitch than is normal. He would want to show musically the contrast between the uncomprehending repetition of the word "break" in the first stanza, like the ceaseless pounding of the sea on the stones, and the repetition of the same word in the last stanza, which must now convey the sense of personal loss that the sound brings to the mind of the poet.

The fact that Tennyson, in this very well-known poem, used not one sound pattern throughout, but two main sound patterns in alternation, might seem bewildering to those who have learned to SCAN poetry by identifying the conventional FEET. Too often students get the notion that the meter of poetry is a fairly mechanical business, in which the poet selects his basic foot and then simply runs off his poem in it. If that were the case, poetry would have the rhythmical interest of a clock. Actually, poetry relies as much on variation from a prevailing pattern as upon the pattern itself. The poet modulates the pattern when he wants to heighten an effect.

It is useful to know at least the most commonly used feet, however, in order to know more clearly how the poet works with rhythm. The most common ones are either DUPLE or TRIPLE: two-syllable feet or three-syllable feet.

Duple.

IAMBIC (˘/˘/)	Ănd snátch ă gráce bĕyónd thĕ réach ŏf árt . . . .
TROCHAIC (/˘/˘)	Ónce ŭpón ă mídnĭght dréarў . . . .
SPONDEE (//)	Práise hím . . . .

Triple.

ANAPESTIC (˘˘/˘˘/)	Ĭn thĕ dárknĕss ŏf tíme, ĭn thĕ déeps ŏf thĕ yéars . . . .
DACTYLIC (/˘˘/˘˘)	Thís ĭs thĕ fórĕst prĭméval; thĕ múrmŭrĭng pínes ănd thĕ hémlŏcks . . . .

A number of other meters have been used in English poetry, but familiarity with iamb, trochee, spondee, anapest, and dactyl will give one an adequate layman's knowledge of the subject.

We would like to say again that the feet described here are very rarely used without variation throughout a whole poem. To say that a poem is written in iambic meter means merely that iambic is the *prevailing* foot, the one the poet uses as his basic beat to provide a metrical structure on which he can work his rhythmical effects. Sometimes the variations he makes of the basic beat defy scansion according to any scheme. The spondee is most used as a variation of another foot, but the spondee is technically a duple meter. Sometimes, as in the poem by Tennyson which began this chapter, a poet will use three accented syllables in a row, for which there is no commonly accepted name.

Verse is classified and described by the length of lines as well as by feet. And the length of the line is expressed by the number of feet in it: iambic pentameter, for instance, is a line of five iambs. The numerical names are derived from Greek.

Monometer	one foot
Dimeter	two feet
Trimeter	three feet
Tetrameter	four feet
Pentameter	five feet
Hexameter	six feet
Heptameter	seven feet
Octometer	eight feet

Lines rarely go beyond this, and even the longest ones in this list usually break down into alternating shorter lines. Heptameter, for instance, usually sounds like alternating four-foot and three-foot lines, a kind of verse called "galloping fourteeners" because of the fourteen syllables in an iambic line of seven feet. Certain specialized names have become attached to some lines. An iambic hexameter, for instance, is called an ALEXANDRINE, iambic pentameter that does not rhyme is called BLANK VERSE, and two iambic pentameter lines that rhyme following each other are called a HEROIC COUPLET.

The iambic foot is the most common in English, because it fits the natural stress patterns of our language. We speak iambic feet all the time without even knowing it ("Ĭ háte tŏ wálk ĭo wórk ălóne"). It is the foot used in the plays of Shakespeare and others, and the blank verse line is the typical line of long poems, like Milton's *Paradise Lost,* Wordsworth's *The Prelude* (though other lines are used too).

Many poets of today write in yet another kind of line, called—rather misleadingly—FREE VERSE, verse which has lines of irregular length and relatively irregular stress patterns. Free verse might seem at first glance to be completely irregular, like prose, and this impression tempts student poets to write in it, because they don't have to worry about making their verse fit any kind of predetermined pattern. Actually, the freedom of this kind of verse is a delusion, for it requires a very sensitive ear to write it well, and usually the poets who write good free verse have had a great deal of discipline in writing metrical verse. The flexibility of free verse must be justified by the results. The musical effects, with varying stress patterns, must be perfectly suited to the words and must produce an entirely satisfactory rhythmical structure of a kind not possible with regular rhythms.

Tennyson's "Break, Break, Break" is musically a relatively simple and regular poem. Let us now look as some parts of poems in which the pulsation of the meter and sounds of the words are manipulated in other ways to produce other effects.

From *The Iliad*

Murmuring they move, as when old ocean roars,
And heaves huge surges to the trembling shores;
The groaning banks are burst with bellowing sound,
The rocks remurmur and the deeps rebound.
At length the tumult sinks, the noises cease.
And a still silence lulls the camp to peace.

Translated, Alexander Pope

Questions.

1. What is the underlying stress pattern in these lines?
2. How is the stress pattern manipulated in the second and third lines to vary from the underlying pattern and why?
3. What effects are achieved by the repetition of "b" sounds in the third line and "s" and "l" sounds in the final line?
4. Read the poem aloud giving appropriate emphasis to the underlying pulse, the sound effects, and the end rimes.

In the next passage from this same translation of *The Iliad*, Pope is attempting to convey a different kind of movement in his verse as he portrays the angered Neptune, father of the floods:

He mounts the car, the golden scourge applies,
He sits superior, and the chariot flies;
His whirling wheels the glassy surface sweep;
The enormous monsters rolling o'er the deep
Gambol around him on the watery way,

And heavy whales in awkward measures play;
The sea subsiding spreads a level plain,
Exults, and owns the monarch of the main;
The parting waves before his coursers fly;
The wondering waters leave his axle dry.

Questions.

1. What sounds does the poet seem to associate with swiftness and smoothness?
2. How does he simultaneously convey through sounds a sense of underlying turbulence?
3. Explain the redundancy of lines 3 and 7.

In the poems we have examined thus far, sounds have been used in a fairly obvious, though effective, manner. Even the person unskilled in poetry is likely to recognize the heavy thrust of certain consonants or the liquid smoothness of certain vowels and consonants. Some poets use sound effects with great subtlety to express complex mixtures of several emotions. Or perhaps the poet moves in a short poem from a somber tone to a happier one and expresses this movement not only in the sense of his words, but also, to a certain extent, in the sounds.

Sonnet 29

When in disgrace with fortune and men's eyes,
I all alone beweep my outcast state,
And trouble deaf heaven with my bootless cries,
And look upon myself and curse my fate,
Wishing me like to one more rich in hope,
Featured like him, like him with friends possessed,
Desiring this man's art, and that man's scope,
With what I most enjoy contented least;
Yet in these thoughts myself almost despising,
Haply I think on thee, and then my state,
Like to the lark at break of day arising
From sullen earth, sings hymns at heaven's gate;
For thy sweet love remembered such wealth brings
That then I scorn to change my state with kings.

WILLIAM SHAKESPEARE

Questions.

1. Compare and contrast the tonal effects of the sounds used in the first four lines of this poem with those in the last four lines.
2. Identify the underlying stress pattern in this poem.
3. Why do lines 5 and 6 begin with strong rather than weak stresses?

The sound of this sonnet is not liquid and smooth, but it has a musical quality nonetheless, which arises from the appropriateness of the sound to the sense—from the support given the meaning of the words by sound repetitions, rhyme variation, and stress. All these help the poem to develop a propulsive and dynamic movement. It should be stressed that in this poem, as in all others in which sound and sense are distinguishable, sound would be discovered to depend more on sense (imagery, metaphor, grammatical assertion) than the other way around.

An aspect of sound in poetry that must be taken into account is the pattern of end rhyme—the recurrence of like sounds occurring at the end of the lines. Giving each different end rhyme a different alphabetical value, we can notate the rhyme pattern of Shakespeare's poem as follows: *abab cdcd efef gg.* (It is a Shakespearean sonnet.) As we saw in Chapter 7, the rhyme pattern organizes the sonnet into parts in such a way that the poem has a larger structural rhythm in addition to the rhythm of the lines. A reader should feel this larger pulse.

Let us now turn back to sort out the various kinds of sounds at work in the poem and to see how far an analysis of the "meaning" of these sounds can be carried. Perhaps in order to "hear" the sounds, we could compare them to the playing of a relatively simple tune on a carillon. We notice that the prevailing metrical beat of the poem is iambic, five heavy stresses per line, alternating ordinarily in a pattern of light-heavy, light-heavy, and that the ending note of each line is repeated at the alternate line until the concluding two lines. We notice too, that the darker atmosphere of the first four lines is expressed somewhat discordantly by the deeper-toned bells as harsh consonantal sounds and booming open vowel sounds tumble over one another; but that as the poem develops, the higher bells begin to sound their more silvery notes, and the discord changes to a smooth assonance with a pealing finale in the concluding couplet. The comparison is exaggerated and simplified, but it may serve to convey at least some idea of the remarkable sound shifts which occur in the poem.

Shakespeare, who was primarily a man of the theatre and spent most of his working life as an actor, was probably more aware of the dramatic effects of sounds than is the poet who writes non-dramatic poetry only. His sonnets resemble, in some of their grander moments, the great soliloquies from his plays. Some of the poems in this chapter and elsewhere are considerably less dramatic than Shakespeare's sonnets, but one thing that all the poetic examples investigated thus far have in common is that they all show both freedom and variety in the use of sound effects. The examples of poetry that we have discussed, however, seem to rely considerably more on sound effects than do certain other kinds of poetry, which through their less obvious patterning of line length and stress are called free verse.

A Noiseless Patient Spider

A noiseless patient spider,
I marked where on a little promontory it stood isolated,
Marked how to explore the vacant vast surrounding,
It launched forth filament, filament, filament, out of itself,
Ever unreeling them, ever tirelessly speeding them.

And you O my soul where you stand,
Surrounded, detached, in measureless oceans of space,
Ceaselessly musing, venturing, throwing, seeking the spheres to connect them,
Till the bridge you will need be formed, till the ductile anchor hold,
Till the gossamer thread you fling catch somewhere, O my soul.

WALT WHITMAN

Questions.

1. In how many specific respects is the spider's standing place compared to the soul's?
2. What does Whitman's comparison reveal about his attitude toward the soul?
3. In what respects do similar actions performed by spiders and souls differ in quality?

An attempt to determine the underlying stress pattern of Whitman's line is likely to yield something like this:

˘/ ˘/˘/˘
˘/˘˘˘/ ˘/˘/˘/ ˘˘///˘,
/˘˘˘/ ˘/ ˘/ ˘/˘
˘/ ˘/˘˘, /˘˘, /˘˘, /˘˘/,

We are likely to find ourselves in greater disagreement about the details of this stress pattern, than about the patterning of regular verses. As a result, we are more likely to emphasize in varying degrees the ends of lines, finding ourselves becoming more conscious of other kinds of sound effects, for example, the repetition of the word *filament* in line 4. Other important sounds here are the repetitions of vowel and consonantal sounds in lines 3 and 4, repetition of the double *ee* sound in line 5, and repetition of the *ing* sound in line 8. Despite the absence of rhyme and a regularly stressed rhythm, a considerable amount of carefully calculated repetition of sound occurs in these lines.

Another important aspect of the structure of this poem is the stanza length. The first stanza, which contains the description of the spider, begins with a relatively short line, but the succeeding lines become longer. The number of syllables in the first five-line stanza is as follows: 7, 17, 12, 16, 15; the second five-line stanza, where the spider becomes a metaphor for the soul, contains the following number of syllables: 8, 13, 18, 15, 14. The syllabic length of these lines, with the exception of lines 2 and 3, which are reversed in length in 7 and 8, differs in every case by only a single stress. The speaking length of the lines, except for the reversal noted, is almost the same, but we are allowed greater freedom in the matter of stress.

Several readings of the poem aloud, however, will show that another rhythmical feature is controlled with considerable care by the poet. This is pause, sometimes called by the more technical name of CAESURA. When the English-speaking person speaks more than a few syllables in a line of poetry, he finds himself wanting to pause, and the more marked pauses in poetry, deliberately used for rhythmical purposes, are termed caesuras. Although we make no pause in line 1, we tend to make brief pauses after *where* and after *promontory* in line 2, after *how* in line 3, and after the commas in lines 4 and 5. The second stanza of the poem, in contrast, demands many more such pauses than the first, and the effect it produces, despite a similar number of syllables, is much more measured and stately.

Free verse, then, as written by Whitman, is in its own special way just as carefully contrived as poetry with a regular metrical pattern and rhyme scheme. In his use of a carefully arranged pattern of syllables per line, Whitman was returning to a kind of verse that is still practiced regularly in Italian and other languages descended from the Latin. Because the English language falls more easily into an accentual rather than a quantitative pattern, using accent or stress rather than length of syllables to mark rhythm, English and American poets customarily use a metrical line. Not all of Whitman's poems, of course, yield such a regular syllabic pattern upon analysis. But one of the best of modern poets, Dylan Thomas, uses quantitative patterns in his poems frequently and quite consciously, as in

"Fern Hill" (page 454). Both Whitman and Thomas were fond of reciting their poetry aloud, and Thomas's readings are really musical performances.

The caesura appears in almost any pentameter line, usually after the second or the third foot. Some poets, especially those of the neoclassical period, use this slight pause with very conscious effect to give their line a graceful balance, even in devastating satire, such as John Dryden's poem on Thomas Shadwell.

From *MacFlecknoe*

Sh[adwell] alone my perfect image bears,
Mature in dulness from his tender years;
Sh[adwell] alone, of all my sons, is he
Who stands confirmed in full stupidity.
The rest to some faint meaning make pretence,
But Sh[adwell] never deviates into sense.
Some beams of wit on other souls may fall,
Strike thro', and make a lucid interval;
But Sh[adwell]'s genuine night admits no ray,
His rising fogs prevail upon the day.

JOHN DRYDEN

Questions.

1. Where do the caesuras fall in each line? (In some they are more pronounced than in others.)
2. What effect do they produce in each case?
3. Is the imagery in the last four lines effective for Dryden's purpose?

Poetry is, among other things, an aural art; it is intended to be heard whether it is read silently or aloud. The patterns of sound in themselves contribute a good deal to our pleasure in poetry. Hearing poetry is enjoyable even when it is written in a language one does not understand, if it is read well. The rhythm, the sound patterns, the rise and fall of the poetic line even without meaning somehow manage to produce a kind of esthetic response. This is a limited kind of pleasure, of course, and one does not ordinarily read poetry merely for the sound. But the sound is important, both because it makes a contribution to poetic structure and because it helps to convey the sense.

Poems for Further Study:

Sudden Light

I have been here before,
But when or how I cannot tell:
I know the grass beyond the door,
The sweet keen smell,
The sighing sound, the lights around the shore.

You have been mine before,—
How long ago I may not know:
But just when at that swallow's soar
Your neck turned so,
Some veil did fall,—I knew it all of yore.

Has this been thus before?
And shall not thus time's eddying flight
Still with our lives our love restore
In death's despite,
And day and night yield one delight once more?

DANTE GABRIEL ROSSETTI

To Night

I

Swiftly walk o'er the western wave,
Spirit of Night!
Out of the misty eastern cave,
Where, all the long and lone daylight,
Thou wovest dreams of joy and fear,
Which make thee terrible and dear,—
Swift by thy flight!

II

Wrap thy form in a mantle gray,
Star-inwrought!
Blind with thine hair the eyes of Day;
Kiss her until she be wearied out,
Then wander o'er city, and sea, and land,
Touching all with thine opiate wand—
Come, long-sought!

III

When I arose and saw the dawn,
I sighed for thee;
When light rode high, and the dew was gone,
And noon lay heavy on flower and tree,
And the weary Day turned to his rest,
Lingering like an unloved guest,
I sighed for thee.

IV

Thy brother Death came, and cried,
Wouldst thou me?
Thy sweet child Sleep, the filmy-eyed,
Murmured like a noontide bee,
Shall I nestle near thy side?
Wouldst thou me?—And I replied,
"No, not thee!"

V

Death will come when thou art dead,
Soon, too soon—
Sleep will come when thou are fled;
Of neither would I ask the boon
I ask of thee, belovéd Night—
Swift be thine approaching flight,
Come soon, soon!

PERCY BYSSHE SHELLEY

What Thing Is Love?

What thing is love? for, well I wot, love is a thing.
It is a prick, it is a sting,
It is a pretty pretty thing;
It is a fire, it is a coal.
Whose flame creeps in at every hole;
And as my wit doth best devise,
Love's dwelling is in ladies' eyes:
From whence do glance love's piercing darts
That make such holes into our hearts;

And all the world herein accord
Love is a great and mighty lord,
And when he list to mount so high,
With Venus he in heaven doth lie,
And evermore hath been a god
Since Mars and she played even and odd.

GEORGE PEELE

Suggested Poems for Further Reading (ANTHOLOGY):

Thomas Campion, "Come You Pretty False-Eyed Wanton," p. 280
William Collins, "Ode on the Death of Mr. Thomson," p. 307
Robert Frost, "After Apple-Picking," p. 338
Robert Herrick, "His Litany to the Holy Spirit," p. 358

Poetry and its Setting

10

Thus far in this book we have been concerned mainly with the techniques of poetry and have done little more than touch on literary history in connection with the analyses of particular poems. Historical perspective is of great importance in reading some poems. In order for a modern reader to make any sense out of some of the satires of Dryden or Pope, for instance, he must know at least in general the situation referred to in the poem and the people named in it. Though good poetry is "universal" in the sense that it deals with matters of perennial interest to mankind, or at least deals with particular things in a way that makes them of more than particular interest, all poetry cannot help but reflect its milieu. Milton and Keats hoped, of course, that the fame they sought would continue to other ages, but they wrote first for their own.

The term "historical perspective" might be thought of as having two kinds of meaning: (1) a knowledge of the particular circumstances surrounding the writing of a poem and of particular meanings expressed in the text which are unfamiliar to a modern reader, and (2) an understanding of the way in which a poem of the past reflects the general ideas and attitudes, literary tastes, and other characteristics of its age. For the first kind of historical perspective, a reader can get help from annotated editions, from reference works like the *Oxford Companion to English Literature* and the *Oxford Companion to American Literature*, and from a good historical dictionary such as the *Oxford English Dictionary* (usually called the *OED*). The second kind requires some systematic study of literary history such as that pursued in many advanced courses offered by college and university English departments.*

In the brief space allotted to this matter, we can do little more than suggest some meanings perhaps not evident at once which both kinds of historical perspective might supply in readings of poems from different periods of English literature.

A Sonet

His Golden lockes, Time hath to Silver turned,
O Time too swift, O Swiftness never ceasing:
His Youth gainst Time and Age hath ever spurned
But spurned in vain, Youth waineth by increasing.
Beauty Strength, Youth, are flowers, but fading seen
Dutie, Faith, Love are roots, and ever greene.

His Helmet now, shall make a hive for Bees,
And Lovers Sonets, turned to holy Psalmes:
A man at Armes must now serve on his knees,
And feede on praiers, which are Age his almes.
But though from Court to Cottage he depart,
His saint is sure of his unspotted heart.

And when he saddest sits in homely Cell,
Heele teach his Swaines this Carroll for a Song,
Blest be the heartes that wish my soveraigne well,
Curst be the soules that thinke her any wrong.
Goddesse, allow this aged man his right,
To be your Beads-man now, that was your Knight.

George Peele *or* Sir Henry Lee

---

*An ever increasing abundance of historical and other studies of literature is available inexpensively in paperback editions. A standard reference book, found on every librarian's desk, that will direct a reader to studies of various kinds is Constance Winchell's *Guide to Reference Books*, 7th edition, Chicago, 1951, with supplements, 1950-55. The standard bibliography of English literature is F. W. Bateson, editor, *The Cambridge Bibliography of English Literature.* 4 vols. Cambridge, 1941, with supplement (vol. 5), Cambridge, 1957. For American literature, the standard bibliography will be Jacob Blanck, *Bibliography of American Literature,* New Haven, 1955—, when it is completed. Meanwhile, the third volume of Robert E. Spiller and others, *Literary History of the United States,* New York, 1948, with supplement, 1949, is very useful. The standard current bibliography of English, American, and other literatures is that found annually in the May issue (the "B" issue) of *Publications of the Modern Language Association* ("*PMLA*"), which lists virtually everything published during the previous year, including a great many specialized studies of little interest to anyone but the scholar.

Despite its odd spelling and the curious form of the possessive in line 10 ("his" for 's), most readers can readily take pleasure in this poem without knowing its date, the circumstances of its production, or the courtly milieu out of which it grew. The poem speaks of a lover and his lady in terms fairly conventional to a reader familiar with the custom of some poets to think of themselves as knightly lovers held in bonds of obeisance to courtly ladies. It seems clear enough that the aging lover's relationship with the younger lady suggests that he is considerably older than she, and he wishes to adore her from the safer vantage point of a hermit's cell or a countryman's cottage.

A reader may also enjoy the clever paradoxes of the poem: gold turning to silver, the unceasing swiftness of time, the waning of youth by increasing. He may be struck by the aptness of the poet's observation that duty, faith, and love are more enduring qualities than beauty, strength, and youth, for the poem shows the active force of mortality, which can be resisted only by the greater force of ethical values. A sensitive reader might also enjoy the smoothness of the verse, the skill with which the figure of the knight and his lady are woven into the poem, and the pleasant compliment to the lady, made into a goddess to save her from aging. Most readers might wish to leave the poem at this point, feeling they have gone as far with it as they need to go.

But a little inquiry into the background of the poem will yield several items of specific information which, sharpening the reader's response, may make him enjoy it more. The poem comes, he will find, from a book published in 1590, with the elaborate title, *Polyhymnia, describing the honourable triumpt at Tylt.* The "tilt" or knightly jousting was held on the thirty-second anniversary of Queen Elizabeth's accession, and the occasion also marked Sir Henry Lee's retirement as the queen's champion for those thirty-two years, a knightly office surviving from the Middle Ages. The event described in the first part of the poem, then, is a historical fact, although the role of beadsman was metaphorical to Sir Henry, who did not retire to a cell, but remained a successful courtier to King James after the death of his "Goddess," and married a rather lively woman much younger than himself.

Actually, we cannot be sure whether the author was Sir Henry or George Peele, to whom the poem is ascribed by most anthologies and who was responsible for most of the other poems in *Polyhymnia.* The character of the speaker does seem to fit Sir Henry. Perhaps we should say "singer," since "A Sonet" was sung to the queen by the royal lutanist, Robert Hales. To appreciate the poem fully, we really ought to hear it sung together with other songs and poems from the collection. The term "sonet" may seem puzzling, since this poem is not in fourteen lines, but actually many different kinds of lyrics were called sonnets in the sixteenth and early seventeenth centuries.

An amusing glimpse of royal customs is provided the reader who happens to note that Sir Henry was born in the same year as his eulogized queen, 1533, and both were in their late 50's at the time of the joust. Elizabeth loved to be flattered and expected to be treated by her courtiers as a young woman to the end of her days. Sir Henry's (or Peele's) tact and discrimination are revealed in the compliment in which time stands still for the lady but moves swiftly for the gentleman. Yet the compliment, though of course the court was familiar with the queen's real age, is not wholly artificial; for Elizabeth was even then being given some of the attributes of a goddess, a living legend, for whom time had less meaning than for most people.

John Donne's "A Valediction: Forbidding Mourning" may also be understood reasonably well without knowledge of some of the things alluded to in the poem. But just as the Peele-Lee poem becomes richer with added knowledge, so the imagery and metaphor of Donne's poem become more vivid if the reader is aware that the poet draws on a number of ideas more familiar to his contemporaries than to us: medieval doctrines of the body and soul, Renaissance conventions of love poetry, Ptolemaic astronomy, alchemy, metallurgy, geometry, and ancient Greek philosophy.

A Valediction: Forbidding Mourning

As virtuous men pass mildly away,
   And whisper to their souls, to go,
Whilst some of their sad friends do say,
   The breath goes now, and some say, no:

So let us melt, and make no noise
   No tear-floods, nor sigh-tempests move;
'Twere profanation of our joys
   To tell the laity our love.

Moving of th' earth brings harms and fears,
   Men reckon what it did and meant,
But trepidation of the spheres,
   Though greater far, is innocent.

Dull sublunary lovers' love
(Whose soul is sense) cannot admit
Absence, because it doth remove
Those things which elemented it.

But we by a love so much refined
That our selves know not what it is,
Inter-assured of the mind,
Care less, eyes, lips, and hands to miss.

Our two souls therefore, which are one,
Though I must go, endure not yet
A breach, but an expansion,
Like gold to airy thinness beat.

If they be two, they are two so
As stiff twin compasses are two;
Thy soul, the fixed foot, makes no show
To move, but doth, if th' other do.

And though it in the center sit,
Yet when the other far doth roam,
It leans, and hearkens after it,
And grows erect, as that comes home.

Such wilt thou be to me, who must
Like th' other foot, obliquely run;
Thy firmness makes my circle just,
And makes me end, where I begun.

JOHN DONNE

In the first stanza the speaker uses a simile that asks at just what point the virtuous soul leaves the body in death. In the second stanza he presents typical Petrarchan exaggerations in love poems, where tears come in floods and sighs are tempests. In the third and fourth stanzas, he shifts his comparison to astronomy, when he says that movements of the earth, because they are close, have drastic consequences, but motions in the stars in the higher spheres surrounding the earth (in the geocentric conception of the universe) do not affect the earth very much because they are so far away; and the sensual lovers are called *sublunary,* i.e., under the moon, or in the lowest sphere. In words like *elemented,* Donne's speaker refers to the doctrine of the four elements that compose all things, and by implication, as is seen when this metaphor develops, he refers to alchemy and metallurgy. For the love is *refined,* in the fourth stanza, so much so that it passes beyond the state in which it can be identified; it becomes so pure that it is a fifth essence, a quintessence, a word with a highly specialized meaning in alchemy. In stanza five the figure is carried farther and related to gold, the metal that was of greatest interest to alchemy, and given a specific image in gold leaf, gold beaten very thin. In the seventh to the ninth stanzas, he changes the simile to compasses in geometry and develops it, ending in the last two lines with the idea of the eternal perfection of the circle, which was often used as geometrical representation of eternity and God because it is the perfect figure, without beginning or end.

To be sure, some of the imagery of the poem presents no particular difficulties even to a reader who has never heard of Ptolemy or alchemy. A moment's reflection will yield an interpretation of *sublunary* as being under the moon, probably good enough for the casual reader to enjoy the poem. Gold beaten to "airy thinness" is easy enough to grasp, and anyone who has used compasses to draw a circle should have no trouble with the last image. But in order to read the poem thoroughly and accurately enough to appreciate the precision with which Donne uses his images, one must have more exact knowledge of what is going on.

Let us turn now to the second kind of historical perspective we spoke of earlier, the way in which a poem reflects the general ideas and attitudes of its age. Here one encounters the familiar but nonetheless vaguely understood names for historical epochs like Renaissance, Augustan, Romantic, Victorian. Renaissance means literally re-birth. Many scholars, many political historians and historians of science especially, boggle at the implications of the term and deny that there ever was a re-birth of the kind suggested by the term. The names given to the various epochs do not, then, adequately reflect the character of the epochs for the careful reader; the terms are merely convenient conventional designations, not descriptions. Though not all scholars agree as to what are the essential characteristics of various epochs, the epochs themselves have enough characteristics in common to form distinguishable segments of history. Many of these characteristics can be seen in the poetry of any given age.*

Lord Byron's "Prometheus," though it does not seem like the poems popularly associated with the Romantic period (that from about 1790 to

*An interesting book which includes five poems of different periods, noticing attitudes and ideas indigenous to each age, E. M. Tillyard, *Poetry and Its Background Illustrated by Five Poems, 1470-1870* (London, 1955; published earlier, 1948, as *Five Poems, 1470-1870*).

about 1840) and though it is on a classic (Aeschylean) theme, nevertheless reflects some of the important ideas and attitudes of that complex period.

Prometheus was to the Romantics a favorite hero, as rebel against tyranny, sufferer for humanity, and possessor of transcendent knowledge. The values to be seen in Prometheus are not the ones conventionally attached to the Romantic poets, who are all too often thought of as sentimentalists writing poems about nature, escaping in fancy to the far away and long ago, or aspiring to hopeless ideals. Though the Romantics set a high value on emotional intensity, they did not in fact relish emotion for its own sake. Though some of them—by no means all—did write nature poems, they did not do so to "commune" with nature or even merely to celebrate the beauties of nature; for they saw nature symbolically as expressing important truths concerning the nature of man and concerning man's relationship with the cosmos. Though some of the Romantics did write poems set in distant times and places, most of them used exotic settings, when they used them at all, to develop universal or contemporary themes. And, though the Romantics were indeed idealistic, they also faced squarely the bitter facts of life.

Romanticism is easily misunderstood because it is enormously complex, and its ideas are subtle. No single characterization of it can do it justice.* The Romantic movement was not a literary "revolt" by a coterie of poets, but a general European cultural phenomenon that came about as a sort of climactic convergence of developments in politics, philosophy, society, and art. Among its characteristics in England, in addition to those mentioned above, were a profound belief in political liberty; individualism; a belief in the capabilities of man to make a better world—with, however, a fairly realistic recognition of man's shortcomings; a reaction against a mechanistic and material view of the cosmos and of man's mind; a profound belief in the imagination as a means to important knowledge; and a view of poetry which emphasized imagery, symbol, and often myth.

Some but not all of these characteristics may be seen in Byron's "Prometheus" (other characteristics have been suggested in the discussions of "Kubla Khan" and "The Sick Rose," earlier). If one approaches this poem in the context of Romanticism as a whole, its themes, though taken from the Greek dramatist Aeschylus, are also identifiable as Romantic.

---

*A collection of discussions of Romanticism may be found in Robert F. Gleckner and Gerald E. Enscoe, eds., *Romanticism: Points of View* (Englewood Cliffs, N. J., 1962). A recent difficult, but rewarding, essay is Morse Peckham's "Toward a Theory of Romanticism: II. Reconsiderations," *Studies in Romanticism,* I (1961), 1-8. An important group of essays is *Romanticism Reconsidered,* ed. Northrop Frye (New York, 1963).

Prometheus

I

Titan! to whose immortal eyes
  The sufferings of mortality,
  Seen in their sad reality,
Were not as things that gods despise;
What was thy pity's recompense?
A silent suffering, and intense;
The rock, the vulture, and the chain,
All that the proud can feel of pain,
The agony they do not show,
The suffocating sense of woe,
  Which speaks but in its loneliness,
And then is jealous lest the sky
Should have a listener, nor will sigh
  Until its voice is echoless.

II

Titan! to thee the strife was given
  Between the suffering and the will
  Which torture where they cannot kill;
And the inexorable Heaven,
And the deaf tyranny of Fate,
The ruling principle of Hate,
Which for its pleasure doth create
The things it may annihilate,
Refused thee even the boon to die:
The wretched gift eternity
Was thine—and thou hast borne it well.
All that the Thunderer wrung from thee
Was but the menace which flung back
On him the torments of thy rack;
The fate thou didst so well foresee,
But would not to appease him tell;
And in thy Silence was his Sentence,
And in his Soul a vain repentance,
And evil dread so ill dissembled,
That in his hand the lightnings trembled.

III

Thy Godlike crime was to be kind,
  To render with thy precepts less
The sum of human wretchedness,
And strengthen Man with his own mind;
But baffled as thou wert from high,
Still in thy patient energy,
In the endurance, and repulse
  Of thine impenetrable Spirit,
Which Earth and Heaven could not convulse,
  A mighty lesson we inherit:
Thou art a symbol and a sign
  To mortals of their fate and force;
Like thee, Man is in part divine,
  A troubled stream from a pure source;
And Man in portions can foresee
His own funereal destiny;
His wretchedness, and his resistance,
And his sad unallied existence:
To which his Spirit may oppose
Itself—and equal to all woes,
  And a firm will, and a deep sense,
Which even in torture can descry
  Its own concenter'd recompense,
Triumphant where it dares defy,
And making Death a Victory.

George Gordon, Lord Byron

Prometheus as he appears in the work of Romantic poets like Blake, Byron, and Shelley is a symbol of energy, of suffering for man, of superior knowledge, and of a kind of defiance of tyranny that succeeds by a passive resistance in which tyranny is in part overcome by wisdom. He defies Zeus initially in giving man fire, knowledge of the arts and sciences, and Hope; and for this he is punished by a power-loving Zeus, who naturally opposes liberty-loving individualism. He is chained to a rock where a vulture each day eats his liver, which grows back during the night. Since Prometheus knows that Zeus will eventually be overthrown, this knowledge helps him endure the torture. But in the very act of endurance, Prometheus defies Zeus in another way, for, as the Romantics saw him, he does not suffer in quite the way Zeus wanted him to. Despite being chained, he remains superior to his oppressor by refusing to bend his spirit to Zeus's will and by refusing to think in Zeus's terms. Indeed, in Shelley's *Prometheus Unbound* he pities Zeus, thus putting himself outside that conception of life in which Zeus, as the embodiment of "the ruling principle of Hate," must function. For Prometheus to direct his great energy to hating Zeus would be to accept Zeus's principles of hate and force, to play according to Zeus's rules, and, since Zeus actually does have force, to suffer defeat. Instead Prometheus defies by enduring in silence, and triumphs, by passive resistance.

Byron sees Prometheus as "a symbol and a sign" to mortals "of their fate and force," since, like Prometheus, man is "in part divine." Man too must face wretchedness as part of his lot, but he can defy it with a firm will, not succumb in spirit to his wretched fate, and can find a "concentered recompense" in his own being,

Triumphant where it dares defy,
And making Death a Victory.

Byron's view of man is less optimistic—perhaps more realistic—than Shelley's. In Shelley's treatment of the myth, Prometheus' pitying Zeus helps to bring about the end of tyranny, or at least signals its end; and it is followed by a millenium in which the whole world is changed by love. Byron foresees no such change. Men, individually and collectively through institutions, will continue to create "wretchedness" and oppression. However, spirited souls whose vision goes beyond conventional mores—the rebels—can, like Prometheus, successfully but painfully defy the world that would make them wretched, at least to the extent that they can remain true to their own natures.

This is not Stoic doctrine; it is a rebellious individualism (though not of the "rugged" kind), which postulates self-identity as the only certain value in a troubled world, or as the starting point for a search for value. This is a Romantic conception, though Byron's version of it is rather darker than those of the other Romantics. Involved in it are other Romantic traits: individualism conceived as it is here arises from a distrust of rational systems that do not work; and the defiant individualist has, like Prometheus, superior knowledge, which for the Romantics is gained from imagination.

In almost any poem by Byron the more specific historical context of biography is also important. Prometheus in this poem is a projection on a heroic scale of some of Byron's personal values, and Prometheus' situation as that of a rebellious exile being punished for daring to defy the established order of Zeus reflects Byron's own situation in 1816, when he was an outcast of Regency society travelling on the Continent, suffering for what, in some moods, he regarded as a kind of moral rebellion: incest. Aspects of the Prometheus figure also appear in another heroic projection of the poet's life: Manfred, the solitary exile of Byron's lyric drama *Manfred,* written in the same year. It should not be too surprising that Byron expresses certain personal attitudes through a hero who was also a favorite of many of the other Romantics, because he symbolized some ideas and attitudes prevalent at the time. Byron, despite the fascinating contradictions warring within him, was a kind of living dramatization of many of the essential values of the age.

Most of what we have said in this chapter thus far applies to that kind of reading of poetry which becomes a historical *study* of poetry. In reading a good deal of poetry from the past, it is useful and sometimes necessary to have historical information about the poem, the poet, and his age in order to understand what a poem is talking about, and one's reading of anything is enriched by the knowledge he brings to the text. Still, most of us do not make our first approach to a poem with the intention of studying it, but rather with the intention of simply reading it—letting the poem speak to us as it will. Then, if our interest is aroused, we may go on to find out more about it, about other poems by the same writer, about the writer, and about the poem's milieu, if it was written in an age different from our own.

A body of poetry that is directly readable, requiring no study of a bygone age, of course, is the poetry of our own day. We can read it with an understanding that we can never have of poetry of the past, because we can never project ourselves back into history completely enough to make the attitudes and ideas of another age as relevant to our lives as they were to people of that age. Neither, of course, will readers of the year 2100 find our poetry to have the same kind of relevance to them as it has to us. In a few years the poetry of today will have a "historical setting," which serious readers will try to understand; that setting is for us our own society, which may baffle us in some respects but which we have a better chance of understanding than future historians, because we are experiencing it directly. To be sure, some of the values of our society which are so much a part of our lives that we don't even question them, will be sorted out by historical perspective and will be shown to have governed many of our actions, individually and socially, in ways that we do not now suspect. But as confused as the values of contemporary society may seem to us, we are aware of them in a way that no historian can be, because a historian cannot ever recreate the concrete particularity through which they impinge on us.

The poetry of our time reflects the attitudes and issues of our time, but it also clarifies them by giving them form and often by commenting on them directly. One important traditional role of the poet is that of social commentator, frequently a disconcerting one since he often vexes rather than soothes the age. Many of the poems considered in this book thus far have commented directly on social and other values, and the Anthology contains many more that do so. We conclude this chapter by examining a contemporary poem which seems at first reading to be merely a succession of thoughts aroused by a walk along a river, but which touches on some of the central values of our time.

*One Evening**

As I walked out one evening,
Walking down Bristol Street,
The crowds upon the pavement
Were fields of harvest wheat.

And down by the brimming river
I heard a lover sing
Under an arch of the railway:
"Love has no ending.

I'll love you, dear, I'll love you
Till China and Africa meet,
And the river jumps over the mountain
And the salmon sing in the street.

I'll love you till the ocean
Is folded and hung up to dry,
And the seven stars go squawking
Like geese about the sky.

The years shall run like rabbits,
For in my arms I hold
The Flower of the Ages,
And the first love of the world."

But all the clocks in the city
Began to whirr and chime:
"O let not Time deceive you,
You cannot conquer Time.

In the burrows of the Nightmare
Where Justice naked is,
Time watches from the shadow
And coughs when you would kiss.

In headaches and in worry
Vaguely life leaks away,
And Time will have his fancy
To-morrow or to-day.

Into many a green valley
Drifts the appalling snow;
Time breaks the threaded dances
And the diver's brilliant bow.

O plunge your hands in water,
Plunge them in up to the wrist;
Stare, stare in the basin
And wonder what you've missed.

The glacier knocks in the cupboard,
The desert sighs in the bed,
And the crack in the tea-cup opens
A lane to the land of the dead.

Where the beggars raffle the banknotes
And the Giant is enchanting to Jack,
And the Lily-white Boy is a Roarer,
And Jill goes down on her back.

O look, look in the mirror,
O look in your distress;
Life remains a blessing
Although you cannot bless.

O stand, stand at the window
As the tears scald and start;
You shall love your crooked neighbour
With your crooked heart."

It was late, late in the evening
The lovers they were gone;
The clocks had ceased their chiming,
And the deep river ran on.

W. H. Auden

The basic stress pattern throughout the poem is of three heavy stresses with considerable variation among the light stresses. The effect of this meter is to give to a serious poem a jazzy, jerky, nervous quality, which is appropriate to the picture of modern life, with the apparently senseless dynamism of the city, that emerges as the poem develops.

The speaker of the poem, the narrator, is more an observer than doer. He reports two conversations, one of a lover to his girl and the other of Time to the lovers. He seems to report objectively, in a neutral tone at first, but the account he gives is one that is imaginatively modified by the extreme exaggerations of the lover, as they are reported by the narrator. All lovers say substantially the same thing, and the poet depends on our being familiar with lovers' ordinary discourse in order to heighten that here into extraordinarily vivid hyperboles, which not only exaggerate lovers' vows but also develop the theme of time. We know that lovers usually protest that they will love long and faithfully, and the poet uses our familiarity with such talk to abstract its essence, transform it imaginatively, and use it thematically. In the vivid absurdity of the lover's hyperboles, we get a tone that is not neutral but ironic: the lover has much less time than he thinks, and love will not have for him the delights portrayed in his bizarre discourse.

At this point the poem moves to another imaginative plane with the entry of the second speaker, Time, personified by the whirring and chiming clocks. Time's talk, in sharp contrast to the lover's hyperboles, is harshly real. Justice is seldom seen, he says, youth is fleeting, worry is constant, man is lonely, hopes are frequently disappointed, and the naive fairy-tale view of life as pure and right is a delusion. As if these prospects were not sufficiently despairing, Time goes on to say that our optimistic cliches, which we have no basis for believing and little real intention of following, are equally absurd. The poem ends with the lovers gone, the chimes silenced; only the deep river remains, constant in its onward movement.

Does the poem merely represent causes for despair? There is the river, the only natural thing in the poem, and Time's pessimism does not apply to it. Time simply moves on. The river, in this context, becomes by its imperturbability and mystery, another symbol for time and the process of life. Earlier in the poem Time had counseled the lovers to "plunge your hands in water" and wonder what they had missed, suggesting that in the steady movement of the water in the river could be seen the process of life as it really is: steady, inexorable. And in another passage Time remarked in a paradox that "Life remains a blessing / Although you cannot bless."

Time seems, then, to have two aspects: one that coughs when lovers kiss, reminding them that they live in time, that life changes and moves on; the other, the deeply imperturbable process itself. The first aspect arises out of the naive belief in cliches and abstractions, to remind man that if he thinks of his abstractions, including eternal romantic love, as enduring, and things of his values as incorruptible, he is doomed to despair. The second aspect, symbolized by the river, is not subject to man's will, but rather is the process to which man must adapt his enterprises if he is to find any kind of happiness, or peace.

Rather than being merely a representation of despair, therefore, the poem argues, through its images and symbols, for a realistic attitude toward life. It is not a happy poem, nor does it advocate the power of positive thinking. But then ours does not seem to be a happy age, partly because sham values are daily being exposed for what they are in the compression of time that seems to be one of the characteristics of the twentieth century.

The poem speaks of and to the twentieth century. It could not have been written in any other century. To be sure, it does not say all there is to be said about our period, for no one poem could—and there are happier aspects to our lives, as many of the contemporary poems in this book have shown.

To read this contemporary poem with understanding, of course, we should have had enough experience in reading poetry of all ages to be able to respond to the distinctive use of poetic techniques here. The basic stress pattern, as we observed, is three strong accents with a variable number of light accents. However, Auden also uses a number of other rhythmical devices to produce his effects. He achieves an effect of fluency and swiftness in the earlier stanzas of the poem by having the lover address his girl in a rhapsodic rush of words which are punctuated very little. But when Time begins to speak, the tempo of the verse line is immediately slowed down by the sounds of the words and by an increase in the length of the pauses. These pauses become especially noticeable in stanzas 10, 13, 14, and 15; and in these same stanzas certain words (*plunge, stare, look, stand,* and *late*) have an insistent rhythmic quality that give the verse some of the effect of incantation. In stanza 13 the repetition of *look* serves to slow down the movement of the poem from the profuse heaping up of causes for despair, and leads to the demand that the lover look at himself and discover the self to be as ugly and as crooked as others are. Thus the pattern of stress and pause in stanza 13 is a marked contrast to the swift movement of the opening stanzas. Stanzas 14 and 15 are similarly slowed down, and the tonal effect conveyed by this retardation of tempo seems to suggest a diminishing of the dynamism of the city, until late in the evening only the quiet river is left, flowing into eternity.

The language of the poem is quite ordinary, with forceful one-syllable words being usually preferred to orotund polysyllables. Most of the repeated words are monosyllables and serve to reinforce the terse, modern, bitten-off quality of much of the discourse. The imagery of the poem is quite simple, though effective. The personifications are easy to grasp, the materials for comparisons are drawn from familiar experience, and there are references to such familiar objects as closets, washbasins, and mirrors. What Auden does with the comparisons, however, makes them fresh and imaginative, especially in lines 41-44, where a glacier knocks in the cupboard, a desert sighs in bed, and a crack opens in a teacup to become a lane to the land of the dead. These metaphors convey a good deal about the view of life that is being represented in this part of the poem, and they do so poetically, fusing pictorial image, the qualities of things, and ideas.

Even if Auden's poem were not identified, a sensitive reader would immediately recognize it as being modern, not only because its style is modern and because it describes a familiar modern scene, but also because of its attitudes and tone, which are those of our day. Modern poetry—along with modern art and modern music—is sometimes said to be obscure. Some of it is; a good deal of older poetry is too. There is a kind of natural obscurity in poetry that communicates obliquely rather than directly—poetry in which imagery, metaphor, symbol, tone, structure embody important meaning—and if the right to this kind of obscurity be denied, poetry is denied. But sometimes a poet may become too cryptic, elliptical, far-fetched, or private in his symbols for a reader to know what he is talking about, and he makes a poem that seems all but impenetrable. Still, even this apparent impenetrability may be a temporary state of affairs, for a perceptive critic may come along who can make the poem intelligible and show that the obscurity was after all justified by the emotional and intellectual impact of the poem when properly read. A judgment that a poem is obscure is, therefore, at best a contingent one. At any rate, one cannot judge a poem as being obscure until he has given it a fair try. If some modern poems seem a big opaque at first, because they use more of the devices of oblique poetry than do most poems of the past, they will usually yield their meaning on further reading.* In any event, we have one thing to help us: a familiarity with the world they are taking about.

Our very brief discussion of poetry and its setting in this chapter has not dealt with literary history as a discipline or a conceptual structure. An account of that matter would require a whole book in itself. We have been concerned, rather, with the question of the meaning that poetry has in relation to its context, and we have been able to do little more than make a few suggestions concerning that. Poetry can be approached from a number of different points of view, and each one, if pursued far enough, leads to the others.

Poems for Further Study:

The Compleint of Chaucer to His Empty Purse

To you, my purse, and to non other wight   *wight*—person
Compleyne I, for ye be my lady dere!
I am so sory, now that ye be light;
For certes, but ye make hevy chere,   *certes*—certainly
Me were as leef be leyed un-on my bere;
For whiche un-to your mercy thus I crye:
Beth hevy ageyn, or elles mot I dye!

beth—be;
Now voucheth sauf this day, or hit be night,   *mot*—may
That I of you the blisful soun may here,   *voucheth sauf*—vouchsafe
Or see your colour lyk the sonne bright,
That of yelownesse hadde never pere.
Ye be my lyf, ye be myn hertes stere,   *hertes*—heart's;
Quene of comfort and of good companye: *stere*—guide, rudder
Beth hevy ageyn, or elles mot I dye!

Now purs, that be to me my lyves light,
And saveour, as doun in this worlde here,   *sin*—since
Out of this toune help me through your might,   *ny*—close;
Sin that ye wole nat been my tresorere;   *frere*—friar
For I am shave as ny as any frere.
But yit I pray un-to your curtesye:
Beth hevy ageyn, or elles mot I dye!

*An excellent and admirably readable account of obscurity in poetry, especially modern poetry, is John Press, *Checquer'd Shade: Reflections on Obscurity in Poetry*. London, 1958. We owe the distinction between oblique and direct poetry to E. M. W. Tillyard, *Poetry Direct and Oblique*. Revised Edition, London, 1965.

Lenvoy de Chaucer

O conquerour of Brutes Albioun!
Which that by lyne and free eleccioun
Ben verray king, this song to you I sendè;
And ye, that mowen al our harm amende,
Have minde up-on my supplicacioun!

Brutes Albioun—Brutus' Albion (England: Brutus was a lengendary founder of England); *verray*—true

GEOFFREY CHAUCER

Note: The text here uses the spelling of Skeat. The spelling is different in later texts, but there are no radical changes.

The Collar

I struck the board, and cried, "No more; I
will abroad!
What! shall I ever sigh and pine?
My lines and life are free; free as the road
Loose as the wind, as large as store.
Shall I be still in suit?
Have I no harvest but a thorn
To let me blood, and not restore
What I have lost with cordial fruit?
Sure there was wine
Before my sighs did dry it; there was corn
Before my tears did drown it;
Is the year only lost to me?
Have I no bays to crown it,
No flowers, no garlands gay? all blasted,
All wasted?
Not so, my heart, but there is fruit,
And thou hast hands.
Recover all thy sigh-blown age
On double pleasures; leave thy cold dispute
Of what is fit and not; forsake thy cage,
Thy rope of sands
Which petty thoughts have made, and made
to thee
Good cable, to enforce and draw,
And be thy law,
While thou didst wink and wouldst not see.
Away! take heed;
I will abroad.

Call in thy death's head there, tie up thy fears;
He that forbears
To suit and serve his need
Deserves his load."
But as I raved, and grew more fierce and wild
At every word,
Methought I heard one calling, "Child";
And I replied. "My Lord."

George Herbert

Haze

Woof of the sun, ethereal gauze,
Woven of Nature's richest stuffs,
Visible heat, air-water, and dry sea,
Last conquest of the eye;
Toil of the day displayed, sun-dust,
Aerial surf upon the shores of earth,
Ethereal estuary, frith of light,
Breakers of air, billows of heat,
Fine summer spray on inland seas;
Bird of the sun, transparent-winged,
Owlet of noon, soft-pinioned,
From heath or stubble rising without song,—
Establish thy serenity o'er the fields.

Henry David Thoreau

Lady Isabel and the Elf-Knight

Fair lady Isabel sits in her bower sewing,
Aye as the gowans grow gay — *gowan*—daisy
There she heard an elf-knight blawing his horn.
The first morning in May
"If I had yon horn that I hear blawing,
And yon elf-knight to sleep in my bosom."

This maiden had scarcely these words spoken,
Till in at her window the elf-knight has luppen. — *luppen*—leaped
"It's a very strange matter, fair maiden," said he,
"I canna blaw my horn but ye call on me.

"But will ye go to yon greenwood side?
If ye canna gang, I will cause you to ride."

He leapt on a horse, and she on another,
And they rode on to the greenwood together.

"Light down, light down, lady Isabel," said he,
"We are come to the place where ye are to die."

"Hae mercy, hae mercy, kind sir, on me,
Till ance my dear father and mother I see."

"Seven king's daughters here hae I slain,
And ye shall be the eight o them."

She stroakd him sae fast, the nearer he did creep,
Wi' a sma charm she lull'd him fast asleep.

Wi his ain sword-belt sae fast as she ban him,
Wi' his ain dag-durk sae sair as she dang him.

ban—bound
dag-durk—dagger
dang—struck

"If seven king's daughters here ye hae slain,
Lye ye here a husband to them a'."

ANONYMOUS

Questions.

1. Determine as carefully as you can the tone of this ballad.
2. How much do you find out about the appearance of the Lady and the Elf-Knight?

The Lover Complaineth the Unkindness of His Love

My lute, awake! Perform the last
Labor that thou and I shall waste,
And end that I have now begun;
For when this song is sung and past,
My lute, be still, for I have done.

As to be heard where ear is none,
As led to grave in marble stone,
My song may pierce her heart as soon.
Should we then sigh or sing or moan?
  No! No! my lute, for I have done.

The rocks do not so cruelly
Repulse the waves continually
As she my suit and affection.
So that I am past remedy,
  Whereby my lute and I have done.

Proud of the spoil that thou hast got
Of simple hearts, thorough love's shot;
By whom, unkind, thou hast them won,
Think not he hath his bow forgot,
  Although my lute and I have done.

Vengeance shall fall on thy disdain
That makest but game on earnest pain.
Think not alone under the sun
Unquit to cause thy lovers plain,
  Although my lute and I have done.

unquit—unpunished
plain (noun)—plaint, lament

Perchance thee lie withered and old
The winter nights that are so cold,
Plaining in vain unto the moon.
Thy wishes then dare not be told.
  Care then who list, for I have done.

And then may chance thee to repent
The time that thou hast lost and spent
To cause thy lovers sigh and swoon.
Then shalt thou know beauty but lent,
  And wish and want as I have done.

Now cease, my lute. This is the last
Labor that thou and I shall waste,
And ended is that we begun.
Now is this song both sung and past;
  My lute, be still, for I have done.

Sir Thomas Wyatt

*Potency**

The hawk glides
in a high wind over the orchard
acre crows nest in
to the elm and oak forest south of the lake.
A southern rain spreads behind him
and
he is low in an oak
and dry as the near limbs:
he is the jump into the warm wind, and the brown glide
and the fall to green cover, braked and steep.

Down the slate
bank from the plant rain and wind lie on
the river and it
is absent of the drone of motor launches:
turbines turn the generators
at
3,600
rpm, spinning off
the rain, rushed splash of the low waterfall, and on out
to the lake the long, blue and gentle sweep.

When the trout
sinks against rock the men on the bleached
slate laugh, slipping, set
the poles down and climb the steps of the power
plant, watching a hawk fly the green
lake
woods to the river. Rain
has passed. The trout is down
beside a rock and holding under the current the
rise and quick plunge and the swift, silver leap.

GEORGE KEITHLEY

*Reprinted from *Poetry Northwest* (Spring, 1965), with the permission of the poet.

*An Equation**

For instance: $y-xa+mx^2(a^2+1)=0$

Coil upon coil, the grave serpent holds
Its implacable strict pose, under a light
Like marble. The artist's damnation, the rat of time,
Cannot gnaw this form, nor event touch it with age.
Before it was, it existed, creating the mind
Which created it, out of itself. It will dissolve
Into itself, though in another language.
Its changes are not in change, nor its times in time.

And the coiled serpent quivering under a light
Crueler than marble, unwinds slowly, altering
Deliberate the great convolutions, a dancer,
A mime on the brilliant stage. The sudden movement,
Swifter than creases of lightning, renews a statue:
There by its skin a snake rears beaten in copper.

It will not acknowledge the incense on your altars,
Nor hear at night in your room the weeping. . . .

HYAM PLUTZIK

Suggested Poems for Further Reading (ANTHOLOGY):

Anonymous, "The Twa Corbies," p. 246
Robert Burns, "To a Mouse" p. 276
William Shakespeare, "Why Is My Verse So Barren," p. 433
William Wordsworth, "The Solitary Reaper," p. 470
William Butler Yeats, "Lapis Lazuli," p. 476

Judging Poetry

11

It is easy to say that a poem by Milton, admired for over three hundred years, is a good or even great poem, for such a judgment is soundly supported by the test of time. It was not so easy in Milton's time. Judging poetry, especially new poetry, is a rather uncertain business, and the history of literature is full of instances in which otherwise good critics make judgments that have not stood up. Still, judgments are and must be made by any reader of poetry. Or, rather, a reader of poetry must respond strongly enough to a poem to want to make some kind of judgment of it even if only an impressionistic and private one.

Judgments are ordinarily supposed to be based on a disinterested assessment of objective evidence. But, they cannot be so based in poetry, except to a limited extent, because the evidence of the poem is modified by the reader's subjective response to it. Without a strong subjective response, there is no real reading of the poem and hence no real basis for judgment. The initial judgment of a poem must, as Karl Shapiro suggests, be made with "good subjective gusto," in "the first flush of feeling, when the mind is still warm with the pleasure or displeasures of the work."*

Value judgments in poetry, therefore, are not absolute, but are in many respects relative to him who makes them. A critic's judgment is governed by what he is able to respond to in a poem––what, in some cases, he has learned from the taste of his age to respond to. Some of the critics of the past who did not recognize the greatness of certain poems were simply unable to foresee modifications in the poetic tradition which would enable other readers to respond differently to these poems.

**Beyond Criticism.* Lincoln, Nebraska, 1953, p. 72.

All this does not imply that critical judgments are merely subjective or that the only sure test of the quality of a poem is the test of time. The test of time is not some mysterious process that automatically sifts out the bad from the good, but is rather the aggregate of influential individual judgments made over the years. And individual judgments are persuasive to the extent that the judge can communicate the details of his response so that others may see the poem as he does, or at least take his response seriously. This kind of communication can sometimes become an attempt to evoke impressionistically in a sort of "second creation" the effects of the work being discussed, but more usually communication of a critical insight takes the form of displaying features of the work as evidence to support the critical judgment. Literary judgments, therefore, though they may not be objective in the ordinary sense of that term, are objective enough—communicable enough—so that they can be discussed and even debated. Sound literary judgments, though necessarily depending in large measure on subjective responses for evidence, are nevertheless based on evidence that must be discoverable in the poem.

Indeed, the evidence adduced in supporting literary judgments is usually more important than the judgment. In actually giving the results of a judgment, a critic can do little more than assign a poem to broad general categories. Coleridge, for instance, in giving his reactions to some of Blake's lyrics, devised categories like this: "N.B. **I** signifies, It gave me great pleasure. **I̶** still greater—**I̶I̶**, and greater still. **O̶** in the highest degree, **o** in the lowest."* In these categories Coleridge frankly admits that he is judging them in relation to his "pleasure" with them.

Attempting to formulate slightly more "objective" categories, we might say that poetry is considered "great" if it deals with themes of fundamental human importance, gives profound insights into human values, moves us very deeply, and delights us with the perfection of its texture and form. And we could say that poetry is "good"—though not great—if it does well any but not all of the things great poetry does. Of course, merely dealing with a great theme does not necessarily make poetry even good. Good poetry might, for instance, handle a trivial subject with great charm and grace; give us an illuminating insight into something, but have a rather awkward structure; possess a harmonious relationship among its various aspects; contain a number of really memorable lines. "Bad" poetry, on the other hand, could most generally be described as failing in what it sets out to do. It may deal with great themes, but merely give platitudes; have pretensions to elegance, but merely end up being empty and "cute"; strive to be powerful by using intense imagery and succeed only in being grotesque; strive for great

---

**Collected Letters*, ed. Earl Leslie Griggs. Oxford, 1959, IV, p. 833.

simplicity and end up only as rhymed prose; or, confusing difficulty with profundity, it may say something simple in an impenetrable, over-ingenious way. Most poetry described as downright bad, particularly in our own day, relies upon stock emotional responses, usually in connection with religion, love, parents, children, death, and country, and makes tear-jerking sentimental appeals.

Categories such as these, however, are not in themselves very useful because they are so general and because they mean very little except in relation to detailed evidence from particular poems. Judgments are necessary even to apply the categories. We cannot decide, for instance, whether the imagery in a poem fails to be powerful and is only grotesque without judging it in relation to the effectiveness of the poem as a whole. For this reason judging literature becomes more a discussion of particular poems than of determining principles. And though the value of any judgment of a poem depends on the principles according to which it is being judged, it also depends very much on the perception used to produce the evidence. Whoever sets out to make a judgment of a poem, therefore, must be a perceptive reader and have a good knowledge of the various aspects of the art of poetry.

The need for sensitivity and knowledge cannot be stressed enough in learning how to judge poetry. Every instructor has had the time-consuming and distressing experience of having a student judge a poem and cite only his own obtuseness (real or assumed) as evidence: "I don't get it. I see nothing like that in there." Simple fairness requires that only when he *can* see—or understand how others can see—or at least be aware what the poet is trying to do is he justified in making a judgment, especially one he expects others to take seriously. The "good subjective gusto" mentioned by Shapiro means the reader should react to a poem with feeling and make his judgment with feeling too, but it does not imply the soundness of the principle, "I don't know much about poetry, but I know what I like." A reader will often reject something in a poem as being bad, but he ought to know what he is rejecting. In addition, if he is going to talk about his judgment, he ought to be able to make his judgment communicable. The only thing communicable in a judgment based on an unwillingness to respond to a poem is the judge's unwillingness.

To say much more than this would lead us to questions which once brought up would require more space than could be devoted to them here. Instead let us consider a few poems, some of which have enough characteristics in common to justify comparisons, so that we can try to see whether and—more important—*how* one is preferable to another. Please bear in mind that we can illustrate only one or two critical problems.

One of the things a reader of poetry discovers is that good poetry does not indulge emotions for their own sake. Good poetry is often deeply emotional, but its emotions are of a kind we can believe in and respect. Concerned as it is with the human condition, and dark as it may often be about the outlook for improvement, good poetry nevertheless expresses its feelings in a way that preserves a sense of human dignity.

Invictus

Out of the night that covers me,
Black as the Pit from pole to pole,
I thank whatever gods may be
For my unconquerable soul.

In the fell clutch of circumstance
I have not winced nor cried aloud.
Under the bludgeonings of chance
My head is bloody, but unbowed.

Beyond this place of wrath and tears
Looms but the Horror of the shade,
And yet the menace of the years
Finds, and shall find, me unafraid.

It matters not how strait the gate,
How charged with punishments the scroll,
I am the master of my fate;
I am the captain of my soul.

William Ernest Henley

Questions.

1. What seems to be the speaker's situation?
2. To whom does he seem to be talking? Is his talk appropriate for this situation?

Space and Dread and the Dark

Space and dread and the dark—
Over a livid stretch of sky
Cloud-monsters crawling, like a funeral train
Of huge, primeval presences

Stooping beneath the weight
Of some enormous, rudimentary grief;
While in the haunting loneliness
The far sea waits and wanders with a sound
As of the trailing skirts of Destiny.
Passing unseen
To some immitigable end
With her gray henchman, Death

What larve, what specter is this
Thrilling the wilderness to life
As with the Bodily shape of Fear?
What but a desperate sense,
A strong foreboding of those dim
Interminable continents, forlorn
And many-silenced, in a dusk
Inviolable utterly, and dead
As the poor dead it guddles and swarms and styes
In hugger-mugger through eternity?

Life—life—let there be life!
Better a thousand times the roaring hours
When a wave and wind,
Like the Arch-Murderer in flight
From the Avenger at his heel,
Storms through the desolate fastnesses
And wild waste places of the world!

Life—give me life until the end,
That at the very top of being,
The battle-spirit shouting in my blood,
Out of the reddest hell of the fight
I may be snatched and flung
Into the everlasting lull,
The immortal, incommunicable dream.

WILLIAM ERNEST HENLEY

Questions.

1. Apply the questions from the previous poem to this one.

On His Blindness

When I consider how my light is spent
Ere half my days in this dark world and wide,
And that one Talent which is death to hide
Lodged with me useless, though my soul more bent
To serve therewith my Maker, and present
My true account, lest He returning chide;
"Doth God exact day-labor, light denied?"
I fondly ask. But Patience, to prevent
That murmur, soon replies, "God doth not need
Either man's work or his own gifts. Who best
Bear his mild yoke, they serve him best. His state
Is kingly: thousands at his bidding speed,
And post o'er land and ocean without rest;
They also serve who only stand and wait.

JOHN MILTON

Questions.

1. Compare the speaker's situation in this poem with the situations of the speakers in the other two poems.
2. Compare his reaction with theirs.

"Invictus" presents a speaker who is self-consciously courageous. Indeed, in bragging about his ability to stand up to the blows of fate, he becomes somewhat egotistical; and the reader, instead of admiring him for his fortitude, may feel a little embarrassed at his heroic posturing. It is hard to take him as seriously as he must be taken if the poem is to move us, and the poem, instead of dramatically expressing powerful emotions, displays a ranting egotist in whose fate we have little interest. The speaker directs attention to himself alone by saying that the black night covers *him;* he compliments himself for having an unconquerable soul. He is in the grip of triteness as well as circumstance in phrases like "fell clutch," and "place of wrath and tears"; his language generally has the characteristics of high-flown oratory rather than of poetry, especially in the last two lines, so often quoted. The images become grotesque and even ludicrous as the passionate oratory fails to move us, especially in the second stanza; and the poem is so metrically regular, the rhymes so predictable that it fails to have any real music.

The second poem by Henley is much less egotistical in conception. Its tone is still rather forced, with its direct passionate cry for "Life—life—let there be life," and with its demand that the speaker may be "snatched and flung" from the fight when he dies. But the imagery, which here is used to characterize fate, eternity, and the process of life, not only the admirable state of the speaker's soul, better supports the vigorous mood of desire for intense participation in life. Moreover, the use of free verse rather than the metrically regular, even sing-song, verse of "Invictus" better suits the passionate mood. Of this poem it could be said that the imagery of the last stanza again becomes a little extreme, as in lines 32-33, but it is a better poem than "Invictus."

Like Henley's "Invictus," Milton's sonnet also shows courage, but of a deeper, quieter kind. Milton, who as a man was scarcely self-effacing, nevertheless does not represent himself in the poem egotistically. The speaker asks humbly—though with a sense that he is a man who has something to offer—what he can do now that he is blind, and the reply, from personified Patience, is directed not only to the poet but is stated as a general principle, applicable to anyone. It is up to the poet to apply the principle to himself. This poem engages us because we can admire and believe in the speaker and because everything in the poem not only builds this admiration, but expands the context and says something serious about man's relationship to God.

It so happens that Henley suffered from serious physical disability, and Milton became blind. Do those facts affect our judgment of the poems in any way? It may seem cruel to criticize Henley's poems adversely when he was expressing in them some of the admirable, brave determination he showed in his own troubled life. To allow his disability to affect our criticism of his poems, however, would be to confuse criticism with biography. We may very well admire Henley as a man, and we may even read some of his poems biographically to support our admiration of him. When we judge his poems as works of art, however, we must not let sympathy confuse biography and art. Milton asks no such sympathy. He treats his blindness in a way that makes it represent any kind of disabling tragedy to a person, shifting the attention away from himself to man's relationship with God. To be sure, the poet's biography often is helpful in understanding a poem, and knowing something of the circumstances in which a poem was written may contribute to our appreciation of it. But criticism assumes that the poet published his work to be judged on its own merits.

The poems in this chapter have been of uneven quality, and it was possible to pick out some that were better than others. It might even be possible to rank this group of poems along some sort of scale in a way that would be reasonably consistent with general opinion. Many students seem to think that if literary criticism cannot discriminate precisely the relative degrees of goodness or badness of poems, it is merely subjective, and anyone's judgment is as good as anyone else's. Judgments of poetry are always to some extent subjective, and merely removing the authors' names, as is sometimes done, will remove only the subjective influence of brand labels. The more important kinds of subjectivity will still be left. The data on the basis of which judgments are made, for instance, are the affective responses of the reader. And these, furthermore, are not directly communicable, but must be communicated by making someone else respond to the poem in the way that the judge does. This is not to suggest that judgments do not, after all, mean very much, but merely to warn against expecting of literary judgments the kind of artificial precision found in judging cats. Aristotle has a principle that states that one ought to expect in investigating anything only as much precision as the subject is capable of, and with poetry the precision to be expected is not very great. Judging poetry is a more complicated matter than judging automobiles, surely, and even there general agreement as to the order of excellence is lacking.

Some poems could be thought of as being great, some good, some downright bad. But when we attempt to discriminate between two good poems, to decide which is better, we start to run into trouble. Each one offers something that the other does not, and in a way that makes comparative judgment uncertain. Consider, for instance, the following two poems.

*Shortening Days at the Homestead**

The first fire since the summer is lit, and is smoking into the room;
The sun-rays thread it through, like woof-lines in a loom.
Sparrows spurt from the hedge, whom misgivings appall
That winter did not leave last year for ever, after all.
Like shock-headed urchins, spiny-haired,
Stand pollard willows, their twigs just bared.

Who is this coming with pondering pace
Black and ruddy, with white embossed,
His eyes being black, and ruddy face
And the marge of his hair like morning frost?
It's the cider-maker,
And apple tree-shaker,
And behind him on wheels, in readiness,
His mill, and tubs, and vat, and press.

THOMAS HARDY

Questions.

1. Discuss the appropriateness of the rhyme, meter, and sound effects of this poem in relation to its subject matter.
2. Decide on the tone of the poem, and observe any shifts in tone from the first stanza to the second.
3. Are the similes in lines 2 and 5 fresh and apt to the circumstances described in the poem?
4. What does the cider-maker come to represent in the poem?

The picture of Fall presented in this poem is quite concrete, although it is not associated with a specific place or time. The smoking fireplace, the sparrows, the leaf-fallen willows are easily seen in our mind's eye.

In contrast to the specific picture of Fall in "Shortening Days" is the more general reference to the season in the following poem.

*Cold Summer**

Twilight is blue for seven weeks
Upon its borders, and beyond
Pure darkness splits to dagger-peaks
Of flawed and shivered diamond.

Between slim hills the atmosphere
Swims cold as wine in silver jugs;
The summers live minute and clear,
Coloured like Persian praying-rugs.

She whirls above this circumscribed
And patterned carpet, with a pair
Of tame attendant pigeons, bribed
By corn as yellow as her hair.

Elinor Wylie

Questions.

1. Compare and contrast the sound effects of this poem with the one preceding it, and try to arrive at some kind of judgment about the differences between the two poems and the aptness of the effects in the respective poems.

---

2. Discuss the similes in the second line from the point of view of vividness and appropriateness.
3. To what do the "its" of line 2 and the "She" of line 9 refer?

A hasty glance at the diction of the two poems might suggest that the first poem uses a simpler vocabulary than the second to give its more familiar picture. But a closer look reveals that the most unusual word in the second poem is probably *circumscribed,* which we would be likely to know at least as well as *pondering* and *embossed* in the first poem. What does make the diction of the second poem seem a bit strange is not the words, but the kind of comparisons in it. The first poem adheres to familiar details (though the traveling cider-maker has almost completely passed from the country scene), whereas the comparisons of the second poem are exotic: wine swimming in silver jugs and summers "Coloured like Persian praying-rugs."

The diction of the poems affects their tone. The homely comparisons of the first poem give it a kind of colloquial feeling as though the author were taking us into his confidence and at the same time expecting us to be familiar with the natural sequence of events he is describing. We are pleased, if somewhat stifled, by the smoky room, amused by the sparrows and the comparison of willows with urchins, and our appetites may be whetted by the thought of the fresh cider about to be pressed from the crisp new apples. Appeals are made to our senses of sight, smell, hearing, and taste.

Elinor Wylie's diction affects the tone of her poem in a different way. She is not revealing to her reader the familiar paraphernalia of a usual late summer, but she is attempting to convey how different this particular cold summer is from those her reader may be familiar with. She therefore emphasizes the strange way in which twilight comes and is succeeded by a stranger dark. The vigor of the air of this unusual summer is conveyed in the comparison with cold wine in silver jugs, which can be tasted as well as felt. The smoky haze suggested by the opening comparison of Hardy's poem is replaced by the "minute and clear" days *(summers)* of the second poem, suggesting the surprise with which each of these summer days is greeted. The unusual coloring that the clear pure air allows the landscape to assume is effectively expressed in the comparison of the landscape to a Persian prayer rug. The poet seems to be telling us that we have never seen a summer quite like this.

Which poem is better? In this case a comparative judgment is difficult, and does not seem of overwhelming importance, because both poems are good. Trying to rank them objectively is not only hard but rather beside the point, for though they are on a similar subject, they are quite different. Hardy shows us something familiar—at least to readers of his time—and

Miss Wylie, with her brighter, more intense imagery, shows us something new.

Compare the following two poems, both narrative, telling tragic stories of the death of men whose women wait for them. One is a poem by a sophisticated poet, the other a folk-ballad. Which is the better poem? What kind of evidence is relevant in making the decision, if one is possible?

*The Mill**

The miller's wife had waited long,
The tea was cold, the fire was dead;
And there might yet be nothing wrong
In how he went and what he said:
"There are no millers anymore,"
Was all that she had heard him say;
And he had lingered at the door
So long that it seemed yesterday.

Sick with a fear that had no form
She knew that she was there at last;
And in the mill there was a warm
And mealy fragrance of the past.
What else there was would only seem
To say again what he had meant;
And what was hanging from a beam
Would not have heeded where she went.

And if she though it followed her,
She may have reasoned in the dark
That one way of the few there were
Would hide her and would leave no mark:
Black water, smooth above the weir
Like starry velvet in the night,
Though ruffled once, would soon appear
The same as ever to the sight.

EDWIN ARLINGTON ROBINSON

---

*Reprinted with permission of The Macmillan Company from *The Three Taverns* by E. A. Robinson. Copyright 1920 The Macmillan Company, renewed 1948 by Ruth Nivison.

Questions.

1. Does this poem overstate or understate the story it tells?
2. Is the description of the sequence of events sufficient to arouse the reader's interest and sympathy?
3. Describe the sequence of events between stanza 1 and stanza 2. How do you know what happened at this point?

Rare Willy

"Willy's rare, and Willy's fair,
And Willy's wondrous bonny;
And Willy heght to marry me,
Gin e'er he marryd ony.

heght—promised

"Yestreen I made by bed fu' braid,
The night I'll make it narrow,
For a' the live-long winter's night
I lie twin'd of my marrow.

braid—broad, wide
twin'd—deprived
marrow—mate

"O came you by yon water-side?
Pu'd you the rose or lilly?
Or came you by yon meadow green?
Or saw you my sweet Willy?"

She sought him east, she sought him west,
She sought him braid and narrow;
Sine, in the clifting of a craig,
She found him drown'd in Yarrow.

clifting—cleft

ANONYMOUS

The greatest value of making judgments for the reader of poetry who is not a professional student of literature lies not so much in the conclusions arrived at as in the process of making the judgments. The primary end of reading is not making judgments, but responding so fully to the work that judgment is a part of that response. Judgment is a by-product, a sort of formulation of the value that is felt in reading the poem. Such values may be talked about; indeed, one of the pleasures of reading poetry is talking about it with other people. And very likely among a group of people there will be a certain amount of general agreement as to which poems are better than others. The important thing, however, is not the amount of agreement, but the degree of involvement in passing judgments—an involvement that includes not only an intense subjective response but brings to bear on the poem a good deal of knowledge about the art of poetry.

Any judgment one makes may be modified later as one gets to know the poem better. Still, any judgment that is not at some point heavily influenced by a strong direct response to the poem is going to be based on weak and wavering data; and anything that such a judgment can boast in the way of cool clinical detachment is going to be vitiated by not dealing with what matters most: a vital relationship between reader and poem.

Poems for Further Study:

Come Not, When I am Dead

Come not, when I am dead,
To drop thy foolish tears upon my grave,
To trample round my fallen head
And vex the unhappy dust thou wouldst not save.
There let the wind sweep by and the plover cry;
But thou, go by.
Child, if it were thine error or thy crime
I care no longer, being all unblessed
Wed whom thou wilt, but I am sick of time,
And I desire to rest.
Pass on, weak heart, and leave me where I lie;
Go by, go by.

ALFRED LORD TENNYSON

Questions.

1. To whom is the poem addressed?
2. What is meant by "I am sick of time" in line 9?
3. What, specifically, would the "Child" have to do to "save" the person speaking in the poem?

Song

Absent from thee I languish still,
Then ask me not, when I return?
The straying fool 'twill plainly kill
To wish all day, all night to mourn.

Dear, from thine arms then let me fly,
That my fantastic mind may prove
The torments it deserves to try,
That tears my fixed heart from my love.

When, wearied with a world of woe,
To thy safe bosom I retire,
Where love and peace and honor flow,
May I contend there expire.

Lest once more wandering from that heaven
I fall on some base heart unblessed,
Faithless to thee, false, unforgiven,
And lose my everlasting rest.

John Wilmot, Earl of Rochester

Questions.

1. Where does the speaker place the blame for his wandering?
2. What is the speaker's attitude toward himself, and how does it differ from the attitude of the speaker toward himself in "Come Not, When I Am Dead"?
3. Paraphrase carefully and fully the compliment to the lady in the final line of the poem.

Suggested Poems for Further Reading (ANTHOLOGY):

William Ellery Channing, "And the Hermit Sat, and Told His Beads," p. 282
T. S. Eliot, "The Love Song of J. Alfred Prufrock," p. 331
George Meredith, "We Saw the Swallows," p. 398
Sir Philip Sidney, "Song from Arcadia," p. 438
William Wordsworth, "Elegiac Stanzas," p. 467

Hearing Poetry and Reading Aloud

12

Schools have recently placed much emphasis on speeding up our reading so that students can get through their lessons faster and executives can read more reports. Rapid reading is very useful for material that can be read rapidly, but poetry is not of that kind. Poetry must be heard, either by the ear as it is read aloud or by the mind as it is read silently, and therefore, cannot be read any faster than it can be spoken. It would be just as unthinkable to speed through a poem as it would be to ride through an art gallery on a motor scooter or to hear symphonies by playing LP records at 78 rpm. Musicians who are able to curl up with a score and read it silently—which they rarely do for esthetic pleasure—hear it mentally no faster than the tempo at which it would be performed. Readers of poetry must similarly hear poetry no faster than it can be read aloud if they do not actually read it aloud.

There are many fine readings of poems recorded by actors who keep their ability to project emotion in check just enough to allow the poem to be heard as a poem, not realizing it too completely as a dramatic performance, yet giving it some emotional heightening. By and large, however, the most successful readings of poems are those by poets themselves, and in these days of the tape recorder we are fortunate in having recorded readings of virtually all recent major poets. Though not all poets do an equally good job, even the poorer readers somehow make their poems come to life.*

What makes these readings, often given in tight cracked voices by men and women who have obviously never had a speech lesson in their lives, seem more convincing than some of the performances by professional readers? It is difficult to generalize, for the manner of the poets' reading varies, from Vachel Lindsay's hypnotic chanting (of "The Congo"), to the lyrically sustained periods of Dylan Thomas, to the rather dry understatement favored by others. It could be said, however, that in the reading of most poets we feel not only the rhythmical pulse of the sentence, but of the line. The foot furnishes the beat heard throughout the poem, even, or perhaps especially, when the poet makes variations of the foot. This beat is rather like the metrical beat in music: in poetry, as in music, the beat is the meter, not the rhythm. The structural rhythmic pulse that makes the poem move is the line, the equivalent in poetry to the rhythm of the phrase in music.

When next you hear a poet reading his own work, notice the attention he gives to the line. He will often pause ever so slightly at the end of the line, even when grammatical sense makes the line run on to the next one. Or if he does not pause noticeably, he will somehow give the line a rhythmical cadence that lets the listener feel where it ends, especially in unrhymed verse. In a reading in which the emphasis is placed on rendering the dramatic emotion of the words, which actors are trained to do, there is an understandable tendency to slight the line, for in building up a convincing dramatic mood the interruption caused by the pauses at the ends of lines is a hindrance. Students of speech are sometimes told to disregard the line early in their preparation of a poem for oral reading in order to develop a feeling for continuity. We do not think this is good advice, even as a means to develop smoothness in delivery, for it makes poetry into metrical prose, and deëmphasizes the rhythmic pulse. Most college productions of Shakespeare tend to slight the line, and the audience gets little of the rhythmic effect of iambic pentameter because there are no rhymes to mark the ends of the lines.

---

*Recordings of poets reading their own work are now widely available. The recording companies that have produced most of the recordings of poets are Caedmon, Carillon, Spoken Arts, and Angel, all available on long playing records in music shops. Particular disks, with the identifying numbers, may be found in the *Schwann Long Playing Record Catalog*, published monthly by W. Schwann, 137 Newberry Street, Boston 16, Mass., and available in record shops. The most ambitious recording project in poetry recently is the *Yale Series of Recorded Poets,* 202 Davenport Ave., New Haven, Conn., available on subscription through Carillon Records. Other recordings are to be had from the Library of Congress and from The National Council of Teachers of English, 704 South Fifth Street, Champaign, Ill.

Recordings of older poetry, read by actors, can be found on many labels in the Schwann catalog, under "Poetry, Prose, Speech."

No doubt the advice is given to counteract a common tendency to stop completely at the ends of lines. This is just as bad, of course, for such stops destroy the overall rhythmical movement of this poem. To pause long at the ends of lines is just as unthinkable as to pause at the ends of phrases in a song and for the same reason. Stopping completely in either chops the work up into little pieces.

Most of the time the lines will take care of themselves, for though the line in poetry is an important rhythmical unit, it is not arbitrarily imposed on the sense but usually reflects the movement of the language, of sense. In Keat's sonnet "On First Looking into Chapman's Homer," for instance, the first line says the speaker has travelled; the second line, giving the second predicate in the sentence, says he has seen many "goodly states and kingdoms"; the third line starts a new assertion, that he has been round "many western islands"; the fourth line entirely consists of a relative clause modifying islands. Because the ends of the first two lines are marked by punctuation, a pause is natural. But a slight pause is appropriate even at the end of the third line, despite the lack of punctuation, because the relative clause starts in the next line.

Much have I travelled in the realms of gold,
And many goodly states and kingdoms seen;
Round many western islands have I been
Which bards in fealty to Apollo hold.

Rhyme also helps to mark the ends of the line, the most notable example of this being the heroic couplet in which most eighteenth century poetry is written. Indeed, in this poetry the sense is usually made to coincide exactly with the movement of the couplets, as it is in the following passage from Pope's "The Rape of the Lock":

Hither the heroes and the nymphs resort,
To taste awhile the pleasures of a Court;
In various talk th'instructive hours they past,
Who gave the ball, or paid the visit last;
One speaks the glory of the British Queen,
And one describes a charming Indian screen;
A third interprets motions, looks, and eyes;
At ev'ry word a reputation dies.

When Keats uses the iambic pentameter couplet, however, he runs the sense on from one line to the next and softens the rhymes by adding an extra, unaccented syllable to the rhyme words (a "feminine ending"). A passage from *Endymion* will illustrate this:

A thing of beauty is a joy forever:
Its loveliness increases; it will never
Pass into nothingness; but still will keep
A bower quiet for us, and a sleep
Full of sweet dreams, and health, and quiet breathing.
Therefore, on every morrow, are we wreathing
A flowery band to bind us to the earth,
Spite of despondence, of the inhuman dearth
Of noble natures, of the gloomy days,
Of all the unhealthy and o'er-darkened ways
Made for our searching: . . . .

In reading this verse aloud one should probably not give any special attention to the line endings, because they are marked by tight rhymes in a very familiar verse pattern; the rhythmical unit of the line would, therefore, be heard quite easily in almost any reading. However, if there is any doubt as to whether the rhythmical pulse of the line will be heard in your reading, pause a little—but not so much as to destroy the flow of sense.

Another characteristic of the reading of most poets is their rather slow, quite regular pace. At least it is slow a good bit of the time. When most students are asked to read in class, they read much too fast and erratically, destroying the metrical beat and therefore the variations from that beat which give the line its internal rhythmical interest and which often also emphasize the key words. If one's ear is faulty or if he lacks confidence in being able to get the proper pace for any particular poem, he does much better to err on the slow rather than the fast side in reading out loud.

Reading quite slowly will also help one to savor the words. Poets take great care to choose the best words they can find, and in their own readings seem to enjoy speaking them, enunciating them clearly with due regard for their tonal and rhythmical characteristics.

Perhaps this rather deliberate reading and the concern for the unit of the line at first gives the impression that the poet is greatly underplaying. This is especially apt to be the impression if one has become used to hearing quavery-voiced renditions of poetry on the radio, against a background of completely unrelated music with its own rhythmical patterns detracting from the poetry. Except for, notably, Dylan Thomas, who almost intoned his poetry with his rich Welsh baritone, most comtemporary poets do not modulate the pitch of their voices very much, nor do they very obviously emphasize words by varying the intensity of their voices. But the initial impression of emotional flatness is misleading. The music of poetry is subtle music, and if T. S. Eliot or Robert Frost sound a bit subdued on first hearing, we can only say, "Hear them again." Very quickly one begins to hear the quiet music of the verse, the delicate tensions among the metrical beat, the rhythmic pulse of sense, and the cadence of the line.

It is clearly as impossible to demonstrate oral reading of poetry on paper as it would be to try to tell someone how to play the French horn. And no doubt you will get some demonstration in class. Nevertheless, perhaps we might consider one poem briefly from this point of view in the hope that doing so might alert you to a few things worth considering in reading aloud.

Days

Daughters of Time, the hypocritic Days,
Muffled and dumb like barefoot dervishes,
And marching single in an endless file,
Bring diadems and faggots in their hands.
To each they offer gifts after his will,
Bread, kingdoms, stars, and sky that holds them all.
I, in my pleached garden, watched the pomp,
Forgot my morning wishes, hastily
Took a few herbs and apples, and the Day
Turned and departed silent. I, too late,
Under her solemn fillet saw the scorn.

RALPH WALDO EMERSON

The first seven lines all come to marked pauses at the end, with lesser pauses in the caesuras within. However in lines 8 and 9 Emerson varies his rhythmical pulse. In line 8 he makes us pause quite clearly after the comma, and he weakens the sense of line there by running the sense strongly into the next line. Doing this does not destroy the line as a rhythmical unit, for in reading the poem aloud one must still hear the line. What it does is introduce a tension between the irregularity imposed on the line by grammatical sense and the regular pulse of the lines that has been firmly established in the first seven lines of the poem. In reading line 8 and going on to line 9, we should try to hear both the regular rhythm and the natural rhythm dictated by grammatical sense. At the end of line 8 we probably should pause very little, only giving a hint of the end of the line by a slight suspension of the voice or perhaps a lilt, and then go on to the next line. Emerson helps us mark the end of the line by his use of the dactylic *hastily*, so it seems almost impossible to avoid giving the slight suspension that is needed.

Line 9, similarly, is interrupted by the comma, and again the sense runs on. Once more, however, we should hear, and in reading make heard, the end of the line. And once again Emerson gives us some help, this time by giving us one and a half iambic feet after the pause at the comma; the three words *and the Day* are enough to make the pause seem like a caesura, though perhaps it is not really a caesura since it occurs in the middle of a foot. But it gives enough of the effect of a caesura to allow us to pause naturally slightly after *Day* and thus mark the end of the line.

Line 10 contains a period, requiring a dropping of the voice for a full stop. Again the sense runs on to the next line. Once more, however, the poet allows us to keep the line in mind, this time by introducing the parenthetical phrase *too late* and setting it off by commas. We must pause after *I* and again after *late*, with the result that though the sense does run on, we are made to pause slightly at the end of the line anyway. The last line moves steadily in the rhythm of the first seven to close the poem.

Very likely the poet deliberately—or with the unconscious craft that comes with long practice—altered the rhythm in lines 8 to 10, because at this point in the poem the speaker gives an account of having been out of step with time, wasting time. The days move steadily, silently, and only he who does his duty is in harmony with them. The speaker, however, forgot his morning wishes and failed to do his work and thus ceased to be in harmony with time. For the rhythmic irregularity to be heard, of course, the basic rhythm must be kept sounding, though faintly, so that the tension here is felt.

As an exercise, you might try reading this poem aloud in serveral different ways, to test our suggestions and to see which way the sound best fits the patterns of imagery and sense. You might also try reading other poems, especially sonnets, which are tightly constructed poems and often have rhythmical variations even more subtle than those we have been describing in "Days." Anyone who wants to learn to read poetry well can profit greatly from hearing himself on a tape recorder.

A most curious thing happens when one learns to hear and read poetry aloud: quite often a reader begins to understand it better as he hears it better. At least it seems so, and even seeming to understand the poem means that one is getting to know it directly through experience with it so that further understanding will come more easily than it otherwise would have. Abraham Lincoln, who loved to read poetry aloud, also read particularly difficult government documents this way to understand them better.

It is, in fact, hard to separate understanding a poem from hearing it. A poem combines ideas, images, drama, story, with its own music. It is possible, of course, to talk of the various elements of poetry in isolation from each other; we have done so throughout this book. But doing so disregards, for purposes of analysis of the parts, the way in which the poem must be apprehended as a whole. That way is aurally, in time. One must hear it, and while hearing it feel, see, smell, and otherwise imaginatively sense the images it evokes, make the metaphorical and symbolic connections that it suggests, and frame one's mind to its ideas. All this must finally be done *in time*, for poetry, like music, is a temporal art. At some point in our coming to know a poem, we must hear it, in time. And one of the best ways to hear it and learn to hear other poems is to read aloud, quietly, thoughtfully, carefully, allowing the music of the poem, more than the sound of our voices, to reach our ears.

Poems for Reading Aloud:

From *Amoretti*

Men call you fayre, and you doe credit it,
for that your selfe ye dayly such doe see:
but the trew fayre, that is the gentle wit,
and vertuous mind, is much more praysd of me.
For all the rest, how ever fayre it be,
shall turne to nought and loose that glorious hew:
but onely that is permanent and free
from frayle corruption, that doth flesh ensew.
That is true beautie: that doth argue you
to be divine and borne of heavenly seed:
deriv'd from that fayre Spirit, from whom al true
And perfect beauty did at first proceed.
He onely fayre, and what he fayre hath made,
all other fayre lyke flowers untymely fade.

EDMUND SPENSER

From *Doctor Faustus*

Re-enter HELEN.

Faustus. Was this the face that launched a thousand ships,
And burnt the topless towers of Ilium?—
Sweet Helen, make me immortal with a kiss.—
[*Kisses her.*]

Her lips suck forth my soul: see where it
flies!—
Come, Helen, come, give me my soul again.
Here will I dwell, for heaven is in these lips,
And all is dross that is not Helena.
I will be Paris, and for love of thee,
Instead of Troy, shall Wittenberg be sacked
And I will combat with weak Menelaus,
And wear thy colors on my pluméd crest;
Yes, I will wound Achilles in the heel.
And then return to Helen for a kiss.
O, thou art fairer than the evening air
Clad in the beauty of a thousand stars;
Brighter art thou than flaming Jupiter
When he appeared to hapless Semele;
More lovely than the monarch of the sky
In wanton Arethusa's azured arms;
And none but thou shalt be my paramour!

CHRISTOPHER MARLOWE

stinging
gold swarms
upon the spires
silver

chants the litanies the
great bells are ringing with rose
the lewd fat bells

and a tall
wind
is dragging
the
sea

with

dream

–S

E. E. CUMMINGS*

---

*Copyright 1923, 1951, by E. E. Cummings. Reprinted from his volume *Poems 1923-1924* by permission of Harcourt, Brace & World, Inc.

Questions.

1. E. E. Cummings utilizes the typographic placement of the poem on the page to reinforce its effect and to help the reader to hear it. Does this device seem to work?
2. Read the poem aloud several different ways. Is the one suggested by the typography the best?

Suggested Poems for Further Reading (ANTHOLOGY):

George Noel Gordon, Lord Byron, "When We Two Parted," p. 279
Thomas Hood, "I Remember, I Remember," p. 361
A. E. Housman, "Along the Field," p. 363
John Keats, "Lines on the Mermaid Tavern," p. 373
Alfred, Lord Tennyson, "The Splendor Falls on Castle Walls," p. 452

Three Poets at Work

Three Poets at Work

"How do you go about writing a poem anyway?" "Did the poet really mean to put all those things into the poem?" These are questions that seem to be asked in every introductory course in poetry, and they are fair questions which deserve an answer. Unfortunately, it is not possible to describe the process in such a way that the description will be applicable to all poets. The writing of poetry, like any other creative process, seems at times rather mysterious, even to poets. A part of it is just plain hard work, but work alone will not produce poetry.

To clear up a little of the mystery at least, we have enlisted the aid of the best authorities we could find: some poets themselves, talking about their art. As you read you might notice what is common in their experience and what is unique.

From The Name and Nature of Poetry.

A. E. Housman

Poetry indeed seems to me more physical than intellectual. A year or two ago, in common with others, I received from America a request that I would define poetry. I replied that I could no more define poetry than a terrier can define a rat, but that I thought we both recognized the object by the symptoms which it provokes in us. One of these symptoms was described in connexion with another object by Eliphaz the Temanite: 'A spirit passed before my face: the hair of my flesh stood up.' Experience has taught me, when I am shaving of a morning, to keep watch over my thoughts, because, if a line of poetry strays into my memory, my skin bristles so that the razor ceases to act. This particular symptom is accompanied by a shiver down the spine; there is another which consists in a constriction of the throat and a precipitation of water to the eyes; and there is a third which I can only describe by borrowing a phrase from one of Keats's last letters, where he says, speaking of Fanny Brawne, 'everything that reminds me of her goes through me like a spear.' The seat of this sensation is the pit of the stomach.

My opinions on poetry are necessarily tinged, perhaps I should say tainted, by the circumstance that I have come into contact with it on two sides. We were saying a while ago that poetry is a very wide term, and inconveniently comprehensive: so comprehensive is it that is embraces two books, fortunately not large ones, of my own. I know how this stuff came into existence; and though I have no right to assume that any other poetry came into existence in the same way, yet I find reason to believe that some poetry, and quite good poetry, did. Wordsworth for instance says that poetry is the spontaneous overflow of powerful feelings, and Burns has left us this confession, 'I have two or three times in my life composed from the wish rather than the impulse, but I never succeeded to any purpose.' In short I think that the production of poetry, in its first stage, is less an active than a passive and involuntary process; and if I were obliged, not to define poetry, but to name the class of thing to which it belongs, I should call it a secretion; whether a natural secretion, like turpentine in the fir, or a morbid secretion, like the pearl in the oyster. I think that my own case, though I may not deal with the material so cleverly as the oyster does, is the latter; because I have seldom written poetry unless I was rather out of health, and the experience, though pleasurable, was generally agitating and

---

From *The Name and Nature of Poetry* by A. E. Housman, Cambridge University Press, 1933.

exhausting. If only that you may know what to avoid, I will give some account of the process.

Having drunk a pint of beer at luncheon—beer is a sedative to the brain, and my afternoons are the least intellectual portion of my life—I would go out for a walk of two or three hours. As I went along, thinking of nothing in particular, only looking at things around me and following the progress of the seasons, there would flow into my mind, with sudden and unaccountable emotion, sometimes a line or two of verse, sometimes a whole stanza at once, accompanied, not preceded, by a vague notion of the poem which they were destined to form a part of. Then there would usually be a lull of an hour or so, then perhaps the spring would bubble up again. I say bubble up, because, so far as I could make out, the source of the suggestions thus proffered to the brain was an abyss which I have already had occasion to mention, the pit of the stomach. When I got home I wrote them down, leaving gaps, and hoping that further inspiration might be forthcoming another day. Sometimes it was, if I took my walks in a receptive and expectant frame of mind; but sometimes the poem had to be taken in hand and completed by the brain, which was apt to be a matter of trouble and anxiety, involving trial and disappointment, and sometimes ending in failure. I happen to remember distinctly the genesis of the piece which stands last in my first volume.* Two of the stanzas, I do not say which, came into my head, just as they are printed, while I was crossing the corner of Hampstead Heath between Spaniard's Inn and the footpath to Temple Fortune. A third stanza came with a little coaxing after tea. One more was needed, but it did not come: I had to turn to and compose it myself, and that was a laborious business. I wrote it thirteen times, and it was more than a twelvemonth before I got it right.

***I Hoed and Trenched and Weeded**

I hoed and trenched and weeded,
And took the flowers to fair:
I brought them home unheeded;
The hue was not the wear.

So up and down I sow them
For lads like me to find,
When I shall lie below them,
A dead man out of mind.

Some seed the birds devour,
And some the season mars,
But here and there will flower
The solitary stars

And fields will yearly bear them
As light-leaved spring comes on,
And luckless lads will wear them
When I am dead and gone.

A. E. Housman

How a Poem Is Made.

C. Day Lewis

When I talk to schoolboys and schoolgirls about poetry, they often ask, "What is inspiration?" or "Do poets have to be inspired before they can write a poem?" or, point-blank, "Are *you* inspired?" Those are difficult questions to answer (especially the third one!). But I'm going to try and answer them now—to give you some idea of what goes on in a poet's mind when he is composing a poem.

First you must realize that a great deal of the creating of a poem has already taken place before the poet reaches for his pen and starts writing anything down: and I don't mean by this that he makes up most of the poem "in his head," though some poets do. A poem is created by three stages.

1. The seed or germ of a poem strikes the poet's imagination. It may come in the form of a strong but vague feeling, a particular experience, or an idea: sometimes it first appears as an image: perhaps even—as a poetic phrase or a whole line of verse—already clothed in words. The poet jots down the idea or image in his notebook, or just makes a mental note of it. Then he probably forgets all about it.

2. But the seed of the poem has passed into him, into the part of him we call "the unconcious mind." There it grows and begins to take shape (together, maybe, with other poetic "seeds", for a poet may have any number of poems growing inside him at once), till the moment comes when it is ready to be born. For a poem, this second stage may take a few days only or it may take years.

From *Poetry For You* by C. Day Lewis, Harold Matson Company, Inc., 1944.

3. The poet feels an urgent desire to write a poem. It's often an actual physical feeling: I myself get it in my stomach; it's like a mixture of the feeling I have there when I'm hungry and the one I have when I'm particularly excited or frightened about something that's just going to happen to me. Now the poem is beginning to be born. The poet sits very quietly—or he may stride all over the country side at five miles an hour, or go for a ride on a bus—whatever helps him best to concentrate on getting the poem out of himself. He recognizes, in it, the seed which first came to him weeks or months before, which he may have forgotten all about in the meanwhile; but the seed has grown and developed in a remarkable way.

Stage 3 is where the poem bangs at the door, so to speak, and demands to be let out. What comes out first is not the finished poem, though: it is the general shape and idea of the poem, sometimes a whole stanza ready-made, seldom more than that. This *is* where the hard work of writing a poem begins—and it is very hard work indeed, I can tell you. The poet has to get the rest of the poem out, to shape it, to choose every word in it as carefully as you would choose a baseball bat or a new dress for yourself. Some poems are born more easily than others: but there's nearly always a certain amount of hard work about it, and often it's so hard that the poet may take hours—or even days—to write one single line that really satisfies him.

The coal that glows and fades

So don't get the idea that "inspiration" means a great golden flood of words pouring into the poet's mind and marshaling themselves neatly into lines and stanzas. Inspiration is when the first seed of a poem strikes root in him. You'll notice I used the phrase "strikes root": a poet may have many experiences, receive many ideas and images, which *could* be seeds of poems, but somehow they don't strike root—don't get deep enough into his imagination to fertilize it. And he can never tell *which* of his experiences is going to form itself into a poem, until the poem actually starts asking to be born. We might fairly apply the word "inspiration" to this moment of the poetic process too—the moment when, with eager excitement, the poet realizes he is ready to create a poem. The best way I can describe this moment is to say that it's rather like switching on your radio to get some distant station: you move the dials, oh so delicately, there is a long silence, the instrument begins to warm up, and at last a faint voice is heard—words growing gradually more easy to hear and understand.

Where this inspiration comes from, nobody really knows. But obviously, just as you need a radio to receive the sound waves sent out by a broadcasting station, so the poet needs a sensitive apparatus inside himself to receive the messages of inspiration. This apparatus is the poetic imagination. Everyone possesses some imagination: but the poet's has to be developed in special ways. . . . You develop a muscle by exercising it. And the poet develops his imagination by exercising it.

He does this partly by writing poetry: he gets into the *habit* of writing poetry, and this habit is one of the things that distinguishes a real professional poet from the person who just writes a poem now and then for fun. He does it, also, by constantly playing with words, just as a conjuror absent-mindedly plays with coins to keep his hand in: you can never be a poet unless you are fascinated by words—their sounds and shapes and meanings—and have them whirling about in your head all the time. Above all, the poet develops his poetic faculty through contemplation—that is to say, by looking steadily both at the world outside him and the things that happen inside him, by using all his senses to *feel* the wonder, the sadness, and the excitement of life, and by trying all the time to grasp the mysterious pattern which underlies it. Yet, however devoted he is to his profession, however much he contemplates and practices, however skilful a craftsman in words he may become, a poet can never command inspiration. It may stay with him for months, or desert him for years. He does not know when it will come—or go. As Shelley said,

> The mind in creation is as a fading coal, which some invisible influence, like an inconstant wind, awakens to transitory brightness.

"The flags, the roundabouts, the gala day"

Now I'm going to take you behind the scenes and show you how one of my own poems was written. I think it will help you to understand what I've just been saying. Here is the poem:

Children look down upon the morning-gray
Tissue of mist that veils a valley's lap:
Their fingers itch to tear it and unwrap
The flags, the roundabouts, the gala day.
They watch the spring rise inexhaustibly—
A breathing thread out of the eddied sand,
Sufficient to their day: but half their mind
Is on the sailed and glittering estuary.
Fondly we wish their mist might never break,
Knowing it hides so much that best were hidden:
We'd chain them by the spring, lest it should broaden
For them into a quicksand and a wreck.
But they slip through our fingers like the source,
Like mist, like time that has flagged out their course.

The seed of this poem was a strong feeling I had about my own two children. It is a feeling most parents have, at one time or another—a feeling of sadness that their children must grow up, must leave their protection and go out into the dangerous and difficult world. When you are young, you sometimes resent your parents having that feeling: you *want* to grow up and be independent.

Now, if you look at the poem again, you'll see there are two themes, or subjects, in it—the original one, my *own* feeling, which comes out in the last six lines; and the *children's* feeling of impatience and expectation, which comes out in the first eight. These two themes are intended to balance and contrast with each other.

Before I actually start writing a poem, I often find a line of verse comes into my head—a line which gives me a clue to the theme and pattern which the poem will develop: a sort of key-line. When I sat down to begin this sonnet, such a line of verse at once came into my head. That line (it is the only one I didn't have to work for) was "The flags, the roundabouts, the gala day." I thought about this line, and saw that is was an image of a fête or a fair, the sort of thing a child looks forward to; obviously, it symbolized (that is, "stood for") the grown-up world which a child is so impatient to enter. The idea of *impatience* then added some more lines—the first three. Here, the early-morning mist covering the valley represents the veil which the children wish to tear away, as they would tear the tissue paper off a birthday present—the veil which shuts them off from the grown-up world. The image came out of my memory, recalled from a day several years ago when I was taking my children to school in Devonshire, and we paused at the top of a hill and saw the whole of the valley below covered with mist: I remembered thinking at the time that it looked like tissue paper, but I'd forgotten all about the incident until I began to write this poem.

Next, I wanted a second image-sequence, as a variation on the theme expressed in the first four lines. You'll find it in lines 5 to 8—the picture of a spring bubbling up out of the earth, and the children bending down to watch its "breathing thread." The word "breathing" gives you a clue to the meaning of this passage: the spring represents life near its source, *young* life; and the children are only half satisfied with it; "half their mind" is looking forward to the time when their life will have broadened out, as a stream broadens into an estuary, and becomes more important and exciting. The image of the spring, like that of the mist, came out of my memory: it was a particular spring, near a country house in Ireland, which used to fascinate me as a child; I remember spending hours watching it, wondering how such a tiny thread of water managed to force its way out of the earth.

Next, the other theme had to be started—the *parents'* feeling about the children going out into the world. Notice that, although this theme was the original seed of the poem, it now occupies a relatively small space (lines 9 to 12) : it often happens, when you are writing a poem, that you find the poem turning out quite differently from what you expected—in other words, you don't know what a poem is going to be like till you have gone some way with the composing of it; indeed, to a certain extent, a poem *composes itself*. Lines 9–12 say, quite simply, "We grownups wish the mist of childhood might never break for our children, because, when it does, they'll see the world is not such a pleasant place as they imagined. We'd like to chain them to their childhood, to save them from being hurt ('a quicksand and a wreck') as everyone must sometimes be hurt by life when he grows up." But the poem couldn't end like that, could it? After all, a parent can't really prevent his children growing up, even if it was right for him to try and do so—which it isn't. So, in the last two lines, I describe how children grow independent of their parents, slipping away from them like mist or water ("the source") slips through one's fingers: they must fend for themselves, run their own race—and time has already "flagged out their course."

A corridor of mirrors

I wonder whether you have noticed something about those last six lines. Except for the quicksand and the wreck there are no new images in them. Even the phrase "flagged out their course" (which, by the way, is another memory-image of mine, derived from a two-mile steeplechase I ran in as a boy of fourteen)—even this phrase echoes "the flags" of line 4: Instead of using new images, I have repeated those of the first eight lines—mist, the spring, the estuary ("lest it should *broaden* For them into a quicksand and a wreck"), the flags. In the last chapter I told you how important a part is played in poetry by repetition. It is not only words and phrases, but also images, which can be repeated. And they are repeated in this poem, so that you can see the two main themes from a number of different angles, just as you can see many different reflections of yourself if you walk down a corridor of mirrors.

Lastly, what I have told you about the sources of these particular images will help you to understand how a poem grows. The seed of this poem took root in my mind. Then, without my being aware of it, it somehow attracted to itself several experiences I had had at quite different periods of my life and forgotten about. It got hold of a Devonshire mist, an Irish spring, and a steeplechase course in Dorset; it added an estuary with yachts sailing on it (I still don't know where that last picture came from): and, when I began to write the poem, these four images rose out of my mind all ready to illustrate the theme. . . .

The actual process of writing poetry, then, is rather like the process by which a diamond brooch is made. The poet digs into himself, as a miner digs into a hillside, to find the precious stones—the themes and images of his poems. However skilful and hard-working a miner is, he will not find any diamonds unless there are some to be found there: and you won't get any poetry out of yourself either unless it's there already—unless your imagination is so hot and strong that it has fused your experience into the precious stones which are the raw material of poetry, in the same way as certain chemical conditions are necessary for the making of diamonds beneath the earth's surface. You can't, in fact, write a real poem just by wishing to write one. When the diamonds have been mined, they must be selected, graded, and cut before they can be used for an ornament. This process is equivalent to the work a poet has to do to make a finished poem out of the raw material his imagination yields him. And, just as the quality and size of the diamonds available to him affect the *design* of the brooch which the jeweler makes, so the nature and quality of our poetic material help to create the *pattern* of our poem.

Theodore Roethke

How to Write Like Somebody Else

A good deal of nonsense has been written about "influence" in modern poetry, particularly the influence of one contemporary by another—by writers not very secure in their own practice who would have us believe that even their laundry notes are the result of divine visitation; by reviewers of limited taste and sensibility; by anthologists; and by the glib and middle-aging young who sometimes debase the role of *enfant terrible* by applying to the practice of criticism the methods—and often the taste—of the radio gagman.

For them it's all quite simple: any alliteration, any compounding, any enthusiasm before nature equals Hopkins; any concern with man in society or the use of two "definite" articles in a row is "Audenesque"; any associational shifting or developing a theme alternately, as in music, is Eliot; sexual imagery or a dense language structure, Thomas; and so on.

A little humility may be in order. Let us say that some people—often inarticulate simple types—can hear a poem, can recognize the real thing;

From *On the Poet and His Craft* ed. R. J. Mills, University of Washington Press, 1965.

far fewer know what a line is; and fewer yet, I suspect, are equipped to determine finally whether a writer has achieved his own tone, or whether he has been unduly influenced by another; for such a judgment involves a truly intimate knowledge not only of the particular writers concerned, but also the whole tradition of the language; a *very* exact medium sense; and a delicate and perceptive ear. I suggest that the central critical problem remains: whether a real poem has been created. If it has, the matter of influence becomes irrelevant. Think of the sons of Ben; think of Herbert. Is he any less a poet because he took over some of Donne's effects? Is Auden a charlatan because he read and profited by reading Owen, Laura Riding, Robert Graves?

In a shrewd justification of the referential poem, or less charitably, the poem which is an anthology of other men's effects, Eliot said, "Bad poets imitate; good poets steal." In other words, take what you will with authority and see that you give it another, or even better life, in the new context.

All true, but in some ways a terrifying remark for the beginning writer, who is often neither bad nor good, but simply, as yet, unformed. He isn't sure whether he is a thief or a fake. He may, critically, be far ahead of himself emotionally. He may be able to discuss, with real intelligence, Marvell or Pound or Stevens, but when he takes pen in hand the great models of the past may seem far away and even absurd, and the big names of his own time awesome, overwhelming. Particularly if he is a provincial far from a good library, or from any practicing poet, the immediately preceding literary generation, or the more precocious around his own age—and not always the best of these—may exercise a powerful attraction. The sensitive young are always acutely conscious of "fashion," highly aware of the topical, the surfaces of life; there is a peculiar sheen of contemporaneousness—the phrase may be Huxley's—which seems to exist to speak to them alone. They may be attracted by those writers who reflect their own confusions: the roaring-ass "primitive" produced on both sides of the Atlantic; or they can turn to the overneat technicians who simplify experience by forcing it into an arbitrary order.

To such a young man in such a state I introduce the following examples, my own transgressions, in the hope he will take heart and do otherwise:

This Light

This light is the very flush of spring; it is innocent and warm;
It is gentle as celestial rain; it is mellow as gold;
Its pure effulgence may unbind the form
Of a blossoming tree; it may quicken fallow mould.

This light is various and strange; its luminuous hue
May transmute the bleakest dust to silver snow;
Its radiance may be caught within a pool, a bead of dew;
It may contract to the sheerest point; it may arch to a bow.

This light is heaven's transcendent boon, a beam
Of infinite calm; it will never cease;
It will illuminate forever the aether-stream;
This light will lead me to eventual peace.

This example illustrates, certainly, at least two things: a wrong choice of diction; an unfortunate use of a model. The model is Elinor Wylie; the moral is: don't imitate an imitator; pastiche begets pastiche.

One of the great and early temptations is Beautiful Words. How they shimmer, those mellifluous counters that others have used so often. It's the stage Yeats was at when he murmured. "Words alone are certain good." against which can be set Hopkins' "Words alone are only words." But even Hopkins cared for "lovely" for instance.

Now I didn't clutch a copy of Wylie in one hand, and write the piece with the other. Actually, I had been reading a lot of Vaughan and a friend of mine suggested I do a poem on "Light." I took—I suppose from Wylie—the devices of metaphor on a string—as in her piece

> This sorrow was small and vulnerable and shortlived;
> It was neither earth nor stone . . .

which itself derives, I believe, from Shelley.

To adopt the technical device was legitimate: my real blunder was not to make the poem better: it's static; it doesn't develop; the epithets have too much to do; the last line is a banality.

My next spiritual romance was with Léonie Adams—something else again: her rhythms far subtler and more varied, a much richer aura of suggestiveness.

Listen to this:

The Buds Now Stretch

The buds now stretch into the light,
The warm air stirs the fertile bough,
The sap runs free, and in the night
The young emergent leaf is cast;

The leaf is cast, and garish now,
And drunk with mellow gold, the green
Shapes to the accurate wind, though fast
Upon the branch and laggard leaves,
Their shade not finger-dies, but soon
Their patterns swing into the light
And broaden in the blaze of noon.
The substance of the tree is hung,
And all its loveliness unbound,
Its emerald leaves to sky are flung;
But that sweet vertical, the sun,
Repeats those leaves upon the ground
To deepen half a summer field.
And still as dreams that lovely yield
Of shadows bound like garnered sheaves,
A harvest of immobile shade:
But when those shadows move, a sound,
The full and level noise of leaves.

It's the Adams cadence, the hurrying of syllables into speech, as in:

It was life, or so I said,
And I did well, forsaking it,
To go as quickly as the dead.

The technical trick is in the manipulation of the pause, the caesura, on the fourth and sixth syllables. But, alas, there are verbal, as well as rhythmical echoes: in "Kennst du das Land," this Adams has a line

Knew the leaves deepening the green ground.

While I say

To deepen half a summer field.

Maybe that's not so reprehensible; but she also says, elsewhere,

As sweet as bones which stretch from sleep,

and in "Country Summer":

And full and golden is the yield

and I say

As still as dreams that lovely yield
Of shadows bound like garnered sheaves.

I hate to abandon that poem: I feel it's something Miss Adams and I have created: a literary lovechild. Put it this way: I loved her so much, her poetry, that I just *had* to become, for a brief moment, a part of her world. For it *is* her world, and I had filled myself with it, and I *had* to create something that would honor her in her own terms. That, I think, expresses as best I can what really goes on with the hero- or heroine-worshiping young. I didn't cabbage those effects in cold blood; that poem is a true release in its way. I was too clumsy and stupid to articulate my own emotions: she helped me to say something about the external world, helped me convince myself that maybe, if I kept at it, eventually I might write a poem of my own, with the accent on my own speech.

Thus, one can stake out an area of subject matter, hoard up a body of words, even embody fresh observation in a sustained rhythm, in a poem all of a piece, and *still* be too close to somebody else. I limit myself to passages:

Diffuse the outpourings of the spiritual coward,
The rambling lies invented for the sick.
O see the fate of him whose guard was lowered!—
A single misstep and we leave the quick.

The winds of hatred blow
Cold, cold across the flesh
And chill the anxious heart,
Intricate phobias grow
From each malignant wish
To spoil collective life.
Now each man stands apart.

That, of course, is Wystan Hugh Auden, himself a real magpie, with a cormorant's rapacity and the long memory of the elephant. He pillages the past, as in

"O where are you going?" said reader to rider,

from "The Cutty Wren":

"Oh where are you going?" says Milder to Malder

Or the present; here is Graves' "Full Moon":

As I walked out that sultry night,
  I heard the stroke of One.
The moon, attained to her full height,
  Stood beaming like the sun:
She exorcized the ghostly defeat,
  Whose tryst had now begun.
The fields lay sick beneath my tread.

And Auden himself opens up a ballad:

As I walked out one evening,
Walking down Bristol Street,
The crowds upon the pavement
Were fields of harvest wheat.

And writes an entirely different poem. Now whether his conscious or unconscious mind seized on these elements: the "As I walked out," the street, the wheat, the fields, makes no difference. And it's perfectly possible that he might never have seen Graves' poem, or even written his earlier. But Auden, when he does take over a technical device or even another attitude, for the moment, does so with assurance and style. Invariably the poem moves into its own life.

Is this ever the case in my own practice? Well, I offer this as, possibly, an influence survived:

The Dance

Is that dance slowing in the mind of man
That made him think the universe could hum?
The great wheel turns its axle when it can;
I need a place to sing, and dancing-room,
And I have made a promise to my ears
I'll sing and whistle romping with the bears.

For they are all my friends: I saw one slide
Down a steep hillside on a cake of ice,—
Or was that in a book? I think with pride:
A caged bear rarely does the same thing twice
In the same way: O watch his body sway!—
This animal remembering to be gay.

I tried to fling my shadow at the moon,
The while my blood leaped with a wordless song.
Though dancing needs a master, I had none
To teach my toes to listen to my tongue.
But what I learned there, dancing all alone,
Was not the joyless motion of a stone.

I take this cadence from a man named Yeats;
I take it, and I give it back again:
For other tunes and other wanton beats
Have tossed my heart and fiddled through my brain.
Yes, I was dancing-mad, and how
That came to be the bears and Yeats would know.

Oddly enough, the line "I take this cadence, etc." is, in a sense, a fib. I had been reading deeply in Ralegh, and in Sir John Davies; and they rather than Willie are the true ghosts in that piece.

Is it an effrontery to summarize? Imitation, conscious imitation, is one of the great methods, perhaps *the* method of learning to write. The ancients, the Elizabethans, knew this, profited by it, and were not disturbed. As a son of Ben, Herrick more than once rewrote Jonson, who, in turn, drew heavily on the classics. And so on. The poems are not less good for this: the final triumph is what the language does, not what the poet can do, or display. The poet's ultimate loyalty—the phrase belongs to Stanley Kunitz—is to the poem. The language itself is a compound, or, to change the figure, a bitch. The paradoxical thing, as R. P. Blackmur said of the young in the 'thirties, is that the most original poets are the most imitative. The remark is profound: if a writer has something to say, it will come through. The very fact he has the support of a tradition, or an older writer, will enable him to be more himself—or more than himself.

In a time when the romantic notion of the inspired poet still has considerable credence, true "imitation" takes a certain courage. One dares to stand up to a great style, to compete with papa. In my own case, I should like to think I have over-acknowledged, in one way and another, my debt to Yeats. One simple device provides, I believe, an important technical difference: in the pentameter, I end-stop almost every line—a thing more usual when the resources of the language were more limited. This is not necessarily a virtue—indeed, from many points of view, a limitation. But it is part of an effort, however clumsy, to bring the language back to bare, hard, even terrible statement. All this Yeats himself, a bowerbird if there ever was one, would have understood, and, possibly, approved.

Questions.

1. Is the poet "inspired" to write poetry? If so, how does inspiration manifest itself?
2. How much of the work of the poets whose essays you have just read is calculated, deliberate, how much subconscious?

3. Some of the poets use analogies to explain some of the process of creating a poem. What are these analogies?
4. How much do the poets seem to be aware of craft, of technical workmanship?
5. Which aspects of poetry do they seem to talk of most?
6. How seriously do they seem to take writing poetry?
7. All the writers reprinted in this chapter are modern poets, two of them contemporary. Do any of them seem to want to be deliberately obscure, as modern poets are often charged with being?

Suggested Poems for Further Reading (ANTHOLOGY):

Walter Savage Landor, "Yes, I Write Verses Now and Then," p. 392
Sir Walter Raleigh, "His Pilgrimage," p. 422
Alfred, Lord Tennyson, "The Poet's Song," p. 451
Henry Vaughan, "Quickness," p. 463
Walt Whitman, "The Last Invocation," p. 466

Glossary

A Glossary of Useful Terms

Note: The chapters in which the definitions and concepts are most fully discussed or illustrated are given at the ends of the definitions.

ALEXANDRINE — A line of verse containing six IAMBIC FEET, an iambic HEXAMETER. ("That like a wounded snake draws its slow length along.") (9.)

ALLEGORY — A narrative intended to convey in its characters and incidents not only the literal meaning contained in the story but also a parallel, often a moral, meaning. In Bunyan's *Pilgrim's Progress*, for instance, Christian, the main character, encounters obstacles like Giant Despair and the Slough of Despond on his way to the Celestial City, symbolizing the difficulties in the Christian's way to salvation. Related to FABLE and PARABLE. (5.)

ALLITERATION — Repeating the same sound, especially consonant, of the first or the accented syllable of a word or in accented syllables of a neighboring word or words in a line. ("When, in the dreamy decline of a notable nimbus of nebulous noonshine . . ." —an extreme and humorous example in Swinburne's "Nephilidia.") Also sometimes called INITIAL RIME. (9.)

ALLUSION A reference to a person, place, or event, often a mythical one, without explanatory comment in the belief that the reference is widely enough known to be recognized.

AMBIGUITY A term used to describe the presence of two or more relevant meanings in a word or in a passage of poetry. In poetry it does not mean confusion of meaning. (Cordelia. "The jewels of our father, with washed eyes/Cordelia leaves you. I know you what you are." "Washed" in the sense of crying as well as having sight cleared.)

AMELIORATIVE The connotation of a word or a description of a situation which presents things in a good light or gives a better impression than the facts warrant. ("Maintenance engineer" for "janitor.") (4.)

APOSTROPHE An address to an absent person, especially if such an address interrupts the discourse, or an address to a personified abstraction. ("His Golden locks, Time hath to Silver turned, / O Time too swift, O Swiftness never ceasing.") (Whitman's address to the locomotive might be considered an apostrophe. See 5.)

ARCHAISM A word no longer in current use except in poetry, church ritual, etc. ("Doom is dark and deeper than any sea-dingle." "Led forth his flock that had been long ypent.") (4.)

ASSONANCE The device of repeating the same (or closely similar) vowel sounds with different consonants. ("thin bridge a / narrow walk high / over gulphs rolling. . . .") (9.)

BALLAD The popular or folk ballad is a song in short stanzas that tells a popular story, often very vividly but tersely, and sometimes has a REFRAIN. The literary ballad is a poem patterned on folk ballad, but is more sophisticated.

BLANK VERSE — Usually refers to unrhymed IAMBIC PENTAMETER (a 5-stress line of alternating light and heavy stresses), but which may be used in a more general sense to describe any unrhymed poetry with a regular stress pattern. (9.)

CAESURA — A pause, usually produced by grammatical sense, occurring in a line of poetry. ("Many a night I saw the Pleiads, rising through the mellow Shade.") (9.)

CLICHÉ — A stale, obvious, unimaginative phrase ("pretty as a picture"), a stock expression.

CONCEIT — A fanciful notion or conception involving an unusual comparison, which may be expressed in a simile or a metaphor or may be the framework for an entire lyric. (When lovers are separated by travel, they endure not "A breach, but an expansion,/Like gold to ayery thinnesse beat.") (3.)

CONNOTATION — The implied or suggested meanings that a word has, or the attitudes it evokes. To be distinguished from denotation or denotative meaning, which refers to the word's core meaning—what it specifically refers to or names. *Thin, skinny, slender, sylph-like* all refer denotatively to the relative absence of fat on people but each connotatively suggests different attitudes. Connotative meanings arise out of a word's associations, from the situations or contexts in which it is most typically used. *Home, dwelling, domicile, stash, pad* all refer to the place where a person lives, but differ in connotation because of the contexts in which they are found. Connotative meanings are AMELIORATIVE when they suggest a favorable attitude toward the object named (lady) and PEJORATIVE when the attitude is unfavorable (trull). Connotative meanings need not be either ameliorative or pejorative, but may be otherwise suggestive of associations or attitudes. (4.)

CONSONANCE — The repetiton of a pattern of consonants with changes in the intervening vowels. (In Tennyson's "The moan of doves in immemorial elms. / And murmuring of innumerable bees," the reflection of sense in the consonant sounds produces onomatopoeia.)

COUPLET — A pair of rhymed lines of verse. The HEROIC COUPLET, consisting of two rhymed iambic pentameter lines, is most common, and when the heroic couplet forms a complete clause or sentence it is called a closed couplet. ("Whatever spirit careless of his charge,/His post neglects or leaves the fair at large.") (9.)

DECORUM — A term used to describe that which is suitable, proper, appropriate to the subject in style or diction.

DENOTATION — *See* CONNOTATION.

DICTION — As used in poetry the term refers to the selection of words, the vocabulary used by a particular poet. It is used in a more limited sense to describe the vocabulary of a particular poem. (3.)

DIMETER — A line of two feet. *See* FOOT. (9.)

DUPLE — Containing an even number of syllables, two or a multiple of two, to the foot, as in iambic (˘ /) or trochaic (/ ˘) feet. (9.)

ELEGY-ELEGIAC — Usually a lament for someone who has died and especially one which attempts to resolve the grief of the speaker. When the person who has died is represented as being a shepherd, usually with a fanciful name, and the speaker (or PERSONA) is also a shepherd, the poem is called a PASTORAL ELEGY. The term ELEGY is also applied to poems that are melancholy and reflective, such as Thomas Gray's "Elegy Written in a Country Church Yard."

EMBLEM — See SYMBOL.

EPIC — A narrative poem of considerable length dealing with heroic figures and written in elevated diction. Ordinarily the plot is comparatively simple, the subject matter from remote history or mythology, the hero capable of great deeds, and the treatment of the subject objective.

EPIGRAM — A short poem, often a couplet, poking fun at the follies of individuals or of mankind, which is characterized by its wit, brevity, sharpness, and deft expression. ("Upon Peevish." "Peevish doth boast that he's the very first/ Of English poets, and 'tis thought the worst.")

EUPHEMISM — The substitution of a mild, pleasant, or neutral expression for an unpleasant one. "Crossing the Bar" for dying. *See* PERIPHRASIS.

FABLE — An allegorical story that carries a moral lesson. Anthology: Gay, "The Rat-Catcher and Cats."

FOOT—FEET — A group of syllables of varying stress, a pattern of stresses, which determines the basic beat or METER of a line of verse. FEET—a term used to refer to various groups of syllables with different metrical patterns. *See* METER, DUPLE, TRIPLE. (9.)

FREE VERSE — A term used to describe poetry which departs from the regular line rhythm based on meter in favor of a line that rises and falls irregularly as the thought of emotion develops over a group of lines or an entire poem. Anthology: Whitman, "Reconciliation" and "Self-Contained." (9.)

HEPTAMETER — A line of seven feet. *See* FOOT.

HEROIC COUPLET — *See* COUPLET.

HEXAMETER — A line of six feet. *See* FOOT.

HYPERBOLE — Or OVERSTATEMENT involves an exaggeration, sometimes an extravagant exaggeration, of the facts as when Macbeth describes the difficulty of washing the blood of Duncan from his hands. ("This my hand will rather/ The multitudinous seas incarnadine,/ Making the green one red.")

IMAGERY—IMAGES — The sense impressions evoked by the poem, including those evoked by the objects named, by METAPHOR, SIMILE, SYMBOL, and CONNOTATION. Most imagery in poetry is visual, but it can also be auditory (sounds), olfactory (smells), kinesthetic (having to do with physical sensation of pressure and movement), or gustatory (taste). (2.)

INITIAL RHYME — *See* ALLITERATION.

IRONY — A way of speaking which implies a point of view or points of view at variance, sometimes considerably, from those that are literally expressed. Saying one thing and meaning another. (7.)

METAPHOR — The identification of one thing with another with which it is not ordinarily associated. "The crowds upon the pavement,/ Were fields of harvest wheat." Like compressed simile. *See* SIMILE, PERSONIFICATION. (3.)

METER — The dominant accentual pattern of a poem, referring to the pattern and number of stresses found in most of its lines. The meter of the sonnet, for example, is iambic pentameter or a 5-foot line with alternating light (˘) and heavy (/) stresses as in the following perfectly regular line.
"When I consider everything that grows." (9.)

METONYMY — The use of the name of one thing for that of another associated with or suggested by it. *See* SYNECDOCHE. (3.)

MYTH — The general meaning is that of a legend or story, especially of ancient origin, often associated with natural phenomena as a sort of imaginative explanation of them (e.g., the actions of sun-gods, fertility gods). In this sense myths often involve belief and are also associated with religion (e.g., the myth of the Fall). A system of myths is called a mythology. Poets and other writers often draw on existing myths, especially Greek and Roman, directly and explicitly in ALLUSION, or implicitly in constructing narratives that repeat in modern circumstances the patterns of certain myths. The significance attached to myths as expressing in imaginative form certain fundamental (archetypal) human attitudes by the psychologists Freud and even more Jung has created a great deal of new interest in myth among writers and critics in recent years, but poets have always found myth attractive. Sometimes a poet feels the need to create his own myth, his own imaginative structure that is not subject to the limitations of events in the ordinary world, to express what he wants to represent (e.g., William Blake). Such a poet is called mythopoeic (myth-making).

OCTAVE — A stanza of eight lines, particularly in the sonnet. *See* SESTET.

ODE — To the ancient Greeks any kind of a poem intended to be sung to music, but now usually a lyric, without musical accompaniment, of dignified language and mood. The pseudo-Pindaric ode is identified by a lack of uniformity in the length of its lines and stanzas. The Horatian ode follows a uniform stanzaic pattern.

ONOMATOPOEIA — A term used to describe a similarity between the sound or sounds of the words and the thing or things they are describing. ("The murmuring of innumerable bees").

ORGANIC — A term pertaining to the functionally unifying elements of a poem as opposed to the purely mechanical ones. The carefully integrated or closely articulated structural relationships in the poem among such elements as imagery, meter, diction, irony. Form generated by idea. (8.)

OVERSTATEMENT — *See* HYPERBOLE.

OXYMORON — A locution producing its effect by an internal contradiction, especially between a noun and its modifier. ("darkness visible," "a durable fire," " a sweet mistake.")

PARADOX — A statement affirming or suggesting the co-existence of two things that according to the ordinary rules of logic cannot exist simultaneously. ("Black shade, fair nurse, shadow my white hair.").

PARODY — A work imitating the manner of another work with the intent of ridicule. *See* Lewis Carroll's version of Southey's "The Old Man's Comforts," p. 117.

PARAPHRASE — To convey as precisely and fully as possible in *different* words (with the exception of particles and connectives) the meaning of a poem. A paraphrase differs considerably from a SUMMARY, which attempts only to convey in a general way the substance of a poem. (1.)

PEJORATIVE — The connotation of a word or a description of a situation which presents things in a bad light or gives a worse impression than the facts objectively warrant. *See* AMELIORATIVE. ("If snow be white, why then her breasts are dun." "Mop jockey" for "janitor.") (4.)

PENTAMETER — A line of five feet. *See* FOOT.

PERIPHRASIS — Roundabout expression. Often used in the "softening" process of EUPHEMISM.

PERSONA — A term that meant, literally, the face mask of an actor, hence the imagined character who plays a role in a poem or a play. The speaker of a poem, especially when he is clearly not the poet himself. (6.)

PERSONIFICATION — A metaphor that gives human characteristics to abstract or non-human things. ("Time watches from the shadow/ And coughs when you would kiss"). (3.)

PETRARCHAN SONNET — *See* SONNET.

QUATRAIN — A four-line stanza. *See* STANZA.

REFRAIN — The repetition from stanza to stanza of one or more lines of poetry, which are usually the same, but occasionally differ slightly, as in William Butler Yeats's "The Black Tower," page 111.

REPETITION — An echoing of a single word or phrase or a recurring refrain.

RHYME (RIME) — The repetition of similar sounds at the ends of lines of poetry—succeeding or alternating or in any pattern, sometimes both within (internal rhyme) and at the end of a poetic line. (8.)

SARCASM — A crudely ironic statement intended to wound. Not a literary device—though, like anything else, it may appear in literature—but more typically an attitude that appears in personal relationships. (7.)

SATIRE — A work of literature that ridicules by showing its object as having departed or deviated from a norm or standard of value, and hence is intended to lead its readers to approve the norm and hold deviations from it in amused contempt. The satiric tone may range from light and playful to savage, but it is always critical and to some extent humorous. SARCASM is not satire. See "Holy Willie's Prayer," p. 102 and Johnson, "A Short Song of Congratulation" in Anthology, p. 365.

SCAN—SCANSION — The technical analysis of the form of verse in a poem. It involves: (1) the classification of syllables accented or unaccented, and the grouping of them into feet; (2) the classification of lines according to number of lines; (3) the indication of the rhyme scheme and the application of special names such as SONNET, ODE. (9.)

SENTIMENTALISM — Attaching excessive feeling or mawkish emotionalism to circumstances or occurrences. Indulging in feeling for its own sake. (11.)

SESTET — A stanza of six lines, particularly in the sonnet. *See* OCTAVE.

SHAKESPEAREAN SONNET — *See* SONNET.

SIMILE — The comparison (using *like* or *as*) of one thing with another, often with something with which it may not ordinarily be associated. In poetry it resembles metaphor in effect but makes a weaker identification. *See* METAPHOR. (3.)

SONNET — A poem consisting of fourteen IAMBIC PENTAMETER lines which may be divided in two parts of eight lines (the OCTAVE) and six lines (the SESTET) as in the PETRARCHAN form, or in four parts of three four-line segments (QUATRAINS), and a concluding COUPLET as in the SPENSERIAN and SHAKESPEAREAN forms. Here are the usual rhyme schemes for the three forms:

PETRARCHAN	abbaabba cdecde
SHAKESPEAREAN	abab cdcd efef gg
SPENSERIAN	abab bcbc cdcd ee

SPENSERIAN SONNET — *See* SONNET

SPONDEE — A FOOT of two accented syllables. (9.)

STANZA — A subdivision of a poem, a group of lines marked by recurring patterns of RHYME or by other means. (11.)

STOCK RESPONSE — A generalized conventional attitude likely to appear in response to certain subjects regardless of the particular nature of the stimuli. An automatic or typical attitude. All moms are loveable and all children cute. *See* CLICHÉ. (11.)

SUMMARY — *See* PARAPHRASE.

SYMBOL — The term as ordinarily used means an object that stands for something else, as the American flag stands for the nation. In poetry a symbol does not usually have such specific meanings (in this book symbols with specific limited meanings are called EMBLEMS). A literary symbol—a good one —cannot adequately be translated into a particular equivalent because it suggests too much, and translating it into other terms limits its power to suggest. (5.)

SYMBOLISM — A way of presenting ideas through the use of emblems or symbols. (5.)

SYNECDOCHE — A figure of speech in which the part is used for the whole, the whole for the part, the more general for the less general, the abstract for the concrete. (3.)

TETRAMETER — A line of four feet. *See* FOOT.

TONE — A term used to describe the attitudes implied in a poem toward the subject matter and the audience. (7.)

TRIMETER — A line of three feet. *See* FOOT.

TRIPLE — Containing three or a multiple of three syllables to the foot as in anapestic (˘˘ /) or dactylic (/ ˘˘) feet. (9.)

UNDERSTATEMENT — A form of irony in which a statement is made with less emphasis or seems to be given less importance than the circumstances call for. (11.)

VARIORUM TEXT — An edition of a poem or poems which gives what the editor considers the best version of the poem but also gives, usually in notes, all other important versions of the poem, line by line, from manuscripts and earlier editions. Sometimes, as with the poems of W. B. Yeats, a variorum text thus preserves a record of the poet's revisions. (11.)

Anthology

Questions for poems:

1. Who, and what kind of a person, is the speaker?
2. At what point in time (century, year, day, hour) is the poem spoken?
3. To whom is the poem addressed?
4. What is the attitude (tone) the poem takes toward itself and toward the reader?
5. What do the meter, rhyme, alliteration, assonance and other rhythmical devices contribute to the atmosphere, mood or quality of the poem?
6. Identify any metaphors, similes, personifications, etc., in the poem and discuss their function.
7. Discuss the connotations of words in the poem, indicating what they tell about the speaker, mood, etc.?
8. Paraphrase the poem as carefully as you may, using only particles, conjunctions and verb forms of *to be* from the text.
9. What is the underlying outlook on life conveyed by the poem?
10. Discuss the rhetorical elements of the poem other than those listed under #6: parallelism, periodicity, oxymoron, etc.
11. Are there any symbols or allegorical elements in the poem? Identify and discuss.
12. What is your opinion of the esthetic value of the passage or poem, based on your answers to the foregoing questions?

Back and Side Go Bare

Chorus

Back and side go bare, go bare,
  Both foot and hand go cold;
But, belly, God send thee good ale enough,
  Whether it be new or old.

I cannot eat but little meat,
  My stomach is not good;
But sure I think that I can drink
  With him that wears a hood.
Though I go bare, take ye no care,
  I am nothing a-cold;
I stuff my skin so full within
  Of jolly good ale and old.

I love no roast but a nutbrown toast,
  And a crab laid in the fire;
A little bread shall do me stead,
  Much bread I not desire.
No frost nor snow, no wind, I trow,
  Can hurt me if I would,
I am so wrapped and thoroughly lapped
  Of jolly good ale and old.

And Tib my wife, that as her life
  Loveth well good ale to seek,
Full oft drinks she, till ye may see
  The tears run down her cheek.
Then doth she trowl to me the bowl,
  Even as a maltworm should,
And saith "Sweetheart, I have take my part
  Of this jolly good ale and old."

Now let them drink till they nod and wink,
  Even as good fellows should do;
They shall not miss to have the bliss
  Good ale doth bring men to.
And all poor souls that have scoured bowls,
  Or have them lustily trowled,
God save the lives of them and their wives,
  Whether they be young or old.

Anonymous

I Sing of a Maiden

I sing of a maiden
  That is makeless; *makeless*—matchless
King of all kings
  To her son she ches. *ches*—chose

He came all so still
  Where his mother was,
As dew in April
  That falleth on the grass.

He came all so still
  To his mother's bower,
As dew in April
  That falleth on the flower.

He came all so still
  Where his mother lay,
As dew in April
  That falleth on the spray.

Mother and maiden
  Was never none but she;
Well may such a lady
  Godès mother be.

ANONYMOUS

Kemp Owyne

Her mother died when she was young,
  Which gave her cause to make great moan;
Her father married the warst woman
  That ever lived in Christendom.

She served her with foot and hand,
  In every thing that she could dee,
Till once, in an unlucky time,
  She threw her in ower Craigy's sea.

Says, "Lie you there, dove Isabel,
 And all my sorrows lie with thee;
Till Kemp Owyne come ower the sea,
 And borrow you with kisses three,
Let all the world do what they will,
 Oh borrowed shall you never be!"

Her breath grew strang, her hair grew lang,
 And twisted thrice about the tree,
And all the people, far and near,
 Thought that a savage beast was she.

These news did come to Kemp Owyne,
 Where he lived, far beyond the sea;
He hasted him to Craigy's sea,
 And on the savage beast looked he.

Her breath was strang, her hair was lang,
 And twisted was about the tree,
And with a swing she came about:
 "Come to Craigy's sea, and kiss with me.

"Here is a royal belt," she cried,
 "That I have found in the green sea;
And while your body it is on,
 Drawn shall your blood never be;
But if you touch me, tail or fin,
 I vow my belt your death shall be."

He stepped in, gave her a kiss,
 The royal belt he brought him wi;
Her breath was strang, her hair was lang,
 And twisted twice about the tree,
And with a swing she came about:
 "Come to Craigy's sea, and kiss with me.

"Here is a royal ring," she said,
 "That I have found in the green sea;
And while your finger it is on,
 Drawn shall your blood never be;
But if you touch me, tail or fin,
 I swear my ring your death shall be."

He stepped in, gave her a kiss,
The royal ring he brought him wi;
Her breath was strang, her hair was lang,
And twisted ance about the tree,
And with a swing she came about:
"Come to Craigy's sea, and kiss with me.

"Here is a royal brand," she said,
"That I have found in the green sea;
And while your body it is on,
Drawn shall your blood never be;
But if you touch me, tail or fin,
I swear my brand your death shall be."

He stepped in, gave her a kiss,
The royal brand he brought him wi;
Her breath was sweet, her hair grew short,
And twisted nane about the tree,
And smilingly she came about,
As fair a woman as fair could be.

ANONYMOUS

The Twa Corbies

As I was walking all alane,
I heard twa corbies making a mane:
The tane unto the tither did say,
"Whar sall we gang and dine the day?"

"—In behint yon auld fail dyke *fail*—turf
I wot there lies a new-slain knight;
And næbody kens that he lies there
But his hawk, his hound, and his lady fair.

"His hound is to the hunting gane,
His hawk to fetch the wild-fowl hame,
His lady's ta'en anither mate,
So we may mak' our dinner sweet.

"Ye'll sit on his white hause-bane, *hause-bane*—neck-bone
And I'll pike out his bonny blue e'en:
Wi' æ lock o' his gowden hair
We'll theek our nest when it grows bare. *theek*—thatch

"Mony a one for him maks mane,
But nane sall ken whar he is gane:
O'er his white banes, when they are bare,
The wind sall blaw for evermair."

ANONYMOUS

Thomas Rymer

True Thomas lay oer yon grassy bank,
And he beheld a ladie gay,
A ladie that was brisk and bold,
Come riding oer the fernie brae.

Her skirt was of the grass-green silk,
Her mantel of the velvet fine,
And ilka tett of her horse's mane
Hung fifty silver bells and nine.

True Thomas he took off his hat,
And bowed him low down till his knee:
"All hail, thou mighty Queen of Heaven!
For your peer on earth I never did see."

"O no, O no, True Thomas," she says,
"That name does not belong to me;
I am but the queen of fair Elfland,
And I'm come here for to visit thee.

"But ye maun go wi me now, Thomas,
True Thomas, ye maun go wi me,
For ye maun serve me seven years,
Thro weel or wae as may chance to be."

She turned about her milk-white steed,
And took True Thomas up behind,
And aye wheneer her bridle rang,
The steed flew swifter than the wind.

For forty days and forty nights
He wade thro red blude to the knee,
And he saw neither sun nor moon,
But heard the roaring of the sea.

O they rade on, and further on,
Until they came to a garden green:
"Light down, light down, ye ladie free,
Some of that fruit let me pull to thee."

"O no, O no, True Thomas," she says,
"That fruit maun not be touched by thee,
For a' the plagues that are in hell
Light on the fruit of this countrie.

"But I have a loaf here in my lap,
Likewise a bottle of claret wine,
And now ere we go farther on,
We'll rest a while, and ye may dine."

When he had eaten and drunk his fill,
"Lay down your head upon my knee,"
The lady sayd, "ere we climb yon hill,
And I will show you fairlies three.

"O see not ye yon narrow road,
So thick beset wi thorns and briers?
That is the path of righteousness,
Tho after it but a few enquires.

"And see not ye that braid braid road,
That lies across yon lillie leven?
That is the path of wickedness,
Tho some call it the road to heaven.

"And see not ye that bonny road,
Which winds about the fernie brae?
That is the road to fair Elfland,
Where you and I this night maun gae.

"But Thomas, ye maun hold your tongue,
 Whatever you may hear or see,
For gin ae word you should chance to speak,
 You will neer get back to your ain countrie."

He has gotten a coat of the even cloth,
 And a pair of shoes of velvet green,
And till seven years were past and gone
 True Thomas on earth was never seen.

ANONYMOUS

Weep You No More

Weep you no more, sad fountains;
 What need you flow so fast?
Look how the snowy mountains
 Heaven's sun doth gently waste!
But my sun's heavenly eyes
 View not your weeping,
 That now lies sleeping
Softly, now softly lies
 Sleeping.

Sleep is a reconciling,
 A rest that peace begets;
Doth not the sun rise smiling
 When fair at ev'n he sets?
Rest you then, rest, sad eyes!
 Melt not in weeping,
 While she lies sleeping,
Softly, now softly lies
 Sleeping.

ANONYMOUS

Requiescat

Strew on her roses, roses,
 And never a spray of yew!
In quiet she reposes;
 Ah, would that I did too!

Her mirth the world required;
  She bathed it in smiles of glee.
But her heart was tired, tired,
  And now they let her be.

Her life was turning, turning,
  In mazes of heat and sound.
But for peace her soul was yearning,
  And now peace laps her round.

Her cabined, ample spirit,
  It fluttered and failed for breath.
Tonight it doth inherit
  The vasty hall of death.

MATTHEW ARNOLD

The Buried Life

Light flows our war of mocking words, and yet,
Behold, with tears mine eyes are wet!
I feel a nameless sadness o'er me roll.
Yes, yes, we know that we can jest,
We know, we know that we can smile!
But there's a something in this breast,
To which thy light words bring no rest,
And thy gay smiles no anodyne.
Give me thy hand, and hush awhile,
And turn those limpid eyes on mine,
And let me read there, love! thy inmost soul.

Alas! is even Love too weak
To unlock the heart, and let it speak?
Are even lovers powerless to reveal
To one another what indeed they feel?
I knew the mass of men concealed
Their thoughts, for fear that if revealed
They would by other men be met
With blank indifference, or with blame reproved;
I knew they lived and moved
Tricked in disguises, alien to the rest
Of men, and alien to themselves—and yet
The same heart beats in every human breast!

But we, my love!—doth a like spell benumb
Our hearts, our voices?—must we too be dumb?

Ah! well for us, if even we,
Even for a moment, can get free
Our heart, and have our lips unchained;
For that which seals them both hath been deep-ordained!

Fate, which foresaw
How frivolous a baby man would be—
By what distractions he would be possessed,
How he would pour himself in every strife,
And well-nigh change his own identity—
That it might keep from his capricious play
His genuine self, and force him to obey
Even in his own despite his being's law,
Bade through the deep recesses of our breast
The unregarded River of our Life
Pursue with indiscernible flow its way;
And that we should not see
The buried stream, and seem to be
Eddying at large in blind uncertainty,
Though driving on with it eternally.

But often, in the world's most crowded streets,
But often, in the din of strife,
There rises an unspeakable desire
After the knowledge of our buried life;
A thirst to spend our fire and restless force
In tracking out our true, original course;
A longing to inquire
Into the mystery of this heart which beats
So wild, so deep in us—to know
Whence our lives come and where they go.
And many a man in his own breast then delves,
But deep enough, alas! none ever mines.
And we have been on many thousand lines,
And we have shown, on each, spirit and power;
But hardly have we, for one little hour,
Been on our own line, have we been ourselves—
Hardly had skill to utter one of all
The nameless feelings that course through our breast,
But they course on forever unexpressed.
And long we try in vain to speak and act
Our hidden self, and what we say and do
Is eloquent, is well—but 'tis not true!

And then we will no more be racked
With inward striving, and demand
Of all the thousand nothings of the hour
Their stupefying power;
Ah yes, and they benumb us at our call!
Yet still, from time to time, vague and forlorn,
From the soul's subterranean depth upborne
As from an infinitely distant land,
Comes airs, and floating echoes, and convey
A melancholy into all our day.

Only—but this is rare—
When a belovéd hand is laid in ours,
When, jaded with the rush and glare
Of the interminable hours,
Our eyes can in another's eyes read clear,
When our world-deafened ear
Is by the tones of a loved voice caressed—
A bolt is shot back somewhere in our breast,
And a lost pulse of feeling stirs again:
The eye sinks inward, and the heart lies plain,
And what we mean, we say, and what we would, we know.
A man becomes aware of his life's flow,
And hears its winding murmur; and he sees
The meadows where it glides, the sun, the breeze.

And there arrives a lull in the hot race
Wherein he doth forever chase
That flying and elusive shadow, Rest.
An air of coolness plays upon his face,
And an unwonted calm pervades his breast.
And then he thinks he knows
The Hills where his life rose,
And the Sea where it goes.

MATHEW ARNOLD

The Last Word

Creep into thy narrow bed,
Creep, and let no more be said!
Vain thy onset! all stands fast.
Thou thyself must break at last.

Let the long contention cease!
Geese are swans, and swans are geese.
Let them have it how they will!
Thou art tired; best be still.

They out-talked thee, hissed thee, tore thee?
Better men fared thus before thee;
Fired their ringing shot and passed,
Hotly charged—and sank at last.

Charge once more, then, and be dumb!
Let the victors, when they come,
When the forts of folly fall,
Find thy body by the wall!

MATHEW ARNOLD

We Do Lie Beneath the Grass

We do lie beneath the grass
  In the moonlight, in the shade
Of the yew-tree. They that pass
  Hear us not. We are afraid
    They would envy our delight,
    In our graves by glow-worm night.
Come follow us, and smile as we;
  We sail to the rock in the ancient waves,
Where the snow falls by thousands into the sea,
  And the drowned and the shipwrecked have
      happy graves.

THOMAS LOVELL BEDDOES

A Dream

Once a dream did weave a shade
O'er my Angel-guarded bed,
That an Emmet lost its way
Where on grass methought I lay.

Troubled, 'wildered, and forlorn,
Dark, benighted, travel-worn,
Over many a tangled spray,
All heart-broke I heard her say:

"Oh, my children! do they cry?
Do they hear their father sigh?
Now they look abroad to see:
Now return and weep for me."

Pitying, I dropped a tear;
But I saw a glow-worm near,
Who replied: "What wailing wight
Calls the watchman of the night?

"I am set to light the ground,
While the beetle goes his round:
Follow now the beetle's hum;
Little wanderer, hie thee home."

William Blake

A Poison Tree

I was angry with my friend:
I told my wrath, my wrath did end.
I was angry with my foe:
I told it not, my wrath did grow.

And I watered it in fears,
Night and morning with my tears;
And I sunned it with smiles,
And with soft deceitful wiles.

And it grew both day and night,
Till it bore an apple bright;
And my foe beheld it shine,
And he knew that it was mine,

And into my garden stole
When the night had veiled the pole:
In the morning glad I see
My foe outstretched beneath the tree.

WILLIAM BLAKE

Holy Thursday I

'Twas on a Holy Thursday, their innocent faces clean,
The children walking two and two, in red and blue and green,
Gray-headed beadles walked before, with wands as white as snow,
Till into the high dome of Paul's they like Thames' waters flow.

Oh, what a multitude they seemed, these flowers of London town!
Seated in companies they sit with radiance all their own.
The hum of multitudes was there, but multitudes of lambs,
Thousands of little boys and girls raising their innocent hands.

Now like a mighty wind they raise to Heaven the voice of song,
Or like harmonious thunderings the seats of Heaven among.
Beneath them sit the aged men, wise guardians of the poor;
Then cherish pity, lest you drive an angel from your door.

WILLIAM BLAKE

Holy Thursday II

Is this a holy thing to see
In a rich and fruitful land,
Babes reduced to misery,
Fed with cold and usurous hand?

Is that trembling cry a song?
Can it be a song of joy?
And so many children poor?
It is a land of poverty!

And their sun does never shine,
And their fields are bleak and bare,
And their ways are filled with thorns:
It is eternal winter there.

For where'er the sun does shine,
And where'er the rain does fall,
Babe can never hunger there,
Nor poverty the mind appall.

WILLIAM BLAKE

London

I wander through each chartered street,
Near where the chartered Thames does flow,
And mark in every face I meet
Marks of weakness, marks of woe.

In every cry of every Man,
In every Infant's cry of fear,
In every voice, in every ban,
The mind-forged manacles I hear.

How the Chimney-sweeper's cry
Every blackening Church appalls,
And the hapless Soldier's sigh
Runs in blood down Palace walls.

But most through midnight streets I hear
How the youthful Harlot's curse
Blasts the new born Infant's tear,
And blights with plagues the Marriage hearse.

WILLIAM BLAKE

Never Seek to Tell Thy Love

Never seek to tell thy love,
Love that never told can be;
For the gentle wind does move
Silently, invisibly.

I told my love, I told my love,
I told her all my heart,
Trembling, cold, in ghastly fears—
Ah, she doth depart.

Soon as she was gone from me
A traveller came by
Silently, invisibly—
O, was no deny.

WILLIAM BLAKE

The Clod and the Pebble

"Love seeketh not itself to please,
Nor for itself hath any care,
But for another gives its ease,
And builds a Heaven in Hell's despair."

So sung a little Clod of Clay
Trodden with the cattle's feet,
But a Pebble of the brook
Warbled out these meters meet:

"Love seeketh only Self to please,
To bind another to Its delight,
Joys in another's loss of ease,
And builds a Hell in Heaven's despite."

WILLIAM BLAKE

The Garden of Love

I went to the Garden of Love,
And saw what I never had seen:
A Chapel was built in the midst,
Where I used to play on the green.

And the gates of this Chapel were shut,
And "Thou shalt not" writ over the door;
So I turned to the Garden of Love,
That so many sweet flowers bore:

And I saw it was filled with graves,
And tombstones where flowers should be;
And Priests in black gowns were walking their rounds,
And binding with briars my joys and desires.

William Blake

The Lamb

Little Lamb, who made thee?
Dost thou know who made thee?
Gave thee life, and bid thee feed,
By the stream and o'er the mead;
Gave thee clothing of delight,
Softest clothing, woolly, bright;
Gave thee such a tender voice,
Making all the vales rejoice?
Little Lamb, who made thee?
Dost thou know who made thee?

Little Lamb, I'll tell thee,
Little Lamb, I'll tell thee:
He is called by thy name,
For he calls himself a Lamb,
He is meek, and he is mild;
He became a little child.
I a child, and thou a lamb,
We are called by his name.
Little Lamb, God bless thee!
Little Lamb, God bless thee!

William Blake

The Little Black Boy

My mother bore me in the southern wild,
And I am black, but O! my soul is white;
White as an angel is the English child,
But I am black, as if bereaved of light.

My mother taught me underneath a tree,
And sitting down before the heat of day,
She took me on her lap and kissed me,
And, pointing to the east, began to say:

"Look on the rising sun: there God does live,
And gives his light, and gives his heat away;
And flowers and trees and beasts and men receive
Comfort in morning, joy in the noonday.

"And we are put on earth a little space,
That we may learn to bear the beams of love;
And these black bodies and this sunburnt face
Is but a cloud, and like a shady grove.

"For when our souls have learned the heat to bear,
The cloud will vanish; we shall hear his voice,
Saying: 'Come out from the grove, my love and care,
And round my golden tent like lambs rejoice.' "

Thus did my mother say, and kissed me;
And thus I say to little English boy:
When I from black and he from white cloud free,
And round the tent of God like lambs we joy,

I'll shade him from the heat, till he can bear
To lean in joy upon our father's knee;
And then I'll stand and stroke his silver hair,
And be like him, and he will then love me.

William Blake

To the Evening Star

Thou fair-haired angel of the evening,
Now, whilst the sun rests on the mountains, light
Thy bright torch of love; thy radiant crown
Put on, and smile upon our evening bed!
Smile on our loves, and, while thou drawest the
Blue curtains of the sky, scatter thy silver dew

On every flower that shuts its sweet eyes
In timely sleep. Let thy west wind sleep on
The lake; speak silence with thy glimmering eyes,
And wash the dusk with silver. Soon, full soon,
Dost thou withdraw; then the wolf rages wide,
And the lion glares through the dun forest:
The fleeces of our flocks are covered with
Thy sacred dew: protect them with thine influence.

WILLIAM BLAKE

Pastoral

Who can live in heart so glad
As the merry country lad?
Who upon a fair green balk
May at pleasure sit and walk,
And amid the azure skies
See the morning sun arise,
While he hears in every spring
How the birds do chirp and sing:
Or before the hounds in cry
See the hare go stealing by:
Or along the shallow brook,
Angling with a baited hook,
See the fishes leap and play
In a blessèd sunny day:
Or to hear the partridge call
Till she have her covey all:
Or to see the subtle fox,
How the villain plies the box;
After feeding on his prey,
How he closely sneaks away,
Through the hedge and down the furrow
Till he gets into his burrow:
Then the bees to gather honey;
And the little black-haired coney,
On a bank for sunny place,
With her forefeet wash her face,—
Are not these, with thousands more
Than the courts of kings do know,
The true pleasing spirit's sights
That may breed true love's delights?

balk—strip of unploughed ground

plies the box—seeks a way into henyard

NICHOLAS BRETON

Often Rebuked, Yet Always Back Returning

Often rebuked, yet always back returning
To those first feelings that were born with me,
And leaving busy chase of wealth and learning
For idle dreams of things which cannot be:

Today, I will seek not the shadowy region;
Its unsustaining vastness waxes drear;
And visions rising, legion after legion,
Bring the unreal world too strangely near.

I'll walk, but not in old heroic traces,
And not in paths of high morality,
And not among the half-distinguished faces,
The clouded forms of long-past history.

I'll walk where my own nature would be leading:
It vexes me to choose another guide:
Where the gray flocks in ferny glens are feeding;
Where the wild wind blows on the mountain-side.

What have those lonely mountains worth revealing?
More glory and more grief than I can tell:
The earth that wakes *one* human heart to feeling
Can center both the worlds of Heaven and Hell.

EMILY BRONTE

To Imagination

When weary with the long day's care,
And earthly change from pain to pain,
And lost, and ready to despair,
Thy kind voice calls me back again—
Oh, my true friend, I am not lone
While thou canst speak with such a tone!

So hopeless is the world without,
The world within I doubly prize;
Thy world where guile and hate and doubt
And cold suspicion never rise;
Where thou and I and Liberty
Have undisputed sovereignty.

What matters it that all around
Danger and grief and darkness lie,
If but within our bosom's bound
We hold a bright unsullied sky,
Warm with ten thousand mingled rays
Of suns that know no winter days?

Reason indeed may oft complain
For Nature's sad reality,
And tell the suffering heart how vain
Its cherished dreams must always be;
And Truth may rudely trample down
The flowers of Fancy newly-blown:

But thou art ever there to bring
The hovering vision back and breathe
New glories o'er the blighted spring
And call a lovelier life from death,
And whisper with a voice divine
Of real worlds as bright as thine.

I trust not to thy phantom bliss,
Yet, still, in evening's quiet hour
With never-failing thankfulness
I welcome thee, benignant power,
Sure solacer of human cares
And brighter hope when hope despairs.

EMILY BRONTE

Boot and Saddle

Boot, saddle, to horse, and away!
Rescue my castle before the hot day
Brightens to blue from its silvery gray,

(CHORUS)
Boot, saddle, to horse, and away!

Ride past the suburbs, asleep as you'd say;
Many's the friend there, will listen and pray
"God's luck to gallants that strike up the lay—

(Chorus)
Boot, saddle, to horse, and away!"

Forty miles off, like a roebuck at bay,
Flouts Castle Brancepeth the Roundheads' array:
Who laughs, "Good fellows ere this, by my fay,

(Chorus)
Boot, saddle, to horse, and away?"

Who? My wife Gertrude; that, honest and gay,
Laughs when you talk of surrendering, "Nay!
I've better counselors; what counsel they?

(Chorus)
Boot, saddle, to horse, and away!"

Robert Browning

Confessions

What is he buzzing in my ears?
"Now that I come to die,
Do I view the world as a vale of tears?"
Ah, reverend sir, not I!

What I viewed there once, what I view again
Where the physic bottles stand
On the table's edge,—is a suburb lane,
With a wall to my bedside hand.

That lane sloped, much as the bottles do,
From a house you could descry
O'er the garden-wall: is the curtain blue
Or green to a healthy eye?

To mine, it serves for the old June weather
Blue above lane and wall;
And that farthest bottle labelled "Ether"
Is the house o'ertopping all.

At a terrace, somewhere near the stopper,
There watched for me, one June,
A girl: I know, sir, it's improper,
My poor mind's out of tune.

Only, there was a way . . . you crept
  Close by the side, to dodge
Eyes in the house, two eyes except:
  They styled their house "The Lodge."

What right had a lounger up their lane?
  But, by creeping very close,
With the good wall's help,—their eyes might strain
  And stretch themselves to Oes,

Yet never catch her and me together,
  As she left the attic, there,
By the rim of the bottle labelled "Ether,"
  And stole from stair to stair,

And stood by the rose-wreathed gate. Alas,
  We loved, sir—used to meet:
How sad and bad and mad it was—
  But then, how it was sweet!

ROBERT BROWNING

Home Thoughts from Abroad

I

Oh, to be in England
Now that April's there,
And whoever wakes in England
Sees, some morning, unaware,
That the lowest boughs and the brushwood sheaf
Round the elm-tree bole are in tiny leaf,
While the chaffinch sings on the orchard bough
In England—now!

II

And after April, when May follows,
And the whitethroat builds, and all the swallows!
Hark, where my blossomed pear-tree in the hedge
Leans to the field and scatters on the clover
Blossoms and dewdrops—at the bent spray's edge—
That's the wise thrush; he sings each song twice over,
Lest you should think he never could recapture

The first fine careless rapture!
And though the fields look rough with hoary dew,
All will be gay when noontide wakes anew
The buttercups, the little children's dower
—Far brighter than this gaudy melon-flower!

ROBERT BROWNING

Home-Thoughts, from the Sea

Nobly, nobly Cape Saint Vincent to the northwest died away;
Sunset ran, one glorious blood-red, reeking into Cadiz Bay;
Bluish 'mid the burning water, full in face Trafalgar lay;
In the dimmest northeast distance dawned Gibraltar grand and gray;
"Here and here did England help me: how can I help England?"—say,
Whoso turns as I, this evening, turn to God to praise and pray,
While Jove's planet rises yonder, silent over Africa.

ROBERT BROWNING

Two in the Campagna

I wonder do you feel today
  As I have felt, since, hand in hand,
We sat down on the grass, to stray
  In spirit better through the land,
This morn of Rome and May?

For me, I touched a thought, I know,
  Has tantalized me many times,
(Like turns of thread the spiders throw
  Mocking across our path) for rhymes
To catch at and let go.

Help me to hold it! First it left
  The yellowing fennel, run to seed
There, branching from the brickwork's cleft,
  Some old tomb's ruin; yonder weed
Took up the floating weft,

Where one small orange cup amassed
   Five beetles,—blind and green they grope
Among the honey-meal: and last,
   Everywhere on the grassy slope
I traced it. Hold it fast!

The champaign with its endless fleece
   Of feathery grasses everywhere!
Silence and passion, joy and peace,
   An everlasting wash of air—
Rome's ghost since her decease.

Such life there, through such length of hours,
   Such miracles performed in play,
Such primal naked forms of flowers,
   Such letting Nature have her way
While Heaven looks from its towers!

How say you? Let us, O my dove,
   Let us be unashamed of soul,
As earth lies bare to heaven above!
   How is it under our control
To love or not to love?

I would that you were all to me,
   You that are just so much, no more.
Nor yours, nor mine—nor slave nor free!
   Where does the fault lie? What the core
O' the wound, since wound must be?

I would I could adopt your will,
   See with your eyes, and set my heart
Beating by yours, and drink my fill
   At your soul's springs,—your part, my part
In life, for good and ill.

No. I yearn upward, touch you close,
   Then stand away. I kiss your cheek,
Catch your soul's warmth,—I pluck the rose
   And love it more than tongue can speak—
Then the good minute goes.

Already how am I so far
  Out of that minute? Must I go
Still like the thistleball, no bar,
  Onward, whenever light winds blow,
Fixed by no friendly star?

Just when I seemed about to learn!
  Where is the thread now? Off again!
The old trick! Only I discern—
  Infinite passion, and the pain
Of finite hearts that yearn.

ROBERT BROWNING

The Pilgrim Song

Who would true valour see,
Let him come hither;
One here will constant be,
Come wind, come weather.
There's no discouragement
Shall make him once relent
His first avow'd intent,
To be a pilgrim.

Who so beset him round
With dismal stories,
Do but themselves confound;
His strength the more is.
No lion can him fright,
He'll with a giant fight,
But he will have a right
To be a pilgrim.

Hobgoblin, nor foul fiend,
Can daunt his spirit:
He knows, he at the end
Shall life inherit.
Then fancies fly away,
He'll fear not what men say,
He'll labour night and day
To be a pilgrim.

JOHN BUNYAN

A Man's a Man for A' That

Is there, for honest poverty,
That hings his head, an' a' that?
The coward slave, we pass him by,
We dare be poor for a' that!
For a' that, an' a' that,
Our toils obscure, an' a' that;
The rank is but the guinea's stamp;
The man's the gowd for a' that.

What tho' on hamely fare we dine,
Wear hodden-gray, an' a' that; *hodden-gray*—gray wool cloth
Gie fools their silks, and knaves their wine,
A man's a man for a' that.
For a' that, an' a' that,
Their tinsel show, an' a' that;
The honest man, tho' e'er sae poor,
Is king o' men for a' that.

Ye see yon birkie, ca'd a lord, *birkie*—young man
Wha struts, an' stares, an' a' that;
Tho' hundreds worship at his word,
He's but a coof for a' that. *coof*—fool
For a' that, an' a' that,
His riband, star, an' a' that
The man o' independent mind,
He looks and laughs at a' that.

A prince can mak a belted knight,
A marquis, duke, an' a' that;
But an honest man's aboon his might,
Guid faith he mauna fa' that!
For a' that, an' a' that,
Their dignities, an' a' that,
The pith o' sense, an' pride o' worth,
Are higher rank than a' that.

Then let us pray that come it may,
As come it will for a' that,
That sense and worth, o'er a' the earth,
May bear the gree, an' a' that.
For a' that, an' a' that,
It's coming yet, for a' that,
That man to man, the warld o'er,
Shall brothers be for a' that.

ROBERT BURNS

Bonie Doon

Ye flowery banks o' bonie Doon,
How can ye blume sae fair?
How can ye chant, ye little birds,
And I sae fu' o' care?

Thou'll break my heart, thou bonie bird,
That sings upon the bough;
Thou minds me o' the happy days,
When my fause luve was true.

Thou'll break my heart, thou bonie bird,
That sings beside thy mate;
For sae I sat, and sae I sang,
And wist na o' my fate.

Aft hae I roved by bonie Doon
To see the woodbine twine,
And ilka bird sang o' its luve,
And sae did I o' mine.

Wi' lightsome heart I pu'd a rose
Frae aff its thorny tree;
And my fause luver staw my rose
But left the thorn wi' me.

Robert Burns

Of A' the Airts

Of a' the airts the wind can blaw
I dearly like the west,
For there the bonie lassie lives,
The lassie I lo'e best.
There wild woods grow, and rivers row,
And monie a hill between,
But day and night my fancy's flight
Is ever wi' my Jean.

I see her in the dewy flowers—
I see her sweet and fair.
I hear her in the tunefu' birds—
I hear her charm the air:
There's not a bonie flower that springs
By fountain, shaw, or green,
There's not a bonie bird that sings,
But minds me o' my Jean.

Robert Burns

O, Wert Thou in the Cauld Blast

O, wert thou in the cauld blast
On yonder lea, on yonder lea,
My plaidie to the angry airt, *airt*—quarter of the wind
I'd shelter thee, I'd shelter thee.
Or did misfortune's bitter storms
Around thee blaw, around thee blaw,
Thy bield should be my bosom,
To share it a', to share it a'.

Or were I in the wildest waste,
Sae black and bare, sae black and bare,
The desert were a paradise,
If thou wert there, if thou wert there.
Or were I monarch o' the globe,
Wi' thee to reign, wi' thee to reign,
The brightest jewel in my crown
Wad be my queen, wad be my queen.

Robert Burns

From *The Jolly Beggars*

Air

tune: *Soldier's Joy*

I am a son of Mars, who have been in many wars,
And show my cuts and scars wherever I come:
This here was for a wench, and that other in a trench
When welcoming the French at the sound of the drum.

My 'prenticeship I past, where my leader breath'd his last,
  When the bloody die was cast on the heights of Abram;
And I serv'd out my trade when the gallant game was play'd,
  And the Moro low was laid at the sound of the drum.

I lastly was with Curtis among the floating batt'ries,
  And there I left for witness an arm and a limb:
Yet let my country need me, with Eliott to head me,
  I'd clatter on my stumps at the sound of the drum.

And now, tho' I must beg, with a wooden arm and leg,
  And many a tatter'd rag hanging over my bum,
I'm as happy with my wallet, my bottle, and my callet,
  As when I us'd in scarlet to follow a drum.

What tho' with hoary locks I must stand the winter shocks,
  Beneath the woods and rocks oftentimes for a home?
When the tother bag I sell, and the tother bottle tell,
  I could meet a troop of hell at the sound of a drum.

Air

TUNE: *Soldier Laddie*

I once was a maid, tho' I cannot tell when,
And still my delight is in proper young men.
Some one of a troop of dragoons was my daddie:
No wonder I'm fond of a sodger laddie!

The first of my loves was a swaggering blade:
To rattle the thundering drum was his trade;
His leg was so tight, and his cheek was so ruddy,
Transported I was with my sodger laddie.

But the godly old chaplain left him in the lurch;
The sword I forsook for the sake of the church;
He ventur'd the soul, and risked the body:
'Twas then I prov'd false to my sodger laddie.

Full soon I grew sick of my sanctified sot;
The regiment at large for a husband I got;
From the gilded spontoon to the fife I was ready:
I asked no more but a sodger laddie.

But the peace it reduc'd me to beg in despair,
Till I met my old boy at Cunningham fair;
His rags regimental they flutter'd so gaudy:
My heart it rejoic'd at a sodger laddie.

And now I have liv'd—I know not how long!
But still I can join in a cup or a song;
But whilst with both hands I can hold the glass steady,
Here's to thee, my hero, my sodger laddie!

AIR
TUNE: *Jolly Mortals, Fill Your Glasses*

See the smoking bowl before us!
  Mark our jovial, ragged ring!
Round and round take up the chorus
  And in raptures let us sing:

Chorus

A fig for those by law protected!
  Liberty's a glorious feast!
Courts for cowards were erected,
  Churches built to please the priest!

What is title? what is treasure?
  What is reputation's care?
If we lead a life of pleasure,
  'Tis no matter, how or where!

With the ready trick and fable
  Round we wander all the day;
And at night, in barn or stable,
  Hug our doxies on the hay.

Does the train-attended carriage
  Thro' the country lighter rove?
Does the sober bed of marriage
  Witness brighter scenes of love?

Life is all a variorum,
  We regard not how it goes;
Let them cant about decorum,
  Who have characters to lose.

Here's to budgets, bags, and wallets!
Here's to all the wandering train!
Here's our ragged brats and callets!
One and all, cry out, Amen!

Chorus

A fig for those by law protected!
Liberty's a glorious feast,
Courts for cowards were erected,
Churches built to please the priest!

ROBERT BURNS

To a Louse

ON SEEING ONE ON A LADY'S BONNET AT CHURCH

Ha! wh'are ye gaun, ye crowlin ferlie?
Your impudence protects you sairly;
I canna say but ye strunt rarely,
Owre gauze and lace,
Tho' faith! I fear ye dine but sparely
On sic a place.

Ye ugly, creepin, blastit wonner,
Detested, shunned by saunt an' sinner,
How dare ye set your fit upon her,
Sae fine a lady?
Gae somewhere else, and seek your dinner
On some poor body.

Swith, in some beggar's hauffet squattle;
There ye may creep, and sprawl, and sprattle
Wi' ither kindred jumping cattle,
In shoals and nations;
Whare horn nor bane ne'er dare unsettle
Your thick plantations.

Now haud you there! ye're out o' sight,
Below the fatt'rils, snug an' tight;
Na, faith ye yet! ye'll no be right
Till ye've got on it,
The very tapmost tow'ring height
O' Miss's bonnet.

My sooth! right bauld ye set your nose out,
As plump an' gray as onie grozet;
O for some rank mercurial rozet,
Or fell red smeddum!
I'd give you sic a hearty does o't,
Wad dress your droddum!

I wad na been surprised to spy
You on an auld wife's flainen toy;
Or aiblins some bit duddie boy,
On's wyliecoat;
But Miss's fine Lunardi! fie,
How daur ye do't?

O Jenny, dinna toss your head,
An' set your beauties a' abread!
Ye little ken what curséd speed
The blastie's makin!
Thae winks and finger-ends, I dread,
Are notice takin!

O wad some Power the giftie gie us
To see oursels as ithers see us!
It wad frae monie a blunder free us,
An' foolish notion:
What airs in dress an' gait wad lea'e us,
An' ev'n devotion!

Robert Burns

To a Mountain Daisy

ON TURNING ONE DOWN WITH THE PLOW
IN APRIL, 1786

Wee, modest, crimson-tipped flow'r,
Thou's met me in an evil hour;
For I maun crush amang the stoure
Thy slender stem:
To spare thee now is past my pow'r,
Thou bonie gem.

Alas! it's no thy neebor sweet,
The bonie lark, companion meet,
Bending thee 'mang the dewy weet,
Wi' spreckled breast!
When upward-springing, blythe, to greet
The purpling east.

Cauld blew the bitter-biting north
Upon thy early, humble birth;
Yet cheerfully thou glinted forth
Amid the storm,
Scarce reared above the parent-earth
Thy tender form.

The flaunting flow'rs our gardens yield,
High shelt'ring woods and wa's maun shield:
But thou, beneath the random bield
O' clod or stane,
Adorns the histie stibble-field,
Unseen, alane.

There, in thy scanty mantle clad,
Thy snawie bosom sunward spread,
Thou lifts thy unassuming head
In humble guise;
But now the share uptears thy bed,
And low thou lies!

Such is the fate of artless maid,
Sweet flow'ret of the rural shade!
By love's simplicity betrayed,
And guileless trust;
Till she, like thee, all soiled, is laid
Low i' the dust.

Such is the fate of simple Bard,
On Life's rough ocean luckless starred!
Unskilful he to note the card
Of prudent lore,
Till billows rage, and gales blow hard,
And whelm him o'er!

Such fate to suffering Worth is giv'n,
Who long with wants and woes has striv'n,
By human pride or cunning driv'n
To mis'ry's brink;
Till, wrenched of ev'ry stay but Heav'n,
He, ruined, sink!

Ev'n thou who mourn'st the Daisy's fate,
That fate is thine—no distant date;
Stern Ruin's plowshare drives elate,
Full on thy bloom,
Till crushed beneath the furrow's weight
Shall be thy doom!

ROBERT BURNS

To a Mouse

ON TURNING UP HER NEST WITH THE PLOW,
NOVEMBER, 1785

Wee, sleekit, cowrin, tim rous beastie,
O, what a panic's in thy breastie!
Thou need na start awa sae hasty
Wi' bickering brattle!
I wad be laith to rin an' chase thee,
Wi' murdering pattle!

I'm truly sorry man's dominion
Has broken Nature's social union,
An' justifies that ill opinion
Which makes thee startle
At me, thy poor, earth-born companion
An' fellow-mortal!

I doubt na, whyles, but thou may thieve;
What then? poor beastie, thou maun live:
A daimen icker in a thrave
'S a sma' request;
I'll get a blessin wi' the lave,
An' never miss 't!

Thy wee-bit housie, too, in ruin!
Its silly wa's the win's are strewin!
An' naething, now, to big a new ane,
O' foggage green!
An' bleak December's win's ensuin,
Baith snell an' keen!

Thou saw the fields laid bare an' waste,
An' weary winter comin' fast,
An' cozie here, beneath the blast,
Thou thought to dwell,
Till, crash! the cruel coulter passed
Out through thy cell.

That wee bit heap o' leaves an' stibble,
Has cost thee monie a weary nibble!
Now thou's turned out, for a' thy trouble,
But house or hald,
To thole the winter's sleety dribble,
An' cranreuch cauld!

But Mousie, thou art no thy lane,
In proving foresight may be vain:
The best-laid schemes o' mice an' men
Gang aft agley,
An' lea'e us naught but grief an' pain,
For promised joy!

Still thou art blest, compared wi' me!
The present only toucheth thee:
But och! I backward cast my e'e,
On prospects drear!
An' forward, though I canna see,
I guess an' fear!

Robert Burns

Willie Brewed a Peck o' Maut

O, Willie brewed a peck o' maut,
And Rob an' Allan cam to see:
Three blyther hearts that lee-lang night
Ye wad na found in Christendie.

Chorus

We are na fou, we're nae that fou,
But just a drappie in our ee;
The cock may craw, the day may daw,
And ay we'll taste the barley bree.

Here are we met, three merry boys,
Three merry boys, I trow, are we;
And monie a night we've merry been,
And monie mae we hope to be!

It is the moon, I ken her horn,
That's blinkin in the lift sae hie;
She shines sae bright to wyle us hame,
But, by my sooth, she'll wait a wee!

Wha first shall rise to gang awa',
A cuckold, coward loun is he!
Wha first beside his chair shall fa',
He is the king amang us three!

Chorus

We are na fou, we're nae that fou,
But just a drappie in our ee;
The cock may craw, the day may daw,
And ay we'll taste the barley bree.

Robert Burns

She walks in beauty

She walks in beauty, like the night
Of cloudless climes and starry skies;
And all that's best of dark and bright
Meet in her aspect and her eyes:
Thus mellowed to that tender light
Which heaven to gaudy day denies.

One shade the more, one ray the less,
Had half impaired the nameless grace
Which waves in every raven tress,
Or softly lightens o'er her face;
Where thoughts serenely sweet express
How pure, how dear their dwelling-place.

And on that cheek, and o'er that brow,
So soft, so calm, yet eloquent,
The smiles that win, the tints that glow,
But tell of days in goodness spent,
A mind at peace with all below,
A heart whose love is innocent!

George Noel Gordon, Lord Byron

When We Two Parted

When we two parted
In silence and tears,
Half broken-hearted
To sever for years,
Pale grew thy cheek and cold,
Colder thy kiss;
Truly that hour foretold
Sorrow to this.

The dew of the morning
Sunk chill on my brow—
It felt like the warning
Of what I feel now.
Thy vows are all broken,
And light is thy fame;
I hear thy name spoken,
And share in its shame.

They name thee before me,
A knell to mine ear;
A shudder comes o'er me—
Why wert thou so dear?
They know not I knew thee,
Who knew thee too well—
Long, long shall I rue thee,
Too deeply to tell.

In secret we met—
In silence I grieve
That thy heart could forget,
Thy spirit deceive.
If I should meet thee
After long years,
How should I greet thee?—
With silence and tears.

George Noel Gordon, Lord Byron

Come, You Pretty False-Eyed Wanton

Come, you pretty false-eyed wanton,
  Leave your crafty smiling!
Think you to escape me now
  With slipp'ry words beguiling?
No; you mocked me th'other day;
  When you got loose, you fled away;
But, since I have caught you now,
I'll clip your wings for flying:
Smoth'ring kisses fast I'll heap
  And keep you so from crying.

Sooner may you count the stars
  And number hail down-pouring,
Tell the osiers of the Thames,
  Or Goodwin sands devouring,
Than the thick-showered kisses here
  Which now thy tired lips must bear.
Such a harvest never was
  So rich and full of pleasure,
But 'tis spent as soon as reaped,
  So trustless is love's treasure.

THOMAS CAMPION

Jabberwocky

'Twas brillig, and the slithy toves
  Did gyre and gimble in the wabe;
All mimsy were the borogoves,
  And the mome raths outgrabe.

"Beware the Jabberwock, my son!
  The jaws that bite, the claws that catch!
Beware the Jubjub bird, and shun
  The frumious Bandersnatch!"

He took his vorpal sword in hand:
  Long time the manxome foe he sought—
So rested he by the Tumtum tree,
  And stood awhile in thought.

And, as in uffish thought he stood,
  The Jabberwock, with eyes of flame,
Came whiffling through the tulgey wood,
  And burbled as it came!

One, two! One, two! And through and through
  The vorpal blade went snicker-snack!
He left it dead, and with its head
  He went galumphing back.

"And hast thou slain the Jabberwock?
  Come to my arms, my beamish boy!
O frabjous day! Callooh! Callay!"
  He chortled in his joy.

'Twas brillig, and the slithy toves
  Did gyre and gimble in the wabe;
All mimsy were the borogoves,
  And the mome raths outgrabe.

LEWIS CARROLL

My Cabinets Are Oyster-Shells

My cabinets are oyster-shells,
In which I keep my orient pearls;
To open them I use the tide,
As keys to locks, which opens wide
The oyster shells, then out I take
Those orient pearls, and crowns do make;
And modest coral I do wear,
Which blushes when it touches air.
On silver waves I sit and sing,
And then the fish lie listening:
Then sitting on a rocky stone
I comb my hair with fishes' bone;
The whilst Apollo with his beams
Doth dry my hair from watery streams.
His light doth glaze the water's face,
Make the large sea my looking-glass:

So when I swim on waters high,
I see myself as I glide by:
But when the sun begins to burn,
I back into my waters turn,
And dive unto the bottom low:
Then on my head the waters flow
In curled waves and circles round,
And thus with waters am I crowned.

MARGARET CAVENDISH, DUCHESS OF NEWCASTLE

And Here the Hermit Sat, and Told His Beads

And here the hermit sat, and told his beads,
And stroked his flowing locks, red as the fire,
Summed up his tale of moon and sun and star:
'How blest are we,' he deemed, 'who so comprise
The essence of the whole, and of ourselves,
As in a Venice flask of lucent shape,
Ornate of gilt Arabic, and inscribed
With Suras from Time's Koran, live and pray,
More than half grateful for the glittering prize,
Human existence! If I note my powers,
So poor and frail a toy, the insect's prey,
Itched by a berry, festered by a plum,
The very air infecting my thin frame
With its malarial trick, whom every day
Rushes upon and hustles to the grave,
Yet raised, by the great love that broods o'er all
Responsive, to a height beyond all thought.'

He ended, as the nightly prayer and fast
Summoned him inward. But I sat and heard
The night-hawks rip the air above my head,
Till midnight o'er the warm, dry, dewless rocks;
And saw the blazing dog-star droop his fire,
And the low comet, trailing to the south,
Bend his reverted gaze, and leave us free.

WILLIAM ELLERY CHANNING

Mark Antony

When as the nightingale chanted her vespers,
And the wild forester couched on the ground,
Venus invited me in the evening whispers
Unto a fragrant field with roses crowned,
Where she before had sent
My wishes' complement;
Until my heart's content
Played with me on the green.
Never Mark Antony
Dallied more wantonly
With the fair Egyptian Queen.

First on her cherry cheeks I mine eyes feasted,
Thence fear of surfeiting made me retire;
Next on her warmer lips, which when I tasted,
My duller spirits made active as fire.
Then we began to dart,
Each at another's heart,
Arrows that knew no smart,
Sweet lips and smiles between.
Never Mark Antony
Dallied more wantonly
With the fair Egyptian Queen.

Wanting a glass to plait her amber tresses,
Which like a bracelet rich decked mine arm,
Gaudier than Juno wears when as she graces
Jove with embraces more stately than warm;
Then did she peep in mine
Eyes' humor crystalline;
I in her eyes was seen,
As if we one had been.
Never Mark Antony
Dallied more wantonly
With the fair Egyptian Queen.

Mystical grammar of amorous glances;
Feeling of pulses, the physic of love;
Rhetorical courtings and musical dances;
Numbering of kisses arithmetic prove;
Eyes like astronomy;
Straight-limbed geometry;
In her arts' ingeny
Our wits were sharp and keen.
Never Mark Antony
Dallied more wantonly
With the fair Egyptian Queen.

ingeny—ingeniousness

JOHN CLEVELAND

Dejection: An Ode

Late, late yestreen I saw the new Moon,
With the old Moon in her arms;
And I fear, I fear, my Master dear!
We shall have a deadly storm.

Ballad of Sir Patrick Spence.

I

Well! If the Bard was weather-wise, who made
The grand old ballad of Sir Patrick Spence,
This night, so tranquil now, will not go hence
Unroused by winds, that ply a busier trade
Than those which mold yon cloud in lazy flakes,
Or the dull sobbing draft, that moans and rakes
Upon the strings of this Aeolian lute,
Which better far were mute.
For lo! the New-moon winter-bright!
And overspread with phantom light,
(With swimming phantom light o'erspread
But rimmed and circled by a silver thread)
I see the old Moon in her lap, foretelling
The coming-on of rain and squally blast.
And oh! that even now the gust were swelling,
And the slant night-shower driving loud and fast!
Those sounds which oft have raised me, whilst they awed,
And sent my soul abroad,
Might now perhaps their wonted impulse give,
Might startle this dull pain, and make it move and live!

II

A grief without a pang, void, dark, and drear,
A stifled, drowsy, unimpassioned grief,
Which finds no natural outlet, no relief,
In word, or sigh, or tear—
O Lady! in this wan and heartless mood,
To other thoughts by yonder throstle wooed,
All this long eve, so balmy and serene,
Have I been gazing on the western sky,
And its peculiar tint of yellow green:
And still I gaze—and with how blank an eye!
And those thin clouds above, in flakes and bars,
That give away their motion to the stars;
Those stars, that glide behind them or between,
Now sparkling, now bedimmed, but always seen:
Yon crescent Moon, as fixed as if it grew

In its own cloudless, starless lake of blue;
I see them all so excellently fair,
I see, not feel, how beautiful they are!

III

My genial spirits fail;
And what can these avail
To lift the smothering weight from off my breast?
It were a vain endeavor,
Though I should gaze for ever
On that green light that lingers in the west:
I may not hope from outward forms to win
The passion and the life, whose fountains are within.

IV

O Lady! we receive but what we give,
And in our life alone does Nature live:
Ours is her wedding-garment, ours her shroud!
And would we aught behold, of higher worth,
Than that inanimate cold world allowed
To the poor loveless ever-anxious crowd,
Ah! from the soul itself must issue for
A light, a glory, a fair luminous cloud
Enveloping the Earth—
And from the soul itself must there be sent
A sweet and potent voice, of its own birth,
Of all sweet sounds the life and element!

V

O pure of heart! thou need'st not ask of me
What this strong music in the soul may be!
What, and wherein it doth exist,
This light, this glory, this fair luminous mist,
This beautiful and beauty-making power.
Joy, virtuous Lady! Joy that ne'er was given.
Save to the pure, and in their purest hour,
Life, and Life's effluence, cloud at once and shower,
Joy, Lady! is the spirit and the power,
Which, wedding Nature to us gives in dower
A new Earth and new Heaven,
Undreamt of by the sensual and the proud—
Joy is the sweet voice, Joy the luminous cloud—
We in ourselves rejoice!
And thence flows all that charms or ear or sight,
All melodies the echoes of that voice,
All colors a suffusion from that light.

VI

There was a time when, though my path was rough,
This joy within me dallied with distress,
And all misfortunes were but as the stuff
Whence Fancy made me dreams of happiness:
For hope grew round me, like the twining vine,
And fruits, and foliage, not my own, seemed mine.
But now afflictions bow me down to earth:
Nor care I that they rob me of my mirth;
But oh! each visitation
Suspends what nature gave me at my birth,
My shaping spirit of Imagination.
For not to think of what I needs must feel
But to be still and patient, all I can;
And haply by abstruse research to steal
From my own nature all the natural man —
This was my sole resource, my only plan:
Till that which suits a part infects the whole,
And now is almost grown the habit of my soul.

VII

Hence, viper thoughts, that coil around my mind,
Reality's dark dream!
I turn from you, and listen to the wind,
Which long has raved unnoticed. What a scream
Of agony by torture lengthened out
That lute sent forth! Thou Wind, that rav'st without,
Bare crag, or mountain-tairn, or blasted tree,
Or pine-grove whither woodman never clomb,
Or lonely house, long held the witches' home,
Methinks were fitter instruments for thee,
Mad Lutanist! who in this month of showers,
Of dark-brown gardens, and of peeping flowers,
Mak'st Devils' yule, with worse than wintry song,
The blossoms, buds, and timorous leaves among.
Thou actor, perfect in all tragic sounds!
Thou mighty Poet, e'en to frenzy bold!
What tell'st thou now about?
'Tis of the rushing of an host in rout,
With groans of trampled men, with smarting wounds—
At once they groan with pain, and shudder with the cold!
But hush! there is a pause of deepest silence!
And all that noise, as of a rushing crowd,
With groans, and tremulous shudderings—all is over—
It tells another tale, with sounds less deep and loud!
A tale of less affright,

And tempered with delight,
As Otway's self had framed the tender lay,—
'Tis of a little child
Upon a lonesome wild,
Not far from home, but she hath lost her way:
And now moans low in bitter grief and fear,
And now screams loud, and hopes to make her mother hear.

VIII

'Tis midnight, but small thoughts have I of sleep:
Full seldom may my friend such vigils keep!
Visit her, gentle Sleep! with wings of healing,
And may this storm be but a mountain-birth,
May all the stars hang bright above her dwelling,
Silent as though they watched the sleeping Earth!
With light heart may she rise,
Gay fancy, cheerful eyes,
Joy lift her spirit, joy attune her voice;
To her may all things live, from pole to pole,
Their life the eddying of her living soul!
O simple spirit, guided from above,
Dear Lady! friend devoutest of my choice,
Thus mayest thou ever, evermore rejoice.

SAMUEL TAYLOR COLERIDGE

The Rime of the Ancient Mariner

ARGUMENT

How a Ship having passed the Line was driven by storms to the cold Country towards the South Pole; and how from thence she made her course to the tropical Latitude of the Great Pacific Ocean; and of the strange things that befell: and in what manner the Ancyent Marinere came back to his own Country.

PART I

It is an ancient Mariner,
And he stoppeth one of three.
'By the long grey beard and glittering eye,
Now wherefore stopp'st thou me?

An ancient Mariner meeteth three Gallants bidden to a wedding-feast, and detaineth one.

The Bridegroom's doors are opened wide,
And I am next of kin;
The guests are met, the feast is set:
May'st hear the merry din.'

He holds him with his skinny hand,
'There was a ship,' quoth he.
'Hold off! unhand me, grey-beard loon!'
Eftsoons his hand dropt he.

He holds him with his glittering eye—
The Wedding-Guest stood still,
And listens like a three years' child:
The Mariner hath his will.

The Wedding-Guest is spellbound by the eye of the old seafaring man, and constrained to hear his tale.

The Wedding-Guest sat on a stone:
He cannot choose but hear;
And thus spake on that ancient man,
The bright-eyed Mariner.

'The ship was cheered, the harbour cleared,
Merrily did we drop
Below the kirk, below the hill,
Below the lighthouse top.

The Mariner tells how the ship sailed southward with a good wind and fair weather, till it reached the Line.

The Sun came up upon the left,
Out of the sea came he!
And he shone bright, and on the right
Went down into the sea.

Higher and higher every day,
Till over the mast at noon—'
The Wedding-Guest here beat his breast,
For he heard the loud bassoon.

The Wedding-Guest heareth the bridal music; but the Mariner continueth his tale.

The bride hath paced into the hall,
Red as a rose is she;
Nodding their heads before her goes
The merry minstrelsy.

The Wedding-Guest he beat his breast,
Ye he cannot choose but hear;
And thus spake on that ancient man,
The bright-eyed Mariner.

'And now the STORM-BLAST came, and he
Was tyrannous and strong:
He struck with his o'ertaking wings,
And chased us south along.

The ship driven by a storm toward the south pole.

With sloping masts and dipping prow,
As who pursued with yell and blow
Still treads the shadow of his foe,
And forward bends his head,
The ship drove fast, loud roared the blast,
And southward aye we fled.

And now there came both mist and snow,
And it grew wondrous cold:
And ice, mast-high, came floating by,
As green as emerald.

And through the drifts the snowy clifts
Did send a dismal sheen:
Nor shapes of men nor beasts we ken—
The ice was all between.

The land of ice, and of fearful sounds where no living thing was to be seen.

The ice was here, the ice was there,
The ice was all around:
It cracked and growled, and roared and howled,
Like noises in a swound!

At length did cross an Albatross,
Through the fog it came;
As if it had been a Christian soul,
We hailed it in God's name.

Till a great sea-bird called the Albatross, came through the snow-fog, and was received with great joy and hospitality.

It ate the food it ne'er had eat,
And round and round it flew.
The ice did split with a thunder-fit;
The helmsman steered us through!

And a good south wind sprung up behind;
The Albatross did follow,
And every day, for food or play,
Came to the mariner's hollo!

And lo! the Albatross proveth a bird of good omen, and followeth the ship as it returned northward through fog and floating ice.

In mist or cloud, on mast or shroud,
It perched for vespers nine;
Whiles all the night, through fog-smoke white,
Glimmered the white Moon-shine.'

'God save thee, ancient Mariner!
From the fiends, that plague thee thus!—
Why look'st thou so?'—With my cross-bow
I shot the ALBATROSS.

The ancient Mariner inhospitably killeth the pious bird of good omen.

PART II

The Sun now rose upon the right:
Out of the sea came he,
Still hid in mist, and on the left
Went down into the sea.

And the good south wind still blew behind,
But no sweet bird did follow,
Nor any day for food or play
Came to the mariners' hollo!

And I had done a hellish thing,
And it would work 'em woe:
For all averred, I had killed the bird
That made the breeze to blow.
Ah wretch! said they, the bird to slay,
That made the breeze to blow!

His shipmates cry out against the ancient Mariner, for killing the bird of good luck.

Nor dim nor red, like God's own head,
The glorious Sun uprist:
Then all averred, I had killed the bird
That brought the fog and mist.
'Twas right, said they, such birds to slay,
That bring the fog and mist.

But when the fog cleared off they justify the same, and thus made themselves accomplices in the crime.

The fair breeze blew, the white foam flew,
The furrow followed free;
We were the first that ever burst
Into that silent sea.

The fair breeze continues; the ship enters the Pacific Ocean, and sails northward, even till it reaches the Line.

Down dropt the breeze, the sails dropt down,
'Twas sad as sad could be;
And we did speak only to break
The silence of the sea!

The ship hath been suddenly becalmed.

All in a hot and copper sky,
The bloody Sun, at noon,
Right up above the mast did stand,
No bigger than the Moon.

Day after day, day after day,
We stuck, nor breath nor motion;
As idle as a painted ship
Upon a painted ocean.

And the Albatross begins to be avenged.

Water, water, every where
And all the boards did shrink;
Water, water, every where,
Nor any drop to drink.

The very deep did rot: O Christ!
That ever this should be!
Yea, slimy things did crawl with legs
Upon the slimy sea.

A Spirit had followed them; one of the invisible inhabitants of this planet, neither departed souls nor angels; concerning whom the learned Jew, Josephus, and the Platonic Constantinopolitan, Michael Psellus, may be consulted. They are very numerous, and there is no climate or element without one or more.

About, about, in reel and rout
The death-fires danced at night;
The water, like a witch's oils,
Burnt green, and blue and white.

And some in dreams assuréd were
Of the Spirit that plagued us so;
Nine fathom deep he had followed us
From the land of mist and snow.

The shipmates, in their sore distress, would fain throw the whole guilt on the ancient Mariner in sign whereof they hang the dead sea-bird round his neck.

And every tongue, through utter drought,
Was withered at the root;
We could not speak, no more than if
We had been choked with soot.

Ah! well a-day! what evil looks
Had I from old and young!
Instead of the cross, the Albatross
About my neck was hung.

PART III

The ancient Mariner beholdeth a sign in the element afar off.

There passed a weary time. Each throat
Was parched, and glazed each eye.
A weary time! a weary time!
How glazed each weary eye,
When looking westward, I beheld
A something in the sky.

At first it seemed a little speck,
And then it seemed a mist;
It moved and moved, and took at last
A certain shape, I wist.

A speck, a mist, a shape, I wist!
And still it neared and neared:
As if it dodged a water-sprite,
It plunged and tacked and veered.

At its nearer approach, it seemeth him to be a ship; and at a dear ransom he freeth his speech from the bonds of thirst.

With throats unslaked, with black lips baked,
We could nor laugh nor wail;
Through utter drought all dumb we stood!
I bit my arm, I sucked the blood,
And cried, A sail! a sail!

A flash of joy;

With throats unslaked, with black lips baked,
Agape they heard me call:
Gramercy! they for joy did grin,
And all at once their breath drew in,
As they were drinking all.

And horror follows. For can it be a ship that comes onward without wind or tide?

See! see! (I cried) she tacks no more!
Hither to work us weal;
Without a breeze, without a tide,
She steadies with upright keel!

The western wave was all a-flame.
The day was well nigh done!
Almost upon the western wave
Rested the broad bright Sun;
When that strange shape drove suddenly
Betwixt us and the Sun.

It seemeth him but the skeleton of a ship.

And straight the Sun was flecked with bars,
(Heaven's Mother send us grace!)
As if through a dungeon-grate he peered
With broad and burning face.

Alas! (thought I, and my heart beat loud)
How fast she nears and nears!
Are those *her* sails that glance in the Sun,
Like restless gossameres?

And its ribs are seen as bars on the face of the setting sun.

Are those *her* ribs through which the Sun
Did peer, as through a grate?
And is that Woman all her crew?
Is that a DEATH? and are there two?
Is DEATH that woman's mate?

The Specter-Woman and her Death-mate, and no other on board the skelton-ship.

Like vessel, like crew!

Her lips were red, *her* looks were free,
Her locks were yellow as gold:
Her skin was as white as leprosy,
The Night-mare LIFE-IN-DEATH was she,
Who thicks man's blood with cold.

Death and Life-in-Death have diced for the ship's crew, and she (the latter) winneth the ancient Mariner.

The naked hulk alongside came,
And the twain were casting dice;
'The game is done! I've won! I've won!'
Quoth she, and whistles thrice,

No twilight within the courts of the Sun.

The Sun's rim dips; the stars rush out:
At one stride comes the dark;
With far-heard whisper, o'er the sea,
Off shot the spectre-bark.

At the rising of the Moon,

We listened and looked sideways up!
Fear at my heart, as at a cup,
My life-blood seemed to sip!
The stars were dim, and thick the night,
The steersman's face by his lamp gleamed white;
From the sails the dew did drip—
Till clomb above the eastern bar
The hornéd Moon, with one bright star
Within the nether tip.

One after one, by the star-dogged Moon,
Too quick for groan or sigh,
Each turned his face with a ghastly pang,
And cursed me with his eye.

One after another,

Four times fifty living men,
(And I heard nor sigh nor groan)
With heavy thump, a lifeless lump,
They dropped down one by one.

His shipmates drop down dead.

The souls did from their bodies fly,—
They fled to bliss or woe!
And every soul, it passed me by,
Like the whizz of my cross-bow!

But Life-in-Death begins her work on the ancient Mariner.

PART IV

'I fear thee, ancient Mariner!
I fear the skinny hand!
And thou art long, and lank, and brown,
As is the ribbed sea-sand.

The Wedding-Guest feareth that a Spirit is talking to him;

I fear thee and thy glittering eye,
And thy skinny hand, so brown.'—
Fear not, fear not, thou Wedding-Guest!
This body dropt not down.

But the ancient Mariner assureth him of his bodily life, and proceedeth to relate his horrible penance.

Alone, alone, all, all alone,
Alone on a wide wide sea!
And never a saint took pity on
My soul in agony.

The many men, so beautiful!
And they all dead did lie:
And a thousand thousand slimy things
Lived on; and so did I.

He despiseth the creatures of the calm.

I looked upon the rotting sea,
And drew my eyes away;
I looked upon the rotting deck,
And there the dead men lay.

And envieth that they should live, and so many lie dead.

I looked to heaven, and tried to pray;
But or ever a prayer had gusht,
A wicked whisper came, and made
My heart as dry as dust.

I closed my lids, and kept them close,
And the balls like pulses beat;
For the sky and the sea, and the sea and the sky
Lay like a load on my weary eye,
And the dead were at my feet.

But the curse liveth for him in the eye of the dead men.

The cold sweat melted from their limbs,
Nor rot nor reek did they:
The look with which they looked on me
Had never passed away.

An orphan's curse would drag to hell
A spirit from on high;
But oh! more horrible than that
Is the curse in a dead man's eye!
Seven days, seven nights, I saw that curse,
And yet I could not die.

In his loneliness and fixedness he yearneth towards the journeying Moon, and the stars that still sojourn, yet still move onward; and everywhere the blue sky belongs to them, and is their appointed rest, and their native country and their own natural homes, which they enter unannounced, as lords that are certainly expected, and yet there is a silent joy at their arrival.

The moving Moon went up the sky,
And no where did abide:
Softly she was going up,
And a star or two beside—

Her beams bemocked the sultry main,
Like April hoar-frost spread;
But where the ship's huge shadow lay,
The charméd water burnt away
A still and awful red.

By the light of the Moon he beholdeth God's creatures of the great calm.

Beyond the shadow of the ship,
I watched the water-snakes:
They moved in tracks of shining white,
And when they reared, the elfish light
Fell off in hoary flakes.

Within the shadow of the ship
I watched their rich attire:
Blue, glossy green, and velvet black,
They coiled and swam; and every track
Was a flash of golden fire.

Their beauty and their happiness.

O happy living things! no tongue
Their beauty might declare:
A spring of love gushed from my heart,
And I blessed them unaware:

He blesseth them in his heart.

Sure my kind saint took pity on me,
And I blessed them unaware.

The spell begins to break.

The self-same moment I could pray;
And from my neck so free
The Albatross fell off, and sank
Like lead into the sea.

PART V

Oh sleep! it is a gentle thing,
Beloved from pole to pole!
To Mary Queen the praise be given!
She sent the gentle sleep from Heaven,
That slid into my soul.

By grace of the holy Mother, the ancient Mariner is refreshed with rain.

The silly buckets on the deck,
That had so long remained,
I dreamt that they were filled with dew;
And when I awoke, it rained.

My lips were wet, my throat was cold,
My garments all were dank;
Sure I had drunken in my dreams,
And still my body drank.

I moved, and could not feel my limbs:
I was so light—almost
I thought that I had died in sleep,
And was a blessèd ghost.

He heareth sounds and seeth strange sights and commotions in the sky and the element.

And soon I heard a roaring wind:
It did not come anear;
But with its sound it shook the sails,
That were so thin and sere.

The upper air burst into life!
And a hundred fire-flags sheen,
To and fro they were hurried about!
And to and fro, and in and out,
The wan stars danced between.

And the coming wind did roar more loud.
And the sails did sigh like sedge;
And the rain poured down from one black cloud;
The Moon was at its edge.

The thick black cloud was cleft, and still
The Moon was at its side:
Like waters shot from some high crag,
The lightning fell with never a jag,
A river steep and wide.

The bodies of the ship's crew are inspired, and the ship moves on;

The loud wind never reached the ship,
Yet now the ship moved on!
Beneath the lightning and the Moon
The dead men gave a groan.

They groaned, they stirred, they all uprose,
Nor spake, nor moved their eyes;
It had been strange, even in a dream,
To have seen those dead men rise.

The helmsman steered, the ship moved on;
Yet never a breeze up-blew;
The mariners all 'gan work the ropes,
Where they were wont to do;
They raised their limbs like lifeless tools—
We were a ghastly crew.

The body of my brother's son
Stood by me, knee to knee:
The body and I pulled at one rope,
But he said nought to me.

But not by the souls of the men, nor by demons of of earth or middle air, but by a blessed troop of angelic spirits, sent down by the invocation of the guardian saint.

'I fear thee, ancient Mariner!'
Be calm, thou Wedding-Guest!
'Twas not those souls that fled in pain.
Which to their corses came again,
But a troop of spirits blest:

For when it dawned—they dropped their arms,
And clustered round the mast;
Sweet sounds rose slowly through their mouths,
And from their bodies passed.

Around, around, flew each sweet sound,
Then darted to the Sun;
Slowly the sounds came back again,
Now mixed, now one by one.

Sometimes a-dropping from the sky
I heard the sky-lark sing;
Sometimes all little birds that are,
How they seemed to fill the sea and air
With their sweet jargoning!

And now 'twas like all instruments,
Now like a lonely flute;
And now it is an angel's song,
That makes the heavens be mute.

It ceased; yet still the sails made on
A pleasant noise till noon,
A noise like of a hidden brook
In the leafy month of June,
That to the sleeping woods all night
Singeth a quite tune.

Till noon we quietly sailed on,
Yet never a breeze did breathe:
Slowly and smoothly went the ship,
Moved onward from beneath.

Under the keel nine fathom deep,
From the land of mist and snow,
The spirit said: and it was he
That made the ship to go.
The sails at noon left off their tune,
And the ship stood still also.

The lonesome Spirit from the South Pole carries on the ship as far as the Line, in obedience to the angelic troop, but still requireth vengeance.

The Sun, right up above the mast,
Had fixed her to the ocean:
But in a minute she 'gan stir,
With a short uneasy motion—
Backwards and forwards half her length
With a short uneasy motion.

Then like a pawing horse let go,
She made a sudden bound:
It flung the blood into my head,
And I fell down in a swound.

The Polar Spirit's fellow demons, the invisible inhabitants of the element, take part in his wrong; and two of them relate, one to the other, that penance long and heavy for the ancient Mariner hath been accorded to the Polar Spirit, who returneth southward.

How long in that same fit I lay,
I have not to declare;
But ere my living life returned,
I heard and in my soul discerned
Two voices in the air.

'Is it he?' quoth one, 'Is this the man?
By him who died on cross,
With his cruel bow he laid full low
The harmless Albatross.

The spirit who bideth by himself
In the land of mist and snow,
He loved the bird that loved the man
Who shot him with his bow.'

The other was a softer voice,
As soft as honey-dew:
Quoth he, 'The man hath penance done,
And penance more will do.'

PART VI

FIRST VOICE

'But tell me, tell me! speak again,
Thy soft response renewing—
What makes that ship drive on so fast?
What is the ocean doing?'

SECOND VOICE

'Still as a slave before his lord,
The ocean hath no blast;
His great bright eye most silently
Up to the Moon is cast—

If he may know which way to go;
For she guides him smooth or grim.
See, brother, see! how graciously
She looketh down on him.'

FIRST VOICE

The Mariner hath been cast into a trance; for the angelic power causeth the vessel to drive northward faster than human life could endure.

'But why drives on that ship so fast,
Without or wave or wind?'

SECOND VOICE

'The air is cut away before,
And closes from behind.

Fly, brother, fly! more high, more high!
Or we shall be belated:
For slow and slow that ship will go,
When the Mariner's trance is abated.'

The supernatural motion is retarded; the Mariner awakes, and his penance begins anew.

I woke, and we were sailing on
As in a gentle weather:
'Twas night, calm night, the moon was high;
The dead men stood together.

All stood together on the deck,
For a charnel-dungeon fitter:
All fixed on me their stony eyes,
That in the Moon did glitter.

The pang, the curse, with which they died,
Had never passed away:
I could not draw my eyes from theirs,
Nor turn them up to pray.

And now this spell was snapt: once more
I viewed the ocean green,
And looked far forth, yet little saw
Of what had else been seen—

The curse is finally expiated.

Like one, that on a lonesome road
Doth walk in fear and dread,
And having once turned round walks on,
And turns no more his head;
Because he knows, a frightful fiend
Doth close behind him tread.

But soon there breathed a wind on me,
Nor sound nor motion made:
Its path was not upon the sea,
In ripple or in shade.

It raised my hair, it fanned my cheek
Like a meadow-gale of spring—
It mingled strangely with my fears,
Yet it felt like a welcoming.

Swiftly, swiftly flew the ship.
Yet she sailed softly too:
Sweetly, sweetly blew the breeze—
On me alone it blew.

And the ancient Mariner beholdeth his native country.

Oh! dream of joy! is this indeed
The light-house top I see?
Is this the hill? is this the kirk?
Is this mine own countree?

We drifted o'er the harbour-bar,
And I with sobs did pray—
O let me be awake, my God!
Or let me sleep alway.

The harbour-bay was clear as glass,
So smoothly it was strewn!
And on the bay the moonlight lay,
And the shadow of the Moon.

The rock shone bright, the kirk no less,
That stands above the rock:
The moonlight steeped in silentness
The steady weathercock.

The angelic spirits leave the dead bodies.

And the bay was white with silent light,
Till rising from the same,
Full many shapes, that shadows were,
In crimson colours came.

A little distance from the prow
Those crimson shadows were:
I turned my eyes upon the deck—
Oh, Christ! what saw I there!

And appear in their own forms of light.

Each corse lay flat, lifeless and flat,
And, by the holy rood!
A man all light, a seraph-man,
On every corse there stood.

This seraph-band, each waved his hand:
It was a heavenly sight!
They stood as signals to the land,
Each one a lovely light;

This seraph-band, each waved his hand,
No voice did they impart—
No voice; but oh! the silence sank
Like music on my heart.

But soon I heard the dash of oars,
I heard the Pilot's cheer;
My head was turned perforce away
And I saw a boat appear.

The Pilot and the Pilot's boy,
I heard them coming fast:
Dear Lord in Heaven! it was a joy
The dead men could not blast.

I saw a third—I heard his voice:
It is the Hermit good!
He singeth loud his godly hymns
That he makes in the wood.
He'll shrieve my soul, he'll wash away
The Albatross's blood.

PART VII

The Hermit of the wood.

This Hermit good lives in that wood
Which slopes down to the sea.
How loudly his sweet voice he rears!
He loves to talk with marineres
That come from a far countree.

He kneels at morn, and noon, and eve—
He hath a cushion plump:
It is the moss that wholly hides
The rotted old oak-stump.

The skiff-boat neared: I heard them talk,
'Why, this is strange, I trow!
Where are those lights so many and fair,
That signal made but now?'

Approacheth the ship with wonder.

'Strange, by my faith!' the Hermit said—
'And they answered not our cheer!
The planks looked warped! and see those sails,
How thin they are and sere!
I never saw aught like to them,
Unless perchance it were

Brown skeletons of leaves that lag
My forest-brook along;
When the ivy-tod is heavy with snow,
And the owlet whoops to the wolf below,
That eats the she-wolf's young.'

'Dear Lord! it hath a fiendish look—
(The Pilot made reply)
I am a-feared'—'Push on, push on!'
Said the Hermit cheerily.

The boat came closer to the ship,
But I nor spake nor stirred;
The boat came close beneath the ship,
And straight a sound was heard.

The ship suddenly sinketh.

Under the water it rumbled on,
Still louder and more dread:
It reached the ship, it split the bay;
The ship went down like lead.

The ancient Mariner is saved in the Pilot's boat.

Stunned by that loud and dreadful sound,
Which sky and ocean smote,
Like one that hath been seven days drowned
My body lay afloat;
But swift as dreams, myself I found
Within the Pilot's boat.

Upon the whirl, where sank the ship,
The boat spun round and round;
And all was still, save that the hill
Was telling of the sound.

I moved my lips—the Pilot shrieked
And fell down in a fit;
The holy Hermit raised his eyes,
And prayed where he did sit.

I took the oars: the Pilot's boy,
Who now doth crazy go,
Laughed loud and long, and all the while
His eyes went to and fro.
'Ha! ha!' quoth he, 'full plain I see,
The Devil knows how to row.'

And now, all in my own countree,
I stood on the firm land!
The Hermit stepped forth from the boat,
And scarcely he could stand.

The ancient Mariner earnestly entreateth the Hermit to shrieve him; and the penance of life falls on him.

'O shrieve me, shrieve me, holy man!'
The Hermit crossed his brow.
'Say quick,' quoth he, 'I bid thee say—
What manner of man art thou?'

Forthwith this frame of mine was wrenched
With a woful agony,
Which forced me to begin my tale;
And then it left me free.

And ever and anon throughout his future life an agony constraineth him to travel from land to land,

Since then, at an uncertain hour,
That agony returns:
And till my ghastly tale is told,
This heart within me burns.

I pass, like night, from land to land;
I have strange power of speech;
That moment that his face I see,
I know the man that must hear me:
To him my tale I teach.

What loud uproar bursts from that door!
The wedding-guests are there:
But in the garden-bower the bride
And bride-maids singing are:
And hark the little vesper bell,
Which biddeth me to prayer!

O Wedding-Guest! this soul hath been
Alone on a wide wide sea:
So lonely 'twas, that God himself
Scarce seeméd there to be.

O sweeter than the marriage-feast,
'Tis sweeter far to me,
To walk together to the kirk
With a goodly company!—

To walk together to the kirk,
And all together pray,
While each to his great Father bends,
Old men, and babes, and loving friends
And youths and maidens gay!

Farewell, farewell! but this I tell
To thee, thou Wedding Guest!
He prayeth well, who loveth well
Both man and bird and beast.

And to teach by his own example love and reverence to all things that God made and loveth.

He prayeth best, who loveth best
All things both great and small;
For the dear God who loveth us,
He made and loveth all.

The Mariner, whose eye is bright,
Whose beard with age is hoar,
Is gone: and now the Wedding-Guest
Turned from the bridegroom's door.

He went like one that hath been stunned,
And is of sense forlorn:
A sadder and a wiser man,
He rose the morrow morn.

SAMUEL TAYLOR COLERIDGE

Ode

How sleep the brave, who sink to rest
By all their country's wishes blest!
When *Spring,* with dewy fingers cold,
Returns to deck their hallowed mold,
She there shall dress a sweeter sod,
Than *Fancy's* feet have ever trod.

By fairy hands their knell is rung,
By forms unseen their dirge is sung;
There *Honor* comes, a pilgrim gray,
To bless the turf that wraps their clay,
And *Freedom* shall awhile repair,
To dwell a weeping hermit there!

WILLIAM COLLINS

Ode on the Death of Mr. Thomson

In yonder grave a druid lies,
Where slowly winds the stealing wave;
The year's best sweets shall duteous rise
To deck its poet's sylvan grave.

In yon deep bed of whispering reeds
His airy harp shall now be laid,
That he, whose heart in sorrow bleeds,
May love through life the soothing shade.

Then maids and youths shall linger here,
And while its sounds at distance swell,
Shall sadly seem in pity's ear
To hear the woodland pilgrim's knell.

Remembrance oft shall haunt the shore
When Thames in summer wreaths is dressed,
And oft suspend the dashing oar,
To bid his gentle spirit rest!

And oft, as ease and health retire
To breezy lawn, or forest deep,
The friend shall view yon whitening spire,
And 'mid the varied landscape weep.

But thou, who own'st that earthy bed,
Ah! what will every dirge avail;
Or tears, which love and pity shed,
That mourn beneath the gliding sail?

Yet lives there one whose heedless eye
Shall scorn thy pale shrine glimmering near?
With him, sweet bard, may fancy die,
And joy desert the blooming year.

But thou, lorn stream, whose sullen tide
  No sedge-crowned sisters now attend,
Now waft me from the green hill's side,
  Whose cold turf hides the buried friend!

And see—the fairy valleys fade;
  Dun night has veiled the solemn view!
Yet once again, dear parted shade,
  Meek nature's child, again adieu!

The genial meads, assigned to bless
  Thy life, shall mourn thy early doom:
Their hinds and shepherd-girls shall dress,
  With simple hands, thy rural tomb.

Long, long, thy stone and pointed clay
  Shall melt the musing Briton's eyes:
O vales and wild woods! shall he say,
  In yonder grave your druid lies!

William Collins

Pious Celinda

Pious Celinda goes to prayers,
  If I but ask the favour;
And yet the tender fool's in tears
  When she believes I'll leave her.

Would I were free from this restraint,
  Or else had hopes to win her;
Would she could make of me a saint,
  Or I of her a sinner.

William Congreve

From *To Della Crusca*

Oh sympathy, of birth divine,
Descend, and round my heart-strings twine!
Touch the fine nerve, whene'er I breathe
Where Della Crusca dropt his wreath!
Lead me to the sacred way of Rome,
Lead me to kneel at Virgil's tomb,
Where he th' enduring marble round
With fresh-wove laurels, graceful bound.
The guide where still with sweeter note
Than flowed from Petrarch's tuneful throat,
On Laura's grave he poured the lay
Amidst the sighs of sinking day:
Then point where on the sod his tear
Fell from its crystal source so clear,
That there my mingling tear may sink,
And the same dust its moisture drink.

HANNAH COWLEY

On the Loss of the Royal George

Toll for the brave—
The brave! that are no more:
All sunk beneath the wave,
Fast by their native shore.
Eight hundred of the brave,
Whose courage well was tried,
Had made the vessel heel
And laid her on her side;
A land-breeze shook the shrouds,
And she was overset;
Down went the *Royal George*,
With all her crew complete.

Toll for the brave—
Brave Kempenfelt is gone,
His last sea-fight is fought,
His work of glory done.
It was not in the battle,
No tempest gave the shock,
She sprang no fatal leak,
She ran upon no rock;
His sword was in the sheath,
His fingers held the pen,
When Kempenfelt went down
With twice four hundred men.

Weigh the vessel up,
Once dreaded by our foes,
And mingle with our cup
The tears that England owes;
Her timbers yet are sound,
And she may float again,
Full charged with England's thunder,
And plow the distant main;
But Kempenfelt is gone,
His victories are o'er;
And he and his eight hundred
Must plow the wave no more.

William Cowper

The Castaway

Obscurest night involved the sky,
Th' Atlantic billows roared,
When such a destined wretch as I ,
Washed headlong from on board,
Of friends, of hope, of all bereft,
His floating home for ever left.

No braver chief could Albion boast
Than he with whom he went,
Nor ever ship left Albion's coast,
With warmer wishes sent.
He loved them both, but both in vain,
Nor him beheld, nor her again.

Not long beneath the whelming brine,
Expert to swim, he lay;
Nor soon he felt his strength decline,
Or courage die away;
But waged with death a lasting strife,
Supported by despair of life.

He shouted: nor his friends had failed
To check the vessel's course,
But so the furious blast prevailed,
That, pitiless perforce,
They left their outcast mate behind,
And scudded still before the wind.

Some succour yet they could afford;
And such as storms allow,
The cask, the coop, the floated cord,
Delayed not to bestow.
But he (they knew) nor ship, nor shore,
Whate'er they gave, should visit more.

Nor, cruel as it seemed, could he
Their haste himself condemn,
Aware that flight, in such a sea,
Alone could rescue them;
Yet bitter felt it still to die
Deserted, and his friends so nigh.

He long survives, who lives an hour
In ocean, self-upheld;
And so long he, with unspent power,
His destiny repelled;
And ever, as the minutes flew,
Entreated help, or cried—Adieu!

At length, his transient respite past,
His comrades, who before
Had heard his voice in every blast,
Could catch the sound no more.
For then, by toil subdued, he drank
The stifling wave, and then he sank.

No poet wept him: but the page
Of narrative sincere,
That tells his name, his worth, his age,
Is wet with Anson's tear.
And tears by bards or heroes shed
Alike immortalize the dead.

I therefore purpose not, or dream,
Descanting on his fate,
To give the melancholy theme
A more enduring date:
But misery still delights to trace
Its 'semblance in another's case.

No voice divine the storm allayed,
No light propitious shone;
When, snatched from all effectual aid,
We perished, each alone:
But I beneath a rougher sea,
And whelmed in deeper gulphs than he.

WILLIAM COWPER

Enjoy Thy April Now

Enjoy thy April now,
Whilst it doth freely shine;
This lightning flash and show,
With that clear spirit of thine,
Will suddenly decline;
And thou, fair murdering eyes,
Shall be Love's tombs, where now his cradle lies.

Thy gold and scarlet shall
Pale silver colour be;
Thy row of pearls shall fall
Like withered leaves from tree;
And thou shall shortly see
Thy face and hair to grow
All ploughed with furrows, over-swoln with snow.

That which on Flora's breast,
All fresh and flourishing,
Aurora, newly dressed,
Saw in her dawning spring;
Quite dry and languishing,
Deprived of honor quite,
Day-closing Hesperus beholds at night.

Fair is the lily, fair
The rose, of flowers the eye;
Both wither in the air,
Their beauteous colours die:
And so at length shall lie
Deprived of former grace,
The lilies of thy breasts, the roses of thy face.

What then will it avail,
O youth, advisèd ill,
In lap of Beauty frail
To nurse a wayward will,
Like snake in sun-warm hill?
Pluck, pluck betime thy flower,
That springs and parcheth in one short hour!

SAMUEL DANIEL

Love is a Sickness

Love is a sickness full of woes,
  All remedies refusing;
A plant that with most cutting grows,
  Most barren with best using.
    Why so?
More we enjoy it, more it dies;
If not enjoyed it sighing cries
    Hey ho.

Love is a torment of the mind,
  A tempest everlasting;
And love hath made it of a kind
  Not well, nor full, nor fasting.
    Why so?
More we enjoy it, more it dies;
If not enjoyed it sighing cries,
    Hey ho.

SAMUEL DANIEL

Golden Slumbers

Golden slumbers kiss your eyes,
Smiles awake you when you rise.
Sleep, pretty wantons, do not cry,
And I will sing a lullaby:
Rock them, rock them, lullaby.

Care is heavy, therefore sleep you;
You are care, and care must keep you.
Sleep, pretty wantons, do not cry,
And I will sing a lullaby:
Rock them, rock them, lullaby.

THOMAS DEKKER

Haymakers, Rakers

Haymakers, rakers, reapers, and mowers,
  Wait on your Summer-queen;
Dress up with musk-rose her eglantine bowers,
  Daffodils strew the green;
    Sing, dance, and play,
    'Tis holiday;
  The sun does bravely shine
  On our ears of corn.
    Rich as a pearl
    Comes every girl,
  This is mine, this is mine, this is mine;
Let us die, ere away they be borne.

Bow to the Sun, to our queen, and that fair one
  Come to behold our sports:
Each bonny lass here is counted a rare one,
  As those in a prince's courts.
    These and we
    With country glee,
  Will teach the woods to resound,
  And the hills with echoes hollow:
    Skipping lambs
    Their bleating dams,
  'Mongst kids shall trip it round;
For joy thus our wenches we follow.

Wind, jolly huntsmen, your neat bugles shrilly,
  Hounds make a lusty cry;
Spring up, you falconers, the partridges freely,
  Then let your brave hawks fly.
    Horses amain,
    Over ridge, over plain,
  The dogs have the stag in chase:
  'Tis a sport to content a king.
    So ho ho! through the skies
    How the proud bird flies,
  And sousing kills with a grace!
Now the deer falls; hark, how they ring!

THOMAS DEKKER

A Face Devoid of Love or Grace

A face devoid of love or grace
A hateful, hard, successful face,
A face with which a stone
Would feel as thoroughly at ease
As were they old acquaintances,—
First time together thrown.

EMILY DICKINSON

Faith is a Fine Invention

Faith is a fine invention
For gentlemen who see;
But microscopes are prudent
In an emergency!

EMILY DICKINSON

I Stepped from Plank to Plank

I stepped from plank to plank
So slow and cautiously;
The stars about my head I felt,
About my feet the sea.

I knew not but the next
Would be my final inch,—
This gave me that precarious gait
Some call experience.

EMILY DICKINSON

It Dropped so Low in My Regard

It dropped so low in my regard
I heard it hit the ground,
And go to pieces on the stones
At bottom of my mind;

Yet blamed the fate that fractured, less
Than I reviled myself
For entertaining plated wares
Upon my silver shelf.

EMILY DICKINSON

Safe

Safe in their alabaster chambers,
Untouched by morning and untouched by noon,
Sleep the meek members of the resurrection,
Rafter of satin and roof of stone.

Light laughs the breeze in her castle of sunshine;
Babbles the bee in a stolid ear;
Pipe the sweet birds in ignorant cadence,—
Ah, what sagacity perished here!

Grand go the years in the crescent above them;
Worlds scoop their arcs, and firmaments row,
Diadems drop and Doges surrender,
Soundless as dots on a disk of snow.

EMILY DICKINSON

Split the Lark and You'll Find the Music

Split the lark and you'll find the music,
Bulb after bulb, in silver rolled,
Scantily dealt to the summer morning,
Saved for your ear when lutes be old.

Loose the flood, you shall find it patent,
Gush after gush, reserved for you;
Scarlet experiment! Sceptic Thomas,
Now, do you doubt that your bird was true?

EMILY DICKINSON

Sweet is the Swamp with its Secrets

Sweet is the swamp with its secrets,
Until we meet a snake;
'Tis then we sigh for houses,
And our departure take
At that enthralling gallop
That only childhood knows.
A snake is summer's treason,
And guile is where it goes.

EMILY DICKINSON

The Brain

The brain within its groove
Runs evenly and true;
But let a splinter swerve,
'Twere easier for you
To put the water back
When floods have slit the hills,
And scooped a turnpike for themselves,
And blotted out the mills!

EMILY DICKINSON

The Mushroom is the Elf of Plants

The mushroom is the elf of plants,
At evening it is not;
At morning in a truffled hut
It stops upon a spot

As if it tarried always;
And yet its whole career
Is shorter than a snake's delay,
And fleeter than a tare.

'Tis vegetation's juggler,
The germ of alibi;
Doth like a bubble antedate,
And like a bubble hie.

I feel as if the grass were pleased
To have it intermit;
The surreptitious scion
Of summer's circumspect.

Had nature any outcast face,
Could she a son contemn,
Had nature an Iscariot,
That mushroom,—it is him.

EMILY DICKINSON

The Pedigree of Honey

The pedigree of honey
Does not concern the bee;
A clover, any time, to him
Is aristocracy.

EMILY DICKINSON

The Rat is the Concisest Tenant

The rat is the concisest tenant.
He pays no rent,—
Repudiates the obligation,
On schemes intent.

Balking our wit
To sound or circumvent,
Hate cannot harm
A foe so reticent.

Neither decree
Prohibits him,
Lawful as
Equilibrium.

EMILY DICKINSON

Upon the Gallows Hung a Wretch

Upon the gallows hung a wretch,
Too sullied for the hell
To which the law entitled him.
As nature's curtain fell
The one who bore him tottered in,
For this was woman's son.
" 'Twas all I had," she stricken gasped;
Oh, what a livid boon!

EMILY DICKINSON

Love's Infiniteness

If yet I have not all thy love,
Dear, I shall never have it all,
I cannot breathe one other sigh, to move,
Nor can intreat one other tear to fall,
And all my treasure, which should purchase thee,
Sigh, tears, and oaths, and letters, I have spent.
Yet no more can be due to me,
Than at the bargain made was meant;
If then thy gift of love were partial,
That some to me, some should to others fall,
  Dear, I shall never have thee all.

Or if then thou gavest me all,
All was but all, which thou hadst then;
But if in thy heart, since, there be or shall,
New love created be, by other men,
Which have their stocks entire, and can in tears,
In sighs, in oaths, and letters outbid me,
This new love may beget new fears,
For, this love was not vowed by thee;
And yet it was, thy gift being general,
The ground, thy heart is mine, what ever shall
  Grow there, dear; I should have it all.

Yet I would not have all yet;
He that hath all can have no more,
And since my love doth every day admit
New growth, thou shouldst have new rewards in store;
Thou canst not every day give me thy heart,
If thou canst give it, then thou never gavest it:
Love's riddles are, that though thy heart depart,
It stays at home, and thou with losing savest it:
But we will have a way more liberal,
Than changing hearts, to join them, so we shall
  Be one, and one another's all.

JOHN DONNE

Song

Go and catch a falling star;
  Get with child a mandrake root;
Tell me where all past years are,
  Or who cleft the Devil's foot;
Teach me to hear mermaids singing,
Or to keep off envy's stinging.
    And find
    What wind
Serves to advance an honest mind.

If thou be'st born to strange sights,
  Things invisible to see,
Ride ten thousand days and nights
  Till age snow white hairs on thee;
Thou, when thou return'st, wilt tell me
All strange wonders that befell thee,
    And swear
    No where
Lives a woman true and fair.

If thou find'st one, let me know;
  Such a pilgrimage were sweet.
Yet do not; I would not go,
  Though at next door we might meet.
Though she were true when you met her,
And last till you write your letter,
    Yet she
    Will be
False, ere I come, to two or three.

John Donne

The Good-Morrow

I wonder by my troth, what thou and I
Did, till we loved? Were we not weaned till then,
But sucked on country pleasures, childishly?
Or snorted we in the seven sleepers' den?
'Twas so; but this, all pleasures fancies be.
If ever any beauty I did see,
Which I desired, and got, 'twas but a dream of thee.

And now good morrow to our waking souls,
Which watch not one another out of fear;
For love all love of other sights controls,
And makes one little room an everywhere.
Let sea-discoverers to new worlds have gone,
Let maps to other, worlds on worlds have shown;
Let us possess one world, each hath one, and is one.

My face in thine eye, thine in mine appears,
And true plain hearts do in the faces rest;
Where can we find two better hemispheres
Without sharp north, without declining west?
Whatever dies was not mixed equally;
If our two loves be one, or thou and I
Love so alike that none do slacken, none can die.

John Donne

The Indifferent

I can love both fair and brown;
Her whom abundance melts, and her whom want betrays;
Her who loves loneness best, and her who masks and plays;
Her whom the country formed, and whom the town;
Her who believes, and her who tries;
Her who still weeps with spongy eyes,
And her who is dry cork and never cries.
I can love her, and her, and you, and you;
I can love any, so she be not true.

Will no other vice content you?
Will it not serve your turn to do as did your mothers?
Or have you all old vices spent and now would find out others?
Or doth a fear that men are true torment you?
O we are not, be not you so;
Le me—and do you—twenty know;
Rob me, but bind me not, and let me go.
Must I, who came to travel thorough you,
Grow your fixed subject, because you are true?

Venus heard me sigh this song;
And by love's sweetest part, variety, she swore,
She heard not this till now; it should be so no more.
She went, examined, and returned ere long,
And said, "Alas! some two or three
Poor heretics in love there be,
Which think to stablish dangerous constancy.
But I have told them, 'Since you will be true,
You shall be true to them, who're false to you.' "

John Donne

Agincourt

Fair stood the wind for France,
When we our sails advance,
Nor now to prove our chance,
Longer will tarry;
But putting to the main,
At Caux, the mouth of Seine,
With all his martial train,
Landed King Harry.

And taking many a fort,
Furnished in warlike sort,
Marcheth towards Agincourt,
In happy hour;
Skirmishing day by day,
With those that stopped his way,
Where the French general lay,
With all his power.

Which in his height of pride,
King Henry to deride,
His ransom to provide
To the King sending.
Which he neglects the while,
As from a nation vile,
Yet with an angry smile,
Their fall portending.

And turning to his men,
Quoth our brave Henry then,
"Though they to one be ten,
Be not amazed.
Yet have we well begun,
Battles so bravely won,
Have ever to the sun,
By fame been raised.

"And for myself," quoth he,
"This my full rest shall be,
England ne'er mourn for me,
Nor more esteem me.
Victor I will remain,
Or on this earth lie slain,
Never shall she sustain
Loss to redeem me.

"Poitiers and Cressy tell,
When most their pride did swell,
Under our swords they fell,
No less our skill is,
Than when our grandsire great,
Claiming the regal seat,
By many a warlike feat,
Lopped the French lilies."

The Duke of York so dread
The eager vaward led;
With the main, Henry sped
Amongst his henchmen.
Excester had the rear,
A braver man not there,
O Lord, how hot they were,
On the false Frenchmen!

They now to fight are gone,
Armor on armor shone,
Drum now to drum did groan,
To hear, was wonder;
That with cries they make,
The very earth did shake,
Trumpet to trumpet spake,
Thunder to thunder.

Well it thine age became,
O noble Erpingham,
Which didst the signal aim
To our hid forces;
When from a meadow by,
Like a storm suddenly,
The English archery
Struck the French horses.

With Spanish yew so strong,
Arrows a cloth-yard long,
That like to serpents stung,
Piercing the weather;
None from his fellow starts,
But playing manly parts,
And like true English hearts,
Stuck close together.

When down their bows they threw
And forth their bilboes drew
And on the French they flew,
Not one was tardy;
Arms were from shoulders sent,
Scalps to the teeth were rent,
Down the French peasants went,
Our men were hardy.

This while our noble King,
His broad-sword brandishing,
Down the French host did ding,
As to o'erwhelm it;
And many a deep wound lent,
His arms with blood besprent,
And many a cruel dent
Bruised his helmet.

Gloster, that duke so good,
Next of the royal blood,
For famous England stood,
With his brave brother;
Clarence, in steel so bright,
Though but a maiden knight,
Yet in that furious fight,
Scarce such another.

Warwick in blood did wade,
Oxford the foe invade,
And cruel slaughter made,
Still as they ran up;
Suffolk his axe did ply,
Beaumont and Willoughby
Bare them right doughtily,
Ferrers, and Fanhope.

Upon Saint Crispin's Day
Fought was this noble fray,
Which Fame did not delay,
To England to carry;
O when shall English men
With such acts fill a pen?
Or England breed again
Such a King Harry?

MICHAEL DRAYTON

Since There's No Help

Since there's no help, come let us kiss and part,
Nay, I have done: you get no more of me;
And I am glad, yea glad with all my heart,
That thus so cleanly, I myself can free,
Shake hands for ever, cancel all our vows,
And when we meet at any time again,
Be it not seen in either of our brows,
That we one jot of former love retain;
Now at the last gasp, of Love's latest breath,
When his pulse failing, Passion speechless lies,
When Faith is kneeling by his bed of death,
And Innocence is closing up his eye,
Now, if thou wouldst, when all have given him over,
From death to life, thou might'st him yet recover.

MICHAEL DRAYTON

Madrigal

The ivory, coral, gold,
Of breast, of lips, of hair,
So lively Sleep doth show to inward sight,
That wake I think I hold
No shadow, but my fair:
Myself so to deceive,
With long-shut eyes I shun the irksome light.
Such pleasure thus I have,
Delighting in false gleams,
If Death Sleep's brother be,
And souls relieved of sense have so sweet dreams,
That I would wish me thus to dream and die.

WILLIAM DRUMMOND

Madrigal

Like the Idalian queen,
Her hair about her eyne,
With neck and breast's ripe apples to be seen,
At first glance of the morn,
In Cyprus' gardens gathering those fair flowers
Which of her blood were born,
I saw, but fainting saw, my paramours.
The Graces naked danced about the place,
The winds and trees amazed
With silence on her gazed;
The flowers did smile, like those upon her face,
And as their aspen stalks those fingers band,
That she might read my case,
A hyacinth I wished me in her hand.

WILLIAM DRUMMOND

My Mind to Me a Kingdom Is

My mind to me a kingdom is;
  Such present joys therein I find
That it excels all other bliss
  That earth affords or grows by kind.
Though much I want which most would have,
Yet still my mind forbids to crave.

No princely pomp, no wealthy store,
  No force to win the victory,
No wily wit to salve a sore,
  No shape to feed a loving eye;
To none of these I yield as thrall—
For why? My mind doth serve for all.

I see how plenty surfeits oft,
  And hasty climbers soon do fall;
I see that those which are aloft
  Mishap doth threaten most of all;
They get with toil, they keep with fear—
Such cares my mind could never bear.

Content to live, this is my stay;
  I seek no more than may suffice;
I press to bear no haughty sway;
  Look, what I lack my mind supplies.
Lo, thus I triumph like a king,
Content with that my mind doth bring.

Some have too much, yet still do crave;
  I little have, and seek no more.
They are but poor, though much they have,
  And I am rich with little store.
They poor, I rich; they beg, I give;
They lack, I leave; they pine, I live.

I laugh not a another's loss;
  I grudge not at another's pain;
No worldly waves my mind can toss;
  My state at one doth still remain.
I fear no foe, I fawn no friend;
I loathe not life, nor dread my end.

Some weigh their pleasure by their lust,
  Their wisdom by their rage of will;
Their treasure is their only trust;
  A cloakéd craft their store of skill.
But all the pleasure that I find
Is to maintain a quiet mind.

My wealth is health and perfect ease;
  My conscience clear my chief defense;
I neither seek by bribes to please,
  Nor by deceit to breed offense,
Thus do I live; thus will I die;
Would all did so as well as I!

Sir Edward Dyer

The Love Song of J. Alfred Prufrock

S'io credesse che mia risposta fosse
A persona che mai tornasse al mondo,
Questa fiamma staria senza piu scosse.
Ma perciocche giammai di questo fondo
Non torno vivo alcun, s'i'odo il vero,
Senza tema d'infamia ti rispondo.

Let us go then, you and I,
When the evening is spread out against the sky
Like a patient etherized upon a table;
Let us go, through certain half-deserted streets,
The muttering retreats
Of restless nights in one-night cheap hotels
And sawdust restaurants with oyster-shells:
Streets that follow like a tedious argument
Of insidious intent
To lead you to an overwhelming question. . . .
Oh, do not ask, "What is it?"
Let us go and make our visit.

In the room the women come and go
Talking of Michelangelo.

The yellow fog that rubs its back upon the window-panes,
The yellow smoke that rubs its muzzle on the window-panes,
Licked its tongue into the corners of the evening,
Lingered upon the pools that stand in drains,
Let fall upon its back the soot that falls from chimneys,
Slipped by the terrace, made a sudden leap,
And seeing that it was a soft October night,
Curled once about the house, and fell asleep.

S'io credesse, etc.—"If I thought
My answer made to one who ever might
Return again up to the living world
This fiery tongue would motionless remain.
But since no living soul has ever left
This pit of Hell, if I hear true report,
I dare to answer without fear of shame."
Dante, *Inferno*, Canto xxvii.

And indeed there will be time
For the yellow smoke that slides along the street,
Rubbing its back upon the window-panes;
There will be time, there will be time
To prepare a face to meet the faces that you meet;
There will be time to murder and create,
And time for all the works and days of hands
That lift and drop a question on your plate;
Time for you and time for me,
And time yet for a hundred indecisions,
And for a hundred visions and revisions,
Before the taking of a toast and tea.

In the room the women come and go
Talking of Michelangelo.

And indeed there will be time
To wonder, "Do I dare?" and, "Do I dare?"
Time to turn back and descend the stair,
With a bald spot in the middle of my hair—
(They will say: "How his hair is growing thin!")
My morning coat, my collar mounting firmly to the chin,
My necktie rich and modest, but asserted by a simple pin—
(They will say: "But how his arms and legs are thin!")
Do I dare
Disturb the universe?
In a minute there is time
For decisions and revisions which a minute will reverse.

For I have known them all already, known them all:
Have known the evenings, mornings, afternoons,
I have measured out my life with coffee spoons;
I know the voices dying with a dying fall
Beneath the music from a farther room.
  So how should I presume?

---

29 *works and days:* Hesiod, a Greek poet of the eighth century B.C., wrote a poem on agriculture called *Works and Days.*

And I have known the eyes already, known them all—
The eyes that fix you in a formulated phrase,
And when I am formulated, sprawling on a pin,
When I am pinned and wriggling on the wall,
Then how should I begin
To spit out all the butt-ends of my days and ways?
  And how should I presume?

And I have known the arms already, known them all—
Arms that are braceleted and white and bare
(But in the lamplight, downed with light brown hair!)
Is it perfume from a dress
That makes me so digress?
Arms that lie along a table, or wrap about a shawl,
  And should I then presume?
  And how should I begin?

. . . .

Shall I say, I have gone at dusk through narrow streets
And watched the smoke that rises from the pipes
Of lonely men in shirt-sleeves, leaning out of windows? . . .

I should have been a pair of ragged claws
Scuttling across the floors of silent seas.

. . . .

And the afternoon, the evening, sleeps so peacefully!
Smoothed by long fingers,
Asleep . . . tired . . . or it malingers,
Stretched on the floor, here beside you and me.
Should I, after tea and cakes and ices,
Have the strength to force the moment to its crisis?
But though I have wept and fasted, wept and prayed,
Though I have seen my head (grown slightly bald) brought in upon a platter,
I am no prophet—and here's no great matter;
I have seen the moment of my greatness flicker,
And I have seen the eternal Footman hold my coat, and snicker,
And in short, I was afraid.

82: John the Baptist's head was delivered to Salome on a platter as her reward for dancing for Herod (Matthew 14:1–11). 92: an allusion to a line in Marvell's "To His Coy Mistress."

And would it have been worth it, after all,
After the cups, the marmalade, the tea,
Among the porcelain, among some talk of you and me,
Would it have been worth while,
To have bitten off the matter with a smile,
To have squeezed the universe into a ball
To roll it toward some overwhelming question,
To say: "I am Lazarus, come from the dead,
Come back to tell you all, I shall tell you all"—
If one, settling a pillow by her head,
  Should say: "That is not what I meant at all;
  That is not it, at all."

And would it have been worth it, after all,
Would it have been worth while,
After the sunsets and the dooryards and the sprinkled streets,
After the novels, after the teacups, after the skirts that trail along the floor—
And this, and so much more?—
It is impossible to say just what I mean!
But as if a magic lantern threw the nerves in patterns on a screen:
Would it have been worth while
If one, settling a pillow or throwing off a shawl,
And turning toward the window, should say:
  "That is not it at all,
  That is not what I meant, at all."

. . . .

No! I am not Prince Hamlet, nor was meant to be;
Am an attendant lord, one that will do
To swell a progress, start a scene or two,
Advise the prince; no doubt, an easy tool,
Deferential, glad to be of use,
Politic, cautious, and meticulous;
Full of high sentence, but a bit obtuse;
At times, indeed, almost ridiculous—
Almost, at times, the Fool.

---

94 *Lazarus:* either or both of the two Lazaruses mentioned in the Bible: the beggar Lazarus or the Lazarus of John II, who was brought back to life by Christ.

113 *progress:* journey of a royal personage.

I grow old. . . . I grow old. . . .
I shall wear the bottoms of my trousers rolled.

Shall I part my hair behind? Do I dare to eat a peach?
I shall wear white flannel trousers, and walk upon the beach.
I have heard the mermaids singing, each to each.

I do not think that they will sing to me.

I have seen them riding seaward on the waves
Combing the white hair of the waves blown back
When the wind blows the water white and black.

We have lingered in the chambers of the sea
By sea-girls wreathed with seaweed red and brown
Till human voices wake us, and we drown.

T. S. Eliot

The Snow-Storm

Announced by all the trumpets of the sky,
Arrives the snow, and, driving o'er the fields,
Seems nowhere to alight: the whited air
Hides hills and woods, the river, and the heaven,
And veils the farm-house at the garden's end.
The sled and traveller stopped, the courier's feet
Delayed, all friends shut out, the housemates sit
Around the radiant fireplace, enclosed
In a tumultuous privacy of storm.

Come see the north wind's masonry.
Out of an unseen quarry evermore
Furnished with tile, the fierce artificer
Curves his white bastions with projected roof
Round every windward stake, or tree, or door.
Speeding, the myriad-handed, his wild work
So fanciful, so savage, nought cares he
For number or proportion. Mockingly,
On coop or kennel he hangs Parian wreaths;
A swan-like form invests the hidden thorn;
Fills up the farmer's lane from wall to wall,
Maugre the farmer's sighs; and at the gate
A tapering turret overtops the work.
And when his hours are numbered, and the world
Is all his own, retiring, as he were not,
Leaves, when the sun appears, astonished Art
To mimic in slow structures, stone by stone,
Built in an age, the mad wind's night-work,
The frolic architecture of the snow.

RALPH WALDO EMERSON

Care-charming Sleep

Care-charming Sleep, thou easer of all woes,
Brother to Death, sweetly thyself dispose
On this afflicted prince; fall like a cloud,
In gentle showers; give nothing that is loud,
Or painful to his slumbers; easy, light,

And as a purling stream, thou son of Night
Pass by his troubled senses; sing his pain,
Like hollow murmuring wind or silver rain;
Into this prince gently, oh, gently slide,
And kiss him into slumbers like a bride.

JOHN FLETCHER

Come Hither, You That Love

Come hither, you that love, and hear me sing
Of joys still growing,
Green, fresh, and lusty as the pride of spring,
And ever blowing.
Come hither, youths that blush, and dare not know
What is desire;
And old men, worse than you, that cannot blow
One spark of fire;
And with the power of my enchanting song,
Boys shall be able men, and old men young.

Come hither, you that hope, and you that cry;
Leave off complaining;
Youth, strength, and beauty, that shall never die,
Are here remaining.
Come hither, fools, and blush you stay so long
From being blessed;
And mad men, worse than you, that suffer wrong,
Yet seek no rest;
And in an hour, with my enchanting song,
You shall be ever pleased, and young maids long.

JOHN FLETCHER

Now the Lusty Spring

Now the lusty spring is seen;
Golden yellow, gaudy blue,
Daintily invite the view.
Everywhere on every green,
Roses blushing as they blow,
And enticing men to pull,
Lilies whiter than the snow,
Woodbines of sweet honey full:
All love's emblems, and all cry,
"Ladies, if not plucked, we die."

Yet the lusty spring hath stayed;
  Blushing red and purest white
  Daintily to love invite
Every woman, every maid.
Cherries kissing as they grow,
  And inviting men to taste,
Apples even ripe below,
  Winding gently to the waist:
    All love's emblems, and all cry.
    "Ladies, if not plucked, we die."

JOHN FLETCHER

After Apple-Picking

My long two-pointed ladder's sticking through a tree
Toward heaven still,
And there's the barrel that I didn't fill
Beside it, and there may be two or three
Apples I didn't pick upon some bough.
But I am done with apple-picking now.
Essence of winter sleep is on the night,
The scent of apples: I am drowsing off.
I cannot rub the strangeness from my sight
I got from looking through a pane of glass
I skimmed this morning from the drinking trough
And held against the world of hoary grass.
It melted, and I let it fall and break.
But I was well
Upon my way to sleep before it fell,
And I could tell
What form my dreaming was about to take.
Magnified apples appear and disappear,
Stem end and blossom end,
And every fleck of russet showing clear.
My instep arch not only keeps the ache,
It keeps the pressure of a ladder-round.
I feel the ladder sway as the boughs bend.
And I keep hearing from the cellar bin
The rumbling sound
Of load on load of apples coming in.
For I have had too much
Of apple-picking: I am overtired
Of the great harvest I myself desired.

There were ten thousand thousand fruit to touch,
Cherish in hand, lift down, and not let fall.
For all
That struck the earth,
No matter if not bruised or spiked with stubble,
Went surely to the cider-apple heap
As of no worth.
One can see what will trouble
This sleep of mine, whatever sleep it is.
Were he not gone,
The woodchuck could say whether it's like his
Long sleep, as I describe its coming on,
Or just some human sleep.

ROBERT FROST

From FABLES

The Hare with Many Friends

Friendship, like love, is but a name,
Unless to one you stint the flame.
The child whom many fathers share,
Hath seldom known a father's care.
'Tis thus in friendship; who depend
On many rarely find a friend.
A Hare, who, in a civil way,
Complied with everything, like Gay,
Was known by all the bestial train,
Who haunt the wood, or graze the plain.
Her care was, never to offend,
And every creature was her friend.
As forth she went at early dawn,
To taste the dew-besprinkled lawn,
Behind she hears the hunter's cries,
And from the deep-mouthed thunder flies.
She starts, she stops, she pants for breath;
She hears the near advance of death;
She doubles, to mislead the hound,
And measures back her mazy round;

Till, fainting in the public way,
Half dead with fear she gasping lay.
  What transport in her bosom grew,
When first the Horse appeared in view!
  "Let me," says she, "your back ascend,
And owe my safety to a friend.
You know my feet betray my flight;
To friendship every burden's light."
  The Horse replied: "Poor honest Puss,
It grieves my heart to see thee thus;
Be comforted; relief is near,
For all your friends are in the rear."
  She next the stately Bull implored;
And thus replied the mighty lord:
"Since every beast alive can tell
That I sincerely wish you well,
I may, without offense, pretend
To take the freedom of a friend;
Love calls me hence; a favorite cow
Expects me near yon barley-mow:
And when a lady's in the case,
You know, all other things give place.
To leave you thus might seem unkind;
But see, the Goat is just behind."
  The Goat remarked her pulse was high,
Her languid head, her heavy eye;
"My back," says he, "may do you harm;
The Sheep's at hand, and wool is warm."
  The Sheep was feeble, and complained
His sides a load of wool sustained:
Said he was slow, confessed his fears,
For hounds eat sheep as well as hares.
  She now the trotting Calf addressed,
To save from death a friend distressed.
"Shall I," says he, "of tender age,
In this important care engage?
Older and abler passed you by;
How strong are those, how weak am I!
Should I presume to bear you hence,
Those friends of mine may take offense.
Excuse me, then. You know my heart.
But dearest friends, alas, must part!
How shall we all lament! Adieu!
For see, the hounds are just in view."

JOHN GAY

From FABLES

The Rat-Catcher and Cats

The rats by night such mischief did,
Betty was every morning chid:
They undermined whole sides of bacon,
Her cheese was sapped, her tarts were taken,
Her pasties, fenced with thickest paste,
Were all demolished and laid waste.
She cursed the cat for want of duty,
Who left her foes a constant booty.
An Engineer, of noted skill,
Engaged to stop the growing ill.
From room to room he now surveys
Their haunts, their works, their secret ways,
Finds where they 'scape an ambuscade,
And whence the nightly sally's made.
An envious Cat, from place to place,
Unseen, attends his silent pace,
She saw that, if his trade went on,
The purring race must be undone,
So, secretly removes his baits,
And every stratagem defeats.
Again he sets the poisoned toils,
And Puss again the labor foils.
"What foe (to frustrate my designs)
My schemes thus nightly countermines?"
Incensed, he cries: "This very hour
The wretch shall bleed beneath my power."
So said. A ponderous trap he brought,
And in the fact poor Puss was caught.
"Smuggler," says he, "thou shalt be made
A victim to our loss of trade."
The captive Cat with piteous mews
For pardon, life, and freedom sues.
"A sister of the science spare,
One interest is our common care."
"What insolence!" the man replied;
"Shall cats with us the game divide?
Were all your interloping band
Extinguished, or expelled the land,
We rat-catchers might raise our fees,
Sole guardians of a nation's cheese!"

JOHN GAY

The Three Pigeons

Let schoolmasters puzzle their brain,
With grammar, and nonsense, and learning;
Good liquor, I stoutly maintain,
Gives genius a better discerning.
Let them brag of their heathenish gods,
Their Lethes, their Styxes, and Stygians,
Their Quis and their Quaes and their Quods,
They're all but a parcel of pigeons.
Toroddle, toroddle, toroll.

When Methodist preachers come down,
A-preaching that drinking is sinful,
I'll wager the rascals a crown,
They always preach best with a skinful.
But when you come down with your pence,
For a slice of their scurvy religion,
I'll leave it to all men of sense,
But you, my good friend, are the pigeon.
Toroddle, toroddle, toroll.

Then come put the jorum about,
And let us be merry and clever,
Our hearts and our liquors are stout,
Here's the Three Jolly Pigeons for ever!
Let some cry up woodcock or hare,
Your bustards, your ducks, and your widgeons;
But of all the gay birds in the air,
Here's a health to the Three Jolly Pigeons!
Toroddle, toroddle, toroll.

OLIVER GOLDSMITH

A Love Story

The full moon easterly rising, furious,
Against a winter sky ragged with red;
The hedges high in snow, and owl's raving—
Solemnities not easy to withstand:
A shiver wakes the spine.

In boyhood, having encountered the scene,
I suffered horror: I fetched the moon home,
With owls and snow, to nurse in my head
Throughout the trials of a new spring,
Famine unassuaged.

But fell in love, and made a lodgement
Of love on those frozen ramparts.
Her image was my ensign: snows melted,
Hedges sprouted, the moon tenderly shone,
The owls trilled with tongues of nightingale.

These were all lies, though they matched the time,
And brought me less than luck: her image
Warped in the weather, turned beldamish.
Then back came winter on me at a bound,
The pallid sky heaved with a moon-quake.

Dangerous it had been with love-notes
To serenade Queen Famine.
In tears I recomposed the former scene,
Let the snow lie, watched the moon rise, suffered the owls,
Paid homage to them of unevent.

Robert Graves

Elegy Written in a Country Churchyard

The curfew tolls the knell of parting day,
The lowing herd wind slowly o'er the lea,
The plowman homeward plods his weary way,
And leaves the world to darkness and to me.

Now fades the glimmering landscape on the sight,
And all the air a solemn stillness holds,
Save where the beetle wheels his droning flight,
And drowsy tinklings lull the distant folds;

Save that from yonder ivy-mantled tower
The moping owl does to the moon complain
Of such as, wandering near her secret bower,
Molest her ancient solitary reign.

Beneath those rugged elms, that yew-tree's shade,
Where heaves the turf in many a moldering heap,
Each in his narrow cell forever laid,
The rude forefathers of the hamlet sleep.

The breezy call of incense-breathing Morn,
The swallow twittering from the straw-built shed,
The cock's shrill clarion, or the echoing horn,
No more shall rouse them from their lowly bed.

For them no more the blazing hearth shall burn,
Or busy housewife ply her evening care;
No children run to lisp their sire's return,
Or climb his knees the envied kiss to share.

Oft did the harvest to their sickle yield,
Their furrow oft the stubborn glebe has broke;
How jocund did they drive their team afield!
How bowed the woods beneath their sturdy stroke!

Let not Ambition mock their useful toil.
Their homely joys, and destiny obscure;
Nor Grandeur hear, with a disdainful smile,
The short and simple annals of the poor.

The boast of heraldry, the pomp of power,
  And all that beauty, all that wealth e'er gave.
Awaits alike the inevitable hour:
  The paths of glory lead but to the grave.

Nor you, ye proud, impute to these the fault,
  If Memory o'er their tomb no trophies raise,
Where through the long-drawn aisle and fretted vault
  The pealing anthem swells the note of praise.

Can storied urn or animated bust
  Back to its mansion call the fleeting breath?
Can Honor's voice provoke the silent dust,
  Or Flattery soothe the dull cold ear of Death?

Perhaps in this neglected spot is laid
  Some heart once pregnant with celestial fire;
Hands that the rod of empire might have swayed,
  Or waked to ecstasy the living lyre.

But Knowledge to their eyes her ample page
  Rich with the spoils of time did ne'er unroll;
Chill Penury repressed their noble rage,
  And froze the genial current of the soul.

Full many a gem of purest ray serene
  The dark unfathomed caves of ocean bear;
Full many a flower is born to blush unseen,
  And waste its sweetness on the desert air.

Some village Hampden that with dauntless breast
  The little tyrant of his fields withstood;
Some mute inglorious Milton here may rest,
  Some Cromwell guiltless of his country's blood.

The applause of listening senates to command,
  The threats of pain and ruin to despise,
To scatter plenty o'er a smiling land,
  And read their history in a nation's eyes,

Their lot forbade; nor circumscribed alone
   Their growing virtues, but their crimes confined;
Forbade to wade through slaughter to a throne,
   And shut the gates of mercy on mankind,

The struggling pangs of conscious truth to hide,
   To quench the blushes of ingenuous shame,
Or heap the shrine of Luxury and Pride
   With incense kindled at the Muse's flame.

Far from the madding crowd's ignoble strife,
   Their sober wishes never learned to stray;
Along the cool sequestered vale of life
   They kept the noiseless tenor of their way.

Yet ev'n these bones from insult to protect
   Some frail memorial still erected nigh.
With uncouth rimes and shapeless sculpture decked,
   Implores the passing tribute of a sigh.

Their name, their years, spelt by the unlettered Muse,
   The place of fame and elegy supply;
And many a holy text around she strews,
   That teach the rustic moralist to die.

For who, to dumb Forgetfulness a prey,
   This pleasing anxious being e'er resigned,
Left the warm precincts of the cheerful day,
   Nor cast one longing, lingering look behind?

On some fond breast the parting soul relies,
   Some pious drops the closing eye requires;
Ev'n from the tomb the voice of Nature cries,
   Ev'n in our ashes line their wonted fires.

For thee, who mindful of the unhonored dead
   Dost in these lines their artless tale relate;
If chance, by lonely Contemplation led,
   Some kindred spirit shall inquire thy fate,

Haply some hoary-headed swain may say,
  "Oft have we seen him at the peep of dawn
Brushing with hasty steps the dews away
  To meet the sun upon the upland lawn.

"There at the foot of yonder nodding beech,
  That wreathes its old fantastic roots so high,
His listless length at noontide would he stretch,
  And pore upon the brook that babbles by.

"Hard by yon wood, now smiling as in scorn,
  Muttering his wayward fancies he would rove,
Now drooping, woeful wan, like one forlorn,
  Or crazed with care, or crossed in hopeless love.

"One morn I missed him on the customed hill,
  Along the heath, and near his favorite tree;
Another came; nor yet beside the rill,
  Nor up the lawn, nor at the wood was he;

"The next with dirges due in sad array
  Slow through the church-way path we saw him borne.
Approach and read (for thou canst read) the lay,
  Graved on the stone beneath yon aged thorn."

THE EPITAPH

Here rests his head upon the lap of Earth
  A youth to Fortune and to Fame unknown.
Fair Science frowned not on his humble birth,
  And Melancholy marked him for her own.

Large was his bounty, and his soul sincere,
  Heaven did a recompense as largely send;
He gave to Misery all he had, a tear,
  He gained from Heaven ('twas all he wished) a friend.

No farther seek his merits to disclose,
  Or draw his frailties from their dread abode,
(There they alike in trembling hope repose),
  The bosom of his Father and his God.

THOMAS GRAY

Ode on the Death of a Favorite Cat

DROWNED IN A TUB OF GOLD FISHES

'Twas on a lofty vase's side,
Where China's gayest art had dyed
The azure flowers, that blow;
Demurest of the tabby kind,
The pensive Selima reclined,
Gazed on the lake below.

Her conscious tail her joy declared;
The fair round face, the snowy beard,
The velvet of her paws,
Her coat, that with the tortoise vies,
Her ears of jet, and emerald eyes,
She saw; and purred applause.

Still had she gazed; but 'midst the tide
Two angel forms were seen to glide,
The Genii of the stream:
Their scaly armor's Tyrian hue
Through richest purple to the view
Betrayed a golden gleam:

The hapless Nymph with wonder saw:
A whisker first and then a claw,
With many an ardent wish,
She stretched in vain to reach the prize.
What female heart can gold despise?
What Cat's averse to fish?

Presumptuous Maid! with looks intent
Again she stretched, again she bent,
Nor knew the gulf between.
(Malignant Fate sat by, and smiled)
The slipp'ry verge her feet beguiled,
She tumbled headlong in.

Eight times emerging from the flood
She mewed to ev'ry wat'ry God,
Some speedy aid to send.
No Dolphin came, no Nereid stirred:
Nor cruel Tom, nor Susan heard.
A Fav'rite has no friend!

From hence, ye Beauties, undeceived,
Know, one false step is ne'er retrieved,
And be with caution bold.
Not all that tempts your wand'ring eyes
And heedless hearts, is lawful prize;
Nor all, that glisters, gold.

THOMAS GRAY

The Bard

I. 1

"Ruin seize thee, ruthless King!
Confusion on thy banners wait,
Though fanned by Conquest's crimson wing
They mock the air with idle state.
Helm, nor hauberk's twisted mail,
Nor even thy virtues, Tyrant, shall avail
To save thy secret soul from nightly fears,
From Cambria's curse, from Cambria's tears!"
Such were the sounds, that o'er the crested pride
Of the first Edward scattered wild dismay,
As down the steep of Snowdon's shaggy side
He wound with toilsome march his long array.
Stout Glo'ster stood aghast in speechless trance;
"To arms!" cried Mortimer, and couched his quivering lance.

I. 2

On a rock, whose haughty brow
Frowns o'er old Conway's foaming flood,
Robed in the sable garb of woe,
With haggard eyes the Poet stood;
(Loose his beard, and hoary hair
Streamed, like a meteor, to the troubled air)
And with a master's hand and prophet's fire,
Struck the deep sorrows of his lyre.
"Hark, how each giant oak, and desert cave,
Sighs to the torrent's awful voice beneath!
O'er thee, oh King! their hundred arms they wave,
Revenge on thee in hoarser murmurs breathe;
Vocal no more, since Cambria's fatal day,
To high-born Hoel's harp, or soft Llewellyn's lay.

I. 3

"Cold is Cadwallo's tongue,
That hushed the stormy main;
Brave Urien sleeps upon his craggy bed;
Mountains, ye mourn in vain
Modred, whose magic song
Made huge Plinlimmon bow his cloud-topped head.
On dreary Arvon's shore they lie,
Smeared with gore, and ghastly pale;
Far, far aloof the affrighted ravens sail;
The famished eagle screams, and passes by.
Dear lost companions of my tuneful art,
Dear, as the light that visits these sad eyes,
Dear, as the ruddy drops that warm my heart,
Ye died amidst your dying country's cries—
No more I weep. They do not sleep.
On yonder cliffs, a grisly band,
I see them sit, they linger yet,
Avengers of their native land;
With me in dreadful harmony they join,
And weave with bloody hands the tissue of thy line.

II. 1

"Weave the warp, and weave the woof,
The winding-sheet of Edward's race.
Give ample room, and verge enough
The characters of Hell to trace.
Mark the year, and mark the night.
When Severn shall re-echo with affright
The shrieks of death, through Berkley's roofs that ring,
Shrieks of an agonizing King!
She-wolf of France, with unrelenting fangs,
That tear'st the bowels of thy mangled mate,
From thee be born, who o'er thy country hangs
The scourge of Heaven. What terrors round him wait!
Amazement in his van, with Flight combined,
And Sorrow's faded form, and Solitude behind.

II. 2

"Mighty victor, mighty lord!
Low on his funeral couch he lies!
No pitying heart, no eye, afford
A tear to grace his obsequies.
Is the sable Warrior fled?
Thy son is gone. He rests among the dead.
Thy swarm, that in thy noon-tide beam were born?
Gone to salute the rising morn.
Fair laughs the morn, and soft the zephyr blows,
While proudly riding o'er the azure realm
In gallant trim the gilded vessel goes;
Youth on the prow, and Pleasure at the helm;
Regardless of the sweeping whirlwind's sway,
That, hushed in grim repose, expects his evening prey.

II. 3

"Fill high the sparkling bowl,
The rich repast prepare,
Reft of a crown, he yet may share the feast;
Close by the regal chair
Fell Thirst and Famine scowl
A baleful smile upon their baffled guest.
Heard ye the din of battle bray,
Lance to lance, and horse to horse?
Long years of havoc urge their destined course,
And through the kindred squadrons mow their way.
Ye towers of Julius, London's lasting shame,
With many a foul and midnight murther fed,
Revere his consort's faith, his father's fame,
And spare the meek usurper's holy head.
Above, below, the rose of snow,
Twined with her blushing foe, we spread;
The bristled boar in infant gore
Wallows beneath the thorny shade.
Now, brothers, bending o'er the accursed loom
Stamp we our vengeance deep, and ratify his doom.

III. 1

"Edward, lo! to sudden fate
(Weave we the woof. The thread is spun.)
Half of thy heart we consecrate.
(The web is wove. The work is done.)
Stay, oh stay! nor thus forlorn,
Leave me unblessed, unpitied, here to mourn;
In yon bright track, that fires the western skies,
They melt, they vanish from my eyes.
But oh! what solemn scenes on Snowdon's height
Descending slow their glittering skirts unroll?
Visions of glory, spare my aching sight,
Ye unborn ages, crowd not on my soul!
No more our long-lost Arthur we bewail.
All hail, ye genuine kings, Britannia's issue, hail!

III. 2

"Girt with many a baron bold
Sublime their starry fronts they rear;
And gorgeous dames, and statesmen old
In bearded majesty, appear.
In the midst a form divine!
Her eye proclaims her of the Briton line;
Her lion-port, her awe commanding face,
Attempered sweet to virgin-grace.
What strings symphonious tremble in the air,
What strains of vocal transport round her play!
Hear from the grave, great Taliessin, hear;
They breathe a soul to animate thy clay.
Bright Rapture calls, and soaring, as she sings,
Waves in the eye of Heaven her many-colored wings.

III. 3

"The verse adorn again
Fierce War, and faithful Love,
And Truth severe, by fairy fiction drest.
In buskined measures move
Pale Grief and pleasing Pain,
With Horror, tyrant of the throbbing breast.
A voice, as of the cherub-choir,
Gales from blooming Eden bear;
And distant warblings lessen on my ear,
That lost in long futurity expire.
Fond impious man, think'st thou, yon sanguine cloud,
Raised by thy breath, has quenched the orb of day?
Tomorrow he repairs the golden flood,
And warms the nations with redoubled ray.
Enough for me. With joy I see
The different doom our fates assign.
Be thine Despair and sceptered Care;
To triumph, and to die, are mine."
He spoke, and headlong from the mountain's height
Deep in the roaring tide he plunged to endless night.

THOMAS GRAY

Sephestia's Song

Weep not, my wanton, smile upon my knee;
When thou art old there's grief enough for thee.
  Mother's wag, pretty boy,
  Father's sorrow, father's joy;
  When thy father first did see
  Such a boy by him and me,
  He was glad, I was woe;
  Fortune changéd made him so,
  When he left his pretty boy
  Last his sorrow, first his joy.

Weep not, my wanton, smile upon my knee;
When thou are old, there's grief enough for thee.
  Streaming tears that never stint,
  Like pearl-drops from a flint,
  Fell by course from his eyes,
  That one another's place supplies;
  Thus he grieved in every part,
  Tears of blood fell from his heart,
  When he left his pretty boy,
  Father's sorrow, father's joy.

Weep not, my wanton, smile upon my knee;
When thou art old, there's grief enough for thee.
  The wanton smiled, father wept,
  Mother cried, baby leapt;
  More he crowed, more he cried,
  Nature could not sorrow hide.
  He must go, he must kiss
  Child and mother, baby bless,
  For he left his pretty boy,
  Father's sorrow, father's joy.
Weep not, my wanton, smile upon my knee;
When thou art old, there's grief enough for thee.

ROBERT GREENE

Sweet Are the Thoughts

Sweet are the thoughts that savor of content;
The quiet mind is richer than a crown;
Sweet are the nights in careless slumber spent;
The poor estate scorns fortune's angry frown.
Such sweet content, such minds, such sleep, such bliss,
Beggars enjoy, when princes oft do miss.

The homely house that harbors quiet rest;
The cottage that affords no pride nor care;
The mean that 'grees with country music best;
The sweet consort of mirth and music's fare;
Obscuréd life sets down a type of bliss:
A mind content both crown and kingdom is.

Robert Greene

Butterfly

In summer spaces a bird rises
Like the juice of trees through the deft
Sidereal animal of creation.

A butterfly spins to my love's hand,
Weaves and drifts, a yellow leaf
With suns and heaven's pebbles in its touch.

Down in the arms of crepuscular grass,
Companion to bears and the smaller deer,
My love receives and blesses her gifts:

Stone draws down water,
Leaves drift on light,
The warm wind waits on its creatures,
And the yellow leaf of summer
Is drawn by the hand of my love.

Water and wind, the grass of spaces,
Currents and floods in the drift of creation,
Move to the center, rise from the core—

My love is a butterfly's hand.

Hugh Hartman

Reprinted by permission of the poet, Hugh Hartman. Unpublished.

Easter Wings

Lord, Who createdst man in wealth and store,
Though foolishly he lost the same,
Decaying more and more,
Till he became
More poore:
With thee
O let me rise,
As larks harmoniously,
And sing this day Thy victories:
Then shall the fall further the flight in me.
My tender age in sorrow did beginne;
And still with sicknesses and shame
Thou didst so punish sinne,
That I became
Most thinne.
With Thee
Let me combine,
And feel this day Thy victorie;
For, if I imp my wing on Thine,
Affliction shall advance the flight in me.

George Herbert

The Pearl

I know the ways of learning, both the head
And pipes that feed the press and make it run;
What reason hath from nature borrowéd,
Or of itself, like a good housewife, spun
In laws and policy; what the stars conspire;
What willing nature speaks, what forced by fire;
Both the old discoveries, and the new-found seas,
The stock and surplus, cause and history;
All these stand open, or I have the keys:
Yet I love Thee.

I know the ways of honor, what maintains
The quick returns of courtesy and wit;
In vies of favors whether party gains
When glory swells the heart, and moldeth it
To all expressions, both of hand and eye,
Which on the world a true-love knot may tie,
And bear the bundle wheresoe'er it goes;
How many drams of spirit there must be
To sell my life unto my friends or foes:
Yet I love Thee.

I know the ways of pleasure, the sweet strains,
The lullings and the relishes of it;
The propositions of hot blood and brains;
What mirth and music mean; what love and wit
Have done these twenty hundred years and more;
I know the projects of unbridled store;
My stuff is flesh, not brass; my senses live,
And grumble oft that they have more in me
Than he that curbs them, being but one to five:
Yet I love Thee.

I know all these, and have them in my hand;
Therefore not seeléd but with open eyes
I fly to Thee, and fully understand
Both the main sale and the commodities;
And at what rate and price I have Thy love,
With all the circumstances that may move.
Yet through the labyrinths, not my groveling wit,
But Thy silk twist let down from heaven to me,
Did both conduct and teach me how by it
To climb to Thee.

George Herbert

Virtue

Sweet Day, so cool, so calm, so bright,
The bridal of the earth and sky,
The dew shall weep thy fall tonight;
For thou must die.

Sweet Rose, whose hue angry and brave
Bids the rash gazer wipe his eye,
Thy root is ever in its grave,
And thou must die.

Sweet spring, full of sweet days and roses,
A box where sweets compacted lie,
My Music shows ye have your closes,
And all must die.

Only a sweet and virtuous soul,
Like season'd timber, never gives;
But though the whole world turn to coal,
Then chiefly lives.

GEORGE HERBERT

His Litany to the Holy Spirit

In the hour of my distress,
When temptations me oppress,
And when I my sins confess,
Sweet Spirit comfort me!

When I lie within my bed,
Sick in heart and sick in head,
And with doubts discomforted,
Sweet Spirit comfort me!

When the house doth sigh and weep,
And the world is drown'd in sleep,
Yet mine eyes the watch do keep;
Sweet spirit comfort me!

When the artless doctor sees
No one hope, but of his fees,
And his skill runs on the lees;
Sweet Spirit comfort me!

When his potion and his pill
Has, or none, or little skill,
Meet for nothing, but to kill;
Sweet Spirit comfort me!

When the passing-bell doth toll,
And the Furies in a shoal
Come to fright a parting soul;
Sweet Spirit comfort me!

When the tapers now burn blue,
And the comforters are few,
And that number more than true;
Sweet Spirit comfort me!

When the priest his last hath prayed,
And I nod to what is said,
'Cause my speech is now decayed;
Sweet Spirit comfort me!

When (God knows) I'm tossed about,
Either with despair, or doubt;
Yet before the glass be out,
Sweet Spirit comfort me!

When the Tempter me pursu'th
With the sins of all my youth,
And half damns me with untruth;
Sweet Spirit comfort me!

When the flames and hellish cries
Fright mine ears, and fright mine eyes,
And all terrors me surprise;
Sweet Spirit comfort me!

When the Judgment is reveal'd,
And that open'd which was seal'd,
When to Thee I have appeal'd;
Sweet Spirit comfort me!

ROBERT HERRICK

The Hag

The hag is astride
This night for to ride,
The devil and she together;
Through thick and through thin,
Now out, and then in,
Though ne'er so foul be the weather.

A thorn or a burr
She takes for a spur,
With a lash of a bramble she rides now;
Through brakes and through briars,
O'er ditches and mires,
She follows the spirit that guides now.

No beast for his food
Dares now range the wood,
But hushed in his lair he lies lurking:
While mischiefs by these,
On land and on seas,
At noon of night are a-working.

The storm will arise
And trouble the skies
This night; and, more for the wonder,
The ghost from the tomb
Affrighted shall come,
Called out by the clap of the thunder.

ROBERT HERRICK

The Wake

Come, Anthea, let us two
Go to feast, as others do.
Tarts and custards, creams and cakes,
Are the junkets still at wakes;
Unto which the tribes resort,
Where the business is the sport.
Morris-dancers thou shalt see;
Marian, too, in pageantry;
And a mimic to devise
Many grinning properties.
Players there will be, and those
Base in action as in clothes;
Yet with strutting they will please
The incurious villages.
Near the dying of the day
There will be a cudgel-play,
Where a coxcomb will be broke,
Ere a good word can be spoke;
But the anger ends all here,
Drenched in ale or drowned in beer.
Happy rustics, best content
With the cheapest merriment,
And possess no other fear
Than to want the wake next year.

ROBERT HERRICK

I Remember, I Remember

I remember, I remember,
The house where I was born,
The little window where the sun
Came peeping in at morn;
He never came a wink too soon,
Nor brought too long a day,
But now, I often wish the night
Had borne my breath away!

I remember, I remember,
The roses, red and white,
The violets, and the lily-cups,
Those flowers made of light!
The lilacs where the robin built,
And where my brother set
The laburnum on his birthday,—
The tree is living yet!

I remember, I remember,
Where I was used to swing,
And thought the air must rush as fresh
To swallows on the wing;
My spirit flew in feathers then,
That is so heavy now,
And summer pools could hardly cool
The fever on my brow!

I remember, I remember,
The fir trees dark and high;
I used to think their slender tops
Were close against the sky:
It was a childish ignorance,
But now 'tis little joy
To know I'm farther off from heaven
Than when I was a boy.

THOMAS HOOD

It Was Not in the Winter

It was not in the winter
Our loving lot was cast!
It was the time of roses,
We plucked them as we passed!

That churlish season never frowned
On early lovers yet!
Oh no—the world was newly crowned
With flowers, when first we met.

'Twas twilight, and I bade you go,
  But still you held me fast;
It was the time of roses—
  We plucked them as we passed!

What else could peer my glowing cheek
  That tears began to stud?
And when I asked the like of Love
  You snatched a damask bud,

And oped it to the dainty core
  Still glowing to the last:
It was the time of roses,
  We plucked them as we passed!

THOMAS HOOD

Along the Field

  Along the field as we came by
A year ago, my love and I,
The aspen over stile and stone
Was talking to itself alone.
"Oh, who are these that kiss and pass?
A country lover and his lass;
Two lovers looking to be wed;
And time shall put them both to bed,
But she shall lie with earth above,
And he beside another love."

  And sure enough beneath the tree
There walks another love with me,
And overhead the aspen heaves
Its rainy-sounding silver leaves;
And I spell nothing in their stir,
But now perhaps they speak to her,
And plain for her to understand
They talk about a time at hand
When I shall sleep with clover clad,
And she beside another lad.

A. E. HOUSMAN

Reveille

Wake! The silver dusk returning
  Up the beach of darkness brims,
And the ship of sunrise burning
  Strands upon the eastern rims.

Wake! The vaulted shadow shatters,
  Trampled to the floor it spanned,
And the tent of night in tatters
  Straws the sky-pavilioned land.

Up, lad, up! 'Tis late for lying.
  Hear the drums of morning play;
Hark, the empty highways crying,
  "Who'll beyond the hills away?"

Towns and countries woo together,
  Forelands beacon, belfries call;
Never lad that trod on leather
  Lived to feast his heart with all.

Up, lad; thews that lie and cumber
  Sunlit pallets never thrive;
Morns abed and daylight slumber
  Were not meant for man alive.

Clay lies still, but blood's a rover;
  Breath's a ware that will not keep.
Up, lad; when the journey's over
  There'll be time enough to sleep.

A. E. Housman

A Short Song of Congratulation

Long-expected one and twenty,
Ling'ring year, at last is flown;
Pomp and pleasure, pride and plenty,
Great Sir John, are all your own.

Loosened from the minor's tether,
Free to mortgage or to sell,
Wild as wind, and light as feather,
Bid the slaves of thrift farewell.

Call the Bettys, Kates, and Jennys,
Every name that laughs at care,
Lavish of your grandsire's guineas,
Show the spirit of an heir.

All that prey on vice and folly
Joy to see their quarry fly,
Here the gamester light and jolly,
There the lender grave and sly.

Wealth, Sir John was made to wander,
Let it wander as it will:
See the jockey, see the pander,
Bid them come, and take their fill.

When the bonny blade carouses,
Pockets full, and spirits high,
What are acres? What are houses?
Only dirt, or wet or dry.

If the guardian or the mother
Tell the woes of wilful waste,
Scorn their counsel and their pother,
You can hang or drown at last.

SAMUEL JOHNSON

Epitaph on Elizabeth, L.H.

Wouldst thou hear what man can say
In a little? Reader, stay.
Underneath this stone doth lie
As much beauty as could die;
Which in life did harbour give
To more virtue than doth live.
If at all she had a fault,
Leave it buried in this vault.
One name was Elizabeth,
Th' other, let it sleep with death:
Fitter, where it died, to tell
Than that it lived at all. Farewell.

BEN JONSON

Slow, Slow, Fresh Fount

Slow, slow, fresh fount, keep time with my salt tears:
  Yet slower, yet; oh, faintly, gentle springs,
List to the heavy part the music bears,
  Woe weeps out her division when she sings.
    Droop herbs and flowers;
    Fall grief in showers,
    Our beauties are not ours;
      Oh, I could still,
Like melting snow upon some craggy hill,
    Drop, drop, drop, drop,
Since nature's pride is now a withered daffodil.

BEN JONSON

Song, to Celia

Drink to me only with thine eyes,
  And I will pledge with mine;
Or leave a kiss but in the cup,
  And I'll not look for wine.
The thirst that from the soul doth rise
  Doth ask a drink divine:
But might I of Jove's nectar sup,
  I would not change for thine.

I sent thee late a rosy wreath,
  Not so much honouring thee,
As giving it a hope that there
  It could not withered be.
But thou thereon didst only breathe,
  And sent'st it back to me:
Since when it grows, and smells, I swear,
  Not of itself, but thee.

BEN JONSON

The Triumph of Charis

See the chariot at hand here of Love,
  Wherein my Lady rideth!
Each that draws is a swan or a dove,
  And well the car Love guideth.
As she goes, all hearts do duty
      Unto her beauty;
And enamored, do wish, so they might
      But enjoy such a sight,
That they still were to run by her side,
Through swords, through seas, whither she would ride.

Do but look on her eyes, they do light
All that Love's world compriseth!
Do but look on her hair, it is bright
As Love's star when it riseth!
Do but mark, her forehead's smoother
Than words that soothe her;
And from her arched brows, such a grace
Sheds itself through the face
As alone there triumps to the life
All the gain, all the good, of the elements' strife.

Have you seen but a bright lily grow
Before rude hands have touched it?
Have you marked but the fall of the snow
Before the soil hath smutched it?
Have you felt the wool of the beaver?
Or swan's down ever?
Or have smelt o' the bud of the briar?
Or the nard in the fire?
Or have tasted the bag of the bee?
Oh so white! Oh so soft! Oh so sweet is she!

BEN JONSON

Though I am Young

Though I am young and cannot tell
Either what Death or Love is well,
Yet I have heard they both bear darts,
And both do aim at human hearts;
And then again, I have been told,
Love wounds with heat, as Death with cold;
So that I fear they do but bring
Extremes to touch, and mean one thing.
As in a ruin we it call
One thing to be blown up, or fall;
Or to our end like way may have
By a flash of lightning, or a wave:
So Love's inflamèd shaft or brand,
May kill as soon as Death's cold hand;
Except Love's fires the virtue have
To fright the frost out of the grave.

BEN JONSON

To the Memory of My Beloved Master, William Shakespeare

To draw no envy, Shakespeare, on thy name,
Am I thus ample to thy book and fame;
While I confess thy writings to be such
As neither man, nor muse, can praise too much.
'Tis true, and all men's suffrage. But these ways
Were not the paths I meant unto thy praise;
For silliest ignorance on these may light,
Which, when it sounds at best, but echoes right;
Or blind affection, which doth ne'er advance
The truth, but gropes, and urgeth all by chance;
Or crafty malice might pretend this praise,
And think to ruin, where it seemed to raise.
These are, as some infamous bawd or whore
Should praise a matron. What could hurt her more?
But thou art proof against them, and, indeed,
Above the ill fortune of them, or the need.
I therefore will begin. Soul of the age!
The applause, delight, the wonder of our stage!
My Shakespeare, rise! I will not lodge thee by
Chaucer, or Spenser, or bid Beaumont lie
A little further, to make thee a room;
Thou art a monument without a tomb,
And art alive still while thy book doth live
And we have wits to read and praise to give.
That I not mix thee so, my brain excuses,
I mean with great, but disproportioned Muses;
For if I thought my judgment were of years,
I should commit thee surely with thy peers,
And tell how far thou didst our Lyly outshine,
Or sporting Kyd, or Marlowe's mighty line.
And though thou hadst small Latin and less Greek,
From thence to honor thee, I would not seek
For names; but call forth thundering Aeschylus,
Euripides, and Sophocles to us;
Pacuvius, Accius, him of Cordova dead,
To life again, to hear thy buskin tread,
And shake a stage; or, when thy socks were on,
Leave thee alone for the comparison
Of all that insolent Greece or haughty Rome
Sent forth, or since did from their ashes come.

Triumph, my Britain, thou hast one to show
To whom all scenes of Europe homage owe.
He was not of an age, but for all time!
And all the Muses still were in their prime,
When, like Apollo, he came forth to warm
Our ears, or like a Mercury to charm!
Nature herself was proud of his designs
And joyed to wear the dressing of his lines!
Which were so richly spun, and woven so fit,
As, since, she will vouchsafe no other wit.
The merry Greek, tart Aristophanes,
Neat Terence, witty Plautus, now not please,
But antiquated and deserted lie,
As they were not of Nature's family.
Yet must I not give Nature all; thy art,
My gentle Shakespeare, must enjoy a part.
For though the poet's matter nature be,
His art doth give the fashion; and, that he
Who casts to write a living line, must sweat
(Such as thine are) and strike the second heat
Upon the Muses' anvil; turn the same
(And himself with it) that he thinks to frame,
Or, for the laurel, he may gain a scorn;
For a good poet's made, as well as born.
And such wert thou! Look how the father's face
Lives in his issue; even so the race
Of Shakespeare's mind and manners brightly shines
In his well turnéd, and true filéd lines;
In each of which he seems to shake a lance,
As brandished at the eyes of ignorance.
Sweet Swan of Avon! what a sight it were
To see thee in our waters yet appear,
And make those flights upon the banks of Thames,
That so did take Eliza, and our James!
But stay, I see thee in the hemisphere
Advanced, and made a constellation there!
Shine forth, thou Star of poets, and with rage
Or influence, chide or cheer the drooping stage,
Which, since thy flight from hence, hath mourned like night,
And despairs day, but for thy volume's light.

BEN JONSON

Processions*

I just want to lie down on the Appian Way
in the sun, like an old pheasant in the off-season
forgetting shotguns and the Plymouth cold
and watch the Pines of Rome tail-feathering
green, into the sky. Under wind, the earth moves
in an ether dream, as when a building sways
for a moment, then stops. Plumage lines the sky
like Caesars coming home. Giddy with heat, my eye
whirls colors, beaded, crested, out of North
Massachusetts, white auditoriums, rainy Sundays
and the intimate ministry,
into Italy like a long distance runner
who runs for the love of his legs
and carries no message.

DONALD JUNKINS

Reprinted from *Poetry* 92, May 1963, with permission of the poet.

The Sunfish*

Slim without diet, he moves toward worms like an early bird.
Soft nibbler, heckler of fishermen, this busyfish hits
and runs. He cleans the steel hook like a dim-wit.

Children love him under boats among the yellow weeds
and under the green shade of wharves for his backbone;
they dangle bait on lines that will not sound his greed.

It is all done by touch. From overhead they cannot
see his soft mail shading into black and blue,
his blood-daubed cheek, his belly as orange as spawn, the hue

of silver fading toward his tail. This Pip, this pun
is the harlequin of the pond. Out of the water
he fades like leather. All anglers fish for the sun.

DONALD JUNKINS

*Reprinted from *The Sunfish and the Partridge*, Pym-Randall Press, copyright 1965, with permission of the poet.

La Belle Dame Sans Merci

O what can ail thee, knight-at-arms,
Alone and palely loitering?
The sedge has withered from the lake,
And no birds sing.

O what can ail thee, knight-at-arms,
So haggard and so woe-begone?
The squirrel's granary is full,
And the harvest's done.

I see a lily on thy brow
With anguish moist and fever dew,
And on thy cheeks a fading rose
Fast withereth too.

I met a lady in the meads,
Full beautiful—a faery's child,
Her hair was long, her foot was light,
And her eyes were wild.

I made a garland for her head,
And bracelets too, and fragrant zone;
She looked at me as she did love,
And made sweet moan.

I set her on my pacing steed
And nothing else saw all day long,
For sidelong would she bend, and sing
A faery's song.

She found me roots of relish sweet,
And honey wild, and manna dew,
And sure in language strange she said—
"I love thee true!"

She took me to her elfin grot,
And there she wept and sighed full sore,
And there I shut her wild, wild eyes
With kisses four.

And there she lulléd me asleep,
  And there I dreamed—ah, woe betide!
The latest dream I ever dreamed
  On the cold hill side.

I saw pale kings, and princes too,
  Pale warriors, death-pale were they all;
They cried—"La Belle Dame sans Merci
  Thee hath in thrall!"

I saw their starved lips in the gloam,
  With horrid warning gapéd wide,
And I awoke and found me here,
  On the cold hill's side.

And this is why I sojourn here,
  Alone and palely loitering,
Though the sedge is withered from the lake,
  And no birds sing.

JOHN KEATS

Lines on the Mermaid Tavern

Souls of Poets dead and gone,
What Elysium have ye known,
Happy field or mossy cavern,
Choicer than the Mermaid Tavern?
Have ye tippled drink more fine
Than mine host's Canary wine?
Or are fruits of Paradise
Sweeter than those dainty pies
Of venison? O generous food!
Drest as though bold Robin Hood
Would, with his maid Marian,
Sup and bowse from horn and can.

I have heard that on a day
Mine host's sign-board flew away,
Nobody knew whither, till
An astrologer's old quill
To a sheepskin gave the story,
Said he saw you in your glory,
Underneath a new old sign
Sipping beverage divine,
And pledging with contented smack
The Mermaid in the Zodiac.

Souls of Poets dead and gone,
What Elysium have ye known,
Happy field or mossy cavern,
Choicer than the Mermaid Tavern?

JOHN KEATS

Ode on a Grecian Urn

1

Thou still unravish'd bride of quietness,
Thou foster-child of silence and slow time,
Sylvan historian, who canst thus express
A flowery tale more sweetly than our rhyme:
What leaf-fring'd legend haunts about they shape
Of deities or mortals, or of both,
In Tempe or the dales of Arcady?
What men or gods are these? What maidens loth?
What mad pursuit? What struggle to escape?
What pipes and timbrels? What wild ecstasy?

2

Heard melodies are sweet, but those unheard
Are sweeter; therefore, ye soft pipes, play on;
Not to the sensual ear, but, more endear'd,
Pipe to the spirit ditties of no tone:
Fair youth, beneath the trees, thou canst not leave
Thy song, nor ever can those trees be bare;
Bold Lover, never, never canst thou kiss,
Though winning near the goal—yet, do not grieve;
She cannot fade, though thou hast not thy bliss,
For ever wilt thou love, and she be fair!

3

Ah, happy, happy boughs! that cannot shed
Your leaves, nor ever bid the Spring adieu;
And, happy melodist, unwearied,
For ever piping songs for ever new;
More happy love! more happy, happy love!
For ever warm and still to be enjoy'd,
For ever panting, and for ever young;
All breathing human passion far above,
That leaves a heart high-sorrowful and cloy'd,
A burning forehead, and a parching tongue.

4

Who are these coming to the sacrifice?
To what green altar, O mysterious priest,
Lead'st thou that heifer lowing at the skies,
And all her silken flanks with garlands drest?
What little town by river or sea shore,
Or mountain-built with peaceful citadel,
Is emptied of this folk, this pious morn?
And, little town, thy streets for evermore
Will silent be; and not a soul to tell
Why thou art desolate, can e'er return.

5

O Attic shape! Fair attitude! with brede
Of marble men and maidens overwrought,
With forest branches and the trodden weed;
Thou, silent form, dost tease us out of thought
As doth eternity: Cold Pastoral!
When old age shall this generation waste,
Thou shalt remain, in midst of other woe
Than ours, a friend to man, to whom thou say'st,
Beauty is truth, truth beauty,—that is all
Ye know on earth, and all ye need to know.

JOHN KEATS

Ode to a Nightingale

My heart aches, and a drowsy numbness pains
  My sense, as though of hemlock I had drunk,
Or emptied some dull opiate to the drains
  One minute past, and Lethe-wards had sunk:
'Tis not through envy of thy happy lot,
  But being too happy in thine happiness—
    That thou, light-wingéd Dryad of the trees,
      In some melodious plot
  Of beechen green, and shadows numberless,
    Singest of summer in full-throated ease.

O, for a draught of vintage! that hath been
  Cooled a long age in the deep-delvéd earth,
Tasting of Flora and the country green,
  Dance, and Provençal song, and sunburnt mirth!
O for a beaker full of the warm South,
  Full of the true, the blushful Hippocrene,
    With beaded bubbles winking at the brim,
      And purple-stainéd mouth;
  That I might drink, and leave the world unseen,
    And with thee fade away into the forest dim:

Fade far away, dissolve, and quite forget
  What thou among the leaves hast never known,
The weariness, the fever, and the fret
  Here, where men sit and hear each other groan;
Where palsy shakes a few, sad, last gray hairs,
  Where youth grows pale, and specter-thin, and dies;
    Where but to think is to be full of sorrow
      And leaden-eyed despairs,
  Where Beauty cannot keep her lustrous eyes,
  Or new Love pine at them beyond tomorrow.

Away! away! for I will fly to thee,
  Not charioted by Bacchus and his pards,
But on the viewless wings of Poesy,
  Though the dull brain perplexes and retards:
Already with thee! tender is the night,
  And haply the Queen-Moon is on her throne,
    Clustered around by all her starry Fays;
      But here there is no light,
  Save what from heaven is with the breezes blown
    Through verdurous glooms and winding mossy ways.

I cannot see what flowers are at my feet,
  Nor what soft incense hangs upon the boughs,
But, in embalméd darkness, guess each sweet
  Wherewith the seasonable month endows
The grass, the thicket, and the fruit-tree wild;
  White hawthorn, and the pastoral eglantine;
    Fast fading violets covered up in leaves;
      And mid-May's eldest child.

The coming musk-rose, full of dewy wine,
  The murmurous haunt of flies on summer eves.
Darkling I listen; and, for many a time,
  I have been half in love with easeful Death,
Called him soft names in many a muséd rime,
  To take into the air my quiet breath;
Now more than ever seems it rich to die,
  To cease upon the midnight with no pain,
    While thou art pouring forth thy soul abroad
      In such an ecstasy!
Still wouldst thou sing, and I have ears in vain—
    To thy high requiem become a sod.

Thou wast not born for death, immortal Bird!
  No hungry generations tread thee down;
The voice I hear this passing night was heard
  In ancient days by emperor and clown:
Perhaps the self-same song that found a path
  Through the sad heart of Ruth, when, sick for home,
    She stood in tears amid the alien corn;
      The same that oft-times hath
  Charmed magic casements, opening on the foam
    Of perilous seas, in faery lands forlorn.

Forlorn! the very word is like a bell
  To toll me back from thee to my sole self,
Adieu! the fancy cannot cheat so well
  As she is famed to do, deceiving elf.
Adieu! adieu! thy plaintive anthem fades
  Past the near meadows, over the still stream,
    Up the hillside; and now 'tis buried deep
      In the next valley glades:
  Was it a vision, or a waking dream?
    Fled is that music—Do I wake or sleep?

John Keats

On the Sea

It keeps eternal whisperings around
Desolate shores, and with its mighty swell
Gluts twice ten thousand caverns, till the spell
Of Hecate leaves them their old shadowy sound.
Often 'tis in such gentle temper found,
That scarcely will the very smallest shell
Be moved for days from whence it sometime fell,
When last the winds of heaven were unbound.
Oh ye! who have your eye-balls vexed and tired,
Feast them upon the wideness of the sea;
Oh ye! whose ears are dinned with uproar rude,
Or fed too much with cloying melody—
Sit ye near some old cavern's mouth, and brood
Until ye start, as if the sea-nymphs quired!

JOHN KEATS

In a Drear-Nighted December

I

In a drear-nighted December,
Too happy, happy tree,
Thy branches ne'er remember
Their green felicity:
The north cannot undo them,
With a sleety whistle through them;
Nor frozen thawings glue them
From budding at the prime.

II

In a drear-nighted December,
Too happy, happy brook,
Thy bubblings ne'er remember
Apollo's summer look;
But with a sweet forgetting,
They stay their crystal fretting,
Never, never petting
About the frozen time.

III

Ah! would 'twere so with many
A gentle girl and boy!
But were there ever any
Writh'd not of passed joy?
"The feel of *not* to feel it,"
When there is none to heal it,
Nor number sense to steel it,
Was never said in rhyme.

JOHN KEATS

The Eve of St. Agnes

St. Agnes' Eve—Ah, bitter chill it was!
The owl, for all his feathers, was a-cold;
The hare limped trembling through the frozen grass,
And silent was the flock in woolly fold:
Numb were the Beadsman's fingers, while he told
His rosary, and while his frosted breath,
Like pious incense from a censer old,
Seem'd taking flight for heaven, without a death,
Past the sweet Virgin's picture, which his prayer he saith.

His prayer he saith, this patient, holy man;
Then takes his lamp, and riseth from his knees,
And back returneth, meager, barefoot, wan,
Along the chapel aisle by slow degrees:
The sculptur'd dead, on each side, seem to freeze,
Emprison'd in black, purgatorial rails:
Knights, ladies, praying in dumb orat'ries,
He passeth by; and his weak spirit fails
To think how they may ache in icy hoods and mails.

Northward he turneth through a little door,
And scarce three steps, ere Music's golden tongue
Flatter'd to tears this agèd man and poor;
But no—already had his deathbell rung;
The joys of all his life were said and sung:
His was harsh penance on St. Agnes' Eve:
Another way he went, and soon among
Rough ashes sat he for his soul's reprieve,
And all night kept awake, for sinners' sake to grieve.

St. Agnes' Eve—Jan. 20, when it was believed that virgins would dream of their future husbands and feast with them.

That ancient Beadsman heard the prelude soft;
And so it chanc'd, for many a door was wide,
From hurry to and fro. Soon, up aloft,
The silver snarling trumpets 'gan to chide:
The level chambers, ready with their pride,
Were glowing to receive a thousand guests:
The carvèd angels, ever eager-eyed,
Star'd, where upon their heads the cornice rests,
With hair blown back, and wings put cross-wise on their breasts.

At length burst in the argent revelry,
With plume, tiara, and all rich array,
Numerous as shadows, haunting fairily
The brain, new stuff'd, in youth, with triumphs gay
Of old romance. These let us wish away.
And turn, sole-thoughted, to one lady there,
Whose heart had brooded, all that wintry day,
On love, and wing'd St. Agnes' saintly care,
As she had heard old dames full many times declare.

They told her how, upon St. Agnes' Eve,
Young virgins might have visions of delight,
And soft adorings from their loves receive
Upon the honey'd middle of the night,
If ceremonies due they did aright;
As, supperless to bed they must retire,
And couch supine their beauties, lily white;
Nor look behind, nor sideways, but require
Of Heaven with upward eyes for all that they desire.

Full of this whim was thoughtful Madeline:
The music, yearning like a God in pain,
She scarcely heard: her maiden eyes divine,
Fix'd on the floor, saw many a sweeping train
Pass by—she heeded not at all: in vain
Came many a tiptoe, amorous cavalier,
And back retir'd: not cool'd by high disdain,
But she saw not: her heart was otherwhere:
She sigh'd for Agnes' dreams, the sweetest of the year.

She danc'd along with vague, regardless eyes,
Anxious her lips, her breathing quick and short:
The hallow'd hour was near at hand: she sighs
Amid the timbrels, and the throng'd resort
Of whisperers in anger, or in sport;
'Mid looks of love, defiance, hate, and scorn,
Hoodwink'd with faery fancy; all amort,
Save to St. Agnes and her lambs unshorn,
And all the bliss to be before tomorrow morn.

So, purposing each moment to retire,
She linger'd still. Meantime, across the moors,
Had come young Porphyro, with heart on fire
For Madeline. Beside the portal doors,
Buttress'd from moonlight, stands he, and implores
All saints to give him sight of Madeline,
But for one moment in the tedious hours,
That he might gaze and worship all unseen;
Perchance speak, kneel, touch, kiss—in sooth such things have been.

He ventures in: let no buzz'd whisper tell:
All eyes be muffled, or a hundred swords
Will storm his heart, Love's fev'rous citadel:
For him, those chambers held barbarian hordes,
Hyena foemen, and hot-blooded lords,
Whose very dogs would execrations howl
Against the lineage: not one breast affords
Him any mercy, in that mansion foul,
Save one old beldame, weak in body and in soul.

Ah, happy chance! the agèd creature came,
Shuffling along with ivory-headed wand,
To where he stood, hid from the torch's flame,
Being a broad hall-pillar, far beyond
The sound of merriment and chorus bland:
He startled her; but soon she knew his face,
And grasped his fingers in her palsied hand,
Saying, "Mercy, Porphyro! hie thee from this place;
They are all here tonight, the whole blood-thirsty race!

"Get hence! get hence! there's dwarfish Hildebrand;
He had a fever late, and in the fit
He cursèd thee and thine, both house and land:
Then there's that old Lord Maurice, not a whit
More tame for his grey hairs—Alas me! flit!
Flit like a ghost away."—"Ah, Gossip dear,
We're safe enough; here in this arm-chair sit,
And tell me how"—"Good Saints! not here, not here;
Follow me, child, or else these stones will be thy bier."

He followed through a lowly archèd way,
Brushing the cobwebs with his lofty plume,
And as she muttered "Well-a—well-a-day!"
He found him in a little moonlight room,
Pale, lattic'd, chill, and silent as a tomb.
"Now tell me where is Madeline," said he,
"O tell me, Angela, by the holy loom
Which none but secret sisterhood may see,
When they St. Agnes' wool are weaving piously."

"St. Agnes! Ah! it is St. Agnes' Eve—
Yet men will murder upon holy days:
Thou must hold water in a witch's sieve.
And be liege-lord of all the Elves and Fays,
To venture so; it fills me with amaze
To see thee, Porphyro!—St. Agnes' Eve!
God's help! my lady fair the conjuror plays
This very night: good angels her deceive!
But let me laugh awhile, I've mickle time to grieve."

Feebly she laugheth in the languid moon,
While Porphyro upon her face doth look,
Like puzzled urchin on an agèd crone
Who keepeth clos'd a wond'rous riddle-book,
As spectacled she sits in chimney nook.
But soon his eyes grew brilliant, when she told
His lady's purpose; and he scarce could brook
Tears, at the thought of those enchantments cold,
And Madeline asleep in lap of legends old.

Sudden a thought came like a full-blown rose,
Flushing his brow, and in his painèd heart
Made purple riot: then doth he propose
A stratagem, that makes the beldame start:
"A cruel man and impious thou art:
Sweet lady, let her pray, and sleep, and dream
Alone with her good angels, far apart
From wicked men like thee. Go, go!—I deem
Thou canst not surely be the same that thou didst seem."

"I will not harm her, by all saints I swear,"
Quoth Prophyro: "O may I ne'er find grace
When my weak voice shall whisper its last prayer,
If one of her soft ringlets I displace,
Or look with ruffian passion in her face:
Good Angela, believe me by these tears;
Or I will, even in a moment's space,
Awake, with horrid shout, my foemen's ears,
And beard them, though they be more fang'd than wolves and bears."

"Ah! why wilt thou affright a feeble soul?
A poor, weak, palsy-stricken, churchyard thing,
Whose passing-bell may ere the midnight toll;
Whose prayers for thee, each morn and evening,
Were never miss'd."—Thus plaining, doth she bring
A gentler speech from burning Porphyro;
So woeful, and of such deep sorrowing,
That Angela gives promise she will do
Whatever he shall wish, betide her weal or woe.

Which was, to lead him, in close secrecy,
Even to Madeline's chamber, and there hide
Him in a closet, of such privacy
That he might see her beauty unespied,
And win perhaps that night a peerless bride,
While legion'd fairies paced the coverlet,
And pale enchantment held her sleepy-eyed.
Never on such a night have lovers met,
Since Merlin paid his Demon all the monstrous debt.

Merlin—The magician of Arthur's court, who, according to legend, was betrayed and imprisoned in a rock by a king's daughter (or a water-fairy) to whom he divulged the secret of his magic power.

"It shall be as thou wishest," said the Dame:
"All cates and dainties shall be storèd there
Quickly on this feast-night: by the tambour frame
Her own lute thou wilt see: no time to spare,
For I am slow and feeble, and scarce dare
On such a catering trust my dizzy head.
Wait here, my child, with patience; kneel in prayer
The while: Ah! thou must needs the lady wed,
Or may I never leave my grave among the dead."

So saying, she hobbled off with busy fear.
The lover's endless minutes slowly pass'd;
The Dame return'd, and whisper'd in his ear
To follow her; with agèd eyes aghast
From fright of dim espial. Safe at last,
Through many a dusky gallery, they gain
The maiden's chamber, silken, hush'd and chaste;
Where Porphyro took covert, pleas'd amain.
His poor guide hurried back with agues in her brain.

Her falt'ring hand upon the balustrade,
Old Angela was feeling for the stair,
When Madeline, St. Agnes' charmèd maid,
Rose, like a mission'd spirit, unaware:
With silver taper's light, and pious care,
She turned, and down the agèd gossip led
To a safe level matting. Now prepare,
Young Porphyro, for gazing on that bed;
She comes, she comes again, like ring-dove fray'd and fled.

Out went the taper as she hurried in;
Its little smoke, in pallid moonshine, died:
She clos'd the door, she panted, all akin
To spirits of the air, and visions wide:
No uttered syllable, or, woe betide!
But to her heart, her heart was voluble,
Paining with eloquence her balmy side;
As though a tongueless nightingale should swell
Her throat in vain, and die, heart-stifled, in her dell.

A casement high and triple-arched there was,
All garlanded with carven imag'ries
Of fruits, and flowers, and bunches of knot-grass,
And diamonded with panes of quaint device,
Innumerable of stains and splendid dyes,
As are the tiger-moth's deep-damask'd wings;
And in the midst, 'mong thousand heraldries,
And twilight saints, and dim emblazonings,
A shielded scutcheon blush'd with blood of queens and kings.

Full on this casement shone the wintry moon,
And threw warm gules on Madeline's fair breast,
As down she knelt for heaven's grace and boon;
Rose-bloom fell on her hands, together prest,
And on her silver cross soft amethyst,
And on her hair a glory, like a saint:
She seem'd a splendid angel, newly dressed,
Save wings, for heaven:—Porphyro grew faint:
She knelt, so pure a thing, so free from mortal taint.

Anon his heart revives: her vespers done,
Of all its wreathèd pearls her hair she frees;
Unclasps her warmèd jewels one by one;
Loosens her fragrant boddice; by degrees
Her rich attire creeps rustling to her knees:
Half-hidden, like a mermaid in sea-weed,
Pensive awhile she dreams awake, and sees,
In fancy, fair St. Agnes in her bed,
But dares not look behind, or all the charm is fled.

Soon, trembling in her soft and chilly nest,
In sort of wakeful swoon, perplex'd she lay,
Until the poppied warmth of sleep oppress'd
Her soothèd limbs, and soul fatigued away;
Flown, like a thought, until the morrow-day;
Blissfully haven'd both from joy and pain;
Clasp'd like a missal where swart Paynims pray;
Blinded alike from sunshine and from rain,
As though a rose should shut, and be a bud again.

Stol'n to the paradise, and so entranced,
Porphyro gazed upon her empty dress,
And listen'd to her breathing, if it chanced
To wake into a slumberous tenderness:
Which when he heard, that minute did he bless,
And breath'd himself: then from the closet crept,
Noiseless as fear in a wide wilderness,
And over the hush'd carpet, silent, stept,
And 'tween the curtains peep'd, where, lo!—how fast she slept.

Then by the bed-side, where the faded moon
Made a dim, silver twilight, soft he set
A table and, half anguish'd, threw thereon
A cloth of woven crimson, gold, and jet:—
O for some drowsy Morphean amulet!
The boisterous, midnight, festive clarion,
The kettledrum, and far-heard clarinet.
Affray his ears, though but in dying tone:—
The hall door shuts again, and all the noise is gone.

And still she slept an azure-lidded sleep,
In blanchèd linen, smooth, and lavender'd,
While he from forth the closet brought a heap
Of candied apple, quince, and plum, and gourd;
With jellies soother than the creamy curd,
And lucent syrops, tinct with cinnamon;
Manna and dates in argosy transferr'd
From Fez; and spicèd dainties, every one,
From silken Samarcand to cedar'd Lebanon.

These delicates he heap'd with glowing hand
On golden dishes and in baskets bright
Of wreathèd silver: sumptuous they stand
In the retirèd quiet of the night,
Filling the chilly room with perfume light.—
"And now, my love, my seraph fair, awake!
Thou art my heaven, and I thine eremite:
Open thine eyes, for meek St. Agnes' sake,
Or I shall drowse beside thee, so my soul doth ache."

Thus whispering, his warm, unnervèd arm
Sank in her pillow. Shaded was her dream
By the dusk curtains:—'twas a midnight charm
Impossible to melt as icèd stream:
The lustrous salvers in the moonlight gleam;
Broad golden fringe upon the carpet lies:
It seem'd he never, never could redeem
From such a steadfast spell his lady's eyes;
So mus'd awhile, entoil'd in woofèd phantasies.

Awakening up, he took her hollow lute,—
Tumultuous,—and, in chords that tenderest be,
He play'd an ancient ditty, long since mute,
In Provence call'd, "La belle dame sans merci":
Close to her ear touching the melody;—
Wherewith disturb'd, she utter'd a soft moan:
He ceased—she panted quick—and suddenly
Her blue affrayèd eyes wide open shone:
Upon his knees he sank, pale as smooth-sculptured stone.

Her eyes were open, but she still beheld,
Now wide awake, the vision of her sleep:
There was a painful change, that nigh expell'd
The blisses of her dream so pure and deep,
At which fair Madeline began to weep,
And moan forth witless words with many a sigh;
While still her gaze on Porphyro would keep;
Who knelt, with joinèd hands and piteous eye,
Fearing to move or speak, she look'd so dreamingly.

"Ah, Porphyro!" said she, "but even now
Thy voice was at sweet tremble in mine ear,
Made tuneable with every sweetest vow;
And those sad eyes were spiritual and clear:
How chang'd thou art! how pallid, chill, and drear!
Give me that voice again, my Porphyro,
Those looks immortal, those complainings dear!
Oh leave me not in this eternal woe,
For if thou diest, my Love, I know not where to go."

Beyond a mortal man impassion'd far
At these voluptuous accents, he arose
Ethereal, flush'd, and like a throbbing star
Seen mid the sapphire heaven's deep repose;
Into her dream he melted, as the rose
Blendeth its odor with the violet,—
Solution sweet: meantime the frost-wind blows
Live Love's alarum pattering the sharp sleet
Against the window-panes; St. Agnes' moon hath set.

'Tis dark: quick pattereth the flaw-blown sleet.
"This is no dream, my bride, my Madeline!"
'Tis dark: the icèd gusts still rave and beat:
"No dream, alas! alas! and woe is mine!
Porphyro will leave me here to fade and pine.—
Cruel! what traitor could thee hither bring?
I curse not, for my heart is lost in thine,
Though thou forsakest a deceivèd thing;—
A dove forlorn and lost with sick unprunèd wing."

"My Madeline! sweet dreamer! lovely bride!
Say, may I be for aye thy vassal blest?
Thy beauty's shield, heart-shap'd and vermeil dyed?
Ah, silver shrine, here will I take my rest
After so many hours of toil and quest,
A famish'd pilgrim,—saved by miracle.
Though I have found, I will not rob thy nest
Saving of thy sweet self; if thou think'st well
To trust, fair Madeline, to no rude infidel.

"Hark! 'tis an elfin-storm from faery land
Of haggard seeming, but a boon indeed:
Arise—arise! the morning is at hand;—
The bloated wassailers will never heed:—
Let us away, my love, with happy speed;
There are no ears to hear, or eyes to see,—
Drown'd all in Rhenish and the sleepy mead:
Awake! arise! my love, and fearless be,
For o'er the southern moors I have a home for thee."

She hurried at his words, beset with fears,
For there were sleeping dragons all around,
At glaring watch, perhaps, with ready spears—
Down the wide stairs a darkling way they found.—
In all the house was heard no human sound.
A chain-droop'd lamp was flickering by each door;
The arras, rich with horseman, hawk, and hound,
Flutter'd in the besieging wind's uproar;
And the long carpets rose along the gusty floor.

They glide, like phantoms, into the wide hall;
Like phantoms, to the iron porch, they glide;
Where lay the Porter, in uneasy sprawl,
With a huge empty flaggon by his side:
The wakeful bloodhound rose, and shook his hide,
But his sagacious eye an inmate owns:
By one, and one, the bolts full easy slide:—
The chains lie silent on the footworn stones;—
The key turns, and the door upon its hinges groans.

And they are gone: ay, ages long ago
These lovers fled away into the storm.
That night the Baron dreamt of many a woe,
And all his warrior-guests, with shade and form
Of witch, and demon, and large coffin-worm,
Were long be-nightmar'd. Angela the old
Died palsy-twitch'd, with meager face deform;
The Beadsman, after a thousand aves told,
For aye unsought-for slept among his ashes cold.

John Keats

After Antietam

The breeze rises
loud off the crisp grass.
The lame in the field scream prayers, and wait
for the bearers. The kindly, the careful. Arriving now.
The deserters crawl in the long grass.

Upstream, McClellan's pursuit hesitates.
His delay, his bloodless pause, spares
Hood's hard-marched, bone lean forces; and Lee's.
Like rumor, the ghosts of these troop off south.
Rewarded with whisky
Colonel Ferrero's thirsty
51sts drink happily.
Lie on.
By the Dunker church in the smoking grove
with Lady Jane the regiment's
laughing-stock.
Autumn in the mauve wood
the farm girls will rein in
and sit their mounts silent . . .
The ponies lap and blow at the shallow stream.
Sunny hills swell.
A detail slips through the ripe corn
fetching out the shattered horses.
In pens the swine are full for the harvest
butchering and the temperate feasts.
These wait, and again all wait.

My love, lie in the day with me, to the shade
and hour of the sane order, when flesh and flesh
breed history, word of the act: Rodman slain,
his men safe, dry; Burnside baffled.
Personal McClellan wary, and loving unto caution
the men walking in at dusk from the blue copse;
their dragging, piling motion orderly
clearing cornfield and hayfield of the carcasses
of cavalry-, wheel-, and pack-horses,
arranging memory on the green valley.
Late September down the valley
the wind smoulders the sweet greasy smoke
of the torched horses,
the wind black, the gristle popping.

Arm turned in arm, my love, lie on with me
as the gusty November snow settles
uneasy against the scattered nettles,
across the black hay, the scorched timothy.
Silent as dormant limbs, as the seasons
freeze terrain north to Pennsylvania's hills;
at thaw the seed distending in the soil
sprouts rapid pasture, green to a weak sun!
Out of May the copper stream rills under
the fume of lilac blooming, the arched stone
bridge. The stand of poplar saplings rises
to the oriole. Into the summer
leaning warm. Lie on with me, my love, low
springs the wind, tall grow the raving grasses.

GEORGE KEITHLEY

Reprinted from *Massachusetts Review*, copyright 1966, with permission of the poet.

Potency

for J. Maritain

The hawk glides
in a high wind over the orchard
acre crows nest in
to the elm and oak forest south of the lake.
and the fall to green cover, braked and steep.
and
he is low in an oak
and dry as the near limbs:
he is the jump into the warm wind, and the brown glide
A southern rain spreads behind him

Down the slate
bank from the plant rain and wind lie on
the river and it
is absent of the drone of motor launches:
turbines turn the generators
at
3,600
rpm, spinning of
the rain, rushed splash of the low waterfall, and on
to the lake the long, blue and gentle sweep.

When the trout
sinks against rock the men on the bleached
slate laugh, slipping, set
the poles down and climb the steps of the power
plant, watching a hawk fly the green
lake
woods to the river. Rain
has passed. The trout is down
beside a rock and holding under the current the
rise and quick plunge and the swift, silver leap.

George Keithley

Reprinted from *Poetry Northwest*, Spring 1965, with permission of the poet.

I Know Not Whether I Am Proud

I know not whether I am proud,
But this I know, I hate the crowd:
Therefore pray let me disengage
My verses from the motley page,
Where others far more sure to please
Pour out their choral song with ease.

And yet perhaps, if some should tire
With too much froth or too much fire,
There is an ear that may incline
Even to words so dull as mine.

Walter Savage Landor

Yes: I Write Verse Now and Then

Yes: I write verses now and then,
But blunt and flaccid is my pen,
No longer talked of by young men
As rather clever.
In the last quarter are my eyes,
You see it by their form and size:
Is it not time then to be wise?
Or now or never!

Fairest that ever sprang from Eve!
While Time allows the short reprieve,
Just look at me! would you believe
'Twas once a lover?
I cannot clear the five-bar gate,
But, trying first its timbers' state,
Climb stiffly up, take breath, and wait
To trundle over.

Thro' gallopade I cannot swing
The entangling blooms of Beauty's spring:
I cannot say the tender thing,
Be't true or false:
And am beginning to opine
Those girls are only half-divine
Whose waists you wicked boys entwine
In giddy waltz.

I fear that arm above that shoulder,
I wish them wiser, graver, older,
Sedater, and no harm if colder,
And panting less.
Ah! people were not half so wild
In former days, when, starchly mild,
Upon her high-heeled Essex smiled
The brave Queen Bess.

WALTER SAVAGE LANDOR

From the train

Lights in the water
and a pale star overhead
as I go through a strange town—
streets and neon signs and dark lots,
taverns on the outskirts,
a red blinker on the radio tower;
then the black farms
and the thin road where truck lights slide.

A place, Where, perhaps,
I might have lived, done a job,
had friends, loved my wife and children,
in ease and gaiety;
not drifted homelessly to the midyear of my life,
nor run so scared at my work,
nor turned from my wife to sulk in the muggy tent of my mind,
nor raged at a small girl and boy.

Cleveland at midnight:
bridges vault over bridges
where a low blocks-long barge-like ship lies
and lights flood the deck of a freighter.
Earlier, in the afternoon,
it was not a place I might have been something I'm not
that made me ache.
but a simple field that sloped gently along a country road
with the long shadows of a row of trees reaching halfway over it.

JACOB LEED

Reprinted from *things*, No. 1, Fall 1964, with permission of the poet.

Disdain Returned

He that loves a rosy cheek,
   Or a coral lip admires,
Or from starlike eyes doth seek
   Fuel to maintain his fires,
As old Time makes these decay,
So his flames must waste away.

But a smooth and steadfast mind,
   Gentle thoughts and calm desires,
Hearts with equal love combined,
   Kindle never-dying fires.
Where these are not, I despise
Lovely cheeks or lips or eyes.

No tears, Celia, now shall win
  My resolved heart to return;
I have searched thy soul within,
  And find naught but pride and scorn;
I have learned thy arts, and now
  Can disdain as much as thou.
Some power, in my revenge, convey
  That love to her I cast away.

RICHARD LOVELACE

The Garden

How vainly men themselves amaze,
To win the palm, the oak, or bays,
And their incessant labors see
Crowned from some single herb or tree
Whose short and narrow-vergéd shade
Does prudently their toils upbraid,
While all the flowers and trees do close
To weave the garlands of repose!

Fair Quiet, have I found thee here
And Innocence, thy sister dear?
Mistaken long, I sought you then
In busy companies of men.
Your sacred plants, if here below,
Only among the plants will grow;
Society is all but rude
To this delicious solitude.

No white nor red was ever seen
So amorous as this lovely green.
Fond lovers, cruel as their flame,
Cut in these trees their mistress' name.
Little, alas! they know or heed,
How far these beauties hers exceed!
Fair trees! wheres'e'r your barks I wound
No name shall but your own be found.

When we have run our passion's heat,
Love hither makes his best retreat.
The gods, that mortal beauty chase,
Still in a tree did end their race;
Apollo hunted Daphne so,
Only that she might laurel grow;
And Pan did after Syrinx speed,
Not as a nymph, but for a reed.

What wondrous life is this I lead!
Ripe apples drop about my head;
The luscious clusters of the vine
Upon my mouth do crush their wine;
The nectarine, and curious peach,
Into my hands themselves do reach;
Stumbling on melons, as I pass,
Ensnared with flowers, I fall on grass.

Meanwhile the mind, from pleasure less,
Withdraws into its happiness;—
The mind, that ocean where each kind
Does straight its own resemblance find;
Yet it creates, transcending these,
Far other worlds, and other seas,
Annihilating all that's made
To a green thought in a green shade.

Here at the fountain's sliding foot,
Or at some fruit-tree's mossy root,
Casting the body's vest aside,
My soul into the boughs does glide:
There, like a bird, it sits and sings,
Then whets and combs its silver wings,
And, till prepared for longer flight,
Waves in its plumes the various light.

Such was that happy garden-state,
While man there walked without a mate.
After a place so pure and sweet,
What other help could yet be meet!
But 'twas beyond a mortal's share
To wander solitary there:
Two paradises 'twere in one,
To live in paradise alone.

How well the skilful gardener drew
Of flowers, and herbs, this dial new;
Where, from above, the milder sun
Does through a fragrant zodiac run,
And, as it works, the industrious bee
Computes its time as well a we!
How could such sweet and wholesome hours
Be reckoned but with herbs and flowers?

ANDREW MARVELL

The Mower to the Glow-Worms

Ye living lamps, by whose dear light
The nightingale does sit so late,
And, studying all the summer night,
Her matchless songs does meditate;

Ye country comets, that portend
No war, nor prince's funeral,
Shining unto no higher end
Than to presage the grasses' fall;

Ye glow-worms, whose officious flame
To wandering mowers shows the way,
That in the night have lost their aim,
And after foolish fires do stray;

Your courteous lights in vain you waste,
Since Juliana here is come;
For she my mind hath so displaced
That I shall never find my home.

ANDREW MARVELL

Father Mapple's Hymn

From *Moby Dick*

The ribs and terrors in the whale,
Arched over me a dismal gloom,
While all God's sunlit waves rolled by,
And left me deepening down to doom.

I saw the opening maw of hell,
With endless pains and sorrows there;
Which none but they that feel can tell—
Oh, I was plunging to despair.

In black distress, I called my God,
When I could scarce believe Him mine,
He bowed his ear to my complaints—
No more the whale did me confine.

With speed He flew to my relief,
As on a radiant dolphin borne;
Awful, yet bright as lightning shone
The face of my Deliverer God.

My song for ever shall record
That terrible, that joyful hour;
I give the glory to my God,
His all the mercy and the power.

HERMAN MELVILLE

We saw the swallows

We saw the swallows gathering in the sky,
And in the osier-isle we heard their noise,
We had not to look back on summer joys,
Or forward to a summer of bright dye:
But in the largeness of the evening earth
Our spirits grew as we went side by side.
The hour became her husband and my bride.
Love, that had robbed us so, thus blessed our dearth!
The pilgrims of the year waxed very loud
In multitudinous chatterings, as the flood
Full brown came from the West, and like pale blood
Expanded to the upper crimson cloud.
Love, that had robbed us of immortal things,
This little moment mercifully gave,
Where I have seen across the twilight wave
The swan sail with her young beneath her wings.

GEORGE MEREDITH

Il Penseroso

Hence, vain deluding Joys,
The brood of Folly without father bred!
How little you bested,
Or fill the fixed mind with all your toys!
Dwell in some idle brain,
And fancies fond with gaudy shapes possess,
As thick and numberless
As the gay motes that people the sun-beams,
Or likest hovering dreams,
The fickle pensioners of Morpheus' train.
But, hail! thou Goddess sage and holy!
Hail, divinest Melancholy!
Whose saintly visage is too bright
To hit the sense of human sight,
And therefore to our weaker view
O'erlaid with black, staid Wisdom's hue;
Black, but such as in esteem
Prince Memnon's sister might beseem.
Or that starred Ethiop queen that strove
To set her beauty's praise above
The Sea-Nymphs, and their powers offended
Yet thou art higher far descended;
Thee bright-haired Vesta long of yore
To solitary Saturn bore;
His daughter she; in Saturn's reign
Such mixture was not held a stain.
Oft in glimmering bowers and glades
He met her, and in secret shades
Of woody Ida's inmost grove,
Whilst yet there was no fear of Jove.
Come, pensive Nun, devout and pure,
Sober, steadfast, and demure,
All in a robe of darkest grain,
Flowing with majestic train,
And sable stole of cypress lawn
Over thy decent shoulders drawn.
Come; but keep thy wonted state,
With even step, and musing gait,
And looks commercing with the skies,
Thy rapt soul sitting in thine eyes;

There, held in holy passion still,
Forget thyself to marble, till
With a sad leaden downward cast
Thou fix them on the earth as fast.
And join with thee calm Peace and Quiet,
Spare Fast, that oft with gods doth diet,
And hears the Muses, in a ring,
Aye round about Jove's altar sing.
And add to these retiréd Leisure,
That in trim gardens takes his pleasure.
But first, and chiefest, with thee bring,
Him that yon soars on golden wing,
Guiding the fiery-wheeléd throne,
The cherub Contemplation;
And the mute silence hist along,
'Less Philomel will deign a song,
In her sweetest saddest plight,
Smoothing the rugged brow of Night,
While Cynthia checks her dragon yoke
Gently o'er the accustomed oak.
Sweet bird, that shunn'st the noise of folly,
Most musical, most melancholy!
Thee, chantress, oft, the woods among,
I woo, to hear thy even-song;
And, missing thee, I walk unseen
On the dry smooth-shaven green,
To behold the wandering moon
Riding near her highest noon,
Like one that had been led astray
Through the heaven's wide pathless way,
And oft, as if her head she bowed,
Stooping through a fleecy cloud.
Oft, on a plat of rising ground,
I hear the far-off curfew sound
Over some wide-watered shore,
Swinging slow with sullen roar;
Or, if the air will not permit,
Some still, removéd place will fit,
Where glowing embers through the room
Teach light to counterfeit a gloom;
Far from all resort of mirth,
Save the cricket on the hearth,
Or the bellman's drowsy charm
To bless the doors from nightly harm.

Or let my lamp, at midnight hour,
Be seen in some high lonely tower
Where I may oft outwatch the Bear
With thrice great Hermes, or unsphere
The spirit of Plato, to unfold
What worlds or what vast regions hold
The immortal mind that hath forsook
Her mansion in this fleshly nook,
And of those demons that are found
In fire, air, flood, or underground,
Whose power hath a true consent,
With planet or with element.
Sometime let gorgeous Tragedy,
In sceptered pall, come sweeping by,
Presenting Thebes, or Pelops' line,
Or the tale of Troy divine,
Or what (though rare) of later age
Ennobled hath the buskined stage.
But, O sad virgin! that thy power
Might raise Musaeus from his bower;
Or bid the soul of Orpheus sing
Such notes as, warbled to the string,
Drew iron tears down Pluto's cheek,
And made hell grant what love did seek;
Or call up him that left half told
The story of Cambuscan bold,
Of Camball, and of Algarsife,
And who had Canacé to wife
That owned the virtuous ring and glass,
And of the wondrous horse of brass,
On which the Tartar king did ride;
And if aught else great bards beside
In sage and solemn tunes have sung,
Of tourneys, and of trophies hung,
Of forests, and enchantments drear,
Where more is meant than meets the ear.
Thus, Night, oft see me in thy pale career,
Till civil-suited Morn appear,
Not tricked and flounced as she was wont
With the Attic boy to hunt,
But kerchiefed in a comely cloud,
While rocking winds are piping loud;
Or ushered with a shower still,
When the gust hath blown his fill,
Ending on the rustling leaves,
With minute-drops from off the eaves.

And, when the sun begins to fling
His flaring beams, me, goddess, bring
To archéd walks of twilight groves,
And shadows brown, that Sylvan loves,
Of pine, or monumental oak,
Where the rude axe with heavéd stroke
Was never heard the nymphs to daunt
Or fright them from their hallowed haunt.
There is close covert by some brook,
Where no profaner eye may look,
Hide me from day's garish eye,
While the bee, with honeyed thigh,
That at her flowery work doth sing,
And the waters murmuring,
With such consort as they keep,
Entice the dewy-feathered sleep;
And let some strange mysterious dream
Wave at his wings, in airy stream
Of lively portraiture displayed,
Softly on my eyelids laid.
And, as I wake, sweet music breathe
Above, about, or underneath,
Sent by some spirit to mortals good,
Or the unseen Genius of the wood.
But let my due feet never fail
To walk the studious cloister's pale,
And love the high embowéd roof,
With antique pillars massy proof,
And storied windows richly dight,
Casting a dim religious light:
There let the pealing organ blow
To the full-voiced choir below
In service high and anthems clear
As may with sweetness, through mine ear,
Dissolve me into ecstasies,
And bring all heaven before mine eyes.
And may at last my weary age
Find out the peaceful hermitage,
The hairy gown and mossy cell,
Where I may sit and rightly spell
Of every star that heaven doth shew,
And every herb that sips the dew,
Till old experience do attain
To something like prophetic strain.
These pleasures, Melancholy, give,
And I with thee will choose to live.

JOHN MILTON

L'allegro

Hence, loathéd Melancholy,
Of Cerberus and blackest Midnight born
In Stygian cave forlorn
'Mongst horrid shapes, and shrieks, and sights unholy!
Find out some uncouth cell,
Where brooding Darkness spreads his jealous wings,
uncouth—unknown
And the night-raven sings;
There, under ebon shades and low-browed rocks,
As ragged as thy locks,
In dark Cimmerian desert ever dwell.
But come, thou Goddess fair and free,
Cimmerian desert—
In heaven yclept Euphrosyne,
a mythical land
And by men heart-easing Mirth;
in perpetual mist
Whom lovely Venus, at a birth,
With two sister Graces more,
To ivy-crownéd Bacchus bore:
Or whether (as some sager sing)
The frolic wind that breathes the spring,
Zephyr, with Aurora playing,
As he met her once a-Maying,
There, on beds of violets blue,
And fresh-blown roses washed in dew,
Filled her with thee, a daughter fair,
So buxom, blithe, and debonair.
buxom—lively
Haste thee, Nymph, and bring with thee
Jest, and youthful Jollity,
Quips and cranks and wanton wiles,
cranks—humorous turns of speech
Nods and becks and wreathéd smiles,
Such as hang on Hebe's cheek,
And love to live in dimple sleek;
Sport that wrinkled Care derides,
And Laughter holding both his sides.
Come, and trip it, as you go,
On the light fantastic toe;
And in thy right hand lead with thee
The mountain-nymph, sweet Liberty;
And, if I give thee honor due,
Mirth, admit me of thy crew,
To live with her, and live with thee,
In unreprovéd pleasures free;
To hear the lark begin his flight,
And, singing, startle the dull night,

From his watch-tower in the skies,
Till the dappled dawn doth rise;
Then to come, in spite of sorrow,
And at my window bid good-morrow,
Through the sweet-briar or the vine,
Or the twisted eglantine;
While the cock, with lively din,
Scatters the rear of darkness thin;
And to the stack, or the barn-door,
Stoutly struts his dames before:
Oft listening how the hounds and horn
Cheerly rouse the slumbering morn,
From the side of some hoar hill,
Through the high wood echoing shrill:
Sometime walking, not unseen,
By hedgegrow elms, on hillocks green,
Right against the eastern gate
Where the great Sun begins his state,
Robed in flames and amber light,
The clouds in thousand liveries dight;
While the plowman, near at hand,
Whistles o'er the furrowed land,
And the milkmaid singeth blithe,
And the mower whets his scythe,
And every shepherd tells his tale
Under the hawthorn in the dale.
Straight mine eye hath caught new pleasures
Whilst the landscape round it measures:
Russet lawns, and fallows gray,
Where the nibbling flocks do stray,
Mountains on whose barren breast
The laboring clouds do often rest;
Meadows trim, with daisies pied;
Shallow brooks, and rivers wide;
Towers and battlements it sees
Bosomed high in tufted trees,
Where perhaps some beauty lies,
The cynosure of neighboring eyes.
Hard by a cottage chimney smokes
From betwixt two agéd oaks,
Where Corydon and Thyrsis met
Are at their savory dinner set
Of herbs and other country messes,
Which the neat-handed Phyllis dresses;

And then in haste her bower she leaves,
With Thestylis to bind the sheaves;
Or, if the earlier season lead,
To the tanned haycock in the mead.
Sometimes, with secure delight,
The upland hamlets will invite,
When the merry bells ring round,
And the jocund rebecks sound
To many a youth and many a maid
Dancing in the checkered shade,
And young and old come forth to play
On a sunshine holiday,
Till the livelong daylight fail:
Then to a spicy nut-brown ale,
With stories told of many a feat,
How Faery Mab the junkets eat.
She was pinched and pulled, she said;
And he, by Friar's lantern led,
Tells how the drudging goblin sweat
To earn his cream-bowl duly set,
When in one night, ere glimpse of morn,
His shadowy flail hath threshed the corn
That ten day-laborers could not end;
Then lies him down, the lubber fiend,
And, stretched out all the chimney's length,
Basks at the fire his hairy strength,
And crop-full out of doors he flings,
Ere the first cock his matin rings.
Thus done the tales, to bed they creep,
By whispering winds soon lulled asleep.
Towered cities please us then,
And the busy hum of men,
Where throngs of knights and barons bold,
In weeds of peace, high triumphs hold,
With store of ladies, whose bright eyes
Rain influence, and judge the prize
Of wit or arms, while both contend
To win her grace whom all commend.
There let Hymen oft appear
In saffron robe, with taper clear,
And pomp, and feast, and revelry,
With mask and antique pageantry;
Such sights as youthful poets dream
On summer eves by haunted stream.

gŏblin—Robin Goodfellow

weeds—clothing

Hymen—god of marriage

Then to the well-trod stage anon,
If Johnson's learnéd sock be on, *sock*—light shoe worn in comedy
Or sweetest Shakespeare. Fancy's child,
Warble his native wood-notes wild.
And ever, against eating cares,
Lap me in soft Lydian airs,
Married to immortal verse,
Such as the meeting soul may pierce,
In notes with many a winding bout *bout*—turn
Of linked sweetness long drawn out
With wanton heed and giddy cunning,
The melting voice through mazes running,
Untwisting all the chains that tie
The hidden soul of harmony;
That Orpheus' self may heave his head
From golden slumber on a bed
Of heaped Elysian flowers, and hear
Such strains as would have won the ear
Of Pluto to have quite set free
His half-regained Eurydice.
These delights if thou canst give,
Mirth, with thee I mean to live.

JOHN MILTON

Lycidas

Yet once more, O ye laurels, and once more,
Ye myrtles brown, with ivy never sear,
I come to pluck your berries harsh and crude,
And with forced fingers rude
Shatter your leaves before the mellowing year.
Bitter constraint and sad occasion dear
Compels me to disturb your season due;
For Lycidas is dead, dead ere his prime,
Young Lycidas, and hath not left his peer.
Who would not sing for Lycidas? He knew
Himself to sing, and build the lofty rime.
He must not float upon his watery bier
Unwept, and welter to the parching wind,
Without the meed of some melodious tear.

Begin, then, Sisters of the sacred well,
That from beneath the seat of Jove doth spring;
Begin, and somewhat loudly sweep the string.
Hence with denial vain and coy excuse;
So may some gentle nurse
With lucky words favor my destined urn,
And as he passes turn
And bid fair peace be to my sable shroud!
For we were nursed upon the selfsame hill,
Fed the same flock, by fountain, shade, and rill;
Together both, ere the high lawns appeared
Under the opening eyelids of the Morn,
We drove afield, and both together heard
What time the gray-fly winds her sultry horn,
Battening our flocks with the fresh dews of night,
Oft till the star that rose at evening, bright,
Toward heaven's descent had sloped his westering wheel.
Meanwhile the rural ditties were not mute,
Tempered to the oaten flute;
Rough Satyrs danced, and Fauns with cloven heel
From the glad sound would not be absent long;
And old Damoetas loved to hear our song.
But, oh! the heavy change, now thou art gone,
Now thou art gone, and never must return!
Thee, Shepherd, thee the woods and desert caves,
With wild thyme and the gadding vine o'ergrown,
And all their echoes, mourn.
The willows, and the hazel copses green,
Shall now no more be seen
Fanning their joyous leaves to thy soft lays.
As killing as the canker to the rose,
Or taint-worm to the weanling herds that graze,
Or frost to flowers, that their gay wardrobe wear,
When first the white-thorn blows—
Such, Lycidas, thy loss to shepherd's ear.
Where were ye, Nymphs, when the remorseless deep
Closed o'er the head of your loved Lycidas?
For neither were ye playing on the steep
Where your old bards, the famous Druids, lie,
Nor on the shaggy top of Mona high,
Nor yet where Deva spreads her wizard stream.
Aye me! I fondly dream
"Had ye been there"—for what could that have done?
What could the Muse herself that Orpheus bore,
The Muse herself, for her enchanting son,

Whom universal nature did lament,
When, by the rout that made the hideous roar,
His gory visage down the stream was sent,
Down the swift Hebrus to the Lesbian shore?
  Alas! what boots it with uncessant care
To tend the homely, slighted shepherd's trade,
And strictly meditate the thankless Muse?
Were it not better done as others use,
To sport with Amaryllis in the shade,
Or with the tangles of Neaera's hair?
Fame is the spur that the clear spirit doth raise
(That last infirmity of noble mind)
To scorn delights, and live laborious days;
But, the fair guerdon when we hope to find,
And think to burst out into sudden blaze,
Comes the blind Fury with the abhorréd shears,
And slits the thin-spun life. "But not the praise,"
Phoebus replied, and touched my trembling ears;
"Fame is no plant that grows on mortal soil,
Nor in the glistering foil
Set off to the world, nor in broad rumor lies,
But lives and spreads aloft by those pure eyes
And perfect witness of all-judging Jove;
As he pronounces lastly on each deed,
Of so much fame in heaven expect thy meed."
  O fountain Arethuse, and thou honored flood,
Smooth-sliding Mincius, crowned with vocal reeds,
That strain I heard was of a higher mood.
But now my oat proceeds,
And listens to the Herald of the Sea
That came in Neptune's plea.
He asked the waves, and asked the felon winds,
What hard mishaps hath doomed this gentle swain!
And questioned every gust of rugged wings
That blows from off each beakéd promontory.
They knew not of his story;
And sage Hippotades their answer brings,
That not a blast was from his dungeon strayed;
The air was calm, and on the level brine
Sleek Panope with all her sisters played.
It was that fatal and perfidious bark,
Built in the eclipse, and rigged with curses dark,
That sunk so low that sacred head of thine.
  Next, Camus, reverend sire, went footing slow,
His mantle hairy, and his bonnet sedge,

Inwrought with figures dim, and on the edge
Like to that sanguine flower inscribed with woe. 106
"Ah! who hath reft," quoth he, "my dearest pledge?"
Last came, and last did go,
The Pilot of the Galilean Lake;
Two massy keys he bore of metals twain
(The golden opes, the iron shuts amain).
He shook his mitered locks, and stern bespake:
"How well could I have spared for thee, young swain,
Enow of such as, for their bellies' sake,
Creep, and intrude, and climb into the fold!
Of other care they little reckoning make
Than how to scramble at the shearers' feast,
And shove away the worthy bidden guest.
Blind mouths! that scarce themselves know how to hold
A sheep-hook, or have learned aught else the least
That to the faithful herdman's art belongs!
What recks it them? What need they? They are sped;
And, when they list, their lean and flashy songs
Grate on their scrannel pipes of wretched straw;
The hungry sheep look up, and are not fed,
But, swoln with wind and the rank mist they draw,
Rot inwardly, and foul contagion spread;
Besides what the grim wolf with privy paw
Daily devours apace, and nothing said.
But that two-handed engine at the door
Stands ready to smite once, and smite no more."
Return, Alpheus, the dread voice is past
That shrunk thy streams; return, Sicilian Muse,
And call the vales, and bid them hither cast
Their bells and flowerets of a thousand hues.
Ye valleys low, where the mild whispers use
Of shades, and wanton winds, and gushing brooks,
On whose fresh lap the swart star sparely looks,
Throw hither all your quaint enameled eyes,
That on the green turf suck the honeyed showers,
And purple all the ground with vernal flowers.
Bring the rathe primrose that forsaken dies,
The tufted crow-toe, and pale jessamine,
The white pink, and the pansy freaked with jet,
The glowing violet,
The musk-rose, and the well-attired woodbine,
With cowslips wan that hang the pensive head,
And every flower that sad embroidery wears;
Bid amaranthus all his beauty shed,

And daffodillies fill their cups with tears,
To strew the laureate hearse where Lycid lies.
For so, to interpose a little ease,
Let our frail thoughts dally with false surmise.
Aye me! Whilst thee the shores and sounding seas
Wash far away, where'er thy bones are hurled,
Whether beyond the stormy Hebrides,
Where thou perhaps under the whelming tide
Visit'st the bottom of the monstrous world;
Or whether thou, to our moist vows denied,
Sleep'st by the fable of Bellerus old,
Where the great Vision of the guarded mount
Looks toward Namancos and Bayona's hold.
Look homeward, Angel, now, and melt with ruth;
And, O ye dolphins, waft the hapless youth.
  Weep no more, woeful shepherds, weep no more,
For Lycidas, your sorrow, is not dead,
Sunk though he be beneath the watery floor;
So sinks the day-star in the ocean bed,
And yet anon repairs his drooping head,
And tricks his beams, and with new-spangled ore
Flames in the forehead of the morning sky.
So Lycidas sunk low, but mounted high,
Through the dear might of Him that walked the waves,
Where, other groves and other streams along,
With nectar pure his oozy locks he laves,
And hears the unexpressive nuptial song,
In the blest kingdoms meek of joy and love.
There entertain him all the Saints above,
In solemn troops, and sweet societies,
That sing, and singing in their glory move,
And wipe the tears forever from his eyes.
Now, Lycidas, the shepherds weep no more;
Henceforth thou art the Genius of the shore,
In thy large recompense, and shalt be good
To all that wander in that perilous flood.
  Thus sang the uncouth swain to the oaks and rills,
While the still morn went out with sandals gray;
He touched the tender stops of various quills,
With eager thought warbling his Doric lay.
And now the sun had stretched out all the hills,
And now was dropped into the western bay.
At last he rose, and twitched his mantle blue;
Tomorrow to fresh woods and pastures new.

John Milton

Believe Me, if all Those Endearing Young Charms

Believe me, if all those endearing young charms,
Which I gaze on so fondly today,
Were to change by tomorrow, and fleet in my arms,
Like fairy-gifts fading away,
Thou wouldst still be adored, as this moment thou art,
Let thy loveliness fade as it will,
And around the dear ruin each wish of my heart
Would entwine itself verdantly still.

It is not while beauty and youth are thine own,
And thy cheeks unprofaned by a tear,
That the fervour and faith of a soul can be known,
To which time will but make thee more dear;
No, the heart that has truly loved never forgets,
But as truly loves on to the close,
As the sun-flower turns on her god, when he sets,
The same look which she turned when he rose.

THOMAS MOORE

Adieu, Fairwell Earth's Bliss

Adieu, farewell earth's bliss,
This world uncertain is,
Fond are life's lustful joys,
Death proves them all but toys,
None from his darts can fly,
I am sick, I must die:
 Lord have mercy on us.

Rich men, trust not in wealth,
Gold cannot buy you health,
Physic himself must fade.
All things, to end are made,
The plague full swift goes by,
I am sick, I must die:
 Lord have mercy on us.

Beauty is but a flower,
Which wrinkles will devour,
Brightness falls from the air,
Queens have died young, and fair,
Dust hath closed Helen's eye.
I am sick, I must die:
  Lord have mercy on us.

Strength stoops unto the grave,
Worms feed on Hector brave,
Swords may not fight with fate,
Earth still holds ope her gate.
Come, come, the bells do cry.
I am sick, I must die:
  Lord have mercy on us.

Wit with his wantonness,
Tasteth death's bitterness:
Hell's executioner,
Hath no ears for to hear
What vain art can reply.
I am sick, I must die:
  Lord have mercy on us.

Haste therefore each degree,
To welcome destiny:
Heaven is our heritage
Earth but a player's stage,
Mount we unto the sky.
I am sick, I must die:
  Lord have mercy on us.

THOMAS NASHE

Spring, the Sweet Spring

Spring, the sweet spring, is the year's pleasant king;
Then blooms each thing, then maids dance in a ring,
Cold doth not sting, the pretty birds do sing:
  "Cuckoo, jug jug, pu-we, to-witta-woo!"

The palm and may make country houses gay,
Lambs frisk and play, the shepherds pipe all day,
And we hear aye birds tune this merry lay:
"Cuckoo, jug jug, pu-we, to-witta-woo!"

The fields breathe sweet, the daisies kiss our feet,
Young lovers meet, old wives a-sunning sit,
In every street these tunes our ears do greet:
"Cuckoo, jug jug, pu-we, to-witta-woo!"
Spring, the sweet spring!

THOMAS NASHE

Gently Dip

Gently dip, but not too deep;
For fear you make the golden beard to weep.
Fair maiden white and red,
Comb me smooth, and stroke my head:
And thou shalt have some cockle bread.
Gently dip, but not too deep,
For fear thou make the golden beard to weep.
Fair maiden, white, and red,
Comb me smooth, and stroke my head;
And every hair, a sheaf shall be,
And every sheaf a golden tree.

GEORGE PEELE

Whenas the Rye

Whenas the rye reach to the chin,
And chopcherry, chopcherry ripe within,
Strawberries swimming in the cream,
And schoolboys playing in the stream;
Then, O, then, O, then, O, my true love said,
'Til that time come again
She could not live a maid.

GEORGE PEELE

Sonnet—To Science

Science! true daughter of Old Time thou art!
 Who alterest all things with thy peering eyes.
Why preyest thou thus upon the poet's heart,
 Vulture, whose wings are dull realities?
How should he love thee? or how deem thee wise,
 Who wouldst not leave him in his wandering
To seek for treasure in the jewelled skies,
 Albeit he soared with an undaunted wing?
Hast thou not dragged Diana from her car?
 And driven the Hamadryad from the wood
To seek a shelter in some happier star?
 Hast thou not torn the Naiad from her flood,
The Elfin from the green grass, and from me
 The summer dream beneath the tamarind tree?

EDGAR ALLAN POE

From *An Essay on Man*

EPISTLE I

Awake, my ST. JOHN! leave all meaner things
To low ambition, and the pride of Kings.
Let us (since Life can little more supply
Than just to look about us and to die)
Expatiate free o'er all this scene of Man;
A mighty maze! but not without a plan;
A wild, where weeds and flow'rs promiscuous shoot;
Or Garden, tempting with forbidden fruit.
Together let us beat this ample field,
Try what the open, what the covert yield;
The latent tracts, the giddy heights, explore
Of all who blindly creep, or sightless soar;
Eye Nature's walks, shoot Folly as it flies,
And catch the Manners living as they rise;
Laugh where we must, be candid where we can;
But vindicate the ways of God to Man.

I.

Say first, of God above, or Man below,
What can we reason, but from what we know?
Of Man, what see we but his station here,
From which to reason, or to which refer?
Through worlds unnumbered though the God be known,
'Tis ours to trace him only in our own.
He, who through vast immensity can pierce,
See worlds on worlds compose one universe,
Observe how system into system runs,
What other planets circle other suns,
What varied Being peoples ev'ry star,
May tell why Heav'n has made us as we are.
But of this frame the bearings, and the ties,
The strong connections, nice dependencies,
Gradations just, has thy pervading soul
Looked through? or can a part contain the whole?
  Is the great chain, that draws all to agree,
And drawn supports, upheld by God, or thee?

II.

Presumptuous Man! the reason wouldst thou find,
Why formed so weak, so little, and so blind?
First, if thou canst, the harder reason guess,
Why formed no weaker, blinder, and no less?
Ask of thy mother earth, why oaks are made
Taller or stronger than the weeds they shade?
Or ask of yonder argent fields above,
Why Jove's satellites are less than Jove?
  Of Systems possible, if 'tis confessed
That Wisdom infinite must form the best,
Where all must full or not coherent be,
And all that rises, rise in due degree;
Then, in the scale of reas'ning life, 'tis plain,
There must be, somewhere, such a rank as Man:
And all the question (wrangle e'er so long)
Is only this, if God has placed him wrong?
  Respecting Man, whatever wrong we call,
May, must be right, as relative to all.
In human works, though labored on with pain,
A thousand movements scarce one purpose gain;
In God's, one single can its end produce;
Yet serves to second too some other use.

So Man, who here seems principal alone,
Perhaps acts second to some sphere unknown,
Touches some wheel, or verges to some goal;
'Tis but a part we see, and not a whole.
When the proud steed shall know why Man restrains
His fiery course, or drives him o'er the plains:
When the dull Ox, why now he breaks the clod,
Is now a victim, and now Egypt's God:
Then shall Man's pride and dullness comprehend
His actions', passions', being's, use and end;
Why doing, suff'ring, checked, impelled; and why
This hour a slave, the next a deity.
Then say not Man's imperfect, Heav'n in fault;
Say rather, Man's as perfect as he ought
His knowledge measured to his state and place;
His time a moment, and a point his space.
If to be perfect in a certain sphere,
What matter, soon or late, or here or there?
The bless'd to-day is as completely so,
As who began a thousand years ago.

III.

Heav'n from all creatures hides the book of Fate,
All but the page prescribed, their present state:
From brutes what men, from men what spirits know:
Or who could suffer Being here below?
The lamb thy riot dooms to bleed to-day,
Had he thy Reason, would he skip and play?
Pleased to the last, he crops the flow'ry food,
And licks the hand just raised to shed his blood.
O blindness to the future! kindly giv'n,
That each may fill the circle marked by Heav'n:
Who sees with equal eye, as God of all,
A hero perish, or a sparrow fall,
Atoms or systems into ruin hurled,
And now a bubble burst, and now a world.
Hope humbly then; with trembling pinions soar;
Wait the great teacher Death: and God adore.
What future bliss, he gives not thee to know,
But gives that Hope to be thy blessing now.
Hope springs eternal in the human breast:
Man never Is, but always To be bless'd:
The soul, uneasy and confined from home,
Rests and expatiates in a life to come.

Lo, the poor Indian! whose untutored mind
Sees God in clouds, or hears him in the wind:
His soul proud Science never taught to stray
Far as the solar walk, or milky way;
Yet simple Nature to his hope has giv'n,
Behind the cloud-topped hill, an humbler heav'n;
Some safer world in depth of woods embraced,
Some happier island in the wat'ry waste,
Where slaves once more their native land behold,
No fields torment, no Christians thirst for gold.
To Be, contents his natural desire,
He asks no Angel's wing, no Seraph's fire;
But thinks, admitted to that equal sky,
His faithful dog shall bear him company.

IV.

Go, wiser thou! and, in thy scale of sense,
Weigh thy Opinion against Providence;
Call imperfection what thou fanci'st such,
Say, here he gives too little, there too much:
Destroy all Creatures for thy sport or gust,
Yet cry, If Man's unhappy, God's unjust;
If Man alone engross not Heav'n's high care,
Alone made perfect here, immortal there:
Snatch from his hand the balance and the rod,
Re-judge his justice, be the God of God.
In Pride, in reas'ning Pride, our error lies;
All quit their sphere, and rush into the skies.
Pride still is aiming at the bless'd abodes,
Men would be Angels, Angels would be Gods
Aspiring to be Gods, if Angels fell,
Aspiring to be Angels, Men rebel:
And who but wishes to invert the laws
Of Order, sins against th' Eternal Cause.

V.

Ask for what end the heav'nly bodies shine,
Earth for whose use? Pride answers, " 'Tis for mine:
For me kind Nature wakes her genial Pow'r,
Suckles each herb, and spreads out ev'ry flow'r;
Annual for me, the grape, the rose renew
The juice nectareous, and the balmy dew;

For me, the mine a thousand treasures brings;
For me, health gushes from a thousand springs;
Seas roll to waft me, suns to light me rise;
My foot-stool earth, my canopy the skies."
  But errs not Nature from his gracious end,
From burning suns when livid deaths descend,
When earthquakes swallow, or when tempests sweep
Towns to one grave, whole nations to the deep?
"No," ('tis replied) "the first Almighty Cause
Acts not by partial, but by gen'ral laws;
Th' exceptions few; some change since all began:
And what created perfect?"—Why then Man?
If the great end be human Happiness,
Then Nature deviates; and can Man do less?
As much that end a constant course requires
Of show'rs and sun-shine, as of Man's desires;
As much eternal springs and cloudless skies,
As Men for ever temp'rate, calm, and wise.
If plagues or earthquakes break not Heav'n's design,
Why then a Borgia, or a Catiline?
Who knows but he, whose hand the lightning forms,
Who heaves old Ocean, and who wings the storms;
Pours fierce Ambition in a Caesar's mind,
Or turns young Ammon, loose to scourge mankind?
From pride, from pride, our very reas'ning springs;
Account for moral as for nat'ral things:
Why charge we Heav'n in those, in these acquit?
In both, to reason right is to submit.
  Better for Us, perhaps, it might appear,
Were there all harmony, all virtue here;
That never air or ocean felt the wind;
That never passion discomposed the mind.
But all subsists by elemental strife;
And Passions are the elements of Life.
The gen'ral Order, since the whole began
Is kept in Nature, and is kept in Man.

VI.

What would this Man? Now upward will he soar,
And, little less than Angel, would be more;
Now looking downwards, just as grieved appears
To want the strength of bulls, the fur of bears.
Made for his use all creatures if he call,

Say what their use, had he the pow'rs of all?
Nature to these, without profusion, kind,
The proper organs, proper pow'rs assign'd;
Each seeming want compensated of course,
Here with degrees of swiftness, there of force;
All in exact proportion to the state;
Nothing to add, and nothing to abate.
Each beast, each insect, happy in its own:
Is Heav'n unkind to Man, and Man alone?
Shall he alone, whom rational we call,
Be pleased with nothing, if not bless'd with all?
  The bliss of Man (could Pride that blessing find)
Is not to act or think beyond mankind;
No pow'rs of body or of soul to share,
But what his nature and his state can bear.
Why has not Man a microscopic eye?
For this plain reason, Man is not a Fly.
Say what the use, were finer optics giv'n,
T' inspect a mite, not comprehend the heav'n?
Or touch, if tremblingly alive all o'er,
To smart and agonize at every pore?
Or quick effluvia darting through the brain,
Die of a rose in aromatic pain?
If Nature thundered in his op'ning ears,
And stunned him with the music of the spheres,
How would he wish that Heav'n had left him still
The whisp'ring Zephyr, and the purling rill?
Who finds not Providence all good and wise,
Alike in what it gives, and what denies?

VII.

Far as Creation's ample range extends,
The scale of sensual, mental pow'rs ascends:
Mark how it mounts, to Man's imperial race,
From the green myriads in the peopled grass:
What modes of sight betwixt each wide extreme,
The mole's dim curtain, and the lynx's beam:
Of smell, the headlong lioness between,
And hound sagacious on the tainted green:
Of hearing, from the life that fills the Flood,
To that which warbles through the vernal wood:
The spider's touch, how exquisitely fine!

Feels at each thread, and lives along the line:
In the nice bee, what sense so subtly true
From pois'nous herbs extracts the healing dew?
How Instinct varies in the grov'ling swine,
Compared, half-reas'ning elephant, with thine!
'Twixt that, and Reason, what a nice barrier,
For ever sep'rate, yet for ever near!
Remembrance and Reflection how allied;
What thin partitions Sense from Thought divide:
And Middle natures, how they long to join,
Yet never pass th' insuperable line!
Without this just gradation, could they be
Subjected, these to those, or all to thee?
The pow'rs of all subdued by thee alone,
Is not thy Reason all these pow'rs in one?

VIII.

See, through this air, this ocean, and this earth,
All matter quick, and bursting into birth.
Above, how high progressive life may go!
Around, how wide! how deep extend below!
Vast chain of Being! which from God began,
Natures ethereal, human, angel, man,
Beast, bird, fish, insect, what no eye can see,
No glass can reach; from Infinite to thee,
From thee to Nothing.—On superior pow'rs
Were we to press, inferior might on ours:
Or in the full creation leave a void,
Where, one step broken, the great scale's destroyed:
From Nature's chain whatever link you strike,
Tenth or ten-thousandth, breaks the chain alike.
And, if each system in gradation roll
Alike essential to th' amazing Whole,
The least confusion but in one, not all
That system only, but the Whole must fall.
Let Earth unbalanced from her orbit fly,
Planets and Suns run lawless through the sky;
Let ruling Angels from their spheres be hurled,
Being on Being wrecked, and world on world;
Heav'n's whole foundations to their center nod,
And Nature tremble to the throne of God.
All this dread Order break—for whom? for thee?
Vile worm!—O Madness! Pride! Impiety!

IX.

What if the foot, ordained the dust to tread,
Or hand, to toil, aspired to be the head?
What if the head, the eye, or ear repined
To serve mere engines to the ruling Mind?
Just as absurd for any part to claim
To be another, in this gen'ral frame:
Just as absurd, to mourn the tasks or pains,
The great directing Mind of all ordains,
All are but parts of one stupendous whole,
Whose body Nature is, and God the soul;
That, changed through all, and yet in all the same;
Great in the earth, as in th' ethereal frame;
Warms in the sun, refreshes in the breeze,
Glows in the stars, and blossoms in the trees,
Lives through all life, extends through all extent,
Spreads undivided, operates unspent;
Breathes in our soul, informs our mortal part,
As full, as perfect, in a hair as heart:
As full, as perfect, in vile Man that mourns,
As the rapt Seraph that adores and burns:
To him no high, no low, no great, no small;
He fills, he bounds, connects, and equals all.

X.

Cease then, nor Order Imperfection name:
Our proper bliss depends on what we blame.
Know thy own point: This kind, this due degree
Of blindness, weakness, Heav'n bestows on thee.
Submit.—In this, or any other sphere,
Secure to be as bless'd as thou canst bear:
Safe in the hand of one disposing Pow'r,
Or in the natal, or the mortal hour.
All Nature is but Art, unknown to thee;
All Chance, Direction, which thou canst not see;
All Discord, Harmony not understood;
All partial Evil, universal Good:
And, spite of Pride, in erring Reason's spite,
One truth is clear, *Whatever is, is right.*

ALEXANDER POPE

His Pilgrimage

Give me my scallop-shell of quiet,
My staff of faith to walk upon,
My scrip of joy, immortal diet,
My bottle of salvation,
My gown of glory, hope's true gage ;
And thus I'll take my pilgrimage.

Blood must be my body's balmer;
No other balm will there be given;
Whilst my soul, like a quiet palmer,
Traveleth toward the land of heaven,
Over the silver mountains,
Where spring the nectar fountains.
There will I kiss
The bowl of bliss,
And drink mine everlasting fill
Upon every milken hill.
My soul will be a-dry before;
But, after, it will thirst no more.

Then by that happy, blissful day
More peaceful pilgrims I shall see,
That have cast off their rags of clay,
And walk appareled fresh like me.
I'll take them first,
To quench their thirst
And taste of nectar suckets,
At those clear wells
Where sweetness dwells,
Drawn up by the saints in crystal buckets.
And when our bottles and all we
Are filled with immortality,
Then the blessed paths we'll travel,
Strowed with rubies thick as gravel,
Ceilings of diamonds, sapphire floors,
High walls of coral, and pearly bowers.

From thence to heaven's bribeless hall,
Where no corrupted voices brawl;
No conscience molten into gold;
No forged accuser bought or sold;
No cause deferred, no vain-spent journey,
For there Christ is the king's attorney,
Who pleads for all, without degrees,
And he hath angels but no fees.
And when the grand twelve million jury
Of our sins, with direful fury,
Against our souls black verdicts give,
Christ pleads his death; and then we live.

Be Thou my speaker, taintless pleader!
Unblotted lawyer! true proceeder!
Thou giv'st salvation, even for alms,
Not with a bribéd lawyer's palms.
And this is mine eternal plea
To Him that made heaven and earth and sea:
That since my flesh must die so soon,
And want a head to dine next noon,
Just at the stroke, when my veins start and spread,
Set on my soul an everlasting head!
Then am I ready, like a palmer fit,
To tread those blest paths, which before I writ.
Of death and judgment, heaven and hell,
Who oft doth think, must needs die well.

SIR WALTER RALEIGH

Love and Life

All my past life is mine no more,
The flying hours are gone:
Like transitory dreams given o'er,
Whose images are kept in store
By memory alone.

The time that is to come is not,
How can it then be mine?
The present moment's all my lot,
And that, as fast as it is got,
Phillis, is only thine.

Then talk not of inconstancy,
False hearts and broken vows;
If I, by miracle, can be
This live-long minute true to thee,
'Tis all that heaven allows.

JOHN WILMOT, EARL OF ROCHESTER

Upon Nothing

Nothing! thou elder brother ev'n to shade,
Thou hadst a being ere the world was made,
And (well fixt) art alone, of ending not afraid.

Ere time and place were, time and place were not,
When primitive *Nothing* something straight begot,
Then all proceeded from the great united—What.

Something the gen'ral attribute of all,
Severed from thee, its sole original,
Into thy boundless self must undistinguished fall.

Yet something did thy mighty pow'r command,
And from thy fruitful emptiness's hand,
Snatched men, beasts, birds, fire, air, and land.

Matter, the wickedst off-spring of thy race,
By Form assisted, flew from thy embrace,
And Rebel Light obscured thy reverend dusky face.

With Form, and Matter, Time and Place did join,
Body, thy foe, with thee did leagues combine,
To spoil thy peaceful realm, and ruin all thy line.

But turn-coat Time assists the foe in vain,
And, bribed by thee, assists thy short-lived reign,
And to thy hungry womb drives back thy slaves again.

Though mysteries are barred from laic eyes,
And the Divine alone, with warrant, pries
Into thy bosom, where the Truth in private lies.

Yet this of thee the wise may freely say,
Thou from the Virtuous nothing tak'st away,
And to be part with thee the Wicked wisely pray.

Great Negative, how vainly would the Wise
Inquire, define, distinguish, teach, devise,
Didst thou not stand to point their dull philosophies?

Is, or *is not*, the two great ends of Fate,
And, true or false, the subject of debate,
That perfect, or destroy, the vast designs of Fate.

When they have racked the Politician's breast,
Within thy bosom must securely rest,
And, when reduced to thee, are least unsafe and best.

But, *Nothing*, why does *Something* still permit,
That sacred Monarchs should at council sit,
With persons highly thought, at best, for nothing fit.

Whilst weighty *Something* modestly abstains,
From Princes' coffers, and from Statesmen's brains,
And nothing there like stately *Nothing* reigns.

Nothing, who dwell'st with fools in grave disguise,
For whom they reverend shapes and forms devise,
Lawn sleeves and furs and gowns, when they like thee look wise.

French truth, Dutch prowess, British policy,
Hibernian learning, Scotch civility,
Spaniards' dispatch, Danes' wit, are mainly seen in thee.

The great man's gratitude to his best friend,
King's promises, Whore's vows, towards thee they bend,
Flow swiftly into thee, and in thee ever end.

JOHN WILMOT, EARL OF ROCHESTER

Song

When I am dead, my dearest,
  Sing no sad songs for me;
Plant thou no roses at my head,
  Nor shady cypress tree.
Be the green grass above me
  With showers and dewdrops wet;
And if thou wilt, remember,
  And if thou wilt, forget.

I shall not see the shadows,
  I shall not feel the rain;
I shall not hear the nightingale
  Sing on as if in pain.
And dreaming through the twilight
  That doth not rise nor set,
Haply I may remember,
  And haply may forget.

CHRISTINA ROSSETTI

Summer

  Winter is cold-hearted,
  Spring is yea and nay,
Autumn is a weathercock
  Blown every way.
  Summer days for me
When every leaf is on its tree;

  When Robin's not a beggar,
  And Jenny Wren's a bride,
And larks hang singing, singing, singing,
  Over the wheat-fields wide,
  And anchored lilies ride,

And the pendulum spider
Swings from side to side;
And blue-black beetles transact business,
And gnats fly in a host,
And furry caterpillars hasten
That no time be lost,
And moths grow fat and thrive,
And ladybirds arrive.

Before green apples blush,
Before green nuts embrown,
Why one day in the country
Is worth a month in town;
Is worth a day and a year
Of the dusty, musty, lag-last fashion
That days drone elsewhere.

CHRISTINA ROSSETTI

Silent Noon

Your hands lie open in the long fresh grass,—
The finger-points look through like rosy blooms:
Your eyes smile peace. The pasture gleams and glooms
'Neath billowing skies that scatter and amass.
All round our nest, far as the eye can pass,
Are golden kingcup-fields with silver edge
Where the cow-parsley skirts the hawthorn-hedge.
'Tis visible silence, still as the hour-glass.

Deep in the sun-searched growths the dragon-fly
Hangs like a blue thread loosened from the sky:—
So this wing'd hour is dropt to us from above.
Oh! clasp we to our hearts, for deathless dower,
This close-companioned inarticulate hour
When twofold silence was the song of love.

DANTE GABRIEL ROSSETTI

The Woodspurge

The wind flapped loose, the wind was still,
Shaken out dead from tree and hill:
I had walked on at the wind's will,—
I sat now, for the wind was still.

Between my knees my forehead was,—
My lips, drawn in, said not Alas!
My hair was over in the grass,
My naked ears heard the day pass.

My eyes, wide open, had the run
Of some ten weeds to fix upon;
Among those few, out of the sun,
The woodspurge flowered, three cups in one.

From perfect grief there need not be
Wisdom or even memory:
One thing then learnt remains to me,—
The woodspurge has a cup of three.

Dante Gabriel Rossetti

A Dog Named Ego, the Snowflakes as Kisses

A dog named Ego, the snowflakes as kisses
Fluttered, ran, came with me in December,
Snuffing the chill air, changing, and halting,
There where I walked toward seven o'clock,
Sniffed at some interests hidden and open,
Whirled, descending, and stood still, attentive
Seeking their peace, the stranger, unknown,
With me, near me, kissed me, touched my wound,
My simple face, obsessed and pleasure bound.

"Not free, no liberty, rock that you carry,"
So spoke Ego in his cracked and harsh voice,
While snowflakes kissed me and satisfied minutes,
Falling from some place half believed and unknown,
"You will not be free, nor ever alone,"
So spoke Ego, "Mine is the kingdom,
Dynasty's bone: you will not be free,
Go, choose, run, you will not be alone."

"Come, come, come," sang the whirling snowflakes,
Evading the dog who barked at their smallness,
"Come!" sang the snowflakes, "Come here! and here!"
How soon at the sidewalk, melted, and done,
One kissed me, two kissed me! So many died!
While Ego barked at them, swallowed their touch,
Ran this way! And that way! While they slipped to the ground,
Leading him further and farther away,
While night collapsed amid the falling,
And left me no recourse, far from my home,
And left me no recourse, far from my home.

DELMORE SCHWARTZ

Get you gone

Get you gone, you will undo me,
If you love me don't pursue me;
Let that inclination persish
Which I dare no longer cherish.
With harmless thoughts I did begin,
But in the crowd love entered in;
I knew him not, he was so gay,
So innocent and full of play.
At every hour, in every place,
I either saw or form'd your face;
All that in plays was finely writ

Fancy for you and me did fit;
My dreams at night were all of you,
Such as till then I never knew.
I sported thus with young desire,
Never intending to go higher;
But now his teeth and claws are grown,
Let me the fatal lion shun.
You found me harmless; leave me so;
For, were I not, you'd leave me too.

SIR CHARLES SEDLEY

128

How Oft, When Thou

How oft, when thou, my music, music playest,
Upon that blessèd wood whose motion sounds
With thy sweet fingers, when thou gently swayest
The wiry concord that mine ear confounds,
Do I envy those jacks that nimble leap
To kiss the tender inward of thy hand,
Whilst my poor lips, which should that harvest reap,
At the wood's boldness by thee blushing stand!
To be so tickled, they would change their state
And situation with those dancing chips,
O'er whom thy fingers walk with gentle gait,
Making dead wood more blest than living lips.
  Since saucy jacks so happy are in this,
  Give them thy fingers, me thy lips to kiss.

WILLIAM SHAKESPEARE

It Was a Lover

It was a lover and his lass,
  With a hey, and a ho, and a hey nonino,
That o'er the green corn-field did pass
  In the spring time, the only pretty ring time,
  When birds do sing, hey ding a ding, ding!
  Sweet lovers love the spring.

Between the acres of the rye,
  With a hey, and a ho, and a hey nonino,
These pretty country folks would lie,
  In spring time, the only pretty ring time,
  When birds do sing, hey ding a ding, ding!
  Sweet lovers love the spring.

This carol they began that hour,
  With a hey, and a ho, and a hey nonino,
How that a life was but a flower
  In the spring time, the only pretty ring time,
  When birds do sing, hey ding a ding, ding!
  Sweet lovers love the spring.

And therefore take the present time,
  With a hey, and a ho, and a hey nonino,
For love is crownéd with the prime
  In the spring time, the only pretty ring time,
  When birds do sing, hey ding a ding, ding!
  Sweet lovers love the spring.

William Shakespeare

60

Like As The Waves

Like as the waves make towards the pebbled shore,
So do our minutes hasten to their end;
Each changing place with that which goes before,
In sequent toil all forwards do contend.
Nativity, once in the main of light,
Crawls to maturity, wherewith being crowned,
Crooked eclipses 'gainst his glory fight,
And Time that gave doth now his gift confound.
Time doth transfix the flourish set on youth
And delves the parallels in beauty's brow,
Feeds on the rarities of nature's truth,
And nothing stands but for his scythe to mow:
  And yet to times in hope my verse shall stand,
  Praising thy worth, despite his cruel hand.

William Shakespeare

O Mistress Mine

O mistress mine, where are you roaming?
O, stay and hear; your true love's coming,
  That can sing both high and low.
Trip no further, pretty sweeting,
Journeys end in lovers meeting,
  Every wise man's son doth know.

What is love? 'Tis not hereafter;
Present mirth hath present laughter;
  What's to come is still unsure;
In delay there lies no plenty;
Then come kiss me, sweet and twenty,
  Youth's a stuff will not endure.

William Shakespeare

Take, Oh, Take

Take, oh, take those lips away,
  That so sweetly were forsworn;
And those eyes, the break of day,
  Lights that do mislead the morn.
But my kisses bring again,
    Bring again;
Seals of love, but sealed in vain,
    Sealed in vain.

William Shakespeare

76

Why Is My Verse So Barren

Why is my verse so barren of new pride,
So far from variation or quick change?
Why with the time do I not glance aside
To new-found methods and to compounds strange?
Why write I still all one, ever the same,
And keep invention in a noted weed,
That every word doth almost tell my name,
Showing their birth, and where they did proceed?
O! know, sweet love, I always write of you,
And you and love are still my argument;
So all my best is dressing old words new,
Spending again what is already spent:
For as the sun is daily new and old,
So is my love still telling what is told.

William Shakespeare

You Spotted Snakes

You spotted snakes with double tongue,
Thorny hedge-hogs, be not seen;
Newts and blind-worms, do no wrong,
Come not near our fairy queen.
Chorus: Philomel, with melody,
Sing in our sweet lullaby:
Lulla, lulla, lullaby; lulla, lulla, lullaby.
Never harm, nor spell, nor charm,
Come our lovely lady nigh;
So good night, with lullaby.

Weaving spiders, come not here.
Hence, you long-legged spinners, hence!
Beetles black, approach not near;
Worm, nor snail, do no offense.
Chorus: Philomel, with melody,
Sing in our sweet lullaby:
Lulla, lulla, lullaby; lulla, lulla, lullaby.
Never harm, nor spell, nor charm,
Come our lovely lady nigh;
So good night, with lullaby.

William Shakespeare

Ode to the West Wind

1

O wild West Wind, thou breath of Autumn's being,
Thou, from whose unseen presence the leaves dead
Are driven, like ghosts from an enchanter fleeing,

Yellow, and black, and pale, and hectic red,
Pestilence-stricken multitudes: O thou,
Who chariotest to their dark wintry bed

The wingéd seeds, where they lie cold and low,
Each like a corpse within its grave, until
Thine azure sister of the Spring shall blow

Her clarion o'er the dreaming earth, and fill
(Driving sweet buds like flocks to feed in air)
With living hues and odors plain and hill:

Wild Spirit, which art moving everywhere;
Destroyer and preserver; hear, oh, hear!

2

Thou on whose stream, mid the steep sky's commotion,
Loose clouds like earth's decaying leaves are shed,
Shook from the tangled boughs of Heaven and Ocean,

Angels of rain and lightning: there are spread
On the blue surface of thine aëry surge,
Like the bright hair uplifted from the head

Of some fierce Maenad, even from the dim verge
Of the horizon to the zenith's height,
The locks of the approaching storm. Thou dirge

Of the dying year, to which this closing night
Will be the dome of a vast sepulcher,
Vaulted with all thy congregated might

Of vapors, from whose solid atmosphere
Black rain, and fire, and hail will burst: oh, hear!

3

Thou who didst waken from his summer dreams
The blue Mediterranean, where he lay,
Lulled by the coil of his crystalline streams,

Beside a pumice isle in Baiae's bay,
And saw in sleep old palaces and towers
Quivering within the wave's intenser day,

All overgrown with azure moss and flowers
So sweet, the sense faints picturing them! Thou
For whose path the Atlantic's level powers

Cleave themselves into chasms, while far below
The sea-blooms and the oozy woods which wear
The sapless foliage of the ocean, know

Thy voice, and suddenly grow gray with fear,
And tremble and despoil themselves: oh, hear!

4

If I were a dead leaf thou mightest bear,
If I were a swift cloud to fly with thee;
A wave to pant beneath thy power, and share

The impulse of thy strength, only less free
Than thou, O uncontrollable! If even
I were as in my boyhood, and could be

The comrade of thy wanderings over Heaven,
As then, when to outstrip thy skyey speed
Scarce seemed a vision; I would ne'er have striven

As thus with thee in prayer in my sore need.
Oh, lift me as a wave, a leaf, a cloud!
I fall upon the thorns of life! I bleed!

A heavy weight of hours has chained and bowed
One too like thee: tameless, and swift, and proud.

5

Make me thy lyre, even as the forest is:
What if my leaves are falling like its own!
The tumult of thy mighty harmonies

Will take from both a deep, autumnal tone,
Sweet though in sadness. Be thou, Spirit fierce,
My spirit! Be thou me, impetuous one!

Drive my dead thoughts over the universe
Like withered leaves to quicken a new birth!
And, by the incantation of this verse,

Scatter, as from an unextinguished hearth
Ashes and sparks, my words among mankind!
Be through my lips to unawakened earth

The trumpet of a prophecy! O Wind,
If Winter comes, can Spring be far behind?

PERCY BYSSHE SHELLEY

On a poet's lips I slept

On a poet's lips I slept
Dreaming like a love-adept
In the sound his breathing kept;
Nor seeks nor finds he mortal blisses,
But feeds on the aëreal kisses
Of shapes that haunt thought's wildernesses.
He will watch from dawn to gloom
The lake-reflected sun illume
The yellow bees in the ivy-bloom,
Nor heed nor see, what things they be;
But from these create he can
Forms more real than living man,
Nurslings of immortality!
One of these awakened me,
And I sped to succour thee.

PERCY BYSSHE SHELLEY

Time

Unfathomable Sea! whose waves are years,
  Ocean of Time, whose waters of deep woe
Are brackish with the salt of human tears!
  Thou shoreless flood, which in thy ebb and flow
Claspest the limits of mortality,
And sick of prey, yet howling on for more,
Vomitest thy wrecks on its inhospitable shore;
Treacherous in calm, and terrible in storm,
    Who shall put forth on thee,
    Unfathomable Sea?

PERCY BYSSHE SHELLEY

Here's to the maiden

Here's to the maiden of bashful fifteen;
Here's to the widow of fifty;
Here's to the flaunting extravagant quean,
And here's to the housewife that's thrifty.

Chorus

Let the toast pass,—
Drink to the lass,
I'll warrant she'll prove an excuse for the glass.

Here's to the charmer whose dimples we prize;
Now to the maid who has none, sir:
Here's to the girl with a pair of blue eyes,
And here's to the nymph with but *one,* sir.
Chorus. Let the toast pass, &c.

Here's to the maid with a bosom of snow;
Now to her that's as brown as a berry:
Here's to the wife with a face full of woe,
And now to the girl that is merry.
Chorus. Let the toast pass, &c.

For let 'em be clumsy, or let 'em be slim,
Young or ancient, I care not a feather;
So fill a pint bumper quite up to the brim,
And let us e'en toast them together.
Chorus. Let the toast pass, &c.

RICHARD BRINSLEY SHERIDAN

Song

If a daughter you have, she's the plague of your life,
No peace shall you know, tho' you've buried your wife,
At twenty she mocks at the duty you taught her,
O. what a plague is an obstinate daughter.
Sighing and whining,
Dying and pining,
O, what a plague is an obstinate daughter.

When scarce in their teens, they have wit to perplex us,
With letters and lovers for ever they vex us,
While each still rejects the fair suitor you've brought her,
O, what a plague is an obstinate daughter.
Wrangling and jangling,
Flouting and pouting,
O, what a plague is an obstinate daughter.

RICHARD BRINSLEY SHERIDAN

Song from Arcadia

Ring out your bells, let mourning shows be spread;
For Love is dead.
All Love is dead, infected
With plague of deep disdain;
Worth as naught worth rejected,
And Faith fair scorn doth gain.
From so ungrateful fancy,
From such a female franzy,
From them that use men thus,
Good Lord, deliver us!

Weep, neighbors, weep; do you not hear it said
That Love is dead?
His death-bed, peacock's folly;
His winding-sheet is shame;
His will, false-seeming holy;
His sole exec'tor, blame.
From so ungrateful fancy,
From such a female franzy,
From them that use men thus,
Good Lord, deliver us!

Let dirge be sung, and trentals rightly read,
For Love is dead;
Sir Wrong his tomb ordaineth
My mistress' marble heart,
Which epitaph containeth,
"Her eyes were once his dart."
From so ungrateful fancy,
From such a female franzy,
From them that use men thus,
Good Lord, deliver us!

Alas, I lie. Rage hath this error bred;
Love is not dead;
Love is not dead, but sleepeth
In her unmatchéd mind,
Where she his counsel keepeth,
Till due deserts she find.
Therefore from so vile fancy,
To call such wit a franzy,
Who Love can temper thus,
Good Lord, deliver us!

SIR PHILIP SIDNEY

From *Jubilato Agno*

For I will consider my cat Jeoffry.
For he is the servant of the living God, duly and daily serving him.
For at the first glance of the glory of God in the east he worships in his way.
For is this done by wreathing his body seven times round with elegant quickness.
For then he leaps up to catch the musk, which is the blessing of God upon his prayer.
For he rolls upon prank to work it in.
For having done duty and received blessing he begins to consider himself.
For this he performs in ten degrees.
For first he looks upon his fore-paws to see if they are clean.
For secondly he kicks up behind to clear away there.
For thirdly he works it upon stretch with the fore paws extended.
For fourthly he sharpens his paws by wood.
For fifthly he washes himself.
For sixthly he rolls upon wash.
For seventhly he fleas himself, that he may not be interrupted upon the beat.
For eighthly he rubs himself against a post.
For ninthly he looks up for his instructions.
For tenthly he goes in quest of food.
For having considered God and himself he will consider his neighbor.
For if he meets another cat he will kiss her in kindness.
For when he takes his prey he plays with it to give it chance.
For one mouse in seven escapes by his dallying.
For when his day's work is done his business more properly begins.
For he keeps the Lord's watch in the night against the adversary.
For he counteracts the powers of darkness by his electrical skin and glaring eyes.
For he counteracts the devil, who is death, by brisking about the life.
For in his morning orisons he loves the sun and the sun loves him.
For he is of the tribe of tiger.

For the Cherub Cat is a term of the Angel Tiger.
For he has the subtlety and hissing of a serpent, which in goodness he suppresses.
For he will not do destruction, if he is well-fed, neither will he spit without provocation.
For he purrs in thankfulness, when God tells him he's a good cat.
For he is an instrument for the children to learn benevolence upon.
For every house is incomplete without him and a blessing is lacking in the spirit.
For the Lord commanded Moses concerning the cats at the departure of the children of Israel from Egypt.
For every family had one cat at least in the bag.
For the English cats are the best in Europe.
For he is the cleanest in the use of his fore-paws of any quadrupede.
For the dexterity of his defence is an instance of the love of God to him exceedingly.
For he is the quickest to his mark of any creature.
For he is tenacious of his point.
For he is a mixture of gravity and waggery.
For he knows that God is his Saviour.
For there is nothing sweeter than his peace when at rest.
For there is nothing brisker than his life when in motion.
For he is of the Lord's poor and so indeed is he called by benevolence perpetually—Poor Jeoffry! poor Jeoffry! the rat has bit thy throat.
For I bless the name of the Lord Jesus that Jeoffry is better.
For the divine spirit comes about his body to sustain it in complete cat.
For his tongue is exceeding pure so that it has in purity what it wants in music.
For he is docile and can learn certain things.
For he can set up with gravity, which is patience upon approbation.
For he can fetch and carry, which is patience in employment.
For he can jump over a stick, which is patience upon proof positive.
For he can spraggle upon waggle at the word of command.
For he can jump from an eminence into his master's bosom.
For he can catch the cork and toss it again.
For he is hated by the hypocrite and miser.
For the former is afraid of detection.
For the latter refuses the charge.
For he camels his back to bear the first notion of business.
For he is good to think on, if a man would express himself neatly.
For he made a great figure in Egypt for his signal services.
For he killed the Icneumon-rat, very pernicious by land.
For his ears are so acute that they sting again.
For from this proceeds the passing quickness of his attention.
For by stroking of him I have found out electricity.
For I perceived God's light about him both wax and fire.
For the electrical fire is the spiritual substance, which God sends from heaven to sustain the bodies both of man and beast.
For God has blessed him in the variety of his movements.

For, though he cannot fly, he is an excellent clamberer.
For his motions upon the face of the earth are more than any other quadrupede.
For he can tread to all the measures upon the music.
For he can swim for life.
For he can creep.

CHRISTOPHER SMART

Coming To Kiss Her Lips

Coming to kiss her lips (such grace I found),
meseemed I smelt a garden of sweet flowers
that dainty odors from them threw around
for damsels fit to deck their lovers' bowers.
Her lips did smell like unto Gillyflowers;
her ruddy cheeks like unto Roses red;
her snowy brows like budded Bellamoures;
her lovely eyes like Pinks but newly spread;
Her goodly bosom like a Strawberry bed;
her neck like to a bunch of Columbines;
her breast like Lilies ere their leaves be shed;
her nipples like young blossomed Jessamines.
Such fragrant flowers do give most odorous smell,
but her sweet odor did them all excell.

EDMUND SPENSER

One Day I Wrote Her Name

One day I wrote her name upon the strand,
but came the waves and washed it away.
agayne I wrote it with a second hand,
but came the tyde, and made my paynes his pray.
Vayne man, sayd she, that doest in vaine assay,
a mortall thing so to immortalize,
for I my selve shall lyke to this decay,
and eek my name bee wyped out lykewize.
Not so, (quod I) let baser things devize
to dy in dust, but you shall live by fame:
my verse your vertues rare shall eternize,
and in the hevens wryte your glorious name.
Where whenas death shall all the world subdew,
our love shall live, and later life renew.

EDMUND SPENSER

Sonnet

Dost see how unregarded now
  That piece of beauty passes?
There was a time when I did vow
    To that alone;
  But mark the fate of faces:
The red and white works now no more in me
Than if it could not charm, or I not see.

And yet the face continues good,
  And I have still desires,
Am still the selfsame flesh and blood,
    As apt to meet
  And suffer from those fires;
O! Some kind power unriddle where it lies,
Whether my heart be faulty, or her eyes?

She every day her man does kill,
  And I as often die;
Neither her power, then, nor my will
    Can question'd be,
  What is the mystery?
Sure Beauty's empires, like to greater states,
Have certain periods set, and hidden fates.

SIR JOHN SUCKLING

Hertha

I am that which began;
  Out of me the years roll;
Out of me God and man;
  I am equal and whole;
God changes, and man, and the form of them
  bodily; I am the soul.

Before ever land was,
  Before ever the sea,
Or soft hair of the grass,
  Or fair limbs of the tree,
Or the flesh-colored fruit of my branches, I
  was, and thy soul was in me.

First life on my sources
    First drifted and swam;
Out of me are the forces
    That save it or damn;
Out of me man and woman, and wild-beast
    and bird; before God was, I am.

Beside or above me
    Naught is there to go;
Love or unlove me,
    Unknow me or know,
I am that which unloves me and loves; I am
    stricken, and I am the blow.

I the mark that is missed
    And the arrows that miss,
I the mouth that is kissed
    And the breath in the kiss,
The search, and the sought, and the seeker,
    the soul and the body that is.

I am that thing which blesses
    My spirit elate;
That which caresses
    With hands uncreate
My limbs unbegotten that measure the length
    of the measure of fate.

But what thing dost thou now,
    Looking Godward, to cry,
"I am I, thou art thou,
    I am low, thou art high"?
I am thou, whom seekest to find him;
    find thou but thyself, thou art I.

I the grain and the furrow,
    The plow-cloven clod
And the plowshare drawn thorough,
    The germ and the sod,
The deed and the doer, the seed and the
    sower, the dust which is God.

Hast thou known how I fashioned thee,
Child, underground?
Fire that impassioned thee,
Iron that bound,
Dim changes of water, what thing of all these
hast thou known of or found?

Canst thou say in thine heart
Thou hast seen with thine eyes
With what cunning of art
Thou wast wrought in what wise,
By what force of what stuff thou wast shapen,
and shown on my breast to the skies?

Who hath given, who hath sold it thee,
Knowledge of me?
Hath it wilderness told it thee?
Hast thou learnt of the sea?
Hast thou communed in spirit with night?
Have the winds taken counsel with thee?

Have I set such a star
To show light on thy brow
That thou sawest from afar
What I show to thee now?
Have ye spoken as brethren together, the sun
and the mountains and thou?

What is here, dost thou know it?
What was, hast thou known?
Prophet nor poet
Nor tripod nor throne
Nor spirit nor flesh can make answer, but only
thy mother alone.

Mother, not maker,
Born, and not made;
Though her children forsake her,
Allured or afraid,
Praying prayers to the God of their fashion,
she stirs not for all that have prayed.

A creed is a rod,
And a crown is of night;
But this thing is God,
To be man with thy might,
To grow straight in the strength of thy spirit,
and live out thy life as the light.

I am in thee to save thee,
As my soul in thee saith;
Give thou as I gave thee,
Thy life-blood and breath,
Green leaves of thy labor, white flowers of thy
thought, and red fruit of thy death.

Be the ways of thy giving
As mine were to thee;
The free life of thy living,
Be the gift of it free;
Not as servant to lord, nor as master to slave,
shalt thou give thee to me.

O children of banishment,
Souls overcast,
Were the lights ye see vanish meant
Alway to last,
Ye would know not the sun overshining the
shadows and stars overpast.

I that saw where ye trod
The dim paths of the night
Set the shadow called God
In your skies to give light;
But the morning of manhood is risen, and the
shadowless soul is in sight.

The tree many-rooted
That swells to the sky
With frondage red-fruited,
The life-tree am I;
In the buds of your lives is the sap of my
leaves; ye shall live and not die.

But the gods of your fashion
That take and that give,
In their pity and passion
That scourge and forgive,
They are worms that are bred in the bark that
falls off; they shall die and not live.

My own blood is what stanches
The wounds in my bark;
Stars caught in my branches
Make day of the dark,
And are worshiped as suns till the sunrise
shall tread out their fires as a spark.

Where dead ages hide under
The live roots of the tree,
In my darkness the thunder
Makes utterance of me;
In the clash of my boughs with each other ye
hear the waves sound of the sea.

That noise is of Time,
As his feathers are spread
And his feet set to climb
Through the boughs overhead,
And my foliage rings round him and rustles,
and branches are bent with his tread.

The storm-winds of ages
Blow through me and cease,
The war-wind that rages,
The spring-wind of peace,
Ere the breath of them roughen my tresses,
ere one of my blossoms increase.

All sounds of all changes,
All shadows and lights
On the world's mountain-ranges
And stream-riven heights,
Whose tongue is the wind's tongue and language
of storm-clouds on earth-shaking nights;

All forms of all faces,
All works of all hands
In unsearchable places
Of time-stricken lands,
All death and all life, and all reigns and all
ruins, drop through me as sands.

Though sore be my burden
And more than ye know,
And my growth have no guerdon
But only to grow,
Yet I fail not of growing for lightnings above
me or deathworms below.

These too have their part in me,
As I too in these;
Such fire is at heart in me,
Such sap is this tree's,
Which hath in it all sounds and all secrets of
infinite lands and of seas.

In the spring-colored hours
When my mind was as May's,
There brake forth of me flowers
By centuries of days,
Strong blossoms with perfume of manhood
shot out from my spirit as rays.

And the sound of them springing
And smell of their shoots
Were as warmth and sweet singing
And strength to my roots;
And the lives of my children made perfect
with freedom of soul were my fruits.

I bid you but be;
I have need not of prayer;
I have need of you free
As your mouths of mine air;
That my heart may be greater within me,
beholding the fruits of me fair.

More fair than strange fruit is
Of faiths ye espouse;
In me only the root is
That blooms in your boughs;
Behold now your God that ye made you to
feed him with faith of your vows.

In the darkening and whitening
Abysses adored,
With dayspring and lightning
For lamp and for sword,
God thunders in heaven, and his angels are
red with the wrath of the Lord.

O my sons, O too dutiful
Toward gods not of me,
Was not I enough beautiful?
Was it hard to be free?
For behold, I am with you, and in you and of
you; look forth now and see.

Lo, winged with world's wonders,
With miracles shod,
With the fires of his thunders
For raiment and rod,
God trembles in heaven, and his angels are
white with the terror of God.

For his twilight is come on him,
His anguish is here;
And his spirits gaze dumb on him,
Grown gray from his fear;
And his hour taketh hold on him stricken, the
last of his infinite year.

Thought made him and breaks him,
Truth slays and forgives;
But to you, as time takes him,
This new thing it gives,
Even love, the beloved Republic, that feeds
upon freedom and lives.

For truth only is living,
Truth only is whole,
And the love of his giving
Man's polestar and pole;
Man, pulse of my center, and fruit of my body, and seed of my soul;

One birth of my bosom;
One beam of mine eye;
One topmost blossom
That scales the sky;
Man, equal and one with me, man that is made of me, man that is I.

ALGERNON CHARLES SWINBURNE

From *In Memoriam*

II

Old Yew, which graspest at the stones
That name the under-lying dead,
Thy fibres net the dreamless head,
Thy roots are wrapt about the bones.

The seasons bring the flower again,
And bring the firstling to the flock;
And in the dusk of thee, the clock
Beats out the little lives of men.

O not for thee the glow, the bloom,
Who changest not in any gale,
Nor branding summer suns avail
To touch thy thousand years of gloom:

And gazing on thee, sullen tree,
Sick for thy stubborn hardihood,
I seem to fail from out my blood
And grow incorporate into thee.

XI

Calm is the morn without a sound,
Calm as to suit a calmer grief,
And only thro' the faded leaf
The chestnut pattering to the ground:

Calm and deep peace on this high wold,
And on these dews that drench the furze,
And all the silvery gossamers
That twinkle into green and gold:

Calm and still light on yon great plain
That sweeps with all its autumn bowers,
And crowded farms and lessening towers,
To mingle with the bounding main:

Calm and deep peace in this wide air,
These leaves that redden to the fall;
And in my heart, if calm at all,
If any calm, a calm despair:

Calm on the seas, and silver sleep,
And waves that sway themselves in rest,
And dead calm in that noble breast
Which heaves but with the heaving deep.

ALFRED, LORD TENNYSON

Now Sleeps the Crimson Petal

Now sleeps the crimson petal, now the white;
Nor waves the cypress in the palace walk;
Nor winks the gold fin in the porphyry font.
The firefly wakens; waken thou with me.

Now droops the milk-white peacock like a ghost,
And like a ghost she glimmers on to me.

Now lies the Earth all Danaë to the stars,
And all thy heart lies open unto me.

Now slides the silent meteor on, and leaves
A shining furrow, as thy thoughts in me.

Now folds the lily all her sweetness up,
And slips into the bosom of the lake.
So fold thyself, my dearest, thou, and slip
Into my bosom and be lost in me.

ALFRED, LORD TENNYSON

The Poet's Song

The rain had fallen, the Poet arose,
  He passed by the town and out of the street,
A light wind blew from the gates of the sun,
  And waves of shadow went over the wheat,
And he sat him down in a lonely place,
  And chanted a melody loud and sweet,
That made the wild-swan pause in her cloud,
  And the lark drop down at his feet.

The swallow stopt as he hunted the fly,
  The snake slipt under a spray,
The wild hawk stood with the down on his beak,
  And stared, with his foot on the prey,
And the nightingale thought, "I have sung many songs,
  But never a one so gay,
For he sings of what the world will be
  When the years have died away."

ALFRED, LORD TENNYSON

The Splendor Falls on Castle Walls

The splendor falls on castle walls
And snowy summits old in story;
The long light shakes across the lakes,
And the wild cataract leaps in glory.
Blow, bugle, blow, set the wild echoes flying,
Blow, bugle; answer, echoes, dying, dying dying.

O hark, O hear! how thin and clear,
And thinner, clearer, farther going!
O sweet and far from cliff and scar
The horns of Elfland faintly blowing!
Blow, let us hear the purple glens replying,
Blow, bugle, answer, echoes, dying, dying, dying.

O love, they die in yon rich sky,
They faint on hill or field or river;
Our echoes roll from soul to soul,
And grow forever and forever.
Blow, bugle, blow, set the wild echoes flying,
And answer, echoes, answer, dying, dying, dying.

ALFRED, LORD TENNYSON

Ulysses

It little profits that an idle king,
By this still hearth, among these barren crags,
Matched with an aged wife, I mete and dole
Unequal laws unto a savage race,
That hoard, and sleep, and feed, and know not me.
I cannot rest from travel; I will drink
Life to the lees. All times I have enjoyed
Greatly, have suffered greatly, both with those
That loved me, and alone; on shore, and when
Through scudding drifts the rainy Hyades
Vexed the dim sea. I am become a name;
For always roaming with a hungry heart

Much have I seen and known—cities of men
And manners, climates, councils, governments,
Myself not least, but honored of them all—
And drunk delight of battle with my peers,
Far on the ringing plains of windy Troy.
I am a part of all that I have met;
Yet all experience is an arch wherethrough
Gleams that untraveled world whose margin fades
Forever and forever when I move.
How dull it is to pause, to make an end,
To rust unburnished, not to shine in use!
As though to breathe were life! Life piled on life
Were all too little, and of one to me
Little remains; but every hour is saved
From that eternal silence, something more,
A bringer of new things; and vile it were
For some three suns to store and hoard myself,
And this gray spirit yearning in desire
To follow knowledge like a sinking star,
Beyond the utmost bound of human thought.
  This is my son, mine own Telemachus,
To whom I leave the scepter and the isle—
Well-loved of me, discerning to fulfill
This labor, by slow prudence to make mild
A rugged people, and through soft degrees
Subdue them to the useful and the good.
Most blameless is he, centered in the sphere
Of common duties, decent not to fail
In offices of tenderness, and pay
Meet adoration to my household gods,
When I am gone. He works his work, I mine.
  There lies the port; the vessel puffs her sail;
There gloom the dark, broad seas. My mariners,
Souls that have toiled, and wrought, and thought with me—
That ever with a frolic welcome took
The thunder and the sunshine, and opposed
Free hearts, free foreheads—you and I are old;
Old age hath yet his honor and his toil.
Death closes all; but something ere the end,
Some work of noble note, may yet be done,
Not unbecoming men that strove with gods.
The lights begin to twinkle from the rocks;
The long day wanes; the slow moon climbs; the deep
Moans round with many voices. Come, my friends.

'Tis not too late to seek a newer world.
Push off, and sitting well in order smite
The sounding furrows; for my purpose holds
To sail beyond the sunset, and the baths
Of all the western stars, until I die.
It may be that the gulfs will wash us down;
It may be we shall touch the Happy Isles,
And see the great Achilles, whom we knew.
Though much is taken, much abides; and though
We are not now the strength which in old days
Moved earth and heaven, that which we are, we are—
One equal temper of heroic hearts,
Made weak by time and fate, but strong in will
To strive, to seek, to find, and not to yield.

ALFRED, LORD TENNYSON

Fern Hill

Now as I was young and easy under the apple boughs
About the lilting house and happy as the grass was green,
The night above the dingle starry,
Time let me hail and climb
Golden in the heydays of his eyes,
And honoured among wagons I was prince of the apple towns
And once below a time I lordly had the trees and leaves
Trail with daisies and barley
Down the rivers of the windfall light.

And as I was green and carefree, famous among the barns
About the happy yard and singing as the farm was home,
In the sun that is young once only,
Time let me play and be
Golden in the mercy of his means,
And green and golden I was huntsman and herdsman, the calves
Sang to my horn, the foxes on the hills barked clear and cold,
And the sabbath rang slowly
In the pebbles of the holy streams.

All the sun long it was running, it was lovely, the hayfields
High as the house, the tunes from the chimneys, it was air
And playing, lovely and watery
And fire green as grass.
And nightly under the simple stars
As I rode to sleep the owls were bearing the farm away,
All the moon long I heard, blessed among stables, the nightjars
Flying with the ricks, and the horses
Flashing into the dark.

And then to awake, and the farm, like a wanderer white
With the dew, come back, the cock on his shoulder: it was all
Shining, it was Adam and maiden,
The sky gathered again
And the sun grew round that very day.
So it must have been after the birth of the simple light
In the first, spinning place, the spellbound horses walking warm
Out of the whinnying green stable
On to the fields of praise.

And honoured among foxes and pheasants by the gay house
Under the new made clouds and happy as the heart was long,
In the sun born over and over,
I ran my heedless ways,
My wishes raced through the house-high hay
And nothing I cared, at my sky blue trades, that time allows
In all his tuneful turning so few and such morning songs
Before the children green and golden
Follow him out of grace,

Nothing I cared, in the lamb white days, that time would take me
Up to the swallow thronged loft by the shadow of my hand,
In the moon that is always rising,
Nor that riding to sleep
I should hear him fly with the high fields
And wake to the farm forever fled from the childless land.
Oh as I was young and easy in the mercy of his means,
Time held me green and dying
Though I sang in my chains like the sea.

DYLAN THOMAS

The Hound of Heaven

I fled Him, down the nights and down the days;
I fled Him, down the arches of the years;
I fled Him, down the labyrinthine ways
Of my own mind; and in the mist of tears
I hid from Him, and under running laughter,
Up vistaed hopes I sped;
And shot, precipitated,
Adown Titanic glooms of chasméd fears,
From those strong Feet that followed, followed after.
But with unhurrying chase,
And unperturbéd pace,
Deliberate speed, majestic instancy,
They beat—and a Voice beat
More instant than the Feet—
"All things betray thee, who betrayest Me."

I pleaded, outlaw-wise,
By many a hearted casement, curtained red,
Trellised with intertwining charities
(For, though I knew His love Who followed,
Yet was I sore adread
Lest, having Him, I must have naught beside);
But, if one little casement parted wide,
The gust of His approach would clash it to.
Fear wist not to evade, as Love wist to pursue.
Across the margent of the world I fled,
And troubled the gold gateways of the stars,
Smiting for shelter on their clangéd bars;
Fretted to dulcet jars
And silvern chatter the pale ports o' the moon.
I said to dawn, Be sudden; to eve, Be soon;
With thy young skyey blossoms heap me over
From this tremendous Lover!
Float thy vague veil about me, lest He see!
I tempted all His servitors, but to find
My own betrayal in their constancy,
In faith to Him their fickleness to me,
Their traitorous trueness, and their loyal deceit.
To all swift things for swiftness did I sue;
Clung to the whistling mane of every wind.
But whether they swept, smoothly fleet,
The long savannahs of the blue;
Or whether, Thunder-driven,

They clanged his chariot 'thwart a heaven
Plashy with flying lightnings round the spurn o' their feet—
Fear wist not to evade as Love wist to pursue.
Still with unhurrying chase,
And unperturbéd pace,
Deliberate speed, majestic instancy,
Came on the following Feet,
And a Voice above their beat—
"Naught shelters thee, who wilt not shelter Me."

I sought no more that after which I strayed
In face of man or maid;
But still within the little children's eyes
Seems something, something that replies;
They at least are for me, surely for me!
I turned me to them very wistfully;
But, just as their young eyes grew sudden fair
With dawning answers there,
Their angel plucked them from me by the hair.
"Come then, ye other children, Nature's—share
With me" (said I) "your delicate fellowship;
Let me greet you lip to lip,
Let me twine with you caresses,
Wantoning
With our Lady-Mother's vagrant tresses,
Banqueting
With her in her wind-walled palace,
Underneath her azured daïs,
Quaffing, as your taintless way is,
From a chalice
Lucent-weeping out of the dayspring."
So it was done;
I in their delicate fellowship was one—
Drew the bolt of Nature's secrecies.
I knew all the swift importings
On the willful face of skies;
I knew how the clouds arise
Spuméd of the wild sea-snortings;
All that's born or dies
Rose and drooped with—made them shapers
Of mine own moods, or wailful or divine—
With them joyed and was bereaven.
I was heavy with the even,
When she lit her glimmering tapers
Round the day's dead sanctities.
I laughed in the morning's eyes.

I triumphed and I saddened with all weather,
 Heaven and I wept together,
And its sweet tears were salt with mortal mine;
Against the red throb of its sunset-heart
  I laid my own to beat,
  And share commingling heat;
But not by that, by that, was eased my human smart.
In vain my tears were wet on Heaven's gray cheek.
For ah! we know not what each other says,
 These things and I; in sound *I* speak—
Their sound is but their stir, they speak by silences.
Nature, poor stepdame, cannot slake my drouth;
 Let her, if she would owe me,
Drop yon blue bosom-veil of sky, and show me
 The breasts o' her tenderness;
Never did any milk of hers once bless
  My thirsting mouth.
  Nigh and nigh draws the chase,
  With unperturbéd pace,
 Deliberate speed, majestic instancy;
  And past those noiséd Feet
  A voice comes yet more fleet—
"Lo! naught contents thee, who content'st not Me."

Naked I wait Thy love's uplifted stroke!
My harness piece by piece Thou hast hewn from me,
  And smitten me to my knee;
 I am defenseless utterly.
 I slept, methinks, and woke,
And, slowly gazing, find me stripped in sleep.
In the rash lustihead of my young powers,
 I shook the pillaring hours
And pulled my life upon me; grimed with smears,
I stand amid the dust o' the mounded years—
My mangled youth lies dead beneath the heap.
My days have crackled and gone up in smoke,
Have puffed and burst as sun-starts on a stream.
 Yea, faileth now even dream
The dreamer, and the lute the lutanist;
Even the linked fantasies, in whose blossomy twist
I swung the earth a trinket at my wrist,
Are yielding; cords of all too weak account
For earth with heavy griefs so overplussed.
 Ah! is Thy love indeed
A weed, albeit an amaranthine weed,

Suffering no flowers except its own to mount?
Ah! must—
Designer infinite!—
Ah! must Thou char the wood ere Thou canst limn with it?
My freshness spent its wavering shower i' the dust;
And now my heart is as a broken fount,
Wherein tear-drippings stagnate, spilt down ever
From the dank thoughts that shiver
Upon the sighful branches of my mind.
Such is; what is to be?
The pulp so bitter, how shall taste the rind?
I dimly guess what Time in mists confounds;
Yet ever and anon a trumpet sounds
From the hid battlements of Eternity;
Those shaken mists a space unsettle, then
Round the half-glimpséd turrets slowly wash again.
But not ere him who summoneth
I first have seen, enwound
With glooming robes purpureal, cypress-crowned;
His name I know, and what his trumpet saith.
Whether man's heart or life it be which yields
Thee harvest, must Thy harvest fields
Be dunged with rotten death?
Now of that long pursuit
Comes on at hand the bruit;
That Voice is round me like a bursting sea:
"And is thy earth so marred,
Shattered in shard on shard?
Lo, all things fly thee, for thou flies Me!
Strange, piteous, futile thing,
Wherefore should any set thee love apart?
Seeing none but I makes much of naught" (He said),
"And human love needs human meriting,
How hast thou merited—
Of all man's clotted clay the dingiest clot?
Alack, thou knowest not
How little worthy of any love thou art!
Whom wilt thou find to love ignoble thee
Save Me, save only Me?
All which I took from thee I did but take,
Not for thy harms,
But just that thou might'st seek it in My arms.
All which thy child's mistake
Fancies as lost, I have stored for thee at home;
Rise, clasp My hand, and come!"
Halts by me that footfall;

Is my gloom, after all,
Shade of His hand, outstretched caressingly?
"Ah, fondest, blindest, weakest,
I am He Whom thou seekest!
Thou dravest love from thee, who dravest Me."

FRANCIS THOMPSON

Rule, Britannia!

When Britain first, at Heaven's command,
Arose from out the azure main,
This was the charter of the land,
And guardian angels sung this strain—
"Rule, Britannia, rule the waves;
Britons never will be slaves."

The nations, not so blessed as thee,
Must in their turns to tyrants fall;
While thou shalt flourish great and free,
The dread and envy of them all.
"Rule, Britannia, rule the waves;
Britons never will be slaves."

Still more majestic shalt thou rise,
More dreadful from each foreign stroke;
As the loud blast that tears the skies
Serves but to root thy native oak.
"Rule," *etc.*

Thee haughty tyrants ne'er shall tame;
All their attempts to bend thee down
Will but arouse thy generous flame,
But work their woe and thy renown.
"Rule," *etc.*

To thee belongs the rural reign;
Thy cities shall with commerce shine;
All thine shall be the subject main,
And every shore it circles thine.
"Rule," *etc.*

The Muses, still with freedom found,
  Shall to thy happy coast repair;
Blessed isle! with matchless beauty crowned,
  And manly hearts to guard the fair.
    "Rule, Britannia, rule the waves;
    Britons never will be slaves."

JAMES THOMSON

Wonder

How like an angel came I down!
  How bright are all things here!
When first among His works I did appear,
  O how their glory me did crown!
The world resembled His eternity,
  In which my soul did walk;
 And everything that I did see
    Did with me talk.

 The skies in their magnificence,
  The lively, lovely air,
Oh, how divine, how soft, how sweet, how fair!
 The stars did entertain my sense;
And all the works of God so bright and pure,
  So rich and great did seem
 As if they ever must endure
    In my esteem.

 A native health and innocence
  Within my bones did grow;
And while my God did all his glories show,
 I felt a vigor in my sense
That was all spirit: I within did flow
  With seas of life like wine;
 I nothing in the world did know
    But 'twas divine.

Harsh, ragged objects were concealed:
Oppressions, tears, and cries,
Sins, griefs, complaints, dissensions, weeping eyes
Were hid, and only things revealed
Which heavenly spirits and the angels prize.
The state of innocence
And bliss, not trades and poverties,
Did fill my sense.

The streets were paved with golden stones;
The boys and girls were mine:
Oh, how did all their lovely faces shine!
The sons of men were holy ones;
In joy and beauty they appeared to me;
And everything which here I found,
While like an angel I did see,
Adorned the ground.

Rich diamond and pearl and gold
In every place was seen;
Rare splendors, yellow, blue, red, white, and green,
Mine eyes did everywhere behold.
Great wonders clothed with glory did appear;
Amazement was my bliss;
That and my wealth was everywhere;
No joy to this!

Cursed and devised proprieties,
With envy, avarice,
And fraud, those fiends that spoil even Paradise,
Flew from the splendor of mine eyes;
And so did hedges, ditches, limits, bounds:
I dreamed not aught of those,
But wandered over all men's grounds,
And found repose.

Proprieties themselves were mine,
And hedges ornaments;
Walls, boxes, coffers, and their rich contents
Did not divide my joys, but all combine.
Clothes, ribbons, jewels, laces I esteemed
My joys by others worn;
For me they all to wear them seemed
When I was born.

THOMAS TRAHERNE

Quickness

False life! a foil and no more, when
Wilt thou be gone?
Thou foul deception of all men,
That would not have the true come on!

Thou art a moon-like toil; a blind
Self-posing state;
A dark contest of waves and wind;
A mere tempestuous debate.

Life is a fix'd, discerning light,
A knowing joy;
No chance, or fit; but ever bright,
And calm, and full, yet doth not cloy,

'Tis such a blissful thing, that still
Doth vivify,
And shine and smile, and hath the skill
To please without eternity.

Thou art a toilsome mole, or less,
A moving mist.
But life is, what none can express,
A quickness, which my God hath kiss'd.

Henry Vaughan

The World

I saw Eternity the other night,
Like a great ring of pure and endless light,
All calm as it was bright;
And round beneath it, Time, in hours, days, years,
Driv'n by the spheres,
Like a vast shadow moved; in which the world
And all her train were hurled.
The doting lover in his quaintest strain
Did there complain;

Near him, his lute, his fancy, and his flights,
    Wit's four delights,
With gloves, and knots, the silly snares of pleasure,   *knots*—love knots
    Yet his dear treasure,
All scattered lay, while he his eyes did pour
    Upon a flower.
The darksome statesman, hung with weights and woe,
Like a thick midnight-fog, moved there so slow,
    He did not stay, nor go;

Condemning thoughts, like sad eclipses, scowl
    Upon his soul,
And clouds of crying witnesses without
    Pursued him with one shout.
Yet digged the mole, and lest his ways be found,
    Worked under ground,
Where he did clutch his prey; but one did see
    That policy.
Churches and altars fed him; perjuries
    Were gnats and flies;
It rained about him blood and tears, but he
    Drank them as free.

The fearful miser on a heap of rust
Sat pining all his life there, did scarce trust
    His own hands with the dust,
Yet would not place one piece above, but lives   *above*—i.e., in heaven
    In fear of thieves.
Thousands there were as frantic as himself,
    And hugged each one his pelf;
The downright epicure placed heaven in sense,
    And scorned pretense;
While others, slipt into a wide excess,
    Said little less;
The weaker sort, slight, trivial wares enslave,
    Who think them brave;
And poor, despiséd Truth sat counting by
    Their victory.
Yet some, who all this while did weep and sing,

And sing and weep, soared up into the ring;
    But most would use no wing.
O fools, said I, thus to prefer dark night
    Before true light!
To live in grots and caves, and hate the day
    Because it shows the way,
The way, which from this dead and dark abode
    Leads up to God;
A way where you might tread the sun, and be
    More bright than he!
But, as I did their madness so discuss,
    One whispered thus,
"This ring the Bridegroom did for none provide
    But for his bride."

HENRY VAUGHAN

Of the Last Verses in the Book

When we for age could neither read nor write,
The subject made us able to indite;
The soul, with nobler resolutions decked,
The body stooping, does herself erect.
No mortal parts are requisite to raise
Her that, unbodied, can her Maker praise.
  The seas are quiet when the winds give o'er;
So, calm are we when passions are nor more!
For then we know how vain it was to boast
Of fleeting things, so certain to be lost.
Clouds of affection from our younger eyes
Conceal that emptiness which age descries.
  The soul's dark cottage, battered and decayed,
Lets in new light through chinks that time has made;
Stronger by weakness, wiser men become,
As they draw near to their eternal home.
Leaving the old, both worlds at once they view,
That stand upon the threshold of the new.

EDMUND WALLER

Reconciliation

Word over all, beautiful as the sky,
Beautiful that war and all its deeds of carnage must in time be utterly lost,
That the hands of the sisters Death and Night incessantly softly wash again, and ever again, this soil'd world;
For my enemy is dead, a man divine as myself is dead,
I look where he lies white-faced and still in the coffin—I draw near,
Bend down and touch lightly with my lips the white face in the coffin.

WALT WHITMAN

Self-Contained

I think I could turn and live with animals,
They are so placid and self-contained.
I stand and look at them, and long, and long.
They do not sweat and whine about their condition,
They do not lie awake in the dark and weep for their sins,
They do not make me sick discussing their duty to God;
Not one is dissatisfied, not one is demented with the mania of owning things;
Not one kneels to another, nor to his kind that lived thousands of years ago.
Not one is respectable and unhappy over the whole earth.

WALT WHITMAN

The Last Invocation

At the last, tenderly,
From the walls of the powerful, fortressed house,
From the clasp of the knitted locks—from the keep of the well-closed doors,
Let me be wafted.

Let me glide noiselessly forth;
With the key of softness unlock the locks—with a whisper
Set ope the doors, O Soul!

Tenderly! be not impatient!
(Strong is your hold, O mortal flesh!
Strong is your hold, O love.)

WALT WHITMAN

Elegiac Stanzas

SUGGESTED BY A PICTURE OF PEELE CASTLE, IN A STORM, PAINTED BY SIR GEORGE BEAUMONT

I was thy neighbor once, thou rugged Pile!
Four summer weeks I dwelt in sight of thee:
I saw thee every day; and all the while
Thy Form was sleeping on a glassy sea.

So pure the sky, so quiet was the air!
So like, so very like, was day to day!
Whene'er I looked, thy Image still was there;
It trembled, but it never passed away.

How perfect was the calm! it seemed no sleep;
No mood, which season takes away, or brings:
I could have fancied that the mighty Deep
Was even the gentlest of all gentle Things.

Ah! then, if mine had been the painter's hand,
To express what then I saw; and add the gleam,
The light that never was, on sea or land,
The consecration, and the poet's dream;

I would have planted thee, thou hoary Pile
Amid a world how different from this!
Beside a sea that could not cease to smile;
On tranquil land, beneath a sky of bliss.

Thou shouldst have seemed a treasure-house divine
Of peaceful years; a chronicle of heaven;—
Of all the sunbeams that did ever shine
The very sweetest had to thee been given.

A picture had it been of lasting ease,
Elysian quiet, without toil or strife;
No motion but the moving tide, a breeze,
Or merely silent Nature's breathing life.

Such, in the fond illusion of my heart,
Such picture would I at that time have made:
And seen the soul of truth in every part,
A steadfast peace that might not be betrayed.

So once it would have been—'tis so no more;
I have submitted to a new control:
A power is gone, which nothing can restore;
A deep distress hath humanized my Soul.

Not for a moment could I now behold
A smiling sea, and be what I have been:
The feeling of my loss will ne'er be old;
This, which I know, I speak with mind serene.

Then, Beaumont, friend! who would have been the friend,
If he had lived, of him whom I deplore,
This work of thine I blame not, but commend;
This sea in anger, and that dismal shore.

O 'tis a passionate Work!—yet wise and well,
Well chosen is the spirit that is here;
That Hulk which labors in the deadly swell,
This rueful sky, this pageantry of fear!

And this huge Castle, standing here sublime,
I love to see the look with which it braves,
Cased in the unfeeling armor of old time,
The lightning, the fierce wind, and trampling waves.

Farewell, farewell the heart that lives alone,
Housed in a dream, at distance from the Kind!
Such happiness, wherever it be known,
Is to be pitied; for 'tis surely blind.

But welcome fortitude, and patient cheer,
And frequent sights of what is to be borne!
Such sights, or worse, as are before me here. —
Not without hope we suffer and we mourn.

WILLIAM WORDSWORTH

I Wandered Lonely as a Cloud

I wandered lonely as a cloud
That floats on high o'er vales and hills,
When all at once I saw a crowd,
A host of golden daffodils;
Beside the lake, beneath the trees,
Fluttering and dancing in the breeze.

Continuous as the stars that shine
And twinkle on the milky way,
They stretched in never-ending line
Along the margin of a bay:
Ten thousand saw I at a glance,
Tossing their heads in sprightly dance.

The waves beside them danced; but they
Out-did the sparkling waves in glee:
A poet could not but be gay,
In such a jocund company:
I gazed—and gazed—but little thought
What wealth the show to me had brought:

For oft, when on my couch I lie
In vacant or in pensive mood,
They flash upon that inward eye
Which is the flash of solitude;
And then my heart with pleasure fills,
And dances with the daffodils.

William Wordsworth

She Was a Phantom of Delight

She was a phantom of delight
When first she gleamed upon my sight;
A lovely apparition, sent
To be a moment's ornament;
Her eyes as stars of twilight fair;
Like twilight's too, her dusky hair;
But all things else about her drawn
From May-time and the cheerful dawn;
A dancing shape, an Image gay,
To haunt, to startle, and waylay.

I saw her upon nearer view,
A spirit, yet a woman too!
Her household motions light and free,
And steps of virgin liberty;
A countenance in which did meet
Sweet records, promises as sweet;
A creature not too bright or good
For human nature's daily food:
For transient sorrows, simple wiles,
Praise, blame, love, kisses, tears, and smiles.

And now I see with eye serene
The very pulse of the machine;
A being breathing thoughtful breath,
A Traveler between life and death;
The reason firm, the temperate will,
Endurance, foresight, strength, and skill,
A perfect woman, nobly planned,
To warn, to comfort, and command;
And yet a spirit still, and bright
With something of angelic light.

WILLIAM WORDSWORTH

The Solitary Reaper

Behold her, single in the field,
Yon solitary Highland lass!
Reaping and singing by herself;
Stop here, or gently pass!
Alone she cuts and binds the grain,
And sings a melancholy strain;
O listen! for the vale profound
Is overflowing with the sound.

No nightingale did ever chaunt
More welcome notes to weary bands
Of travelers in some shady haunt,
Among Arabian sands:
A voice so thrilling ne'er was heard
In springtime from the cuckoo-bird,
Breaking the silence of the seas
Among the farthest Hebrides.

Will no one tell me what she sings?—
Perhaps the plaintive numbers flow
For old, unhappy, far-off things,
And battles long ago:
Or is it some more humble lay,
Familiar matter of today?
Some natural sorrow, loss, or pain,
That has been, and may be again?

Whate'er the theme, the maiden sang
As if her song could have no ending;
I saw her singing at her work,
And o'er the sickle bending;—
I listened, motionless and still;
And, as I mounted up the hill,
The music in my heart I bore,
Long after it was heard no more.

WILLIAM WORDSWORTH

We Are Seven

—A simple Child,
That lightly draws its breath,
And feels its life in every limb,
What should it know of death?

I met a little cottage Girl:
She was eight years old, she said;
Her hair was thick with many a curl
That clustered round her head.

She had a rustic woodland air,
And she was wildly clad:
Her eyes were fair, and very fair;
—Her beauty made me glad.

"Sisters and brothers, little Maid,
How many may you be?"
"How many? Seven in all," she said,
And wondering looked at me.

"And where are they? I pray you tell."
She answered, "Seven are we;
And two of us at Conway dwell,
And two are gone to sea.

"Two of us in the church-yard lie,
My sister and my brother;
And, in the church-yard cottage, I
Dwell near them with my mother."

"You say that two at Conway dwell,
And two are gone to sea,
Yet ye are seven!—I pray you tell,
Sweet Maid, how this may be."

Then did the little Maid reply,
"Seven boys and girls are we;
Two of us in the church-yard lie,
Beneath the church-yard tree."

"You run about, my little Maid,
Your limbs they are alive;
If two are in the church-yard laid,
Then ye are only five."

"Their graves are green, they may be seen,"
The little Maid replied,
"Twelve steps or more from my mother's door,
And they are side by side.

"My stockings there I often knit,
My kerchief there I hem;
And there upon the ground I sit,
And sing a song to them.

"And often after sunset, Sir,
When it is light and fair,
I take my little porringer,
And eat my supper there.

"The first that died was sister Jane;
In bed she moaning lay,
Till God released her of her pain;
And then she went away.

"So in the church-yard she was laid;
And, when the grass was dry,
Together round her grave we played,
My brother John and I.

"And when the ground was white with snow,
And I could run and slide,
My brother John was forced to go,
And he lies by her side."

"How many are you, then," said I,
"If they two are in heaven?"
Quick was the little Maid's reply,
"O Master! we are seven."

"But they are dead; those two are dead!
Their spirits are in heaven!"
'T was throwing words away; for still
The little Maid would have her will,
And said, "Nay, we are seven!"

WILLIAM WORDSWORTH

To His Mistress, the Queen of Bohemia

You meaner beauties of the night,
  That poorly satisfy our eyes
More by your number than your light,
  You common people of the skies,
  What are you when the moon shall rise?

You curious chanters of the wood,
  That warble forth Dame Nature's lays,
Thinking your passions understood
  By your weak accents; what's your praise
  When Philomel her voice shall raise?

You violets that first appear,
  By your pure purple mantles known
Like the proud virgins of the year,
  As if the spring were all your own;
  What are you when the rose is blown?

So, when my mistress shall be seen
In form and beauty of her mind,
By virtue first, then choice, a Queen,
Tell me, if she were not designed
Th' eclipse and glory of her kind.

Sir Henry Wotton

A Face that Should Content Me

A face that should content me wonders well — *wonders*—wondrous
Should not be fair but lovely to behold,
With gladsome cheer all grief for to expel;
With sober looks so would I that it should
Speak without words, such words as none can tell;
The tress also should be of crisped gold;
With wit: amd thus might chance I might be tied,
And knit again the knot that should not slide.

Sir Thomas Wyatt

Farewell all my Welfare

Farewell all my welfare,
My shoe is trod awry;
Now may I cark and care — *cark*—worry, be anxious
To sing *lullay by by.*
Alas! What shall I do thereto?
There is no shift to help me now.

Who made it such offence
To love for love again?
God wot that my pretense
Was but to ease his pain;
For I had ruth to see his woe;
Alas, more fool, why did I so?

For he from me is gone
And makes thereat a game,
And hath left me alone
To suffer sorrow and shame.

Alas! he is unkind doubtless
To leave me thus all comfortless.
It is a grievous smart
To suffer pain and sorrow;
But most grieved my heart
He laid his faith to borrow:
And falsehood hath his faith and troth,
And he forsworn by many an oath.

All ye lovers, perdy,
Hath cause to blame his deed,
Which shall example be
To let you of your speed;
Let never woman again
Trust to such words as men can feign.

For I unto my cost
Am warning to you all,
That they whom you trust most
Soonest decive you shall;
But complaint cannot redress
Of my great grief the great excess.

SIR THOMAS WYATT

My Fair Falcon

Luckes, my fair falcon, and your fellows all,
How well pleasant it were your liberty!
Ye not forsake me that fair might ye befall.
But they that sometime liked my company,
Like lice away from dead bodies they crawl:
Lo, what a proof in light adversity!
But ye, my birds, I swear by all your bells,
Ye be my friends, and so be but few else.

SIR THOMAS WYATT

*Lapis Lazuli**

I HAVE heard that hysterical women say
They are sick of the palette and fiddle-bow,
Of poets that are always gay,
For everybody knows or else should know
That if nothing drastic is done
Aeroplane and Zeppelin will come out,
Pitch like King Billy bomb-balls in
Until the town lie beaten flat.

All perform their tragic play,
There struts Hamlet, there is Lear,
That's Ophelia, that Cordelia;
Yet they, should the last scene be there,
The great stage curtain about to drop,
If worthy their prominent part in the play,
Do not break up their lines to weep.
They know that Hamlet and Lear are gay;
Gaiety transfiguring all that dread.
All men have aimed at, found and lost;
Black out; Heaven blazing into the head:
Tragedy wrought to its uttermost.
Though Hamlet rambles and Lear rages,
And all the drop-scenes drop at once
Upon a hundred thousand stages,
It cannot grow by an inch or an ounce.

On their own feet they came, or on shipboard,
Camel-back, horse-back, ass-back, mule-back,
Old civilisations put to the sword.
Then they and their wisdom went to rack:
No handiwork of Callimachus,
Who handled marble as if it were bronze,
Made draperies that seemed to rise
When sea-wind swept the corner, stands;
His long lamp-chimney shaped like the stem
Of a slender palm, stood but a day;
All things fall and are built again,
And those that build them again are gay.

---

*Reprinted with permission of The Macmillan Company from *Last Poems and Plays* by William Butler Yeats. Copyright 1940 Georgie Yeats. Also, acknowledgments to Mr. M. B. Yeats, The Macmillan Co. of Canada, Ltd., and Macmillan & Co., Ltd.

Two Chinamen, behind them a third,
Are carved in lapis lazuli,
Over them flies a long-legged bird,
A symbol of longevity;
The third, doubtless a serving-man,
Carries a musical instrument.

Every discoloration of the stone,
Every accidental crack or dent,
Seems a water-course or an avalanche,
Or lofty slope where it still snows
Through doubtless plum or cherry-branch
Sweetens the little half-way house
Those Chinamen climb towards, and I
Delight to imagine them seated there;
There, on the mountain and the sky,
On all the tragic scene they stare.
One asks for mournful melodies;
Accomplished fingers begin to play.
Their eyes mid many wrinkles, their eyes,
Their ancient, glittering eyes, are gay.

WILLIAM BUTLER YEATS

First Mate Joseph Conrad

My legs are worn to dangling ropes
By this ball bearing sea which rolls
The world against the frictional sky.
Even these waves which mime
The quarters of the moon are not enough
To hook it to a stop. All is curves and angles.

Even our unwrenchable wake would lead us
To believe our course was like the flicking
Of the sharks and salmons—the creatures
Of this watery, violent world, who know
The tints and foul moods of the sea.

But more than this sea is mutable.
I have stood upon the bridge and watched
The subtle cloudless sky grow dark
And crack like rarest china, and until
The storm has snuffed my smoking pipe
I did not realize the change.

There are no straight lines in the sky,
Or in the sea, or in these seamen.
All is by degrees so changeable
The senses are like earth worms
Nosed against a boulder.

I have been too long upon the water.
Death and danger ring like children's threats.
Is it presumptuous to think I can do more?
Perhaps some day I'll catch the corner
Of the sky and sea before it moves
Beyond my reach.

PAUL ZIMMER

---

*Reprinted with permission of poet—Unpublished.

Ars Poetica

A poem should be palpable and mute
As a globed fruit
Dumb
As old medallions to the thumb
Silent as the sleeve-worn stone
Of casement ledges where the moss has grown—
A poem should be wordless
As the flight of birds
A poem should be motionless in time
As the moon climbs
Leaving, as the moon releases
Twig by twig the night-entangled trees,

Leaving, as the moon behind the winter leaves,
Memory by memory the mind—
A poem should be motionless in time
As the moon climbs
A poem should be equal to:
Not true
For all the history of grief
An empty doorway and a maple leaf
For love
The leaning grasses and two lights above the sea—
A poem should not mean
But be.

ARCHIBALD MACLEISH

Suggestions for Further Reading

Allen, Don Cameron, ed. *The Moment of Poetry*. Baltimore: The Johns Hopkins Press, 1962.

Auden, W. H. *The Enchaféd Flood, or The Romantic Iconography of the Sea*. New York: Random House, Inc., 1950.

*Barfield, Owen. *Poetic Diction: A Study of Meaning*. Second Edition. London: Faber and Faber Ltd., 1952. (Paperback: McGraw-Hill Paperback Series.)

Bateson, F. W. *English Poetry: A Critical Introduction*. London: Longmans, Green and Co., Ltd., 1950.

Berry, F. *Poet's Grammar: Person, Time, and Mood in Poetry*. London: Routledge and Kegan Paul, 1958.

Blackburn, T. *The Price of an Eye: An Introduction to Modern Poetry*. London: Longmans, Green and Co., Ltd., 1961.

Brooke-Rose, Christine. *A Grammar of Metaphor*. London: Secker & Warburg, 1958.

*Brooks, Cleanth. *The Well-Wrought Urn*. New York: Harcourt Brace & World, Inc., 1947. (Paperback: Harvest Books, Harcourt, Brace & World, Inc.)

*Brower, Reuben Arthur. *The Fields of Light: An Experiment in Critical Reading*. London and New York: Oxford University Press, 1951. (Paperback: Galaxy Books, Oxford University Press.)

Books marked with an asterisk are available in paperback editions.

*Crane, Ronald S. *The Languages of Criticism and the Structure of Poetry*. Toronto: University of Toronto Press, 1953. (Paperback: University of Toronto Press.)

Cunningham, J. V. *Tradition and Poetic Structure*. Denver: Alan Swallow, Publisher, 1960.

Davie, Donald. *Articulate Energy: An Inquiry into the Syntax of English Poetry*. London: Routledge and Kegan Paul, 1955.

———. *Purity of Diction in English Verse*. London: Chatto and Windus, 1952; New York: Oxford University Press, 1953.

Day-Lewis, C. *The Poetic Image*. New York and London: Oxford University Press, 1947.

*Drew, Elizabeth, and George Connor. *Discovering Modern Poetry*. New York: Holt, Rinehart and Winston, Inc., 1961. (Paperback: Holt, Rinehart and Winston Inc.)

Durrell, Lawrence. *A Key to Modern Poetry*. Norman, Oklahoma: University of Oklahoma Press, 1952.

*Eliot, T. S. *On Poetry and Poets*. New York: Farrar, Straus & Giroux, Inc., 1957. (Paperback: The Noonday Press.)

Elton, Oliver. *The English Muse*. London: G. Bell and Sons Ltd., 1933.

*Frye, Northrop. *Anatomy of Criticism*. Princeton: Princeton University Press, 1957. (Paperback: Atheneum Publishers.)

Graves, Robert. *Oxford Addresses on Poetry*. London: Cassell, 1962.

Grierson, H. J. C., and J. C. Smith. *A Critical History of English Poetry*. New York and London: Oxford University Press, 1946.

Housman, A. E. *The Name and Nature of Poetry*. New York: Cambridge University Press, 1933.

*Isaacs, J. *The Background of Modern Poetry*. New York: E. P. Dutton & Co., Inc. (Paperback: Dutton Paperbacks.)

Ker, W. P. *The Art of Poetry: Seven Lectures, 1920-1922*. Oxford: The Clarendon Press, 1923.

MacLeish, Archibald. *Poetry and Experience*. Cambridge: Riverside Press, 1961.

MacNeice, Louis. *Modern Poetry*. London: Oxford University Press, 1938.

*Nowottny, Winifred. *The Language Poets Use.* New York: Oxford University Press, 1962. (Paperback: Oxford University Press.)

*Pottle, Frederick A. *The Idiom of Poetry.* Revised Edition. Ithaca, New York: Cornell University Press, 1946. (Paperback: Indiana University Press.)

*Prescott, Frederic Clarke. *The Poetic Mind.* New York: The Macmillan Company, 1922. (Paperback: Cornell Paperbacks.)

*Press, John. *The Chequer'd Shade: Reflections on Obscurity in Poetry.* London and New York: Oxford University Press, 1958. (Paperback: Oxford University Press.)

________. *The Fire and the Fountain.* London, New York: Oxford University Press, 1955.

Read, Sir Herbert. *Form in Modern Poetry.* London: Vision, 1948.

Ridley, M. R. *Poetry and the Ordinary Reader.* New York: E. P. Dutton & Co. Inc., 1939.

Rukeyser, Muriel. *The Life of Poetry.* New York: Current Books, 1949.

Rylands, George H. W. *Words and Poetry.* New York: Payson and Clarke Ltd., 1928

Sansom, Clive, ed. *The World of Poetry: Poets and Critics on the Art and Function of Poetry.* London: Phoenix House, 1959.

Scully, James, ed. *Modern Poetics.* New York: McGraw-Hill Book Company, 1965.

Shapiro, Karl. *Beyond Criticism.* Lincoln, Nebraska: University of Nebraska Press, 1953.

Skelton, Robin. *The Poetic Pattern.* Berkeley: University of California Press, 1956.

*Stauffer, Donald A. *The Nature of Poetry.* New York: W. W. Norton & Company, Inc., 1946. (Paperback: W. W. Norton and Company, Inc.)

Tillyard, E. M. W. *Poetry Direct and Oblique.* Revised Edition. London: Chatts and Windus, 1945.

________. *Poetry and Its Background Illustrated by Five Poems, 1470-1870.* London: Chatto and Windus, 1961. Originally published as *Five Poems, 1470-1870.* London: Chatto and Windus, 1948.

*Tindall, William York. *The Literary Symbol.* New York: Columbia University Press, 1955. (Paperback: Indiana University Press.)

Wells, H. W. *Poetic Imagery.* New York: Columbia University Press, 1924.

Whalley, George. *Poetic Process.* London: Routledge and Kegan Paul, 1953.

Wyld, H. C. K. *Some Aspects of the Diction of English Poetry.* Oxford: Blackwell, 1933.

INDEX OF AUTHORS AND TITLES

INDEX OF FIRST LINES